ORESAMA
TEACHER

Shojo Beat

ORESAMA TEACHER

CHARACTERS AND THE STORY THUS FAR

PUBLIC MORALS CLUB

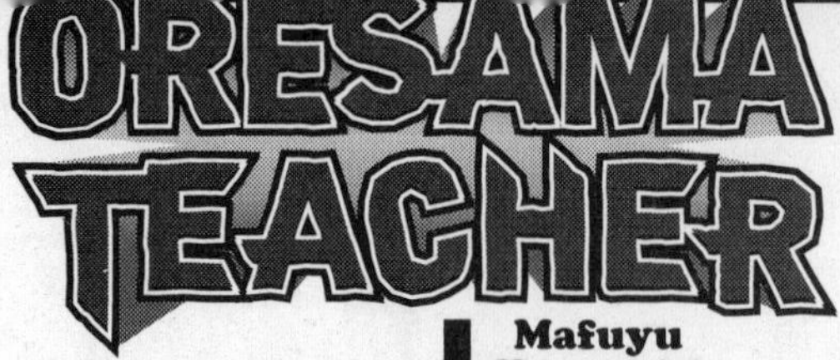

Mafuyu Kurosaki

THE FORMER BANCHO OF SAITAMA EAST HIGH. SHE TRANSFERED TO MIDORIGAOKA ACADEMY AND JOINED THE PUBLIC MORALS CLUB. SHE ALSO PLAYS THE PARTS OF NATSUO AND SUPER BUN. SHE IS CONCERNED BY THE FACT THAT SHE HAS NO FEMALE FRIENDS.

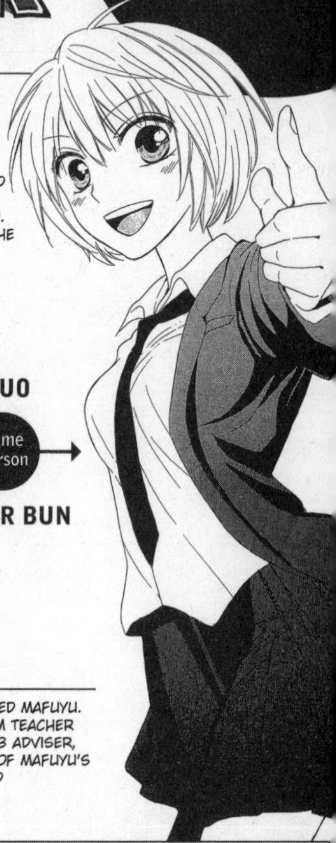

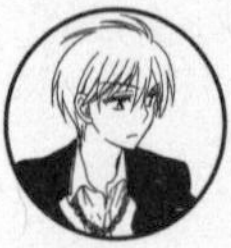

NATSUO

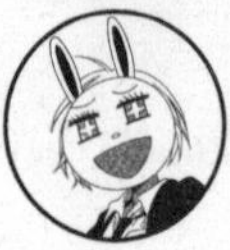

SUPER BUN

Same Person

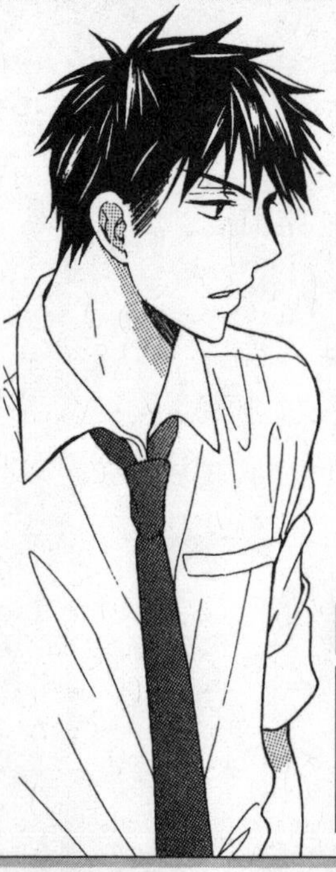

Takaomi Saeki

THE ONE WHO CRUELLY TRAINED MAFUYU. HE WAS MAFUYU'S HOMEROOM TEACHER AND THE PUBLIC MORALS CLUB ADVISER, BUT IN THE FIRST SEMESTER OF MAFUYU'S FINAL YEAR, HE RESIGNED AND DISAPPEARED.

PUBLIC MORALS CLUB

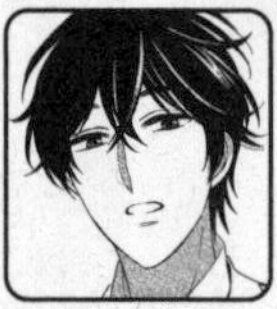

Mr. Maki

A NEW TEACHER. HE REPLACED TAKAOMI AS THE PUBLIC MORALS CLUB ADVISER.

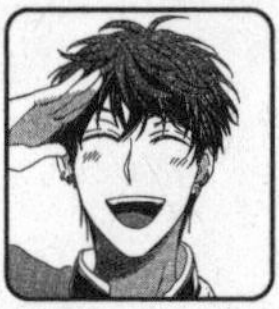

Aki Shibuya

A TALKATIVE AND WOMANIZING UNDERCLASSMAN. HIS NICKNAME IS AKKI. HE'S NOT GOOD AT FIGHTING.

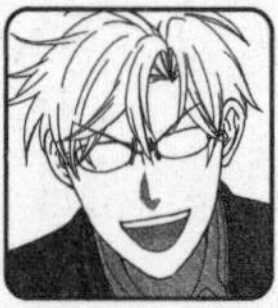

Shinobu Yui

HE WORSHIPS MIYABI, THE FORMER STUDENT COUNCIL PRESIDENT, BUT REJOINED THE PUBLIC MORALS CLUB. HE IS A SELF-PROCLAIMED NINJA.

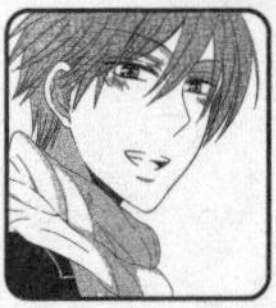

Hayasaka

MAFUYU'S CLASSMATE. HE APPEARS TO BE A PLAIN AND SIMPLE DELINQUENT, BUT HE'S ACTUALLY QUITE DILIGENT.

MIDORIGAOKA

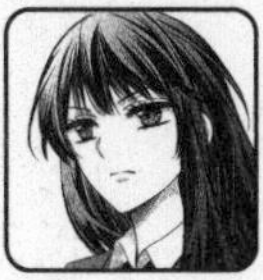

Toko Hanabusa

SHE HAS A STOIC ATTITUDE AND WATCHES OVER HANABUSA, AND SHE HAS FEELINGS FOR YUI. SHE'S THE NEW STUDENT COUNCIL PRESIDENT.

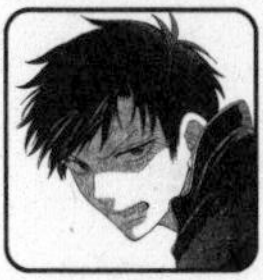

Reito Ayabe

HE LOVES CLEANING. HE GETS STRONGER IN DIRTY PLACES. HE IS A STUDENT COUNCIL OFFICER, BUT HE'S FRIENDS WITH MAFUYU.

EAST HIGH

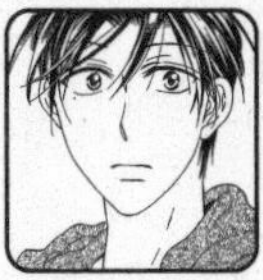

Kohei Kangawa

ONE YEAR YOUNGER THAN MAFUYU. HE IS THE CURRENT BANCHO OF EAST HIGH AND DEEPLY ADMIRES HIS PREDECESSOR, MAFUYU. HE CAN BE CHILDISH.

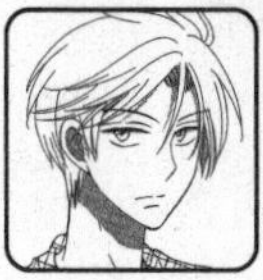

Yuto Maizono

ONE YEAR OLDER THAN MAFUYU AND FORMERLY THE NUMBER TWO AT EAST HIGH. HE CALLS HIMSELF "THE ONE WHO LURES YOU INTO THE WORLD OF MASOCHISM."

WEST HIGH

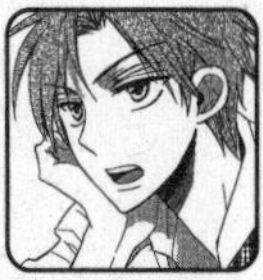

Asahi Sakurada

WEST HIGH'S BANCHO. LIKES CROSSDRESSING. HE MET HAYASAKA AND YUI WHEN WEST HIGH SHARED A SCHOOL TRIP WITH MIDORIGAOKA.

KIYAMA HIGH

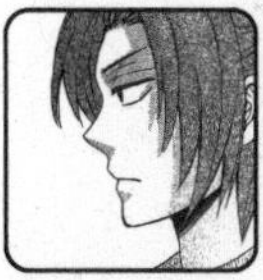

Nogami

THE BANCHO OF KIYAMA HIGH, A RIVAL SCHOOL TO MIDORIGAOKA. HE HAS A PAST WITH KANON NONOGUCHI.

THE GRADUATES

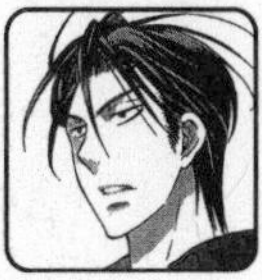

Kyotaro Okegawa

THE FORMER BANCHO OF EAST HIGH. HE IS ATTENDING A LOCAL COLLEGE. HE AND MAFUYU ARE ANONYMOUS PEN PALS.

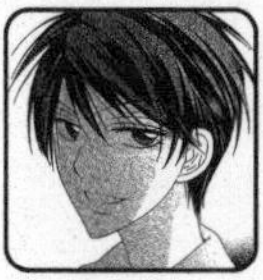

Miyabi Hanabusa

THE SCHOOL DIRECTOR'S SON AND THE FORMER PRESIDENT OF THE STUDENT COUNCIL. HE CAN CHARM OTHERS WITH HIS GAZE. HE IS ATTENDING COLLEGE IN TOKYO.

STORY

★ MAFUYU KUROSAKI WAS A BANCHO WHO CONTROLLED ALL OF SAITAMA, BUT ONCE SHE TRANSFERRED TO MIDORIGAOKA ACADEMY, SHE COMPLETELY CHANGED AND BECAME A SPIRITED HIGH SCHOOL GIRL...OR AT LEAST SHE WAS SUPPOSED TO. TAKAOMI SAEKI, HER CHILDHOOD FRIEND AND HOMEROOM TEACHER, FORCED HER TO JOIN THE PUBLIC MORALS CLUB AND SHE HAS TO CONTINUE TO LIVE A LIFE THAT IS FAR FROM AVERAGE.

★ A FAKE SUPER BUN HAS SHOWN UP AT SCHOOL AND THE MEMBERS OF THE STUDENT COUNCIL HAVE BECOME THE TARGETS OF VERY PERSONAL PRANKS. MAFUYU AND THE PUBLIC MORALS CLUB CHASE DOWN THE IMPOSTER AND DISCOVER THAT IT'S MIYABI HANABUSA! MIYABI IS GRADUATING SOON AND HAS BEEN USING THE FAKE SUPER BUN AS A MEANS TO SEE HOW WELL THE MEMBERS OF THE STUDENT COUNCIL HAVE OVERCOME THEIR ISSUES.

★ MAFUYU AND HER FRIENDS ARE FINALLY THIRD-YEAR STUDENTS. MIYABI HANABUSA'S YOUNGER SISTER, TOKO, HAS ENROLLED AS A FIRST-YEAR STUDENT. BUT AS SOON AS SHE ENTERS THE PICTURE, TAKAOMI RESIGNS AND DISAPPEARS. MEANWHILE, MAFUYU AND HER FRIENDS INVESTIGATE RUMORS THAT NOGAMI OF KIYAMA HIGH IS KEEPING A "BEAST" AS A PET, BUT YUI DISCOVERS THAT THE BEAST IS ACTUALLY TAKAOMI.

★ MAFUYU AND HER FRIENDS HAVE GROWN CONCERNED ABOUT THE STRANGE BEHAVIOR OF MR. MAKI, THE NEW TEACHER AT MIDORIGAOKA. IN ORDER FIND OUT MORE ABOUT HIM, THE PUBLIC MORALS CLUB USES SUMMER BREAK AS AN EXCUSE TO VISIT MAFUYU'S HOMETOWN, NEAR MR. MAKI'S HOME ADDRESS. BUT WHEN IT TURNS OUT HIS ADDRESS IS ACTUALLY WEST HIGH, MAFUYU AND HER FRIENDS HEAD OVER TO INVESTIGATE WITH KANGAWA!

ORESAMA TEACHER

Volume 25
CONTENTS

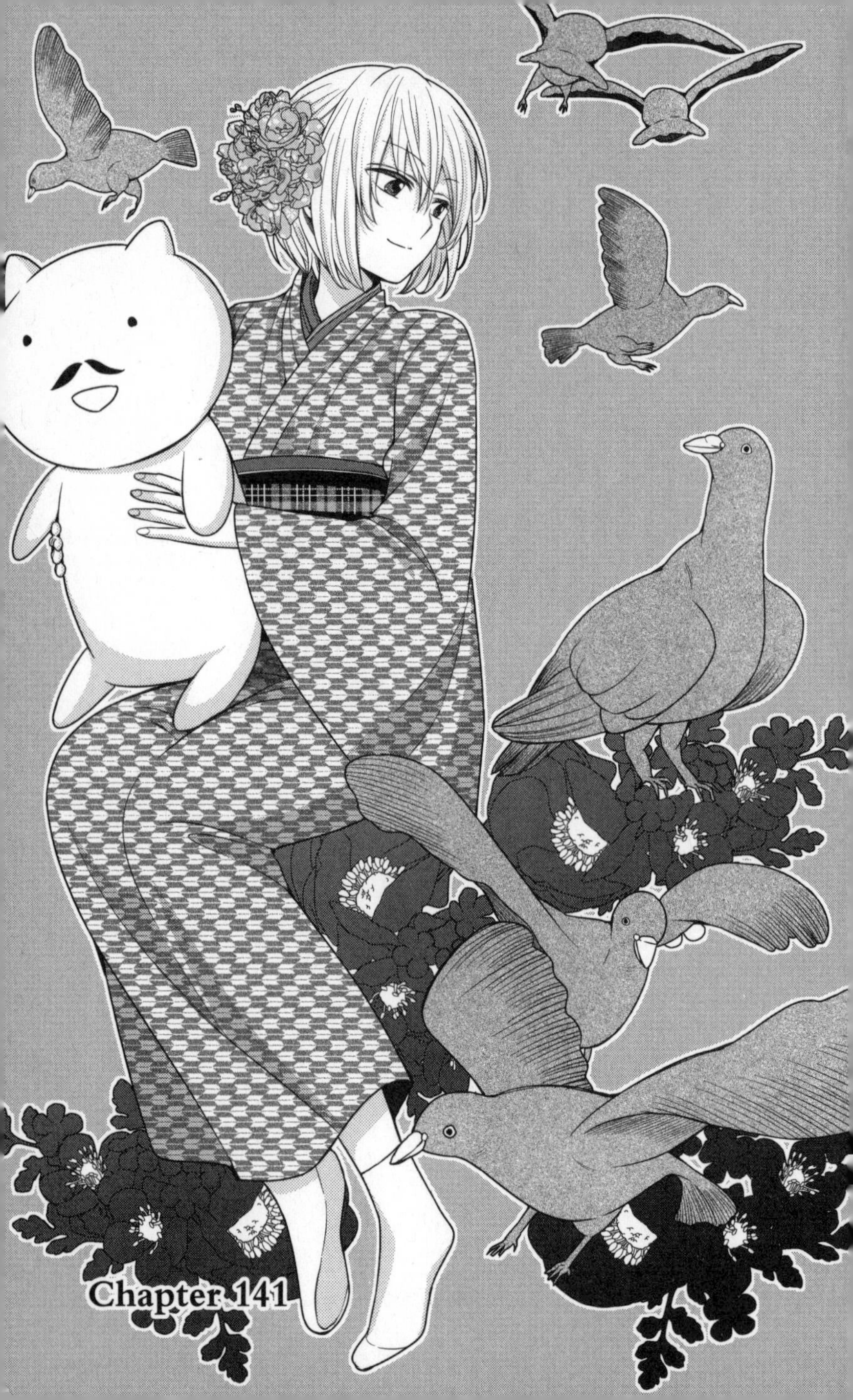
Chapter 141

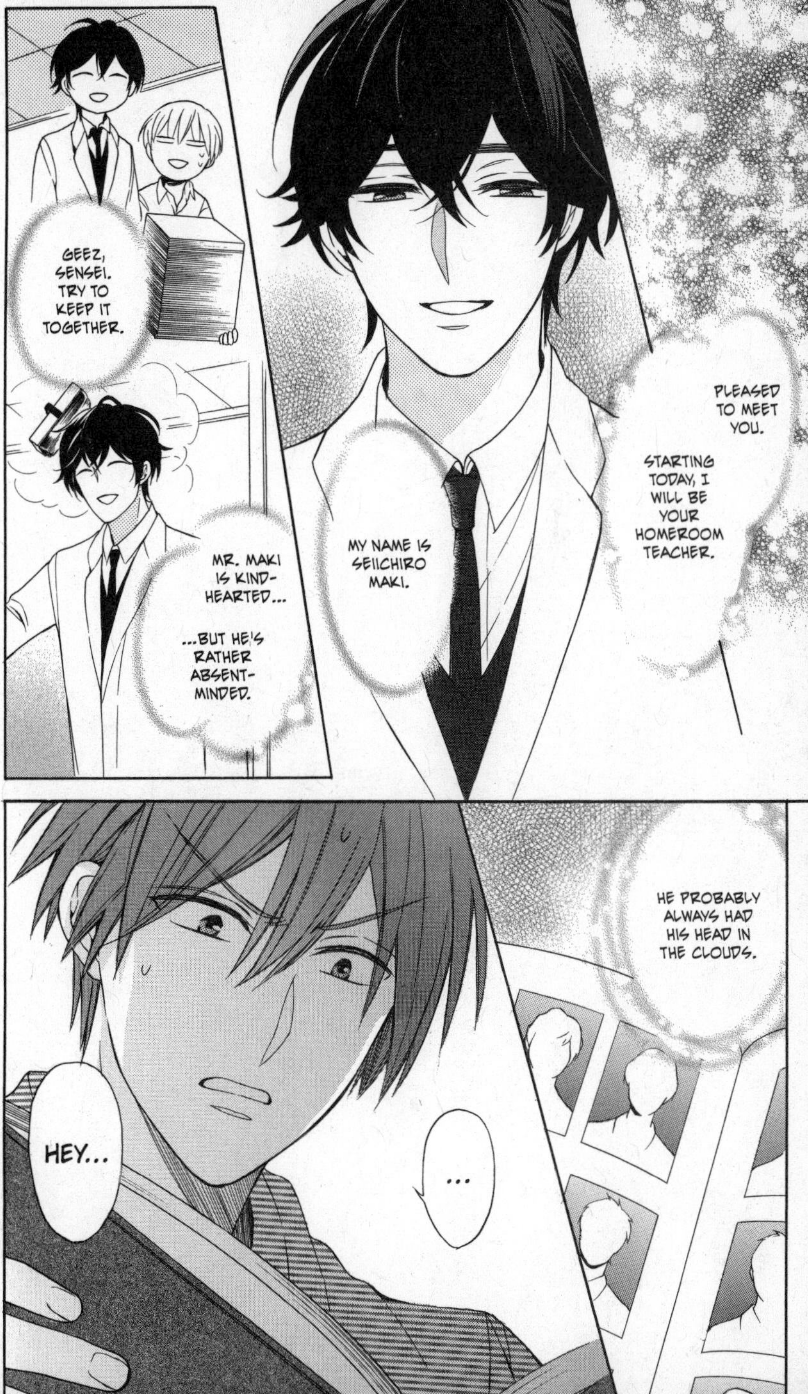
PLEASED TO MEET YOU.
STARTING TODAY, I WILL BE YOUR HOMEROOM TEACHER.
MY NAME IS SEIICHIRO MAKI.
GEEZ, SENSEI. TRY TO KEEP IT TOGETHER.
MR. MAKI IS KIND-HEARTED...
...BUT HE'S RATHER ABSENT-MINDED.
HE PROBABLY ALWAYS HAD HIS HEAD IN THE CLOUDS.
...
HEY...

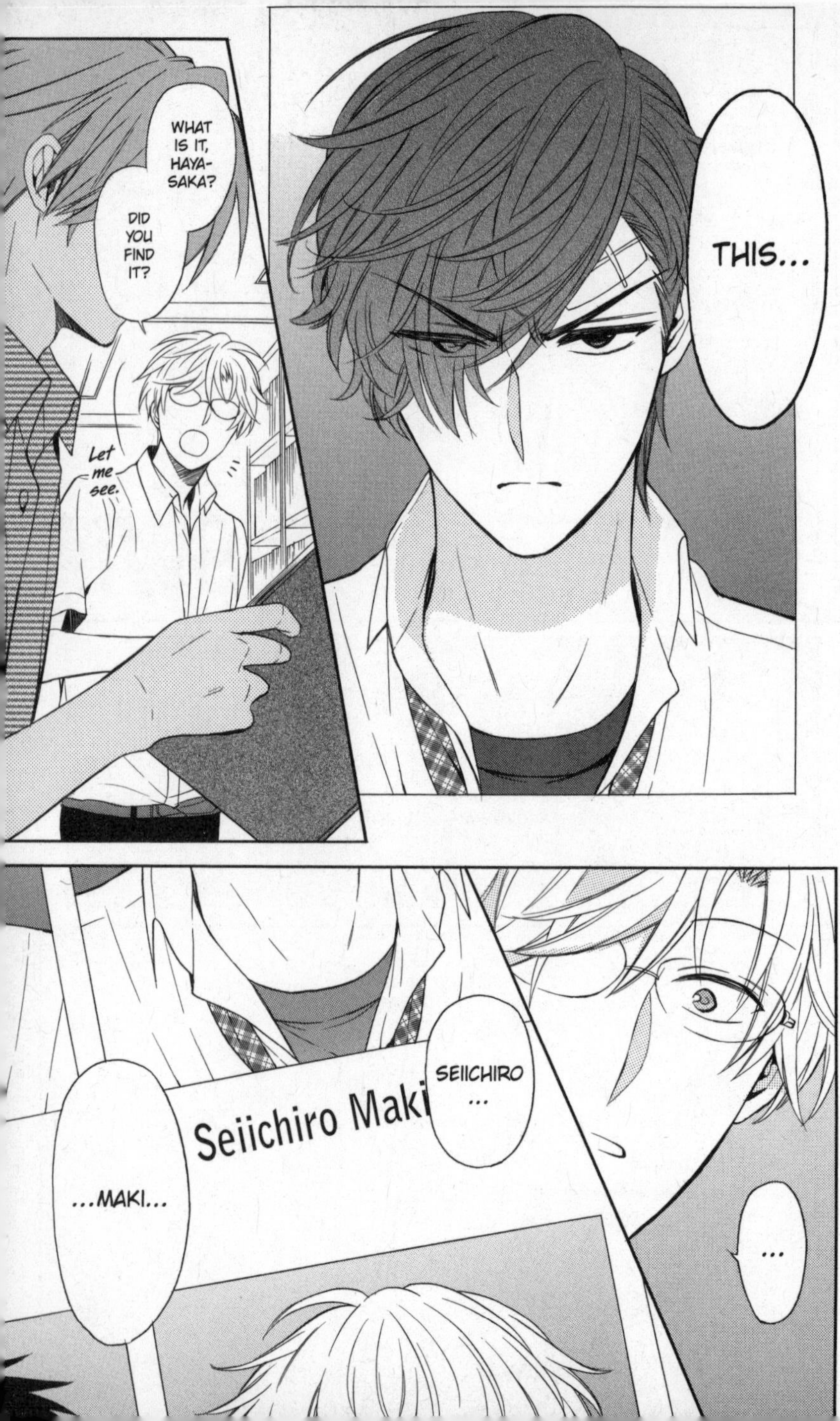
THIS...
WHAT IS IT, HAYA-SAKA?
DID YOU FIND IT?
Let me see.
SEIICHIRO ...
Seiichiro Maki
...
...MAKI...

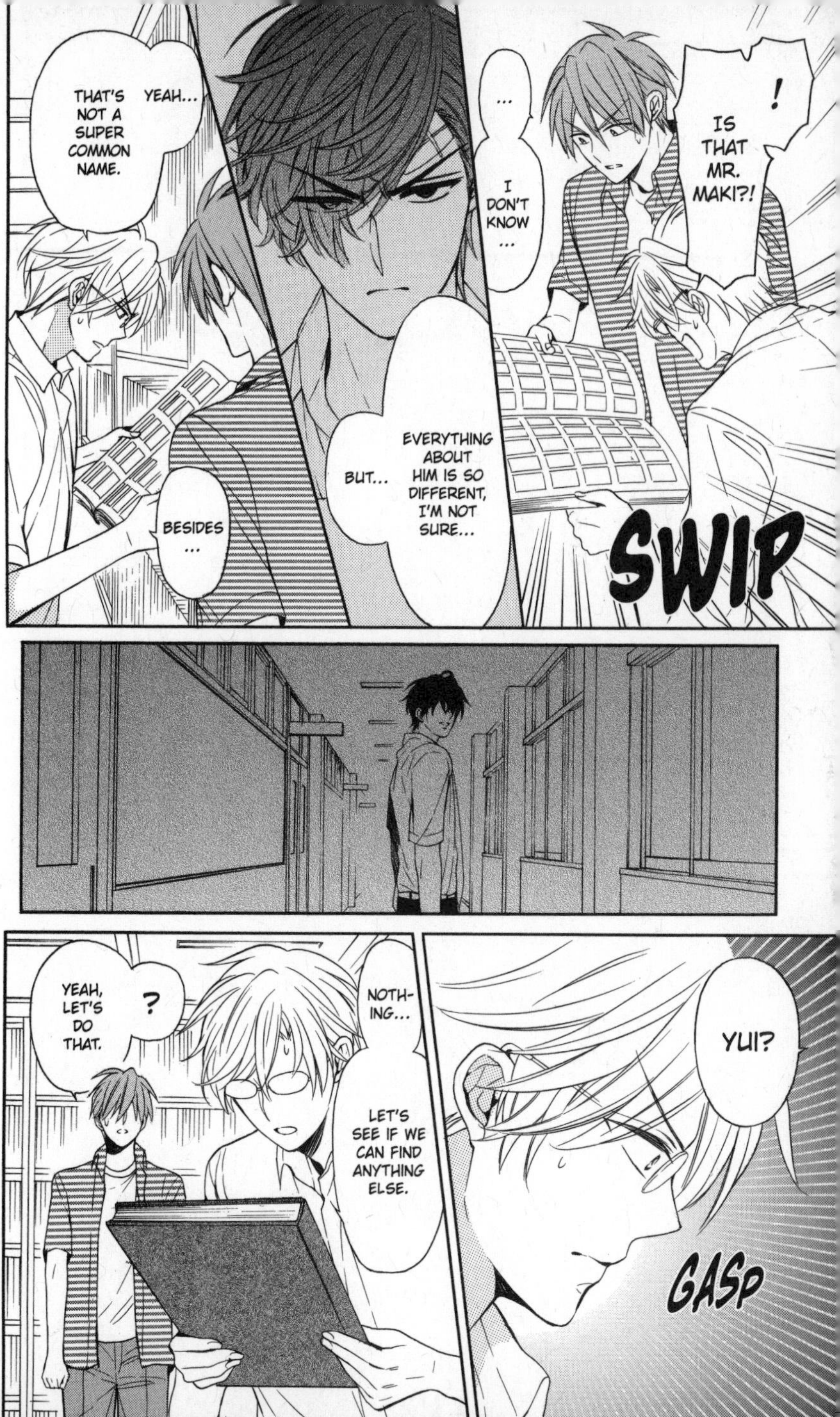
!
IS THAT MR. MAKI?!
SWIP
...
I DON'T KNOW ...
EVERYTHING ABOUT HIM IS SO DIFFERENT, I'M NOT SURE...
BUT...
YEAH...
THAT'S NOT A SUPER COMMON NAME.
BESIDES ...
YUI?
GASP
NOTH-ING...
LET'S SEE IF WE CAN FIND ANYTHING ELSE.
?
YEAH, LET'S DO THAT.

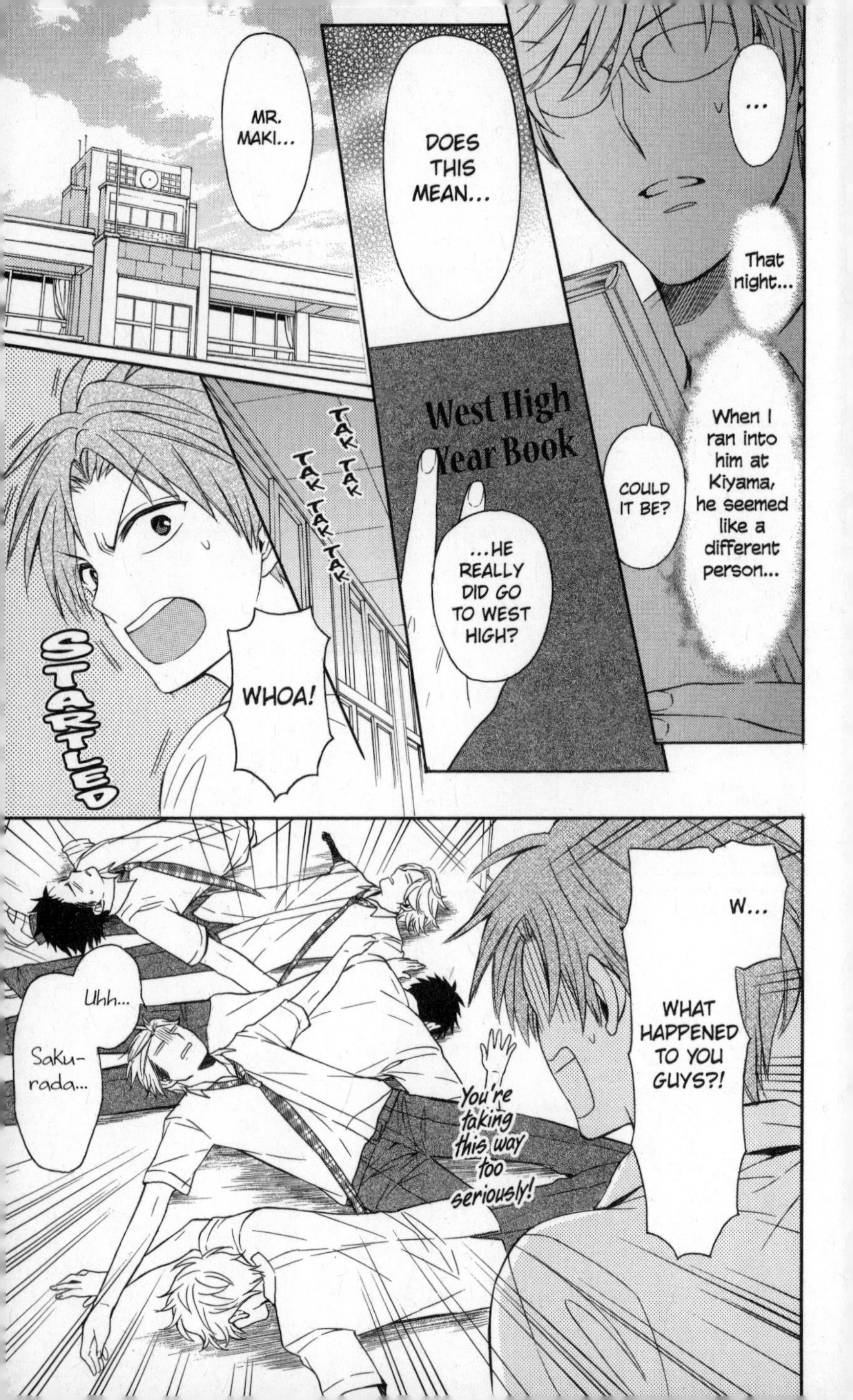
...
That night...
When I ran into him at Kiyama, he seemed like a different person...
COULD IT BE?
DOES THIS MEAN...
West High Year Book
...HE REALLY DID GO TO WEST HIGH?
MR. MAKI...
TAK TAK
TAK TAK TAK
STARTLED
WHOA!
W...
WHAT HAPPENED TO YOU GUYS?!
You're taking this way too seriously!
Uhh...
Saku-rada...

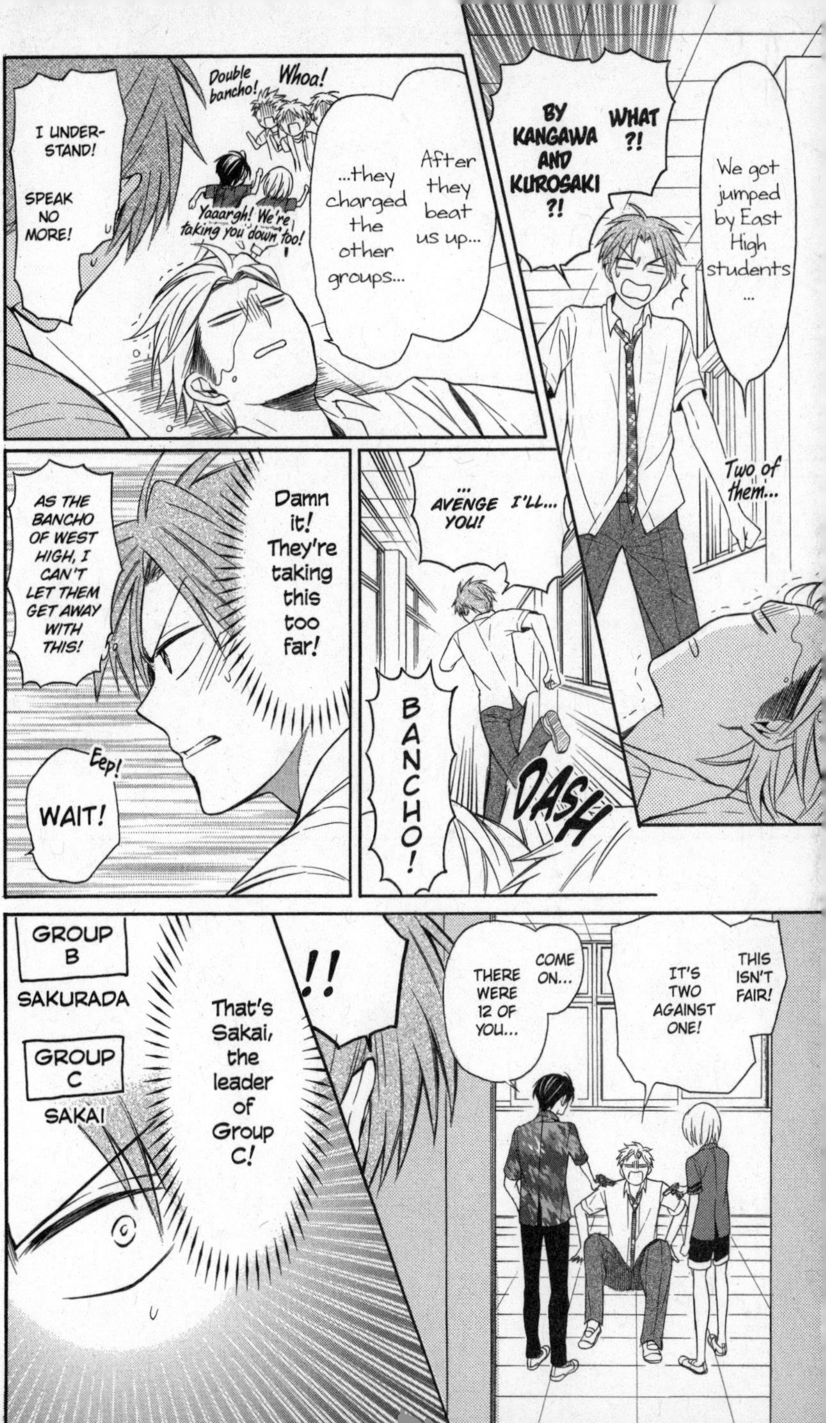
We got jumped by East High students...
WHAT?!
BY KANGAWA AND KUROSAKI?!
Two of them...
After they beat us up...
...they charged the other groups...
Whoa!
Double bancho!
Yaaargh! We're taking you down too!
I UNDERSTAND!
SPEAK NO MORE!
I'LL... ...AVENGE YOU!
BANCHO!
DASH
Damn it! They're taking this too far!
AS THE BANCHO OF WEST HIGH, I CAN'T LET THEM GET AWAY WITH THIS!
Eep!
WAIT!
THIS ISN'T FAIR!
IT'S TWO AGAINST ONE!
COME ON...
THERE WERE 12 OF YOU...
!!
That's Sakai, the leader of Group C!
GROUP B
SAKURADA
GROUP C
SAKAI

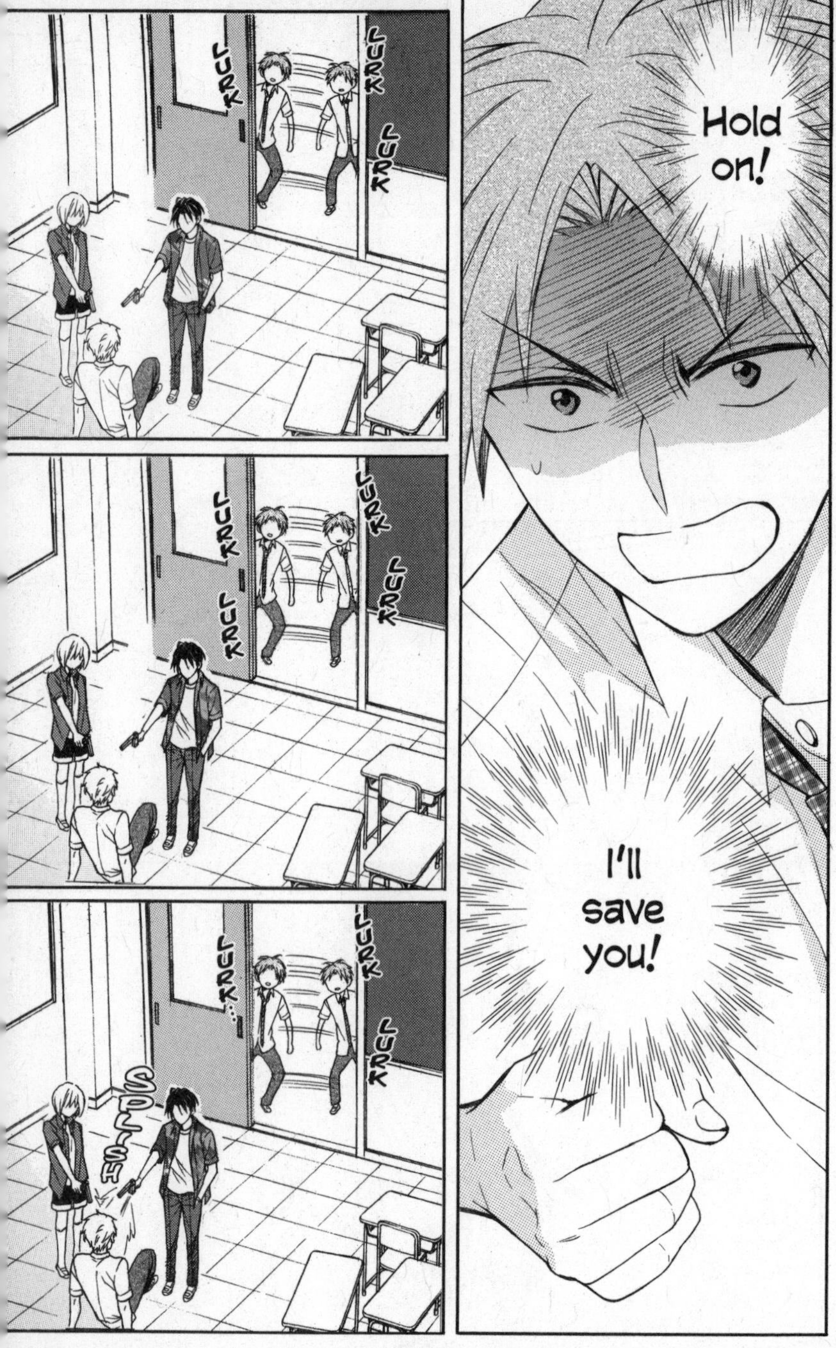
Hold on!
I'll save you!
LURK
LURK
LURK
LURK
LURK
LURK
LURK
LURK
LURK...
LURK
SPLISH

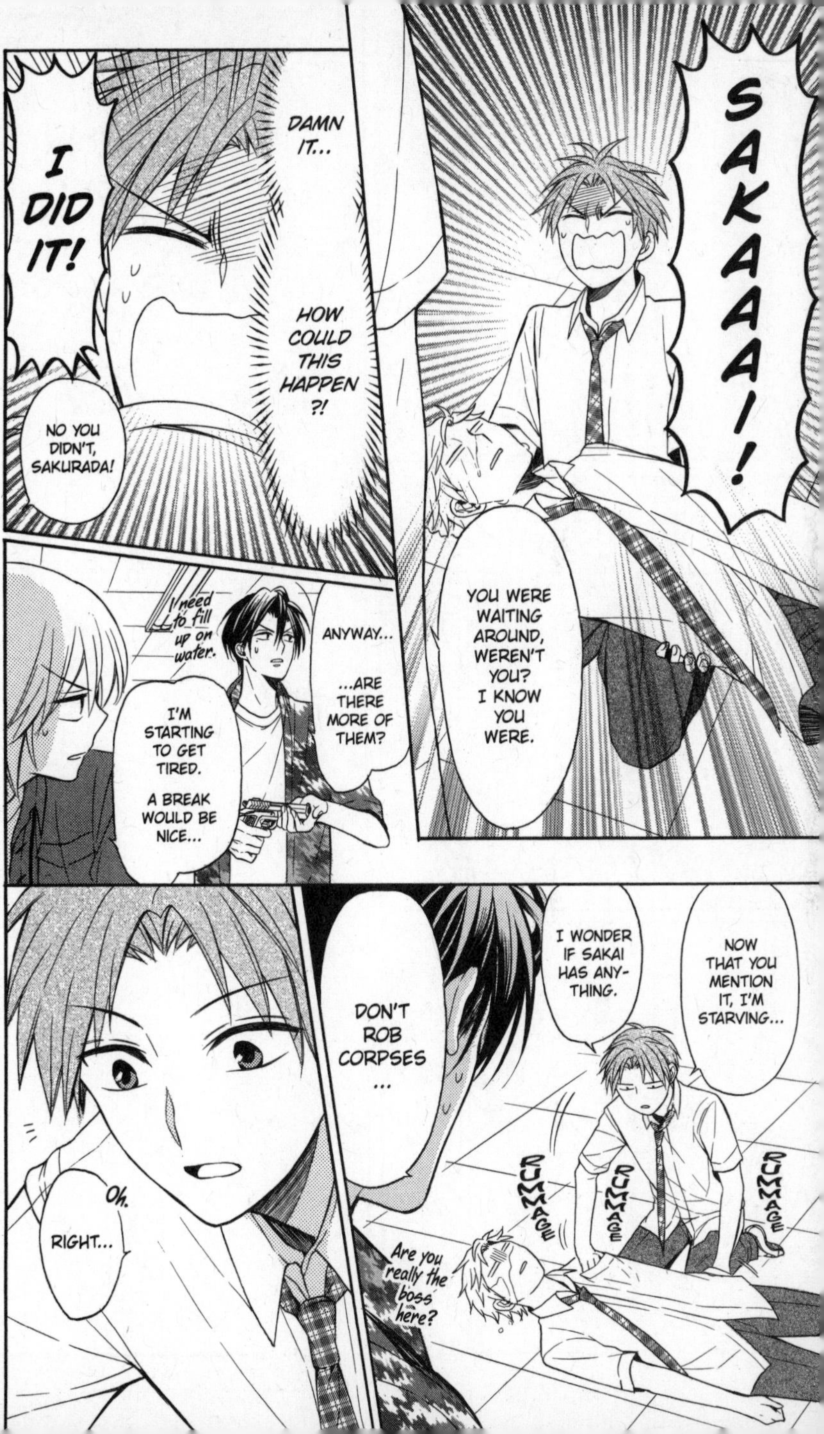
SAKAAAI!
YOU WERE WAITING AROUND, WEREN'T YOU? I KNOW YOU WERE.
DAMN IT...
HOW COULD THIS HAPPEN?!
I DID IT!
NO YOU DIDN'T, SAKURADA!
ANYWAY...
...ARE THERE MORE OF THEM?
I need to fill up on water.
I'M STARTING TO GET TIRED.
A BREAK WOULD BE NICE...
NOW THAT YOU MENTION IT, I'M STARVING...
I WONDER IF SAKAI HAS ANYTHING.
RUMMAGE
RUMMAGE
RUMMAGE
Are you really the boss here?
DON'T ROB CORPSES...
Oh.
RIGHT...

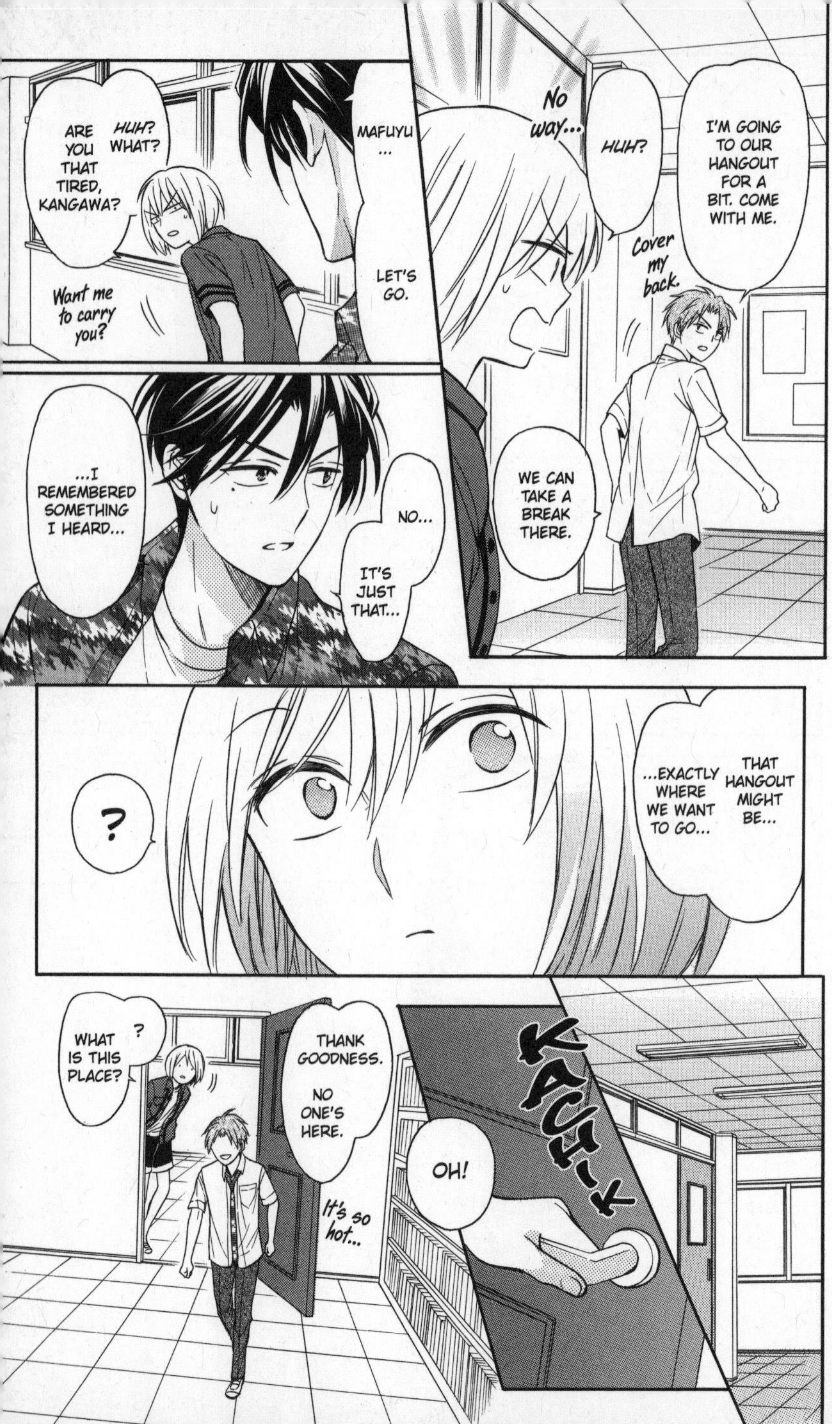

I'M GOING TO OUR HANGOUT FOR A BIT. COME WITH ME.
Cover my back.
HUH?
No way...
WE CAN TAKE A BREAK THERE.
MAFUYU...
LET'S GO.
HUH? WHAT?
ARE YOU THAT TIRED, KANGAWA?
Want me to carry you?
NO...
IT'S JUST THAT...
...I REMEMBERED SOMETHING I HEARD...
THAT HANGOUT MIGHT BE...
...EXACTLY WHERE WE WANT TO GO...
?
KACHI-K
OH!
THANK GOODNESS.
NO ONE'S HERE.
It's so hot...
?
WHAT IS THIS PLACE?

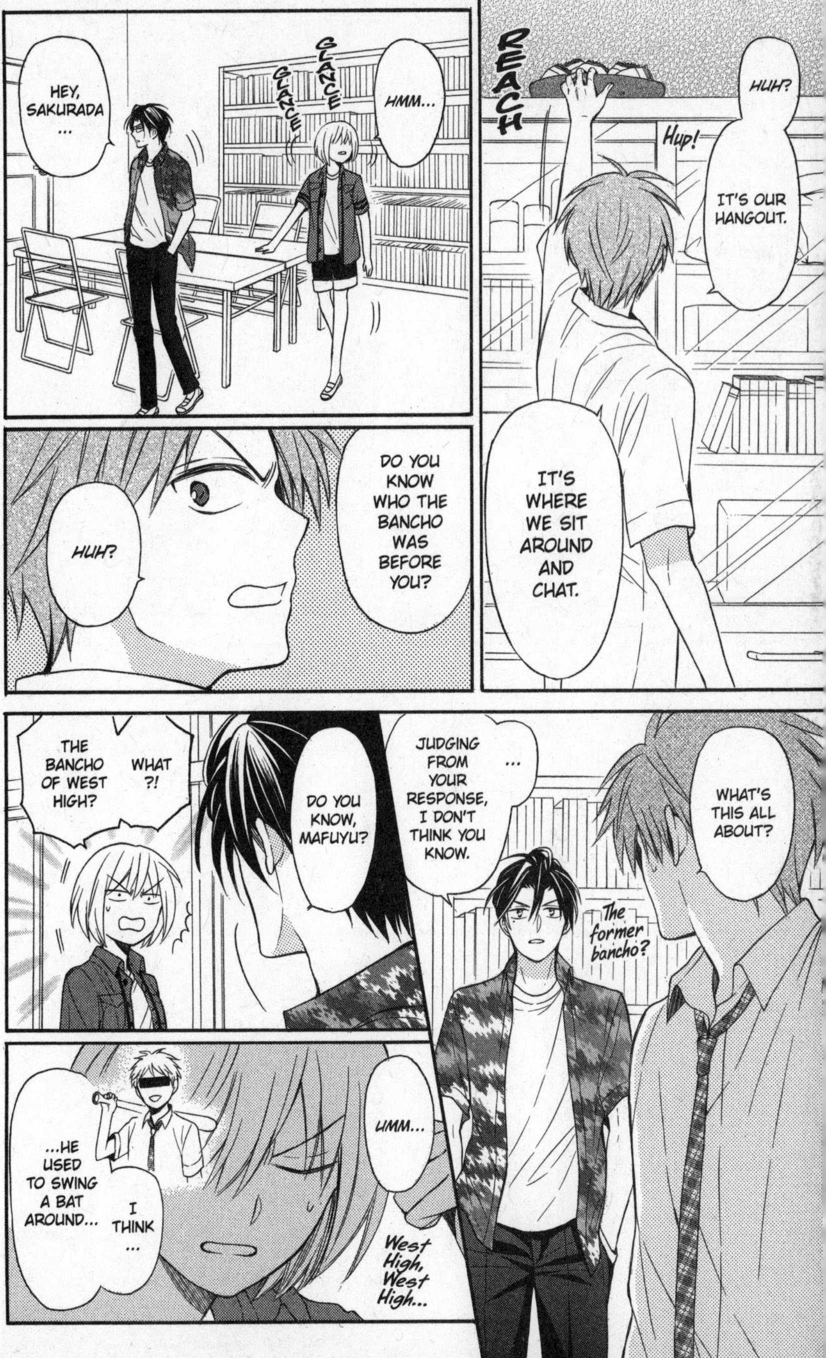
HUH?
REACH
Hup!
IT'S OUR HANGOUT.
IT'S WHERE WE SIT AROUND AND CHAT.
HMM...
GLANCE
GLANCE
HEY, SAKURADA...
DO YOU KNOW WHO THE BANCHO WAS BEFORE YOU?
HUH?
WHAT'S THIS ALL ABOUT?
The former bancho?
...
JUDGING FROM YOUR RESPONSE, I DON'T THINK YOU KNOW.
DO YOU KNOW, MAFUYU?
WHAT?!
THE BANCHO OF WEST HIGH?
UMM...
...HE USED TO SWING A BAT AROUND...
I THINK...
West High, West High...

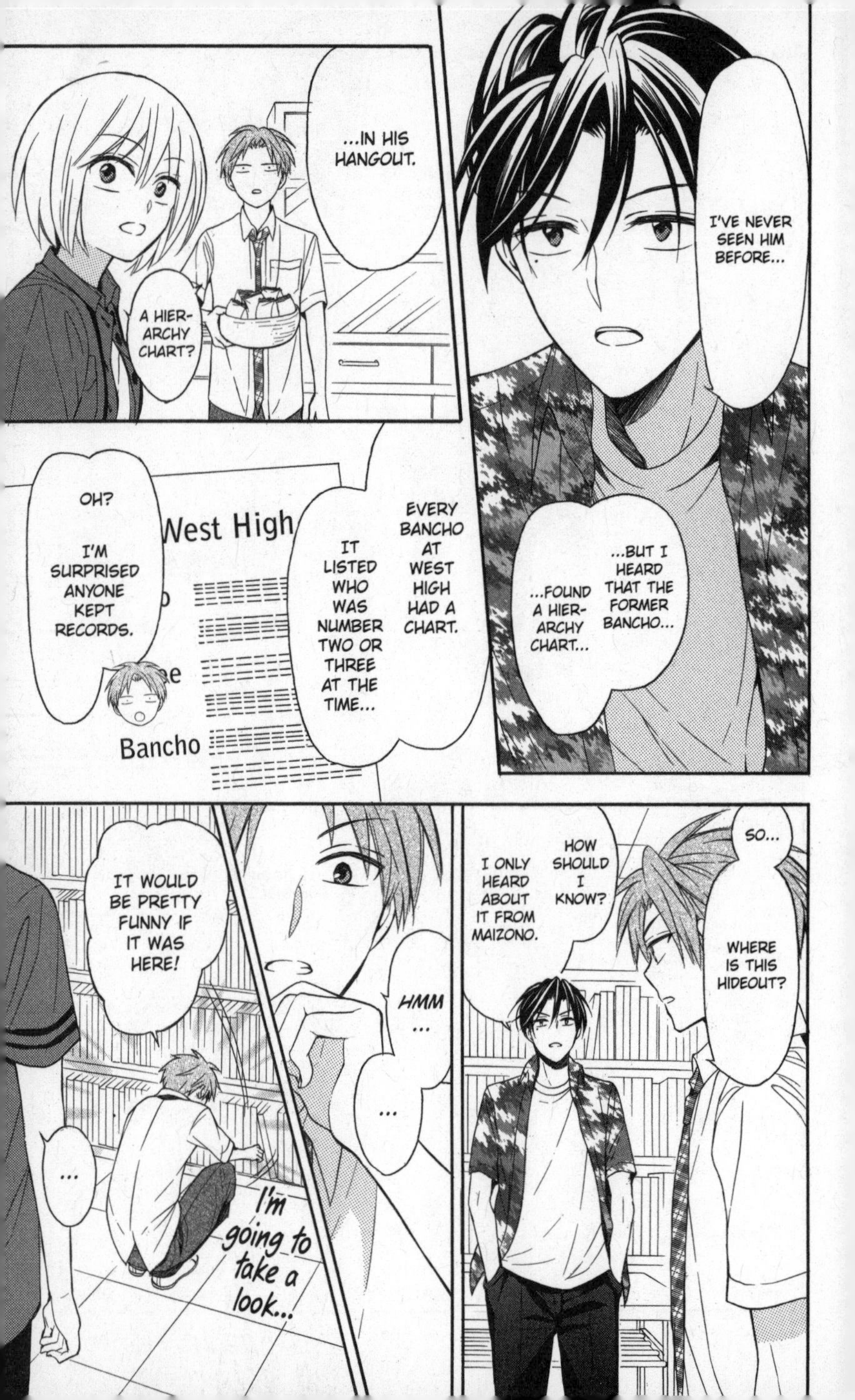
I'VE NEVER SEEN HIM BEFORE...
...BUT I HEARD THAT THE FORMER BANCHO...
...FOUND A HIER-ARCHY CHART...
...IN HIS HANGOUT.
A HIER-ARCHY CHART?
EVERY BANCHO AT WEST HIGH HAD A CHART.
IT LISTED WHO WAS NUMBER TWO OR THREE AT THE TIME...
OH?
I'M SURPRISED ANYONE KEPT RECORDS.
West High
Bancho
SO...
WHERE IS THIS HIDEOUT?
HOW SHOULD I KNOW?
I ONLY HEARD ABOUT IT FROM MAIZONO.
HMM...
...
IT WOULD BE PRETTY FUNNY IF IT WAS HERE!
...
I'm going to take a look...

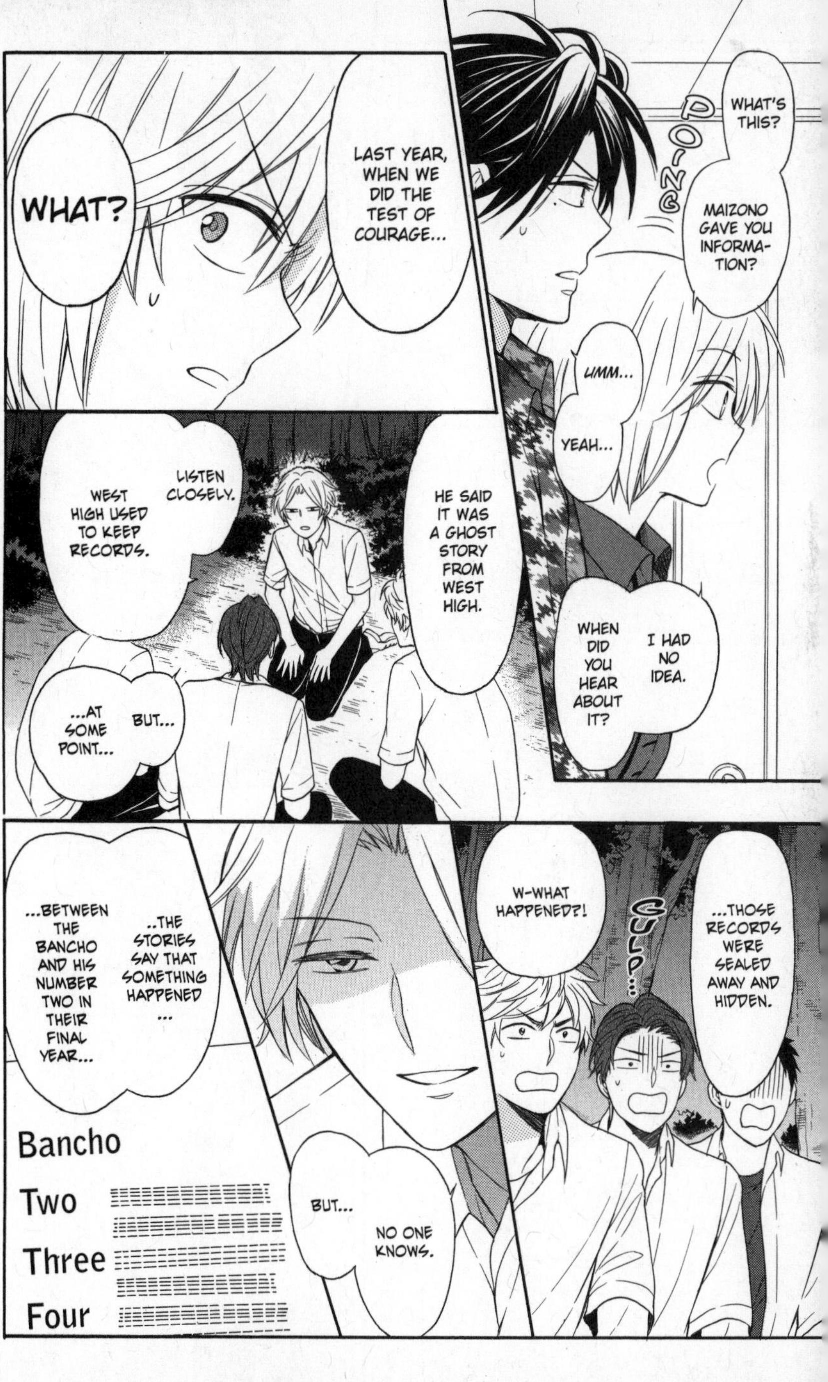
WHAT'S THIS?
POING
MAIZONO GAVE YOU INFORMATION?
UMM...
YEAH...
I HAD NO IDEA.
WHEN DID YOU HEAR ABOUT IT?
LAST YEAR, WHEN WE DID THE TEST OF COURAGE...
WHAT?
HE SAID IT WAS A GHOST STORY FROM WEST HIGH.
LISTEN CLOSELY.
WEST HIGH USED TO KEEP RECORDS.
BUT...
...AT SOME POINT...
...THOSE RECORDS WERE SEALED AWAY AND HIDDEN.
GULP...
W-WHAT HAPPENED?!
..THE STORIES SAY THAT SOMETHING HAPPENED...
...BETWEEN THE BANCHO AND HIS NUMBER TWO IN THEIR FINAL YEAR...
BUT...
NO ONE KNOWS.
Bancho
Two
Three
Four

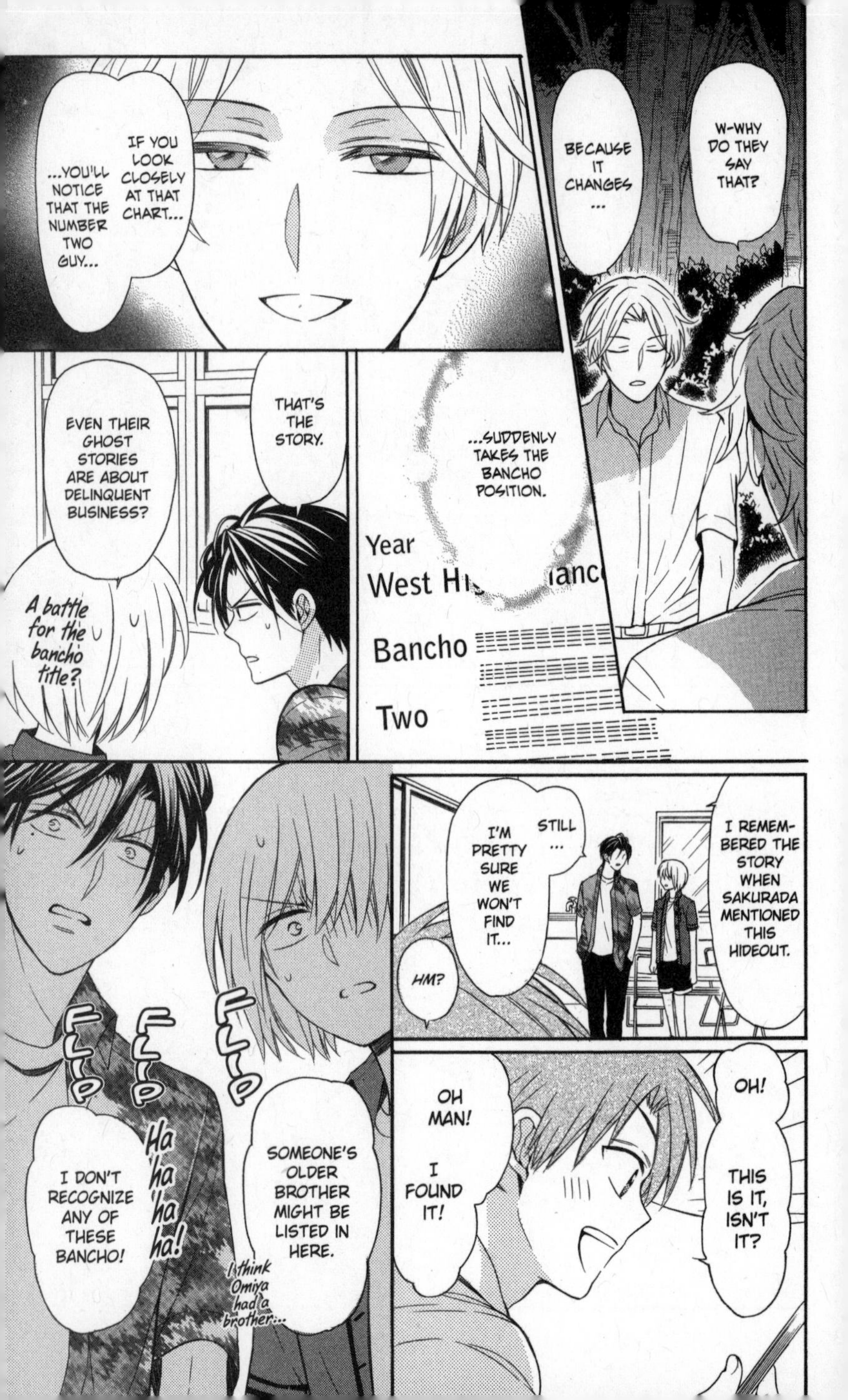

W-WHY DO THEY SAY THAT?
BECAUSE IT CHANGES...
IF YOU LOOK CLOSELY AT THAT CHART...
...YOU'LL NOTICE THAT THE NUMBER TWO GUY...
...SUDDENLY TAKES THE BANCHO POSITION.
Year
Bancho
Two
THAT'S THE STORY.
EVEN THEIR GHOST STORIES ARE ABOUT DELINQUENT BUSINESS?
A battle for the bancho title?
I REMEMBERED THE STORY WHEN SAKURADA MENTIONED THIS HIDEOUT.
STILL...
I'M PRETTY SURE WE WON'T FIND IT...
HM?
OH!
THIS IS IT, ISN'T IT?
OH MAN!
I FOUND IT!
FLIP
FLIP
FLIP
SOMEONE'S OLDER BROTHER MIGHT BE LISTED IN HERE.
Hahahaha!
I DON'T RECOGNIZE ANY OF THESE BANCHO!
I think Omiya had a brother...

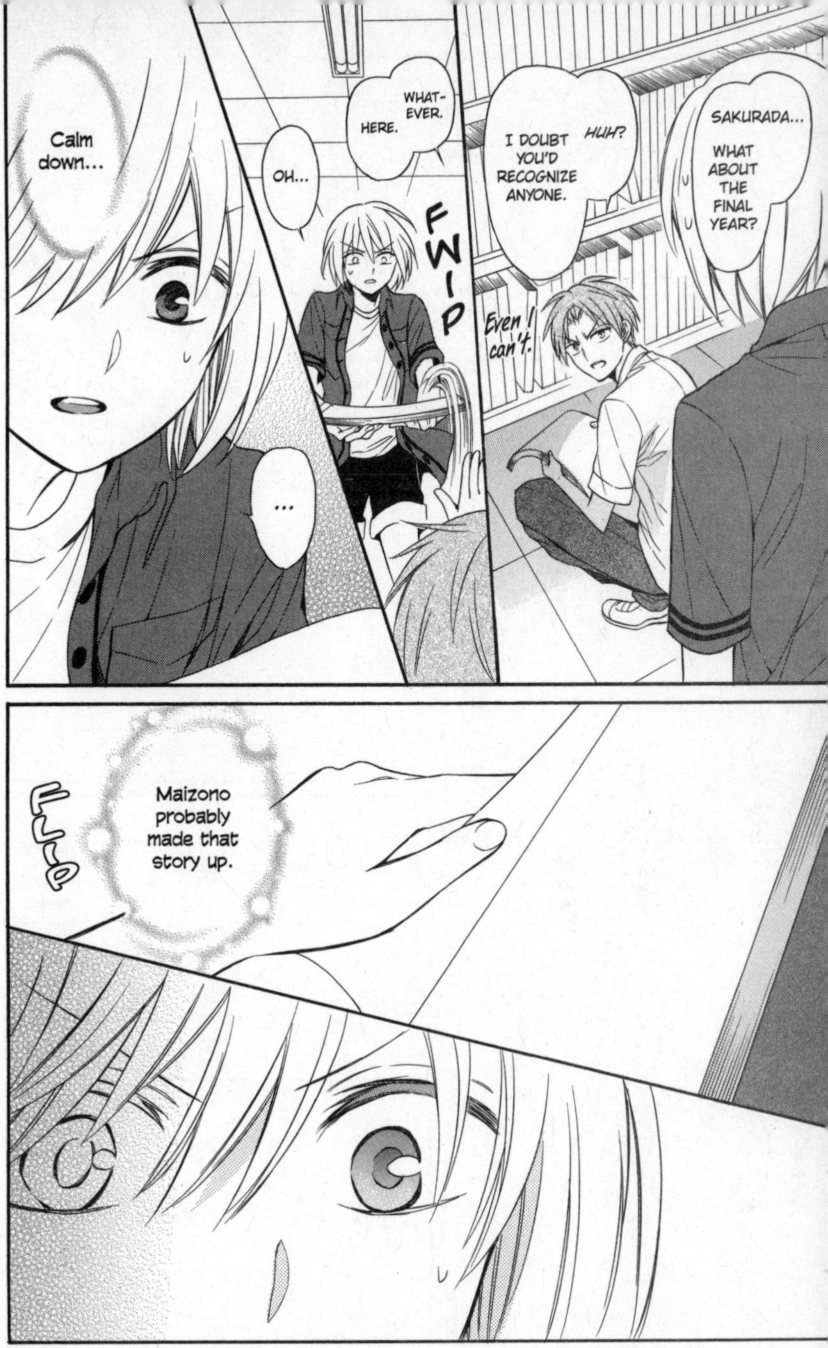
SAKURADA... WHAT ABOUT THE FINAL YEAR?
HUH?
I DOUBT YOU'D RECOGNIZE ANYONE.
Even I can't.
WHAT-EVER. HERE.
OH...
FWIP
...
Calm down...
Maizono probably made that story up.
FLIP

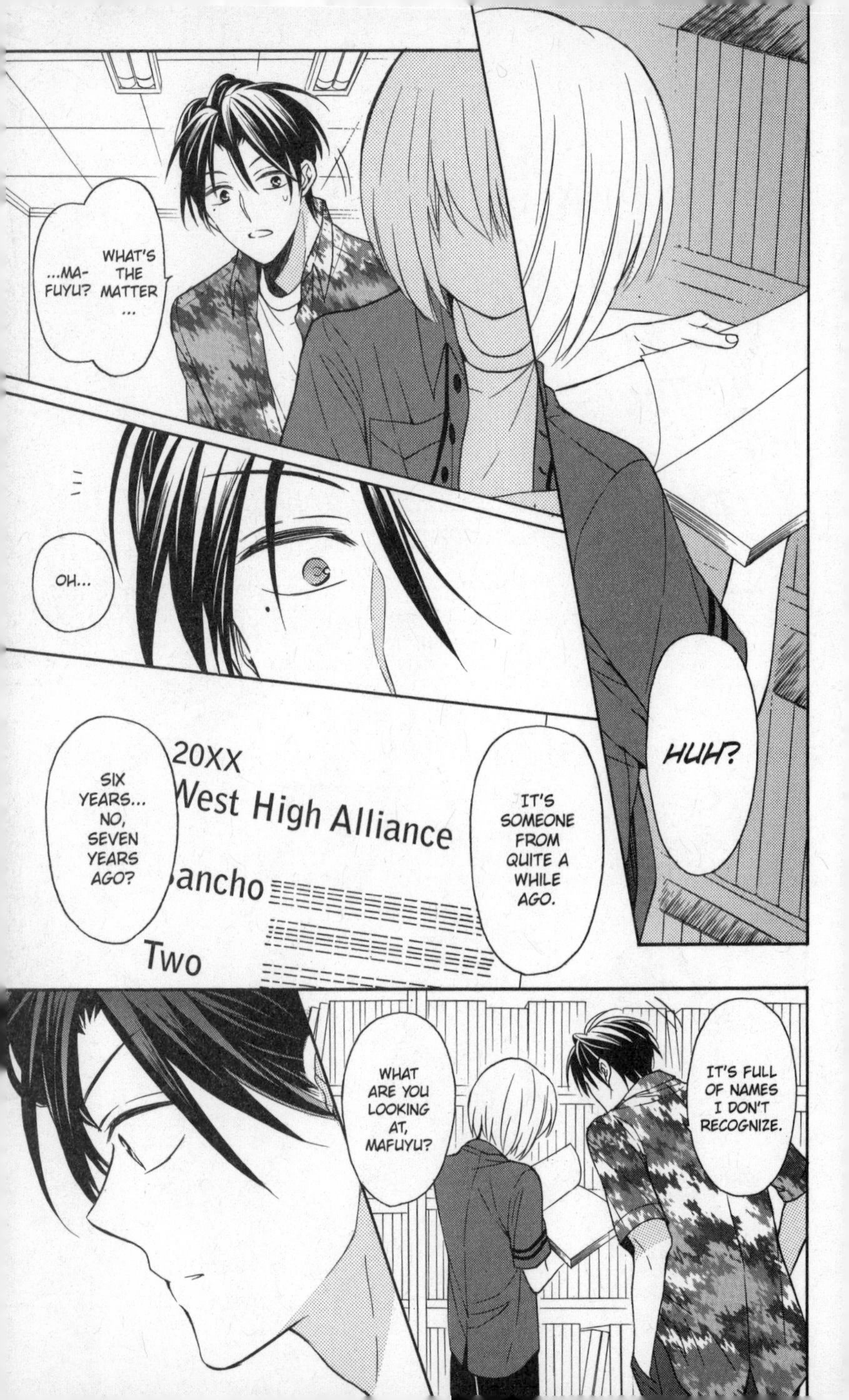
...MA-FUYU? WHAT'S THE MATTER ...
HUH?
OH...
IT'S SOMEONE FROM QUITE A WHILE AGO.
SIX YEARS... NO, SEVEN YEARS AGO?
20XX
West High Alliance
ancho
Two
IT'S FULL OF NAMES I DON'T RECOGNIZE.
WHAT ARE YOU LOOKING AT, MAFUYU?

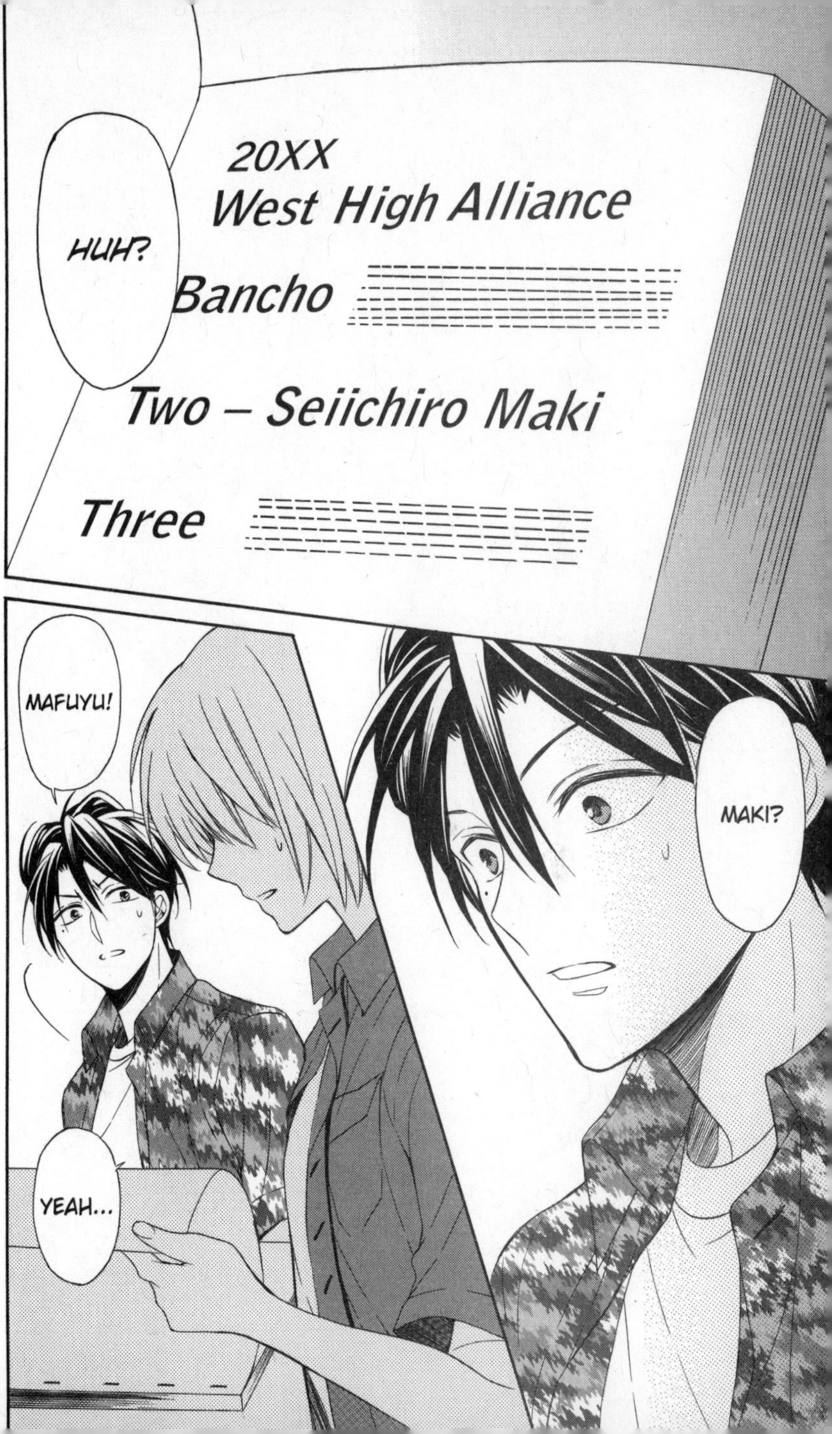
20XX
West High Alliance
Bancho
Two – Seiichiro Maki
Three
HUH?
MAKI?
MAFUYU!
YEAH...

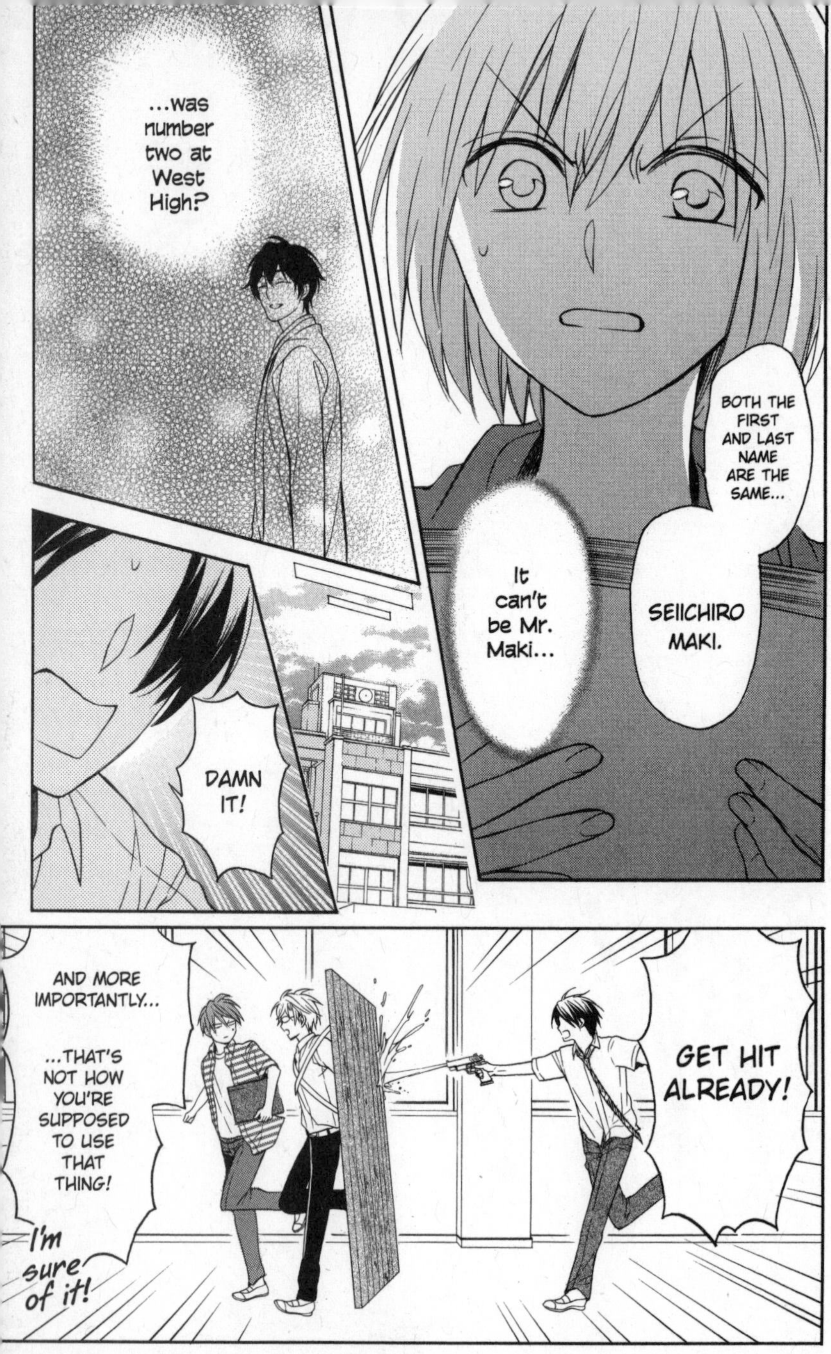
BOTH THE FIRST AND LAST NAME ARE THE SAME...
SEIICHIRO MAKI.
It can't be Mr. Maki...
...was number two at West High?
DAMN IT!
GET HIT ALREADY!
AND MORE IMPORTANTLY...
...THAT'S NOT HOW YOU'RE SUPPOSED TO USE THAT THING!
I'm sure of it!

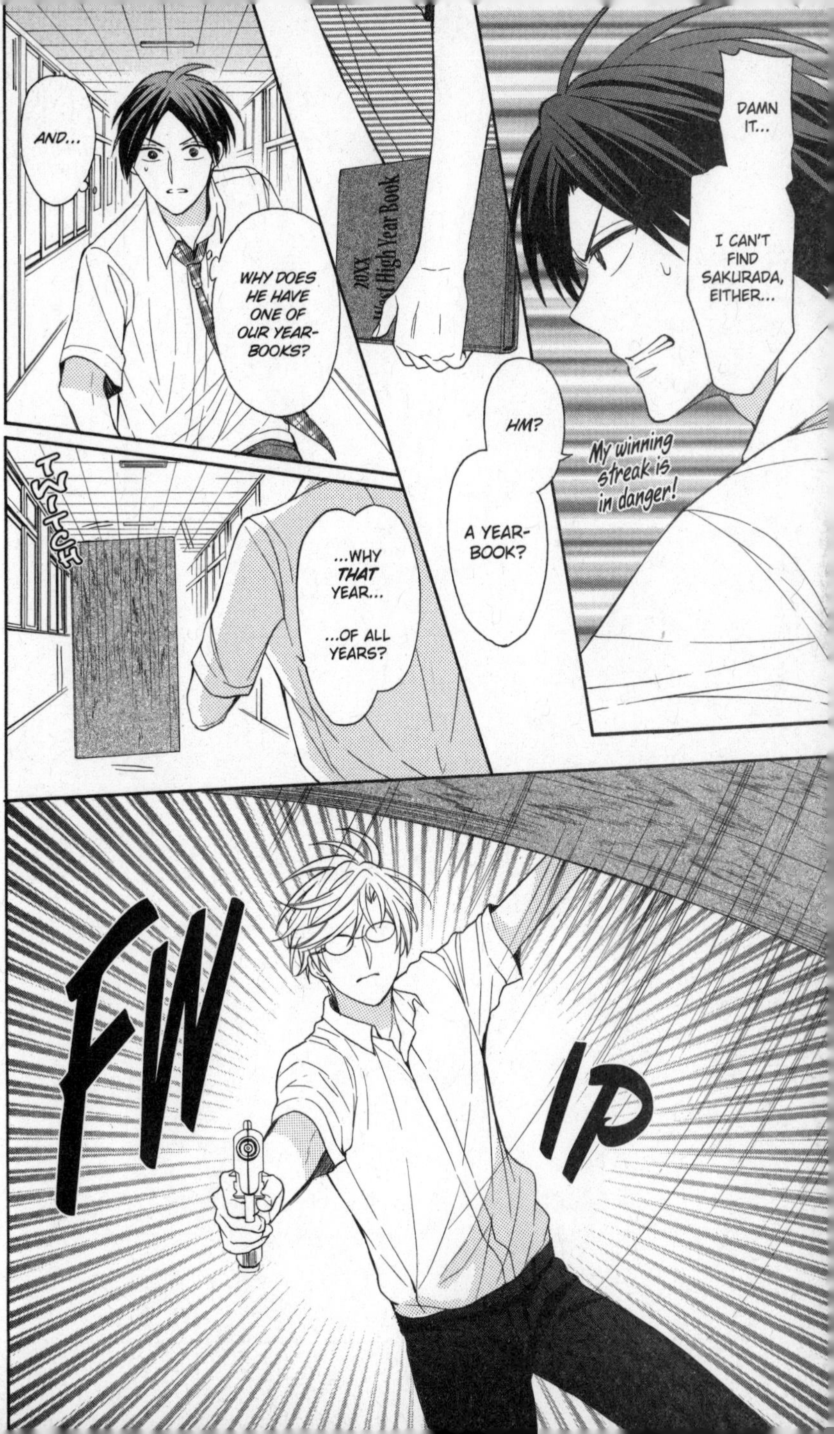
DAMN IT...
I CAN'T FIND SAKURADA, EITHER...
My winning streak is in danger!
HM?
A YEAR-BOOK?
20XX
High Year Book
AND...
WHY DOES HE HAVE ONE OF OUR YEAR-BOOKS?
...WHY THAT YEAR...
...OF ALL YEARS?
TWITCH
FWIP

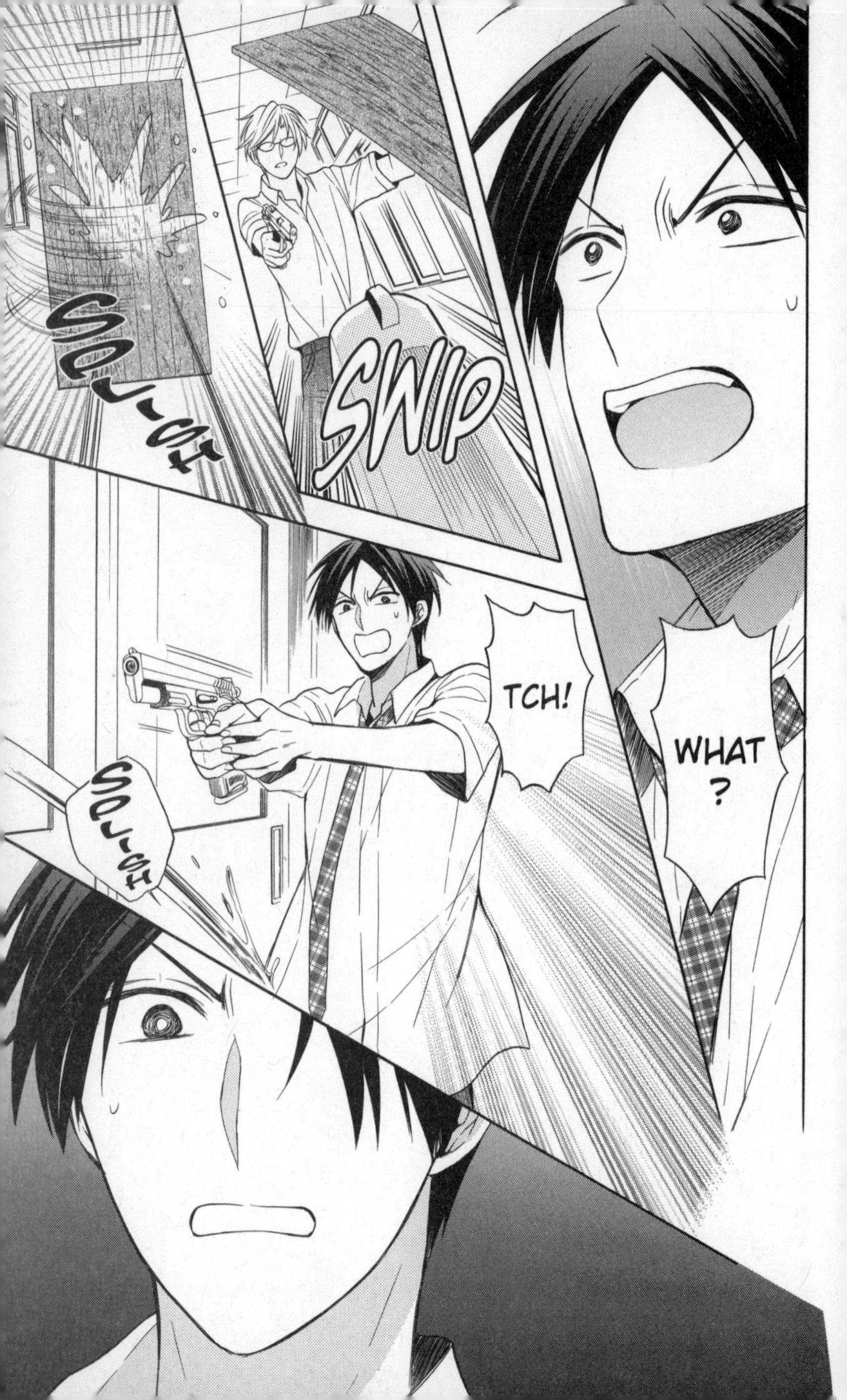
WHAT?
SWIP
SQUISH
TCH!
SQUISH

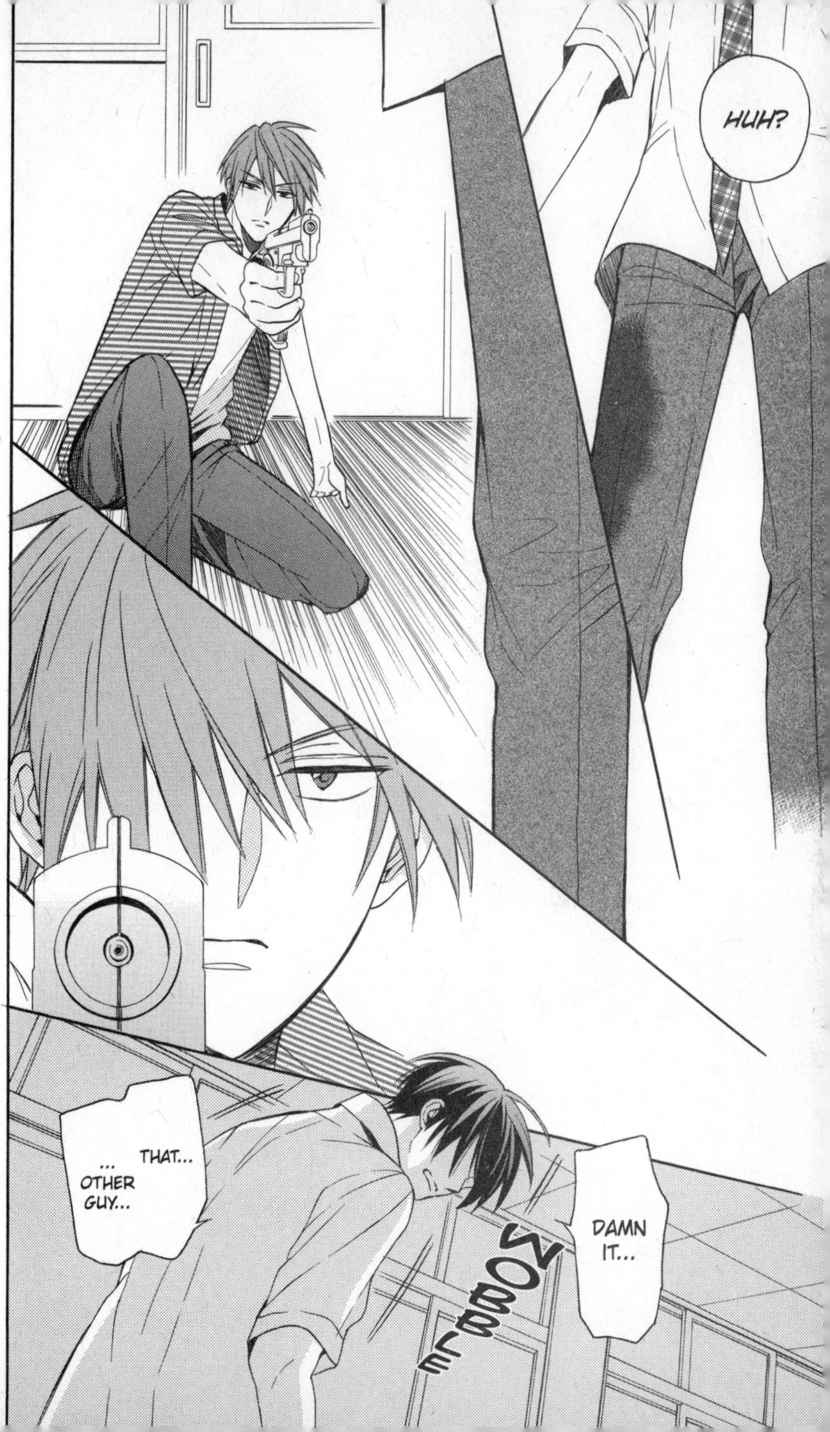
HUH?
DAMN IT...
WOBBLE
... THAT... OTHER GUY...

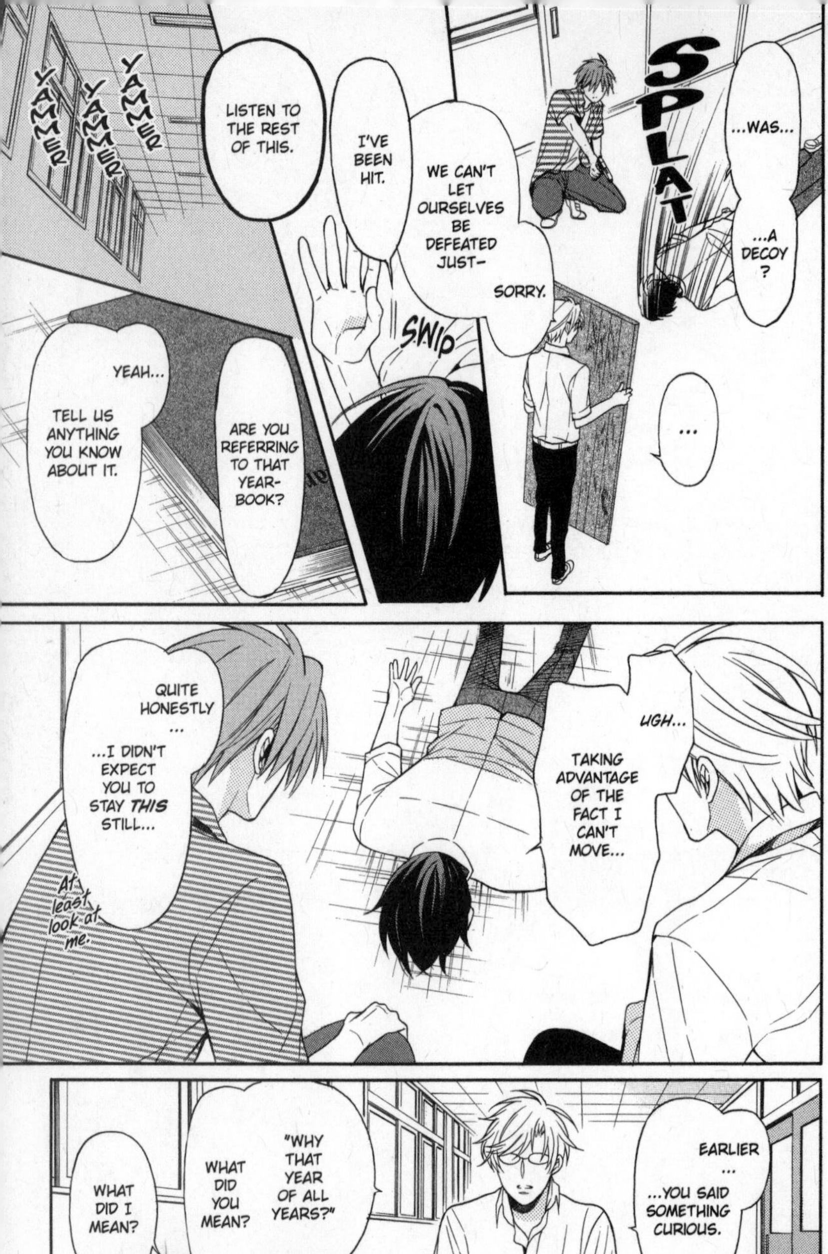
SPLAT
...WAS...
...A DECOY?
...
SORRY.
WE CAN'T LET OURSELVES BE DEFEATED JUST-
I'VE BEEN HIT.
SWIP
LISTEN TO THE REST OF THIS.
YAMMER YAMMER YAMMER
ARE YOU REFERRING TO THAT YEARBOOK?
YEAH...
TELL US ANYTHING YOU KNOW ABOUT IT.
UGH...
TAKING ADVANTAGE OF THE FACT I CAN'T MOVE...
QUITE HONESTLY...
...I DIDN'T EXPECT YOU TO STAY *THIS* STILL...
At least look at me.
EARLIER...
...YOU SAID SOMETHING CURIOUS.
"WHY THAT YEAR OF ALL YEARS?"
WHAT DID YOU MEAN?
WHAT DID I MEAN?

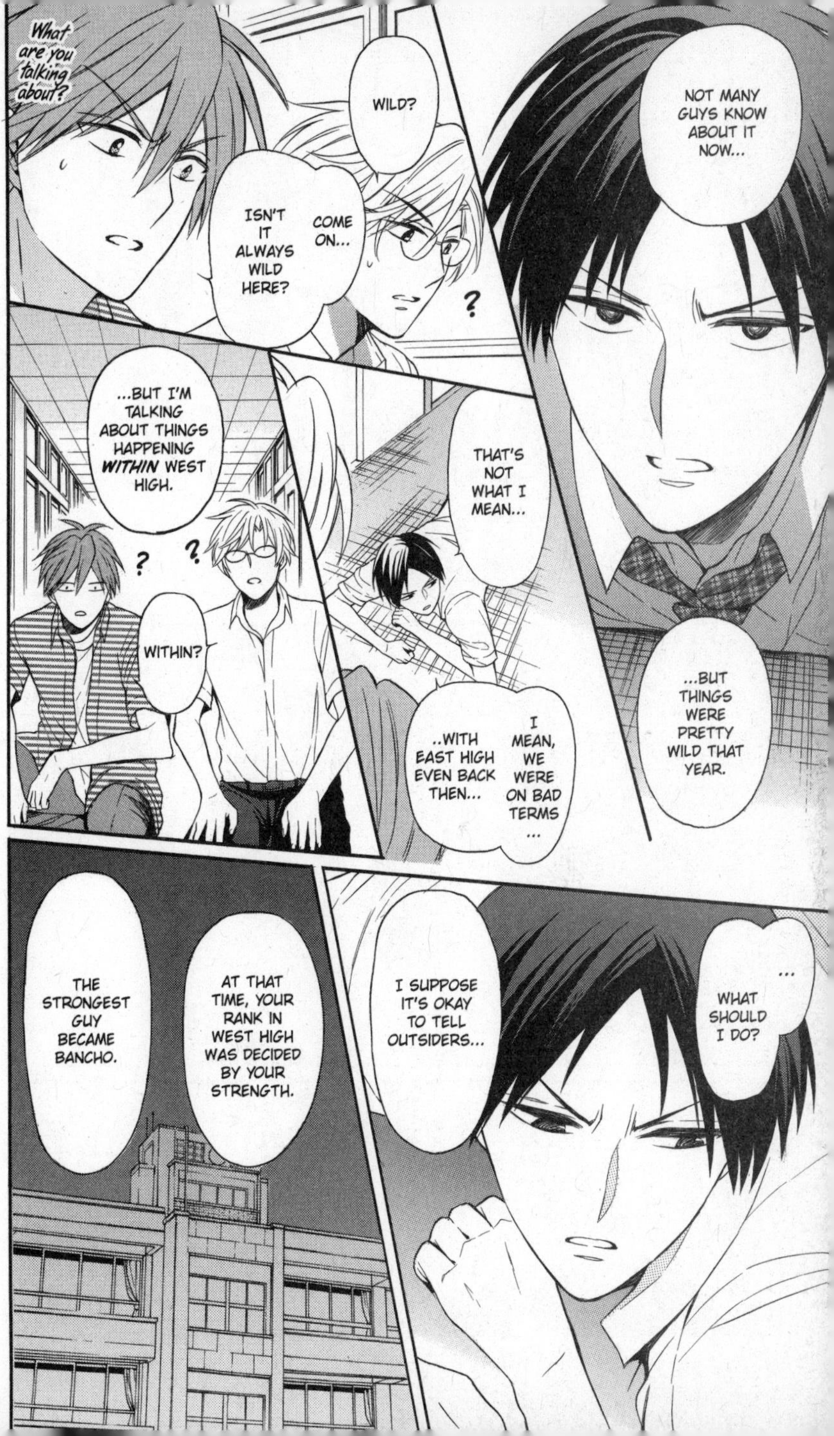
NOT MANY GUYS KNOW ABOUT IT NOW...
...BUT THINGS WERE PRETTY WILD THAT YEAR.
WILD?
COME ON...
ISN'T IT ALWAYS WILD HERE?
What are you talking about?
THAT'S NOT WHAT I MEAN...
I MEAN, WE WERE ON BAD TERMS...
..WITH EAST HIGH EVEN BACK THEN...
...BUT I'M TALKING ABOUT THINGS HAPPENING *WITHIN* WEST HIGH.
WITHIN?
... WHAT SHOULD I DO?
I SUPPOSE IT'S OKAY TO TELL OUTSIDERS...
AT THAT TIME, YOUR RANK IN WEST HIGH WAS DECIDED BY YOUR STRENGTH.
THE STRONGEST GUY BECAME BANCHO.

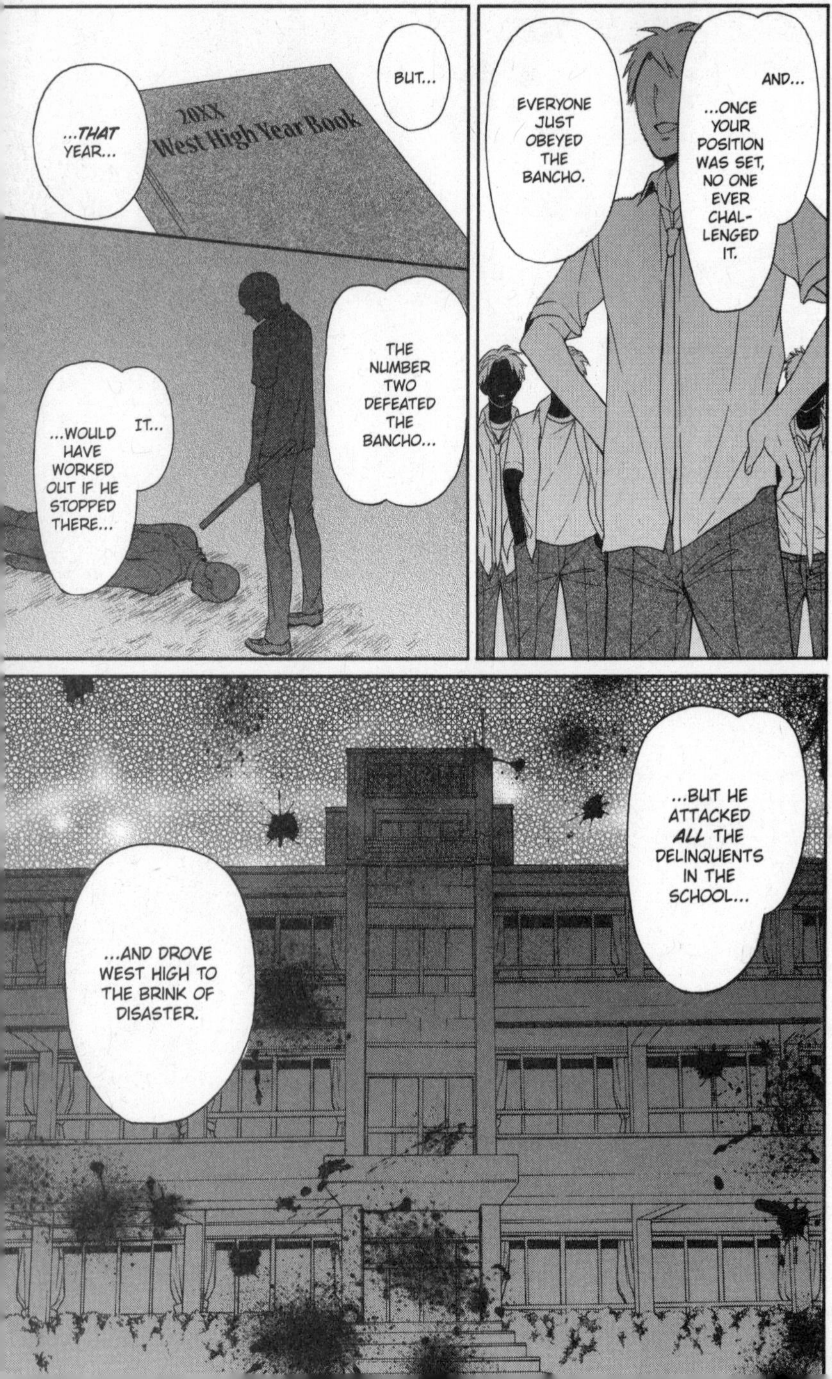
AND...
...ONCE YOUR POSITION WAS SET, NO ONE EVER CHAL-LENGED IT.
EVERYONE JUST OBEYED THE BANCHO.
BUT...
20XX West High Year Book
...*THAT* YEAR...
THE NUMBER TWO DEFEATED THE BANCHO...
IT...
...WOULD HAVE WORKED OUT IF HE STOPPED THERE...
...BUT HE ATTACKED *ALL* THE DELINQUENTS IN THE SCHOOL...
...AND DROVE WEST HIGH TO THE BRINK OF DISASTER.

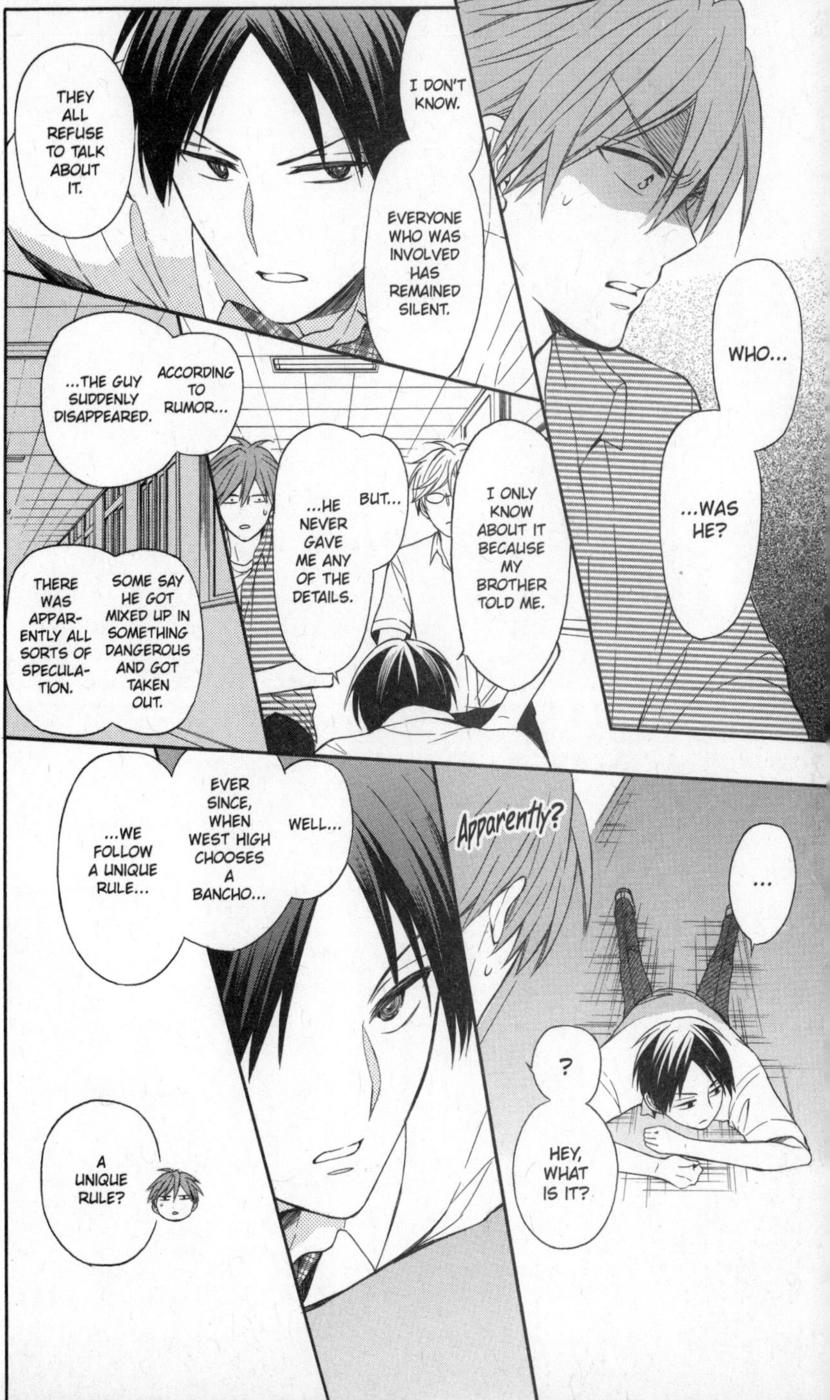
WHO...
...WAS HE?
I DON'T KNOW.
EVERYONE WHO WAS INVOLVED HAS REMAINED SILENT.
THEY ALL REFUSE TO TALK ABOUT IT.
I ONLY KNOW ABOUT IT BECAUSE MY BROTHER TOLD ME.
BUT...
...HE NEVER GAVE ME ANY OF THE DETAILS.
ACCORDING TO RUMOR...
...THE GUY SUDDENLY DISAPPEARED.
SOME SAY HE GOT MIXED UP IN SOMETHING DANGEROUS AND GOT TAKEN OUT.
THERE WAS APPARENTLY ALL SORTS OF SPECULATION.
Apparently?
...
?
HEY, WHAT IS IT?
WELL...
EVER SINCE, WHEN WEST HIGH CHOOSES A BANCHO...
...WE FOLLOW A UNIQUE RULE...
A UNIQUE RULE?

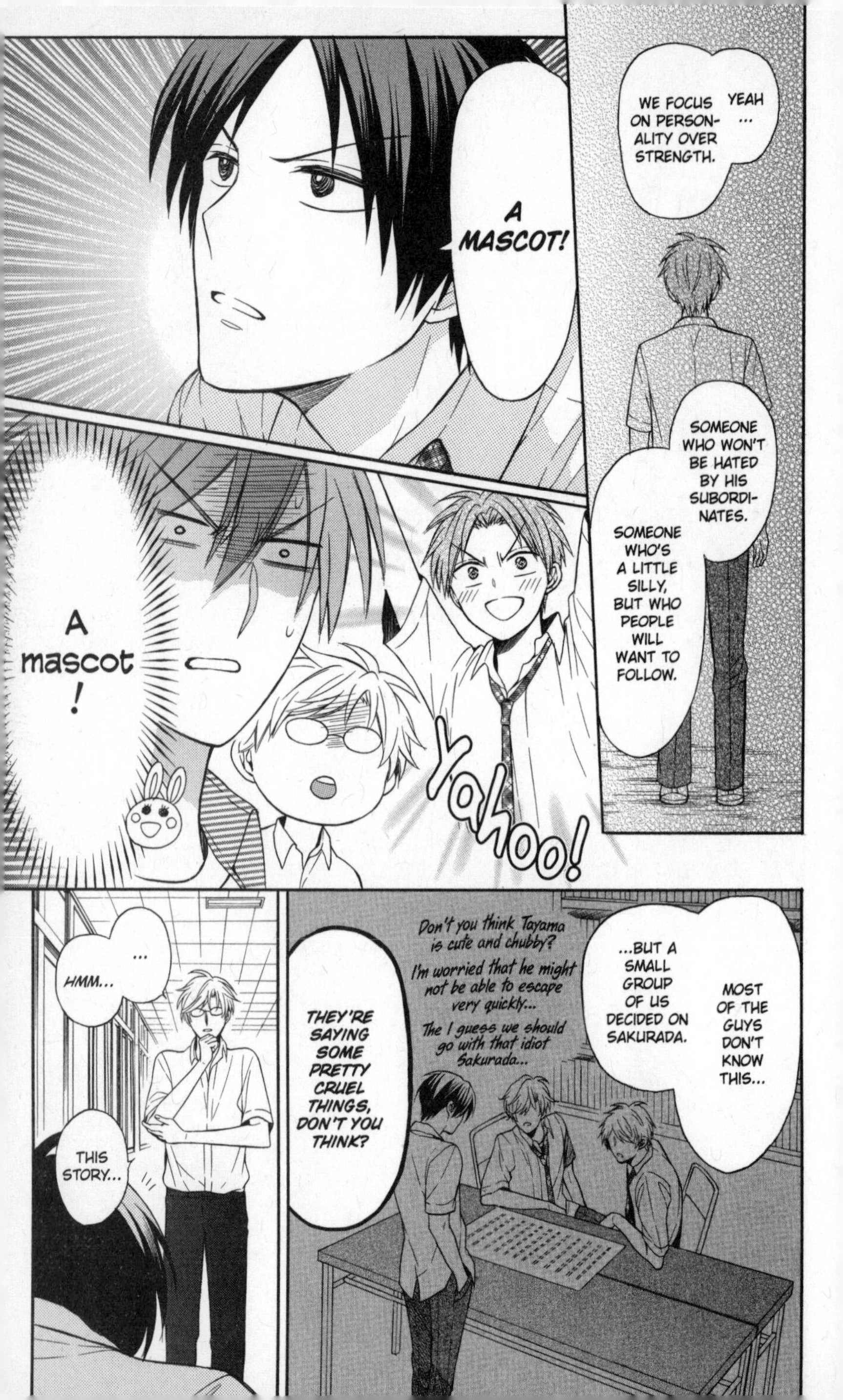
YEAH...
WE FOCUS ON PERSONALITY OVER STRENGTH.
SOMEONE WHO WON'T BE HATED BY HIS SUBORDINATES.
SOMEONE WHO'S A LITTLE SILLY, BUT WHO PEOPLE WILL WANT TO FOLLOW.
A MASCOT!
A mascot!
Yahoo!
MOST OF THE GUYS DON'T KNOW THIS...
...BUT A SMALL GROUP OF US DECIDED ON SAKURADA.
Don't you think Tayama is cute and chubby?
I'm worried that he might not be able to escape very quickly...
The I guess we should go with that idiot Sakurada...
THEY'RE SAYING SOME PRETTY CRUEL THINGS, DON'T YOU THINK?
...
HMM...
THIS STORY...

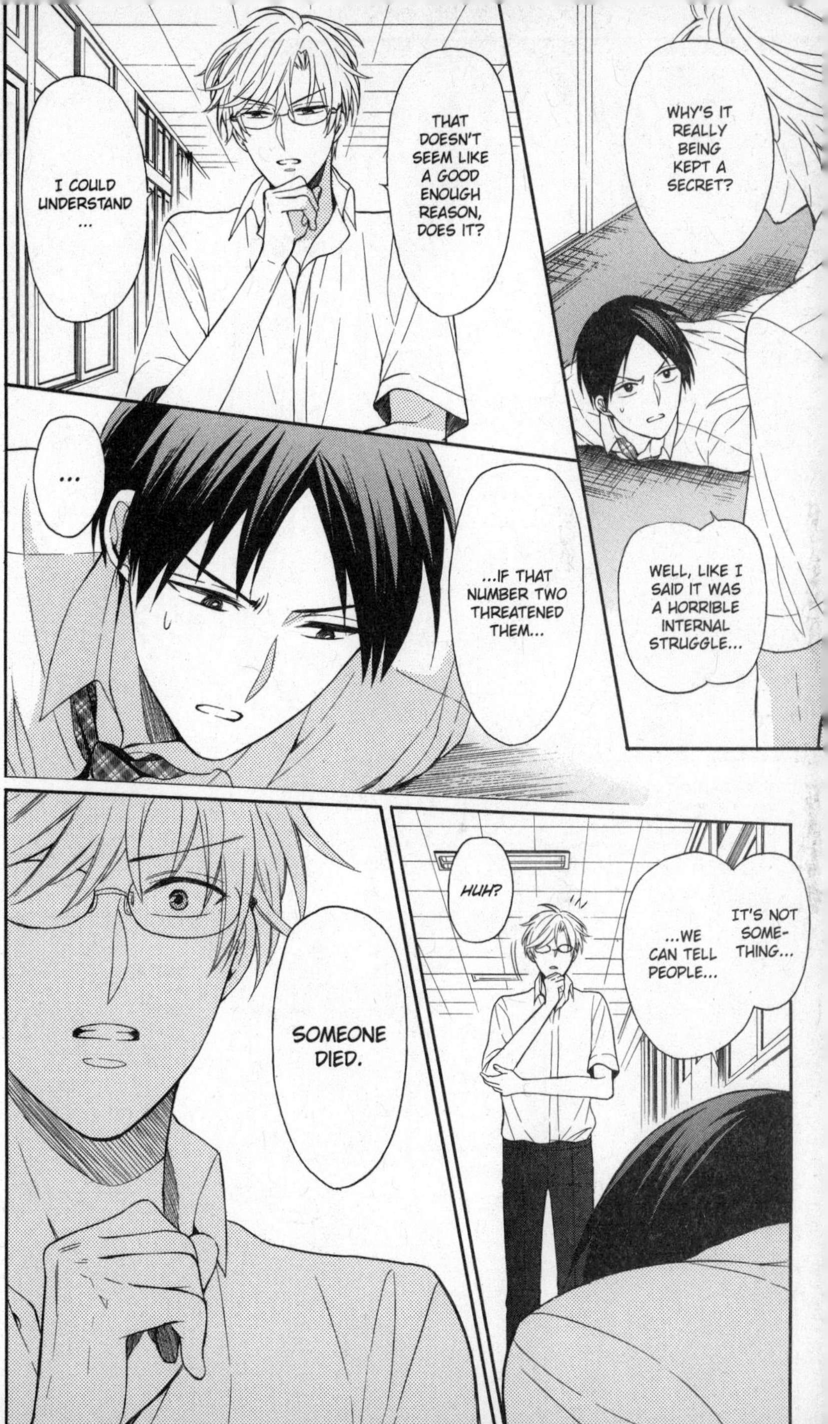
WHY'S IT REALLY BEING KEPT A SECRET?
WELL, LIKE I SAID IT WAS A HORRIBLE INTERNAL STRUGGLE...
THAT DOESN'T SEEM LIKE A GOOD ENOUGH REASON, DOES IT?
I COULD UNDERSTAND ...
...IF THAT NUMBER TWO THREATENED THEM...
...
IT'S NOT SOME-THING...
...WE CAN TELL PEOPLE...
HUH?
SOMEONE DIED.

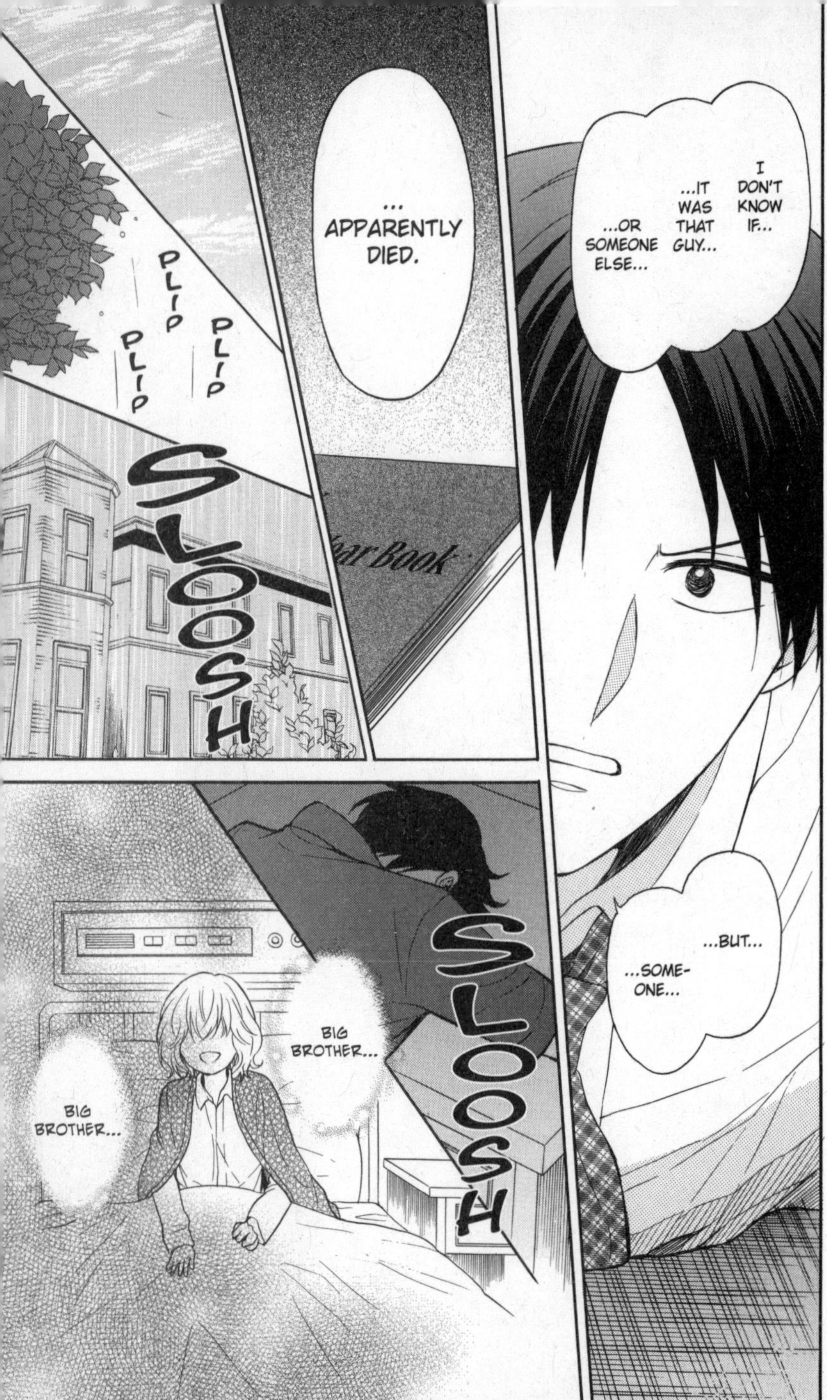
I DON'T KNOW IF...
...IT WAS THAT GUY...
...OR SOMEONE ELSE...
...BUT...
...SOME-ONE...
... APPARENTLY DIED.
PLIP
PLIP
PLIP
SLOOSH
SLOOSH
BIG BROTHER...
BIG BROTHER...

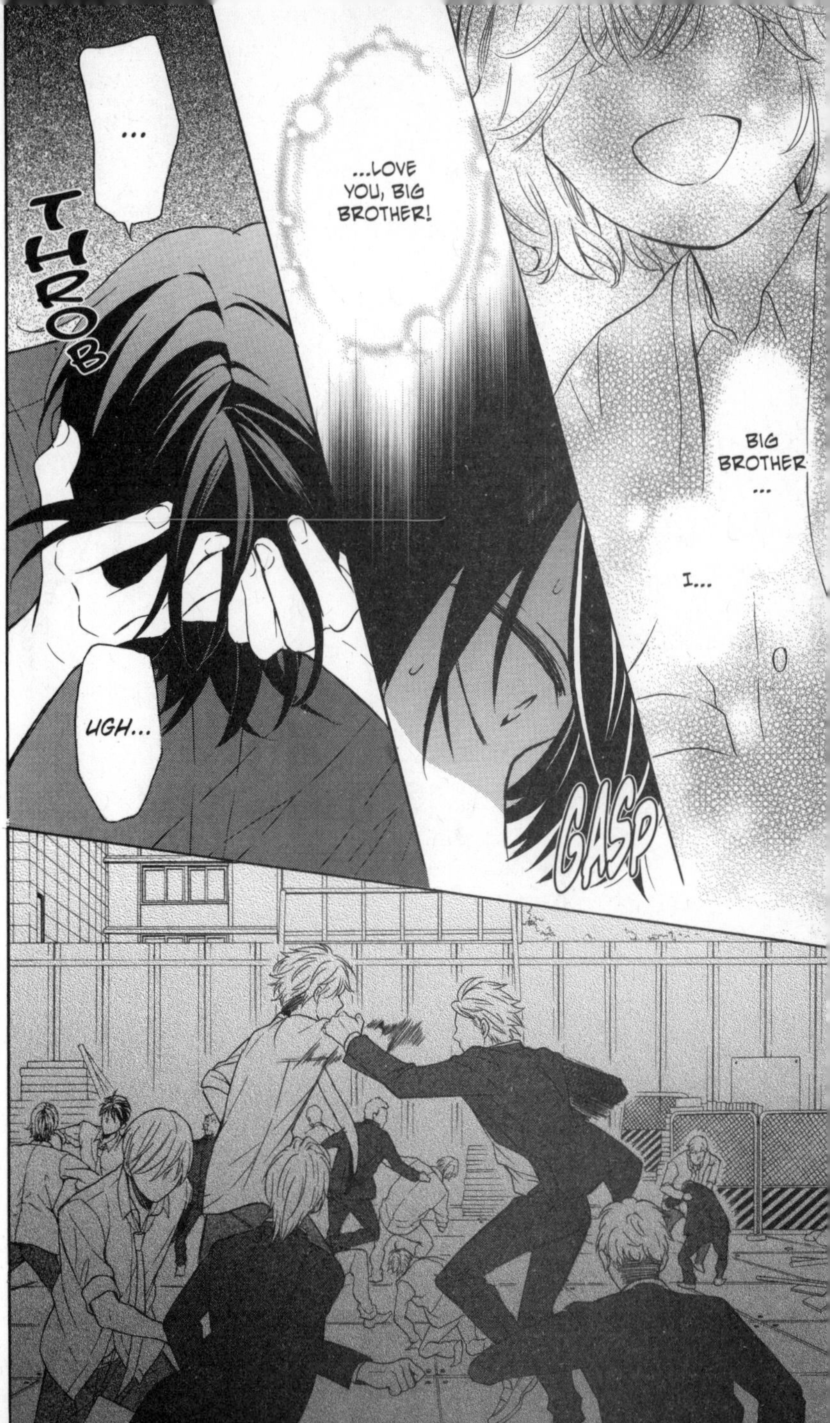
BIG BROTHER...
I...
...LOVE YOU, BIG BROTHER!
GASP
...
THROB
UGH...

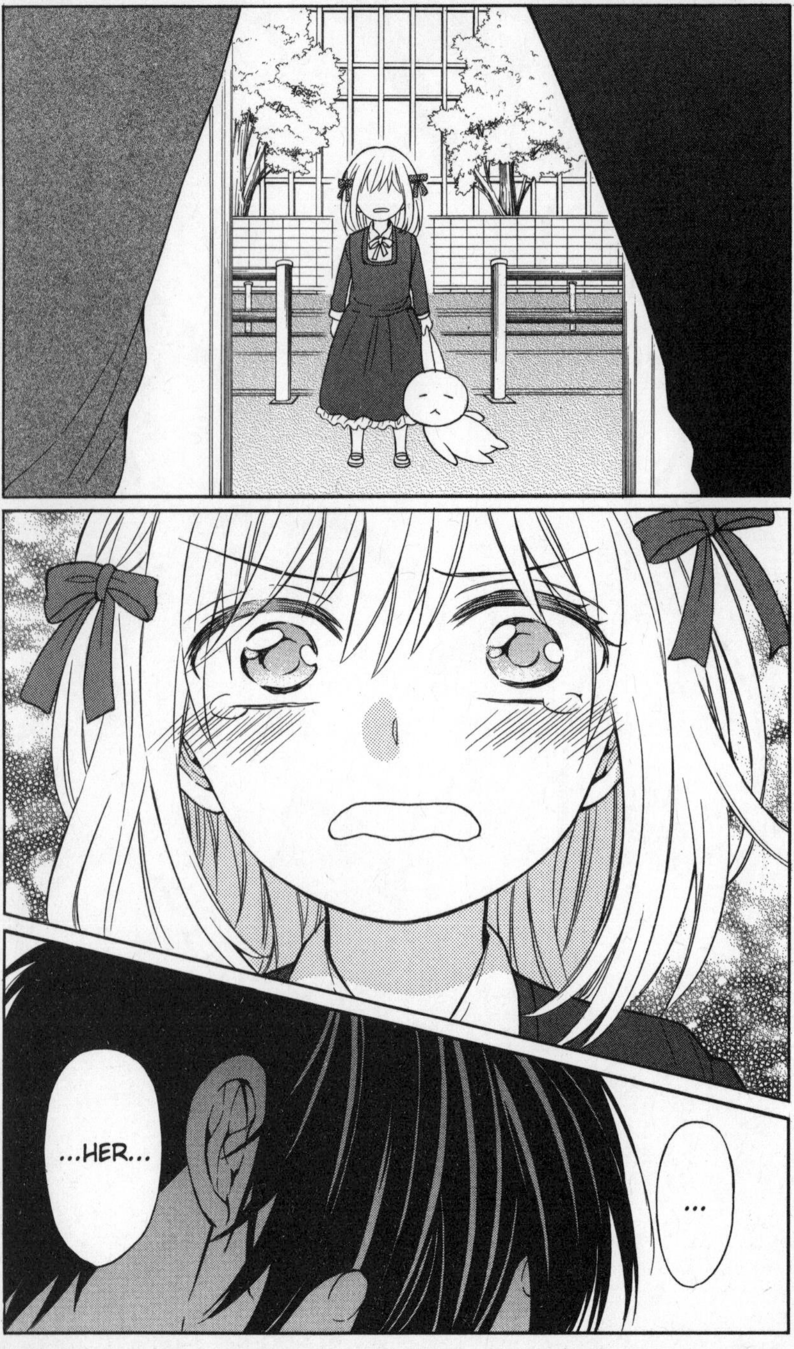
...
...HER...

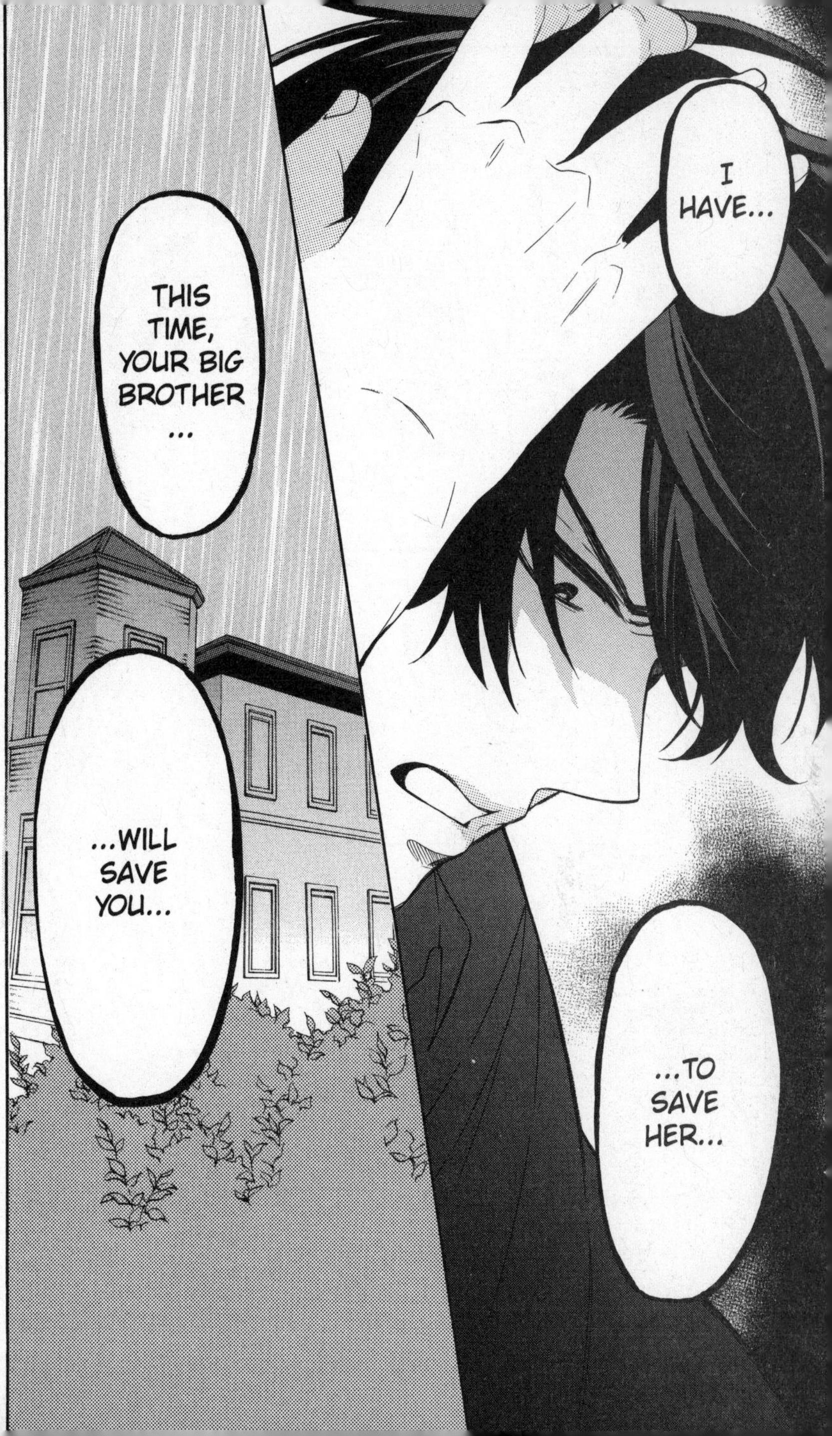
I HAVE...
...TO SAVE HER...
THIS TIME, YOUR BIG BROTHER ...
...WILL SAVE YOU...

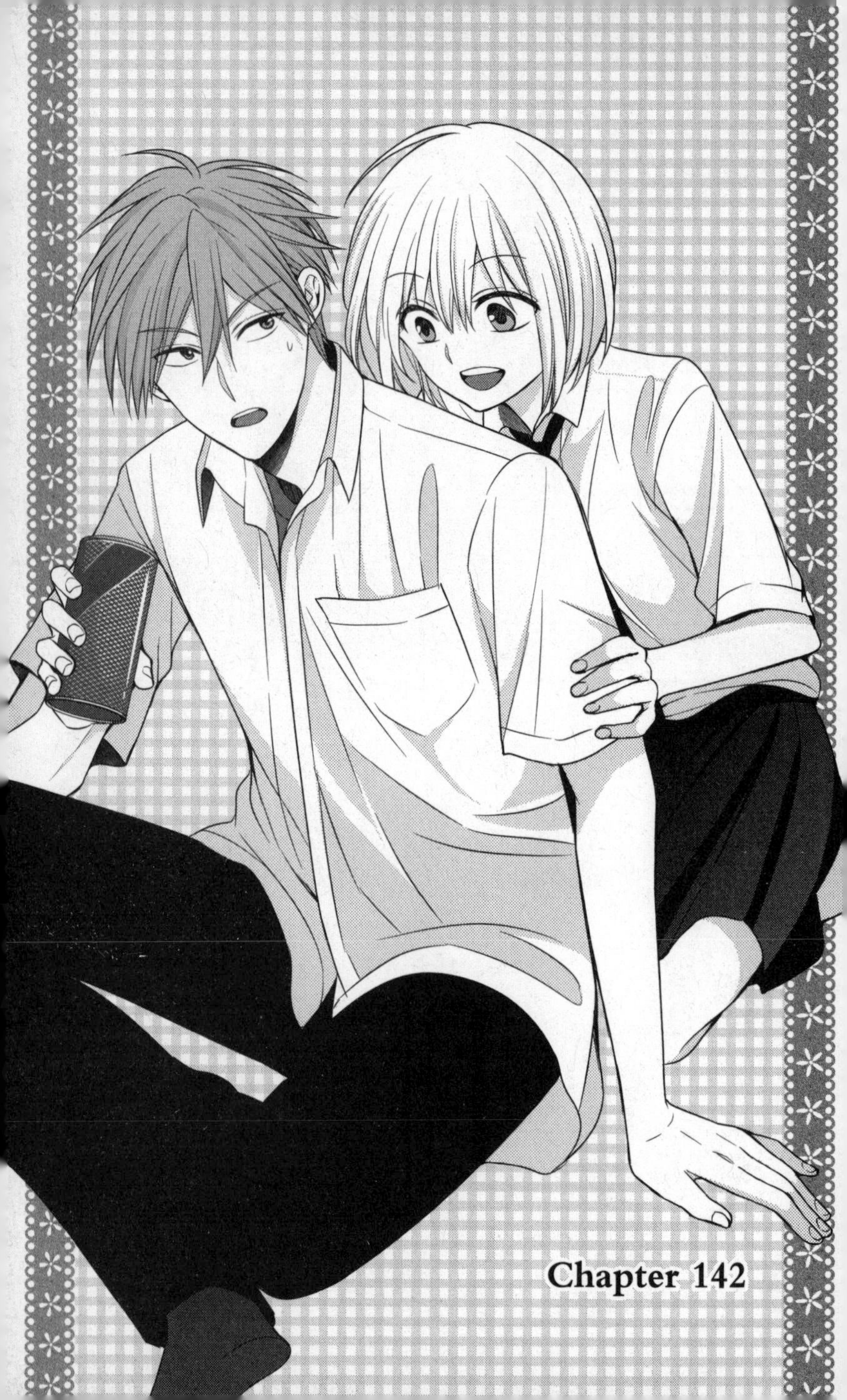
Chapter 142

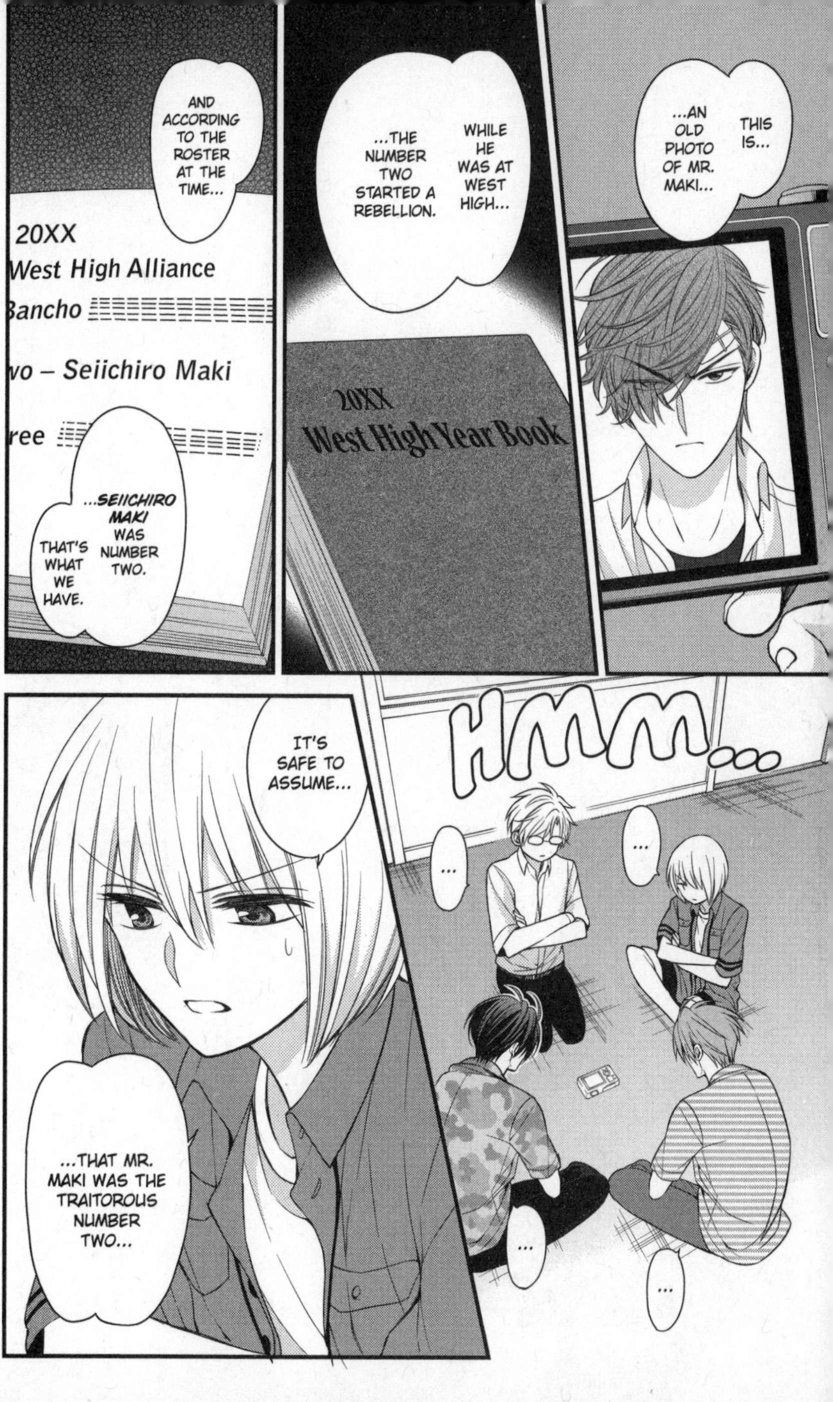
THIS IS...
...AN OLD PHOTO OF MR. MAKI...
WHILE HE WAS AT WEST HIGH...
...THE NUMBER TWO STARTED A REBELLION.
20XX
West High Year Book
AND ACCORDING TO THE ROSTER AT THE TIME...
20XX
West High Alliance
Bancho
wo – Seiichiro Maki
ree
...SEIICHIRO MAKI WAS NUMBER TWO.
THAT'S WHAT WE HAVE.
HMM...
...
...
...
...
IT'S SAFE TO ASSUME...
...THAT MR. MAKI WAS THE TRAITOROUS NUMBER TWO...

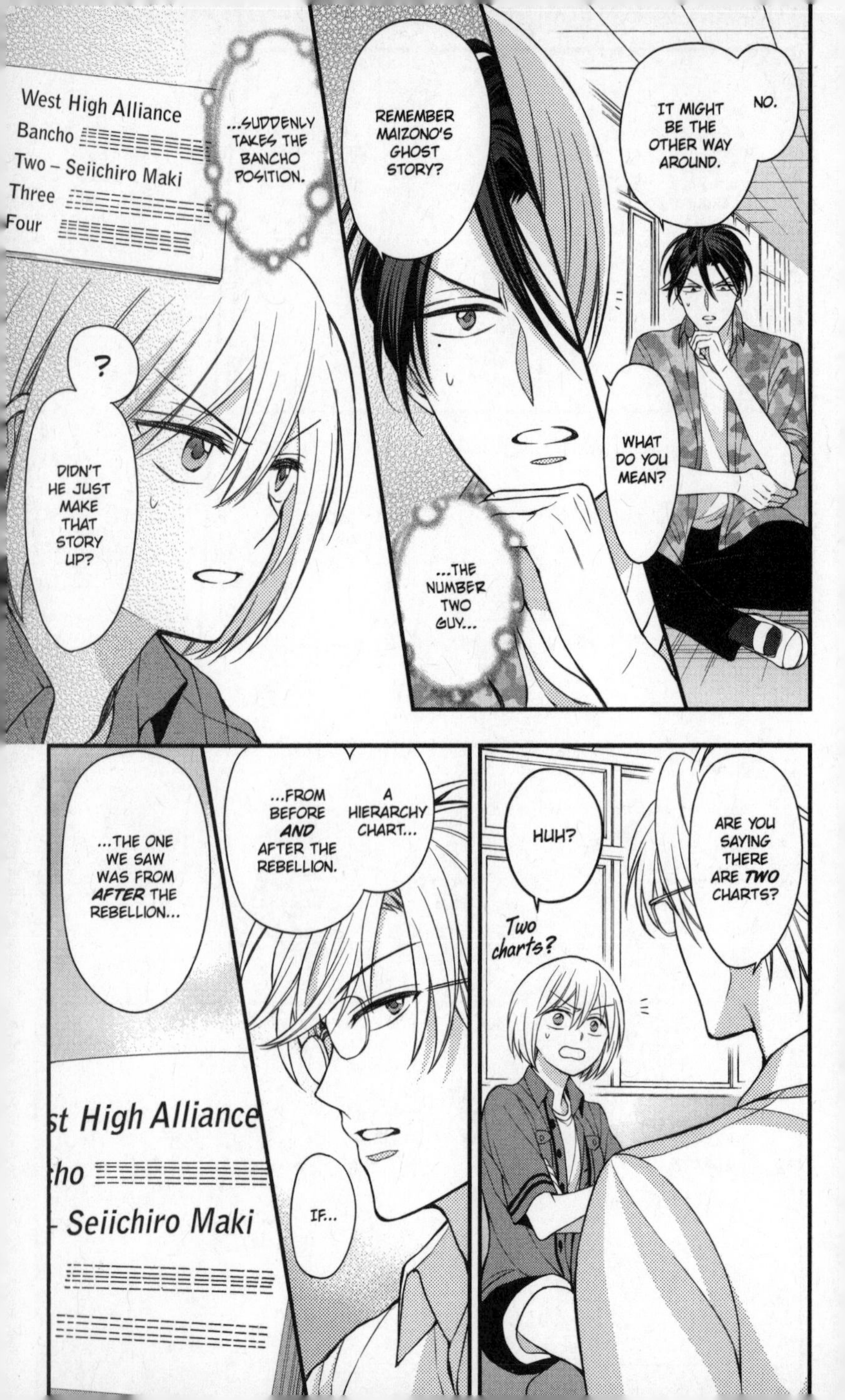
NO.
IT MIGHT BE THE OTHER WAY AROUND.
WHAT DO YOU MEAN?
REMEMBER MAIZONO'S GHOST STORY?
...THE NUMBER TWO GUY...
...SUDDENLY TAKES THE BANCHO POSITION.
West High Alliance
Bancho
Two – Seiichiro Maki
Three
Four
?
DIDN'T HE JUST MAKE THAT STORY UP?
ARE YOU SAYING THERE ARE *TWO* CHARTS?
HUH?
Two charts?
A HIERARCHY CHART...
...FROM BEFORE *AND* AFTER THE REBELLION.
...THE ONE WE SAW WAS FROM *AFTER* THE REBELLION...
IF...
st High Alliance
cho
– Seiichiro Maki

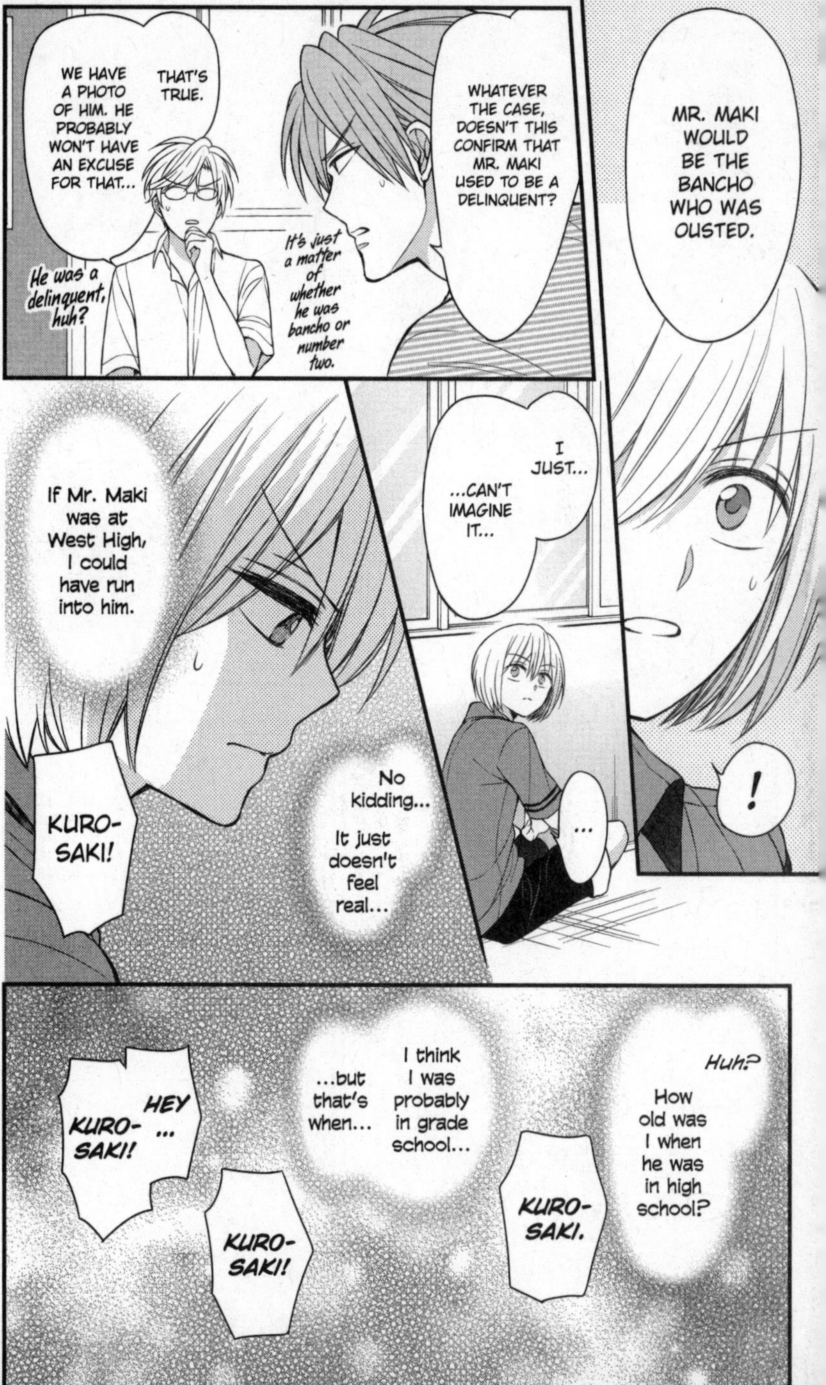
MR. MAKI WOULD BE THE BANCHO WHO WAS OUSTED.
!
WHATEVER THE CASE, DOESN'T THIS CONFIRM THAT MR. MAKI USED TO BE A DELINQUENT?
It's just a matter of whether he was bancho or number two.
THAT'S TRUE.
WE HAVE A PHOTO OF HIM. HE PROBABLY WON'T HAVE AN EXCUSE FOR THAT...
He was a delinquent, huh?
I JUST...
...CAN'T IMAGINE IT...
...
If Mr. Maki was at West High, I could have run into him.
No kidding...
It just doesn't feel real...
KURO-SAKI!
Huh?
How old was I when he was in high school?
KURO-SAKI.
I think I was probably in grade school...
...but that's when...
KURO-SAKI!
HEY ... KURO-SAKI!

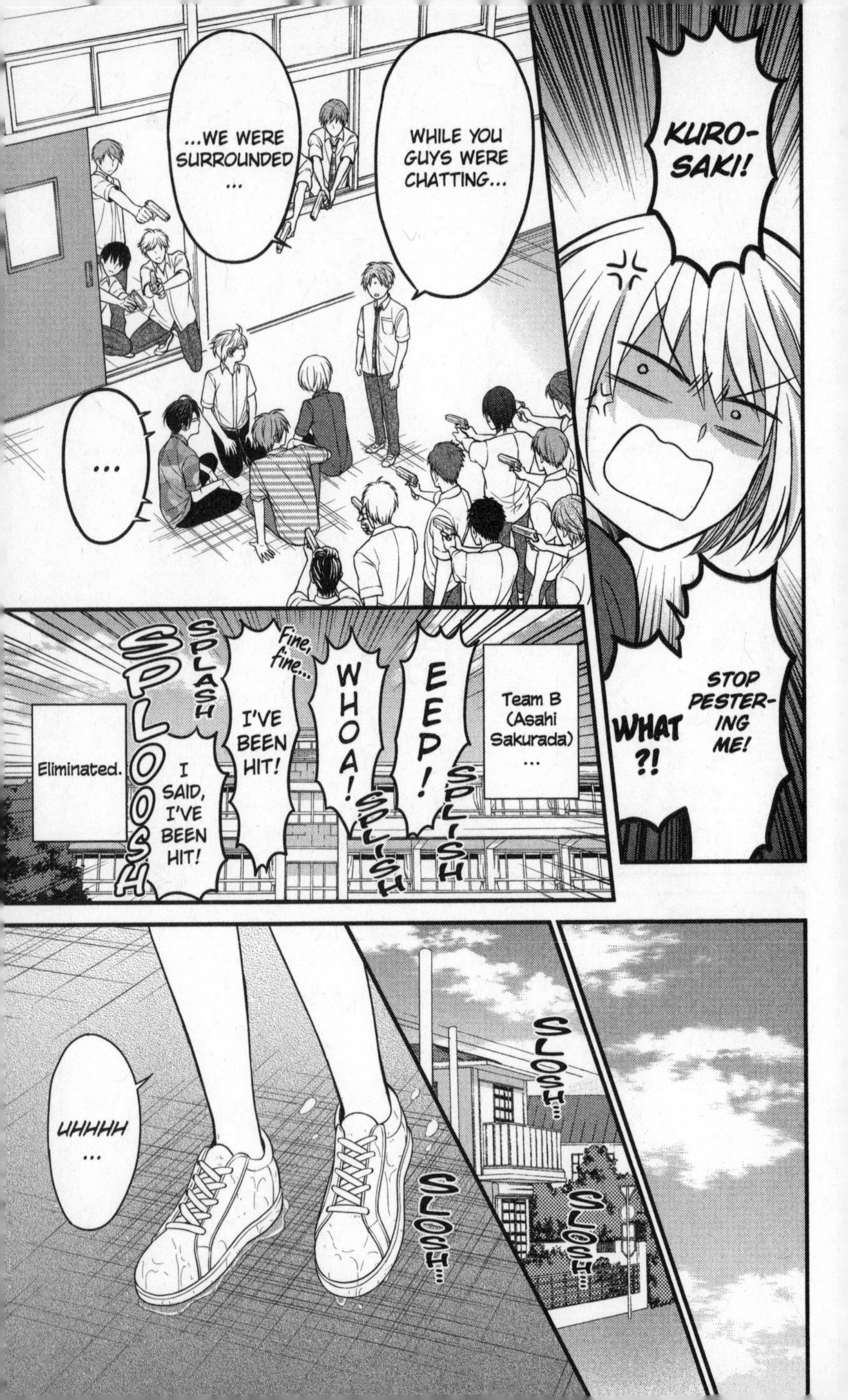
KURO-SAKI!
STOP PESTER-ING ME!
WHAT?!
WHILE YOU GUYS WERE CHATTING...
...WE WERE SURROUNDED...
...
Team B (Asahi Sakurada)...
EEP!
SPLISH
WHOA!
SPLISH
Fine, fine...
I'VE BEEN HIT!
I SAID, I'VE BEEN HIT!
SPLASH
SPLOOSH
Eliminated.
SLOSH...
SLOSH...
SLOSH...
UHHHH...

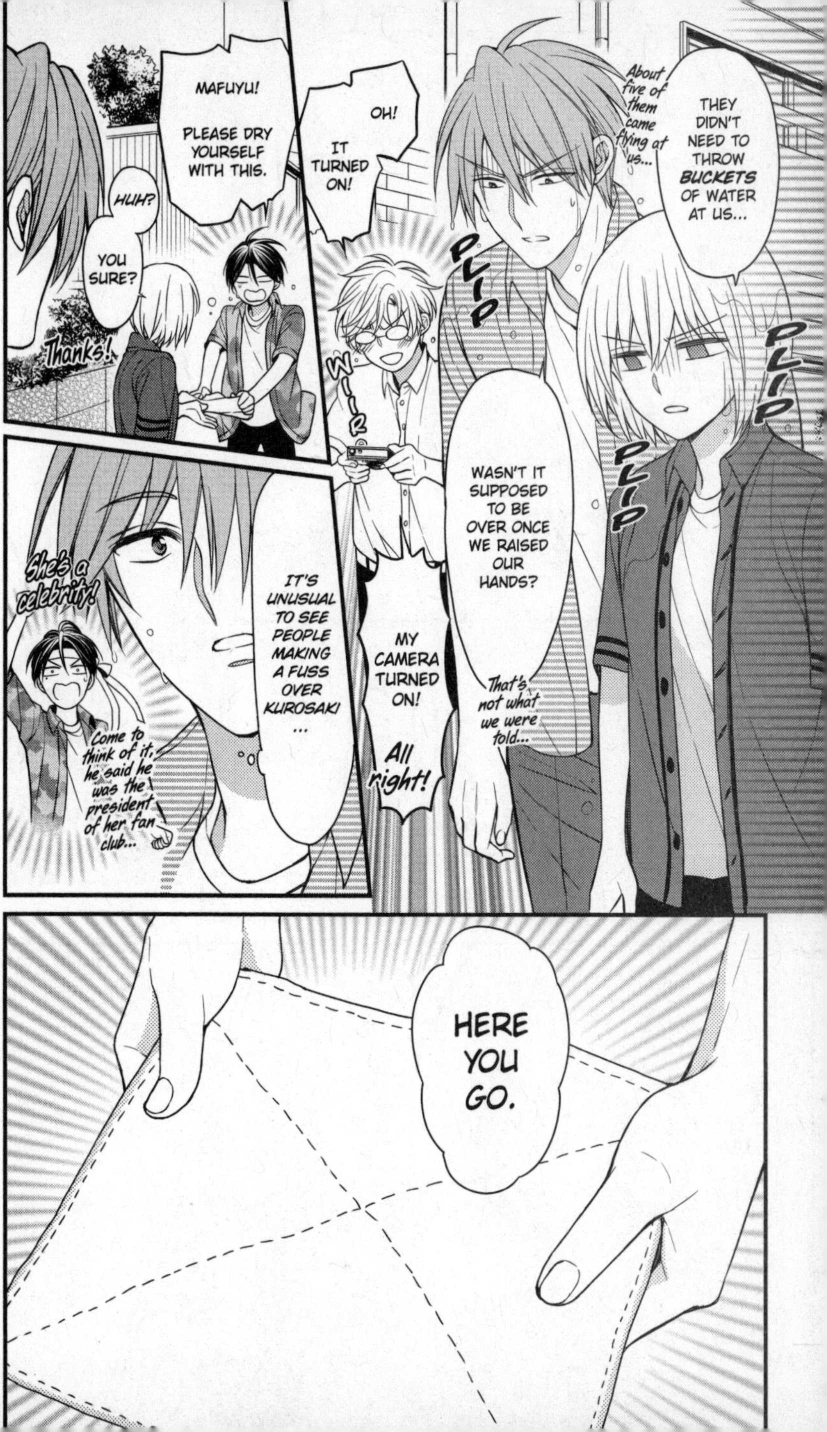

About five of them came flying at us...
THEY DIDN'T NEED TO THROW BUCKETS OF WATER AT US...
PLIP
PLIP
OH!
IT TURNED ON!
WIIR
WASN'T IT SUPPOSED TO BE OVER ONCE WE RAISED OUR HANDS?
That's not what we were told...
PLIP
MY CAMERA TURNED ON!
All right!
MAFUYU!
PLEASE DRY YOURSELF WITH THIS.
HUH?
YOU SURE?
Thanks!
IT'S UNUSUAL TO SEE PEOPLE MAKING A FUSS OVER KUROSAKI...
She's a celebrity!
Come to think of it, he said he was the president of her fan club...
HERE YOU GO.

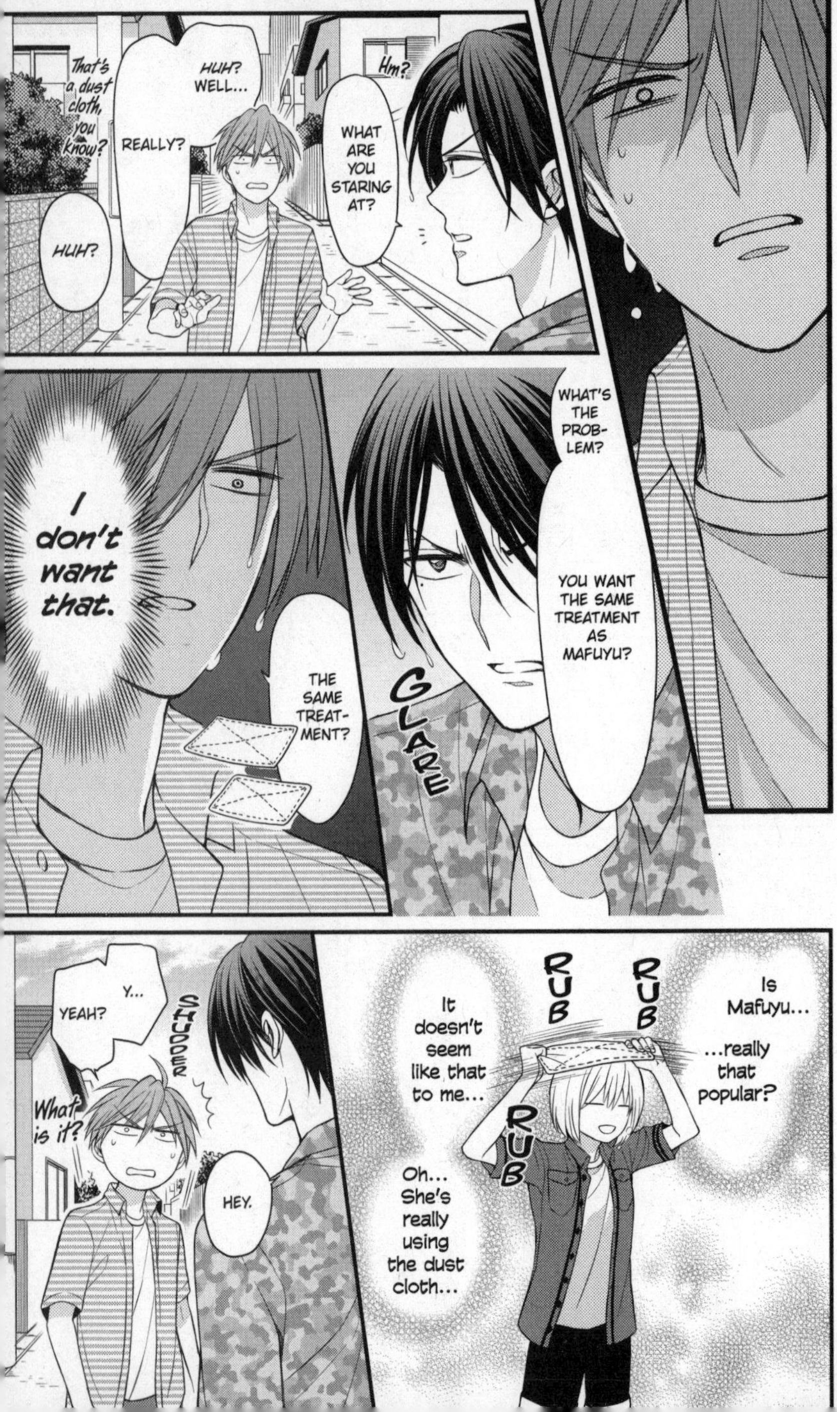
Hm?
WHAT ARE YOU STARING AT?
HUH? WELL...
REALLY?
That's a dust cloth, you know?
HUH?
WHAT'S THE PROBLEM?
YOU WANT THE SAME TREATMENT AS MAFUYU?
GLARE
THE SAME TREATMENT?
I don't want that.
Is Mafuyu...
...really that popular?
RUB RUB RUB
It doesn't seem like that to me...
Oh... She's really using the dust cloth...
HEY.
SHUDDER
Y... YEAH?
What is it?

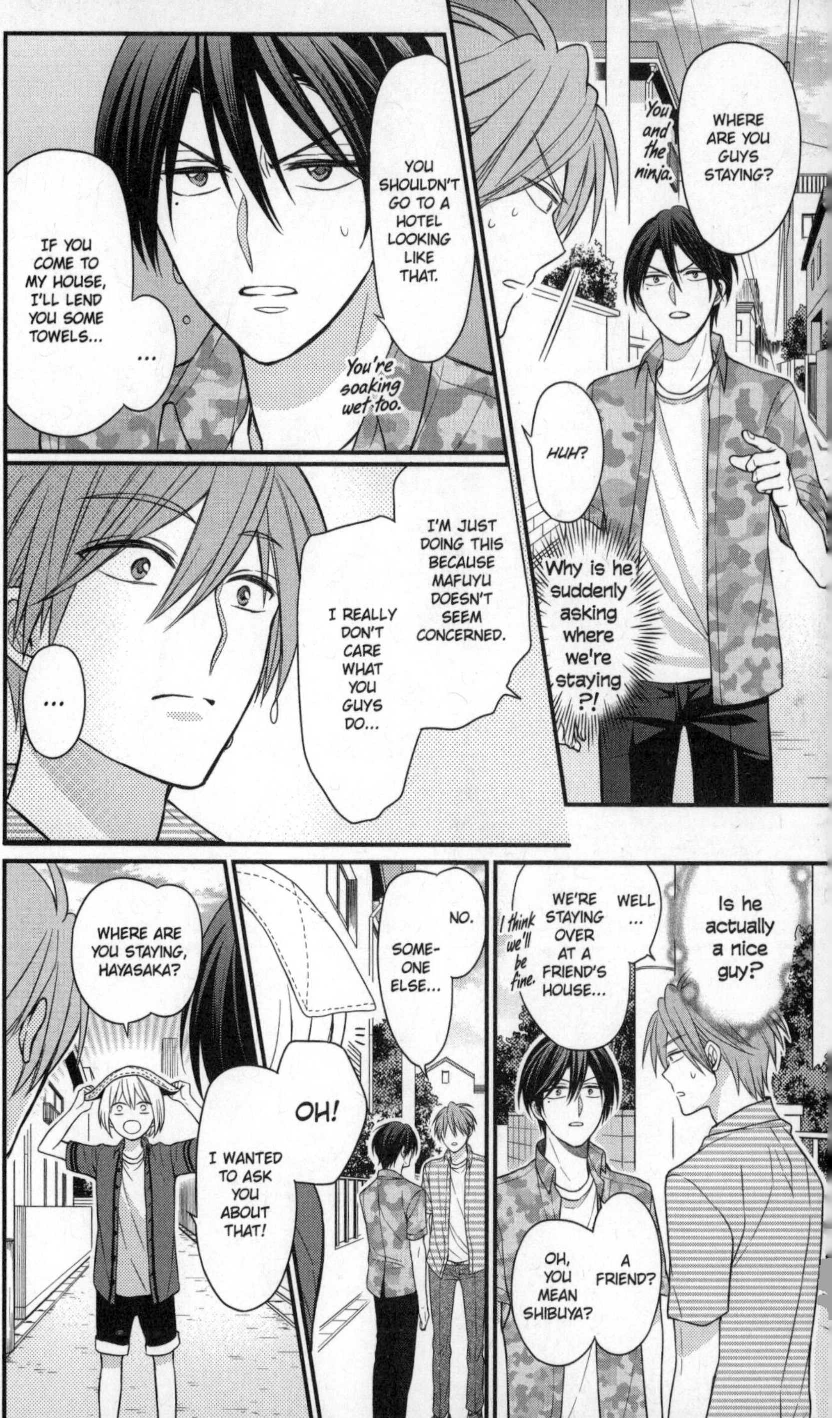
WHERE ARE YOU GUYS STAYING?
You and the ninja.
HUH?
Why is he suddenly asking where we're staying?!
YOU SHOULDN'T GO TO A HOTEL LOOKING LIKE THAT.
You're soaking wet too.
IF YOU COME TO MY HOUSE, I'LL LEND YOU SOME TOWELS...
...
I'M JUST DOING THIS BECAUSE MAFUYU DOESN'T SEEM CONCERNED.
I REALLY DON'T CARE WHAT YOU GUYS DO...
...
Is he actually a nice guy?
WELL ...
WE'RE STAYING OVER AT A FRIEND'S HOUSE...
I think we'll be fine.
A FRIEND?
OH, YOU MEAN SHIBUYA?
NO.
SOME-ONE ELSE...
OH!
I WANTED TO ASK YOU ABOUT THAT!
WHERE ARE YOU STAYING, HAYASAKA?

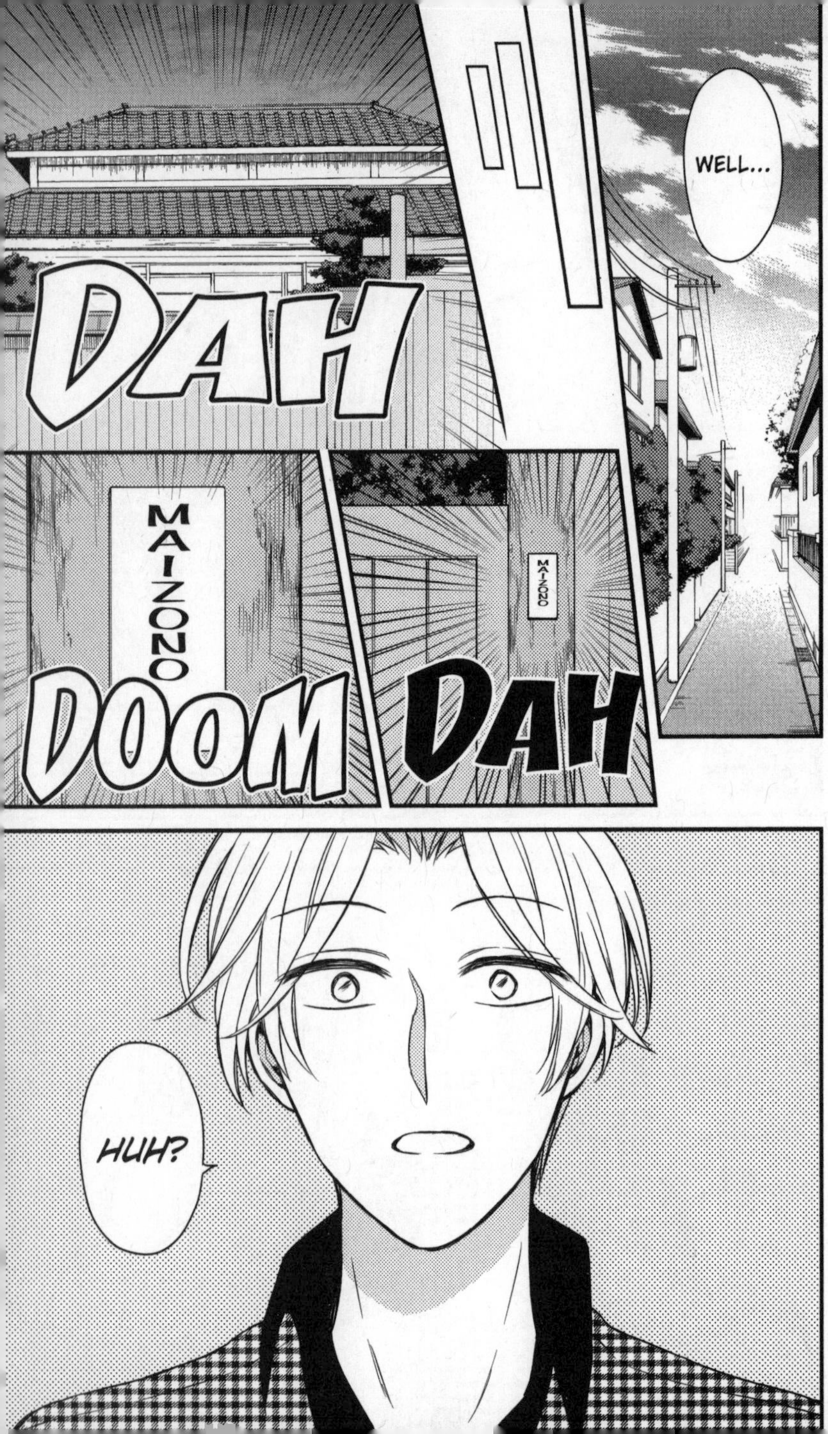
WELL...
DAH
MAIZONO
DAH
MAIZONO
DOOM
HUH?

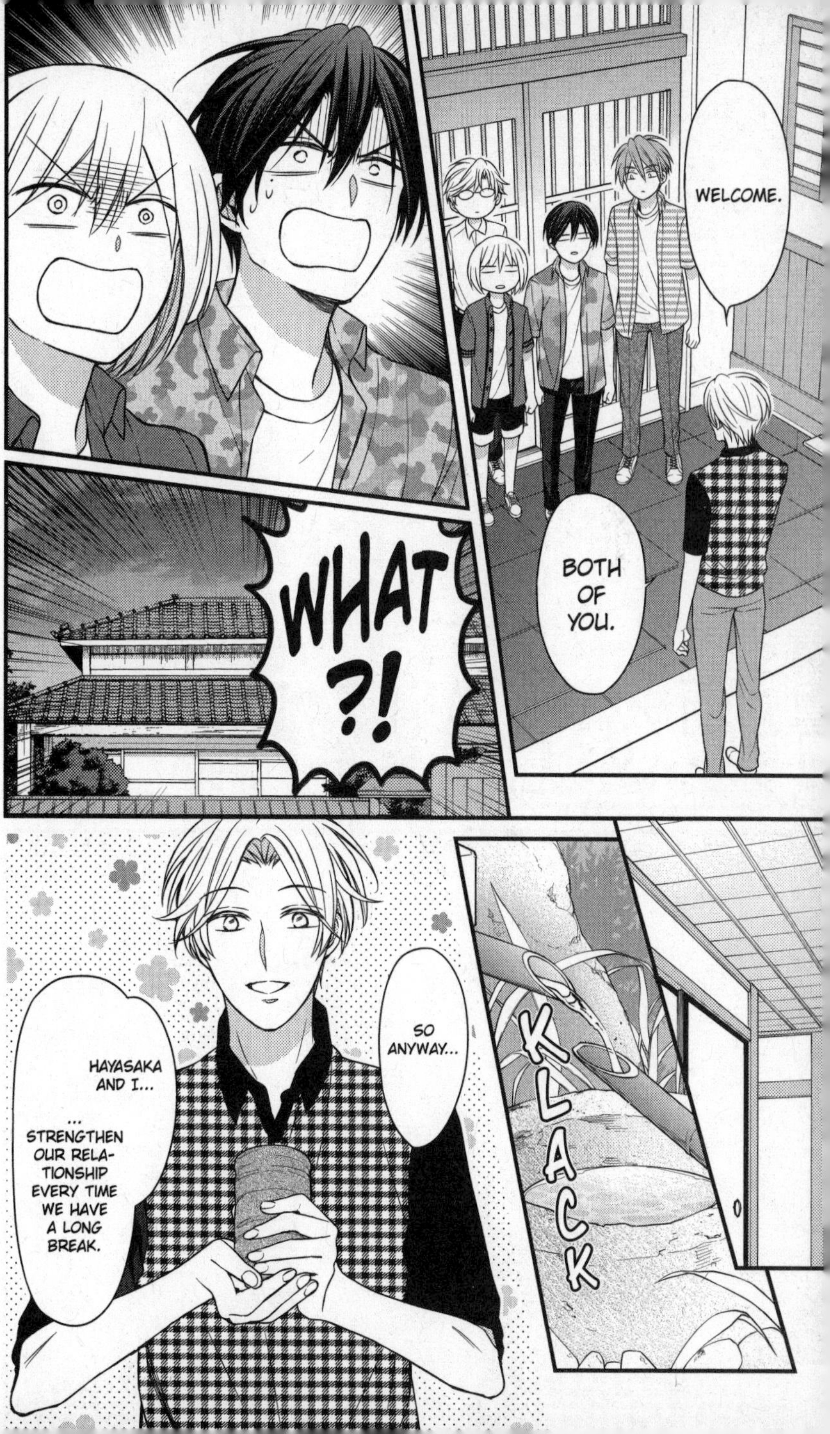
WELCOME.
BOTH OF YOU.
WHAT?!
KLACK
SO ANYWAY...
HAYASAKA AND I...
...STRENGTHEN OUR RELATIONSHIP EVERY TIME WE HAVE A LONG BREAK.

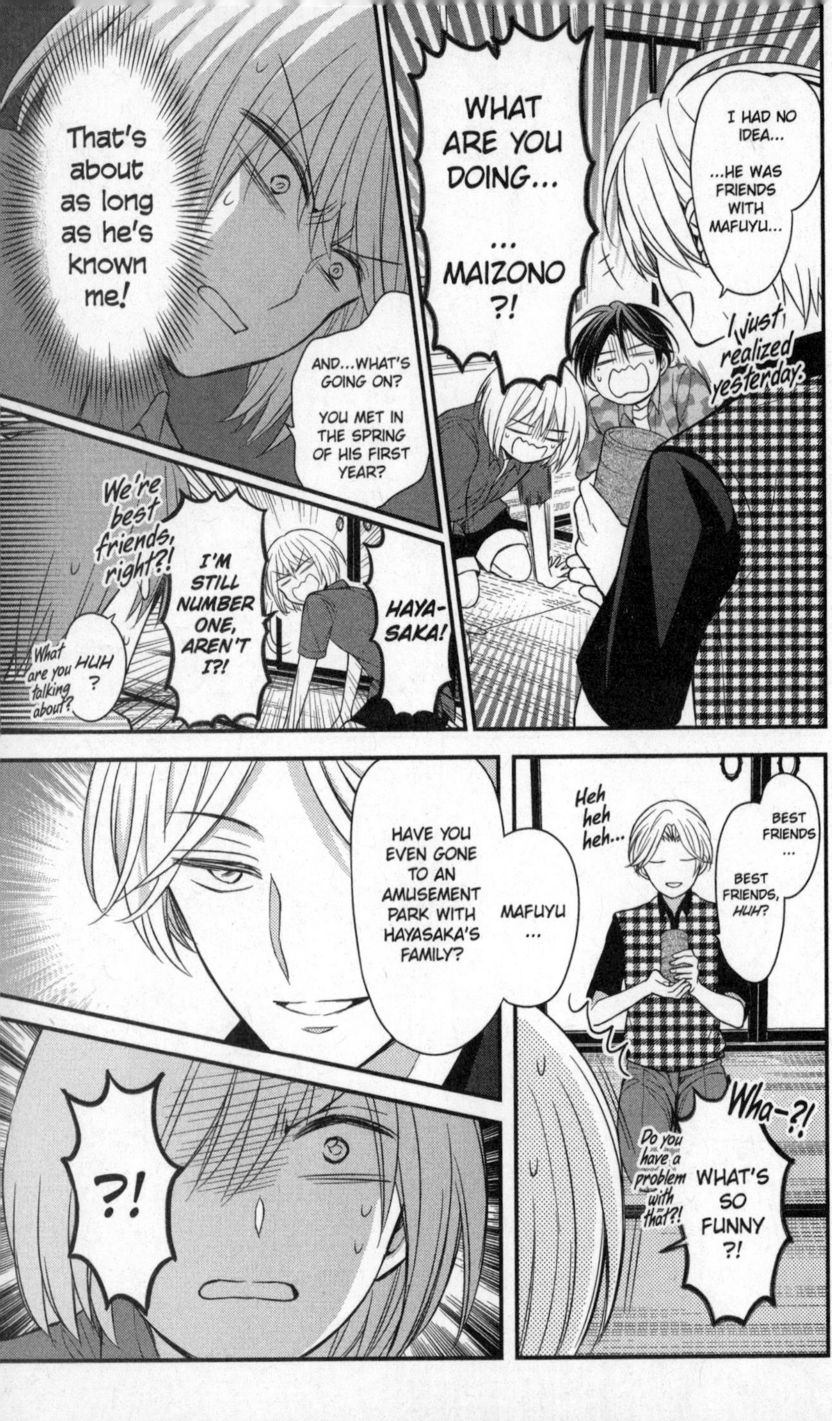
I HAD NO IDEA...
...HE WAS FRIENDS WITH MAFUYU...
WHAT ARE YOU DOING...
...MAIZONO?!
I just realized yesterday.
AND...WHAT'S GOING ON?
YOU MET IN THE SPRING OF HIS FIRST YEAR?
That's about as long as he's known me!
HAYA-SAKA!
I'M STILL NUMBER ONE, AREN'T I?!
We're best friends, right?!
HUH?
What are you talking about?
BEST FRIENDS...
BEST FRIENDS, HUH?
Heh heh heh...
Wha-?!
WHAT'S SO FUNNY?!
Do you have a problem with that?!
MAFUYU...
HAVE YOU EVEN GONE TO AN AMUSEMENT PARK WITH HAYASAKA'S FAMILY?
?!

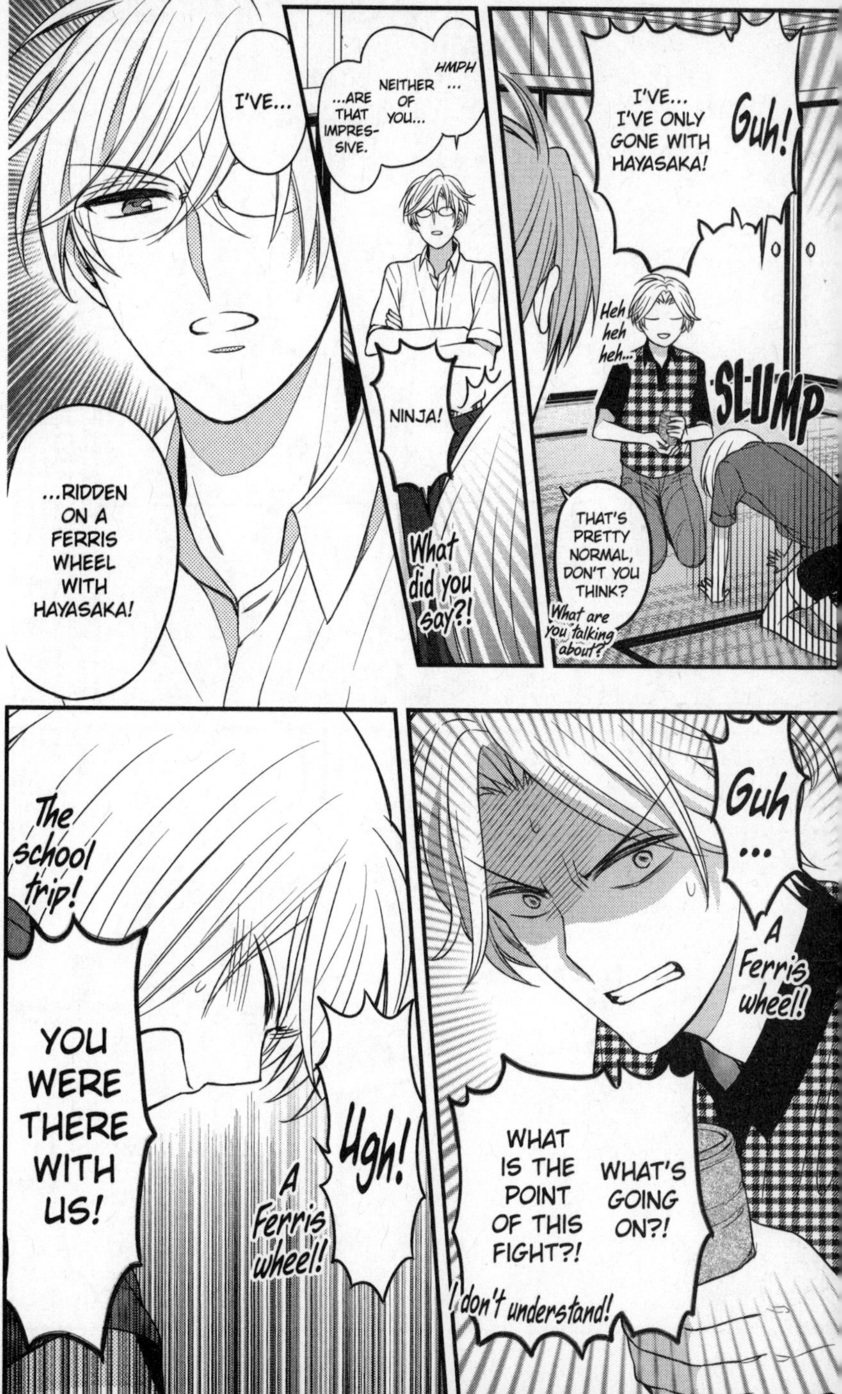
Guh!
I'VE... I'VE ONLY GONE WITH HAYASAKA!
SLUMP
Heh heh heh...
THAT'S PRETTY NORMAL, DON'T YOU THINK?
What are you talking about?
HMPH...
NEITHER OF YOU...
...ARE THAT IMPRESSIVE.
NINJA!
What did you say?!
I'VE...
...RIDDEN ON A FERRIS WHEEL WITH HAYASAKA!
Guh...
A Ferris wheel!
WHAT'S GOING ON?!
WHAT IS THE POINT OF THIS FIGHT?!
I don't understand!
Ugh!
A Ferris wheel!
The school trip!
YOU WERE THERE WITH US!

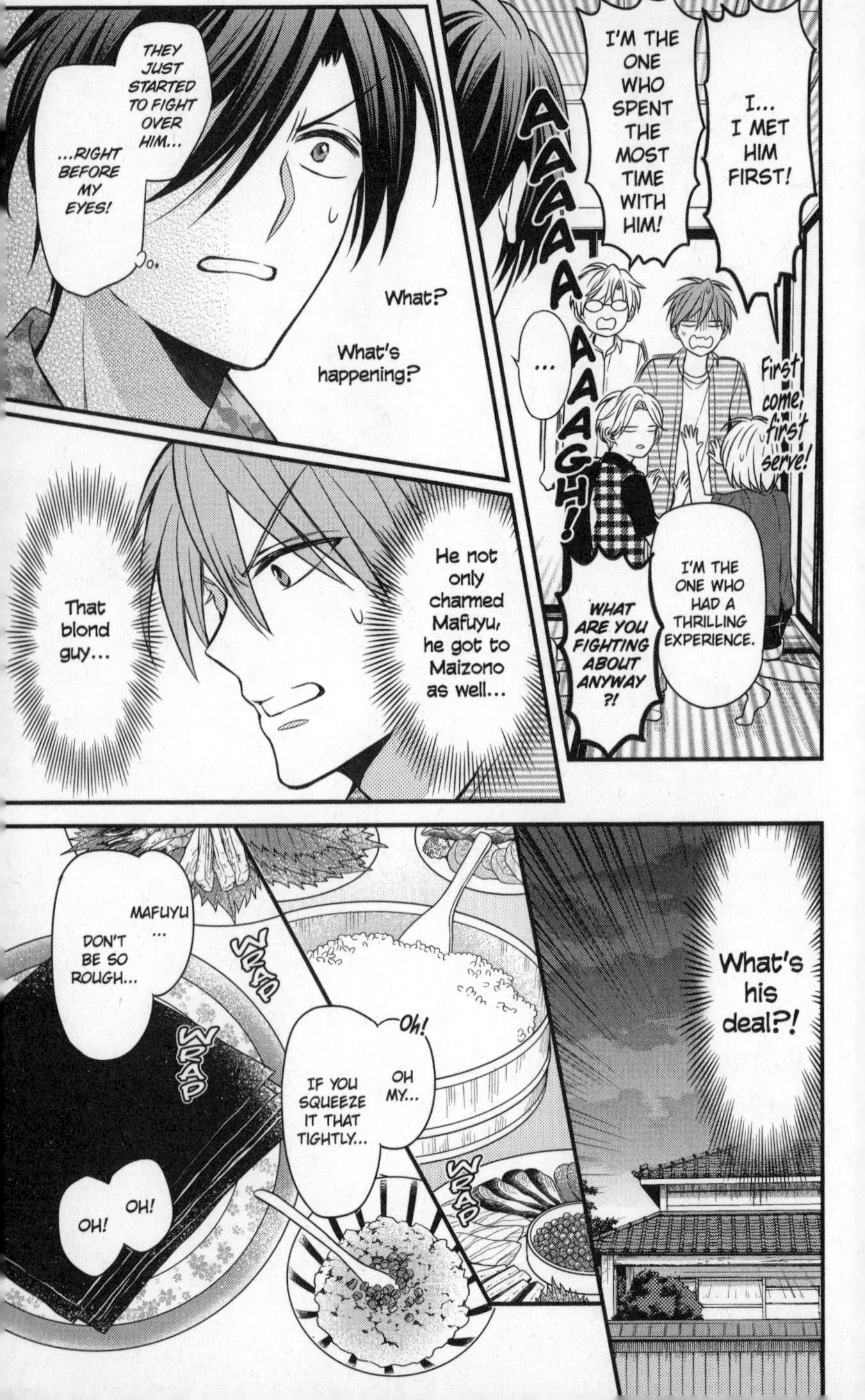
I... I MET HIM FIRST!
I'M THE ONE WHO SPENT THE MOST TIME WITH HIM!
AAAAAAAAGH!
First come, first serve!
...
I'M THE ONE WHO HAD A THRILLING EXPERIENCE.
WHAT ARE YOU FIGHTING ABOUT ANYWAY?!
THEY JUST STARTED TO FIGHT OVER HIM...
...RIGHT BEFORE MY EYES!
What?
What's happening?
He not only charmed Mafuyu, he got to Maizono as well...
That blond guy...
What's his deal?!
-Oh!
OH MY...
IF YOU SQUEEZE IT THAT TIGHTLY...
MAFUYU...
DON'T BE SO ROUGH...
WRAP
WRAP
WRAP
OH!
OH!

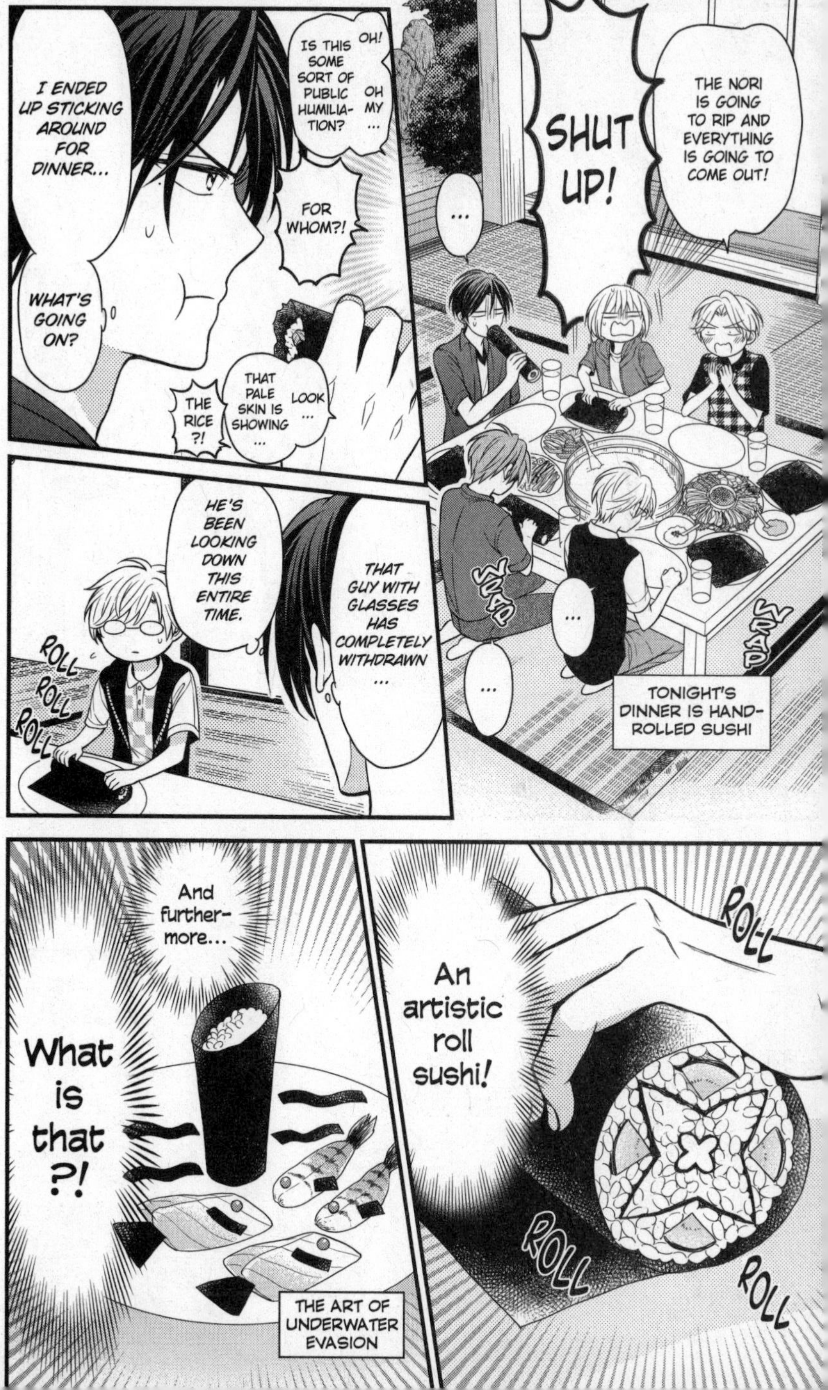
THE NORI IS GOING TO RIP AND EVERYTHING IS GOING TO COME OUT!
SHUT UP!
...
WRAP
...
...
WRAP
TONIGHT'S DINNER IS HAND-ROLLED SUSHI
OH! OH MY ...
IS THIS SOME SORT OF PUBLIC HUMILIATION?
FOR WHOM?!
I ENDED UP STICKING AROUND FOR DINNER...
WHAT'S GOING ON?
LOOK ...
THAT PALE SKIN IS SHOWING ...
THE RICE ?!
THAT GUY WITH GLASSES HAS COMPLETELY WITHDRAWN ...
HE'S BEEN LOOKING DOWN THIS ENTIRE TIME.
ROLL ROLL ROLL
ROLL
An artistic roll sushi!
ROLL
ROLL
And furthermore...
What is that?!
THE ART OF UNDERWATER EVASION

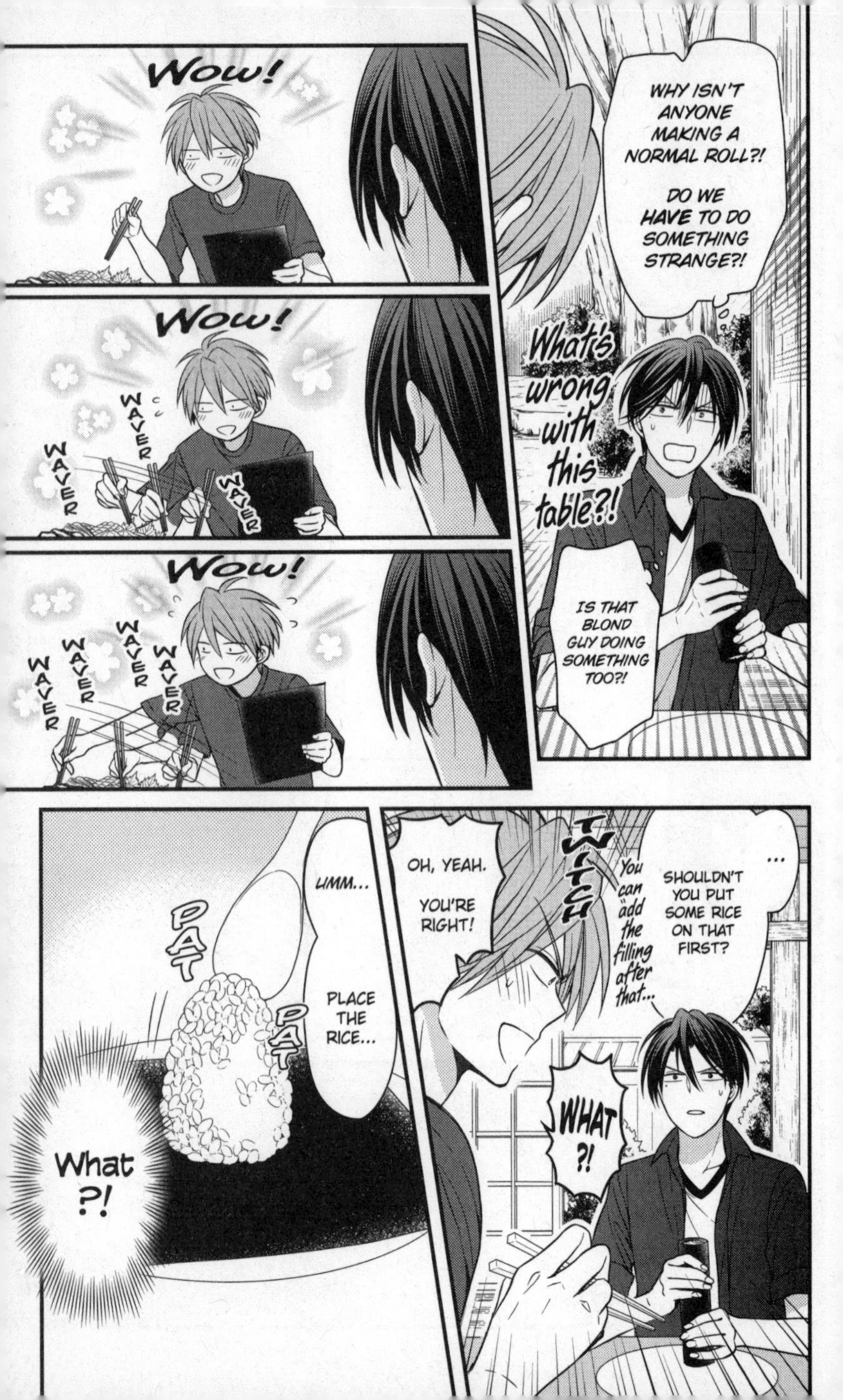
WHY ISN'T ANYONE MAKING A NORMAL ROLL?!
DO WE **HAVE** TO DO SOMETHING STRANGE?!
What's wrong with this table?!
IS THAT BLOND GUY DOING SOMETHING TOO?!
Wow!
Wow!
WAVER
WAVER
WAVER
Wow!
WAVER
WAVER
WAVER
WAVER
...
SHOULDN'T YOU PUT SOME RICE ON THAT FIRST?
You can add the filling after that...
TWITCH
OH, YEAH.
YOU'RE RIGHT!
WHAT ?!
UMM...
PLACE THE RICE...
PAT
PAT
What ?!

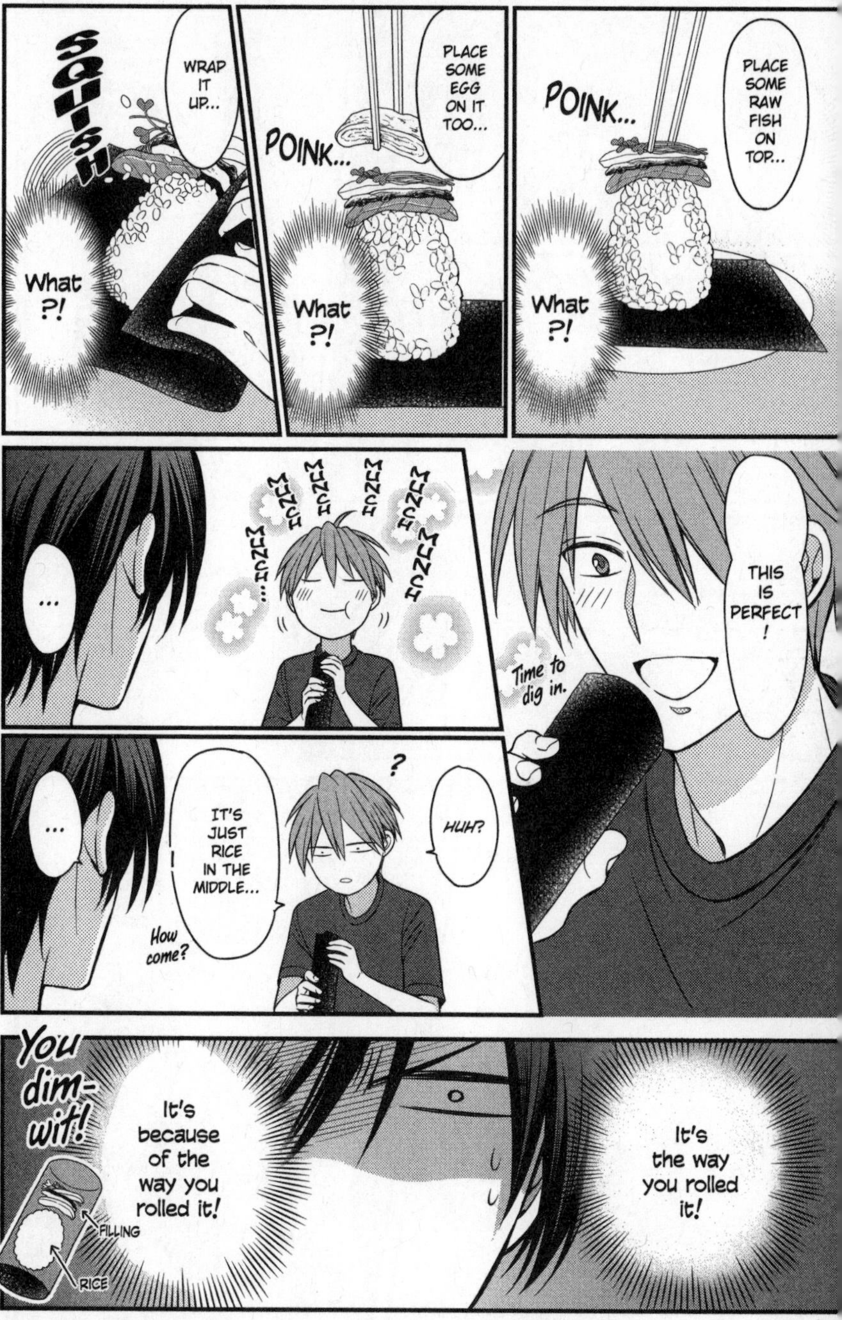
PLACE SOME RAW FISH ON TOP...
POINK...
What?!
PLACE SOME EGG ON IT TOO...
POINK...
What?!
WRAP IT UP...
SQUISH
What?!
THIS IS PERFECT!
Time to dig in.
MUNCH MUNCH
MUNCH
MUNCH
MUNCH
MUNCH...
...
?
HUH?
IT'S JUST RICE IN THE MIDDLE...
How come?
...
It's the way you rolled it!
It's because of the way you rolled it!
You dim-wit!
FILLING
RICE

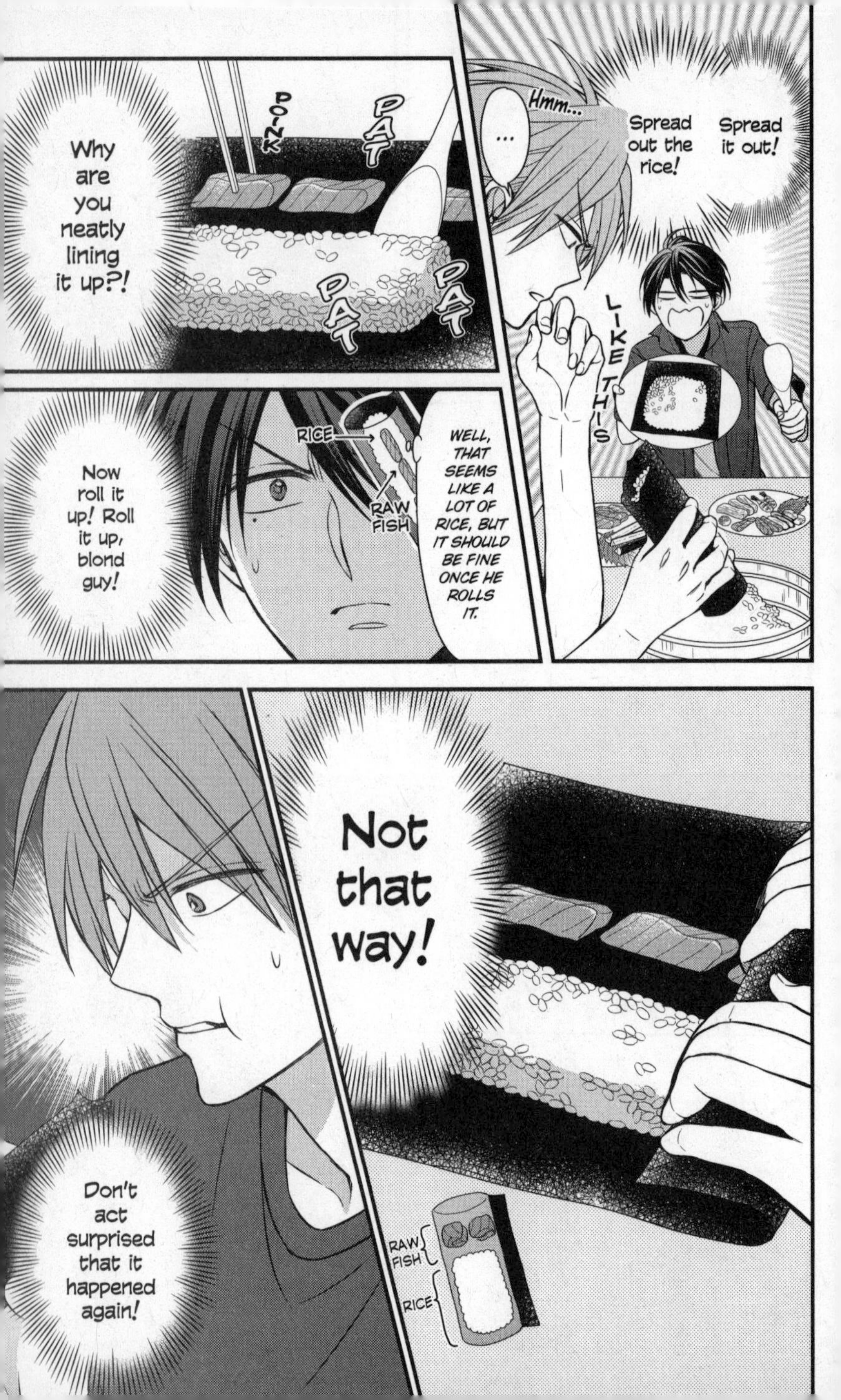
Spread it out!
Spread out the rice!
Hmm...
...
LIKE THIS
PAT
POINK
PAT
PAT
Why are you neatly lining it up?!
WELL, THAT SEEMS LIKE A LOT OF RICE, BUT IT SHOULD BE FINE ONCE HE ROLLS IT.
RICE
RAW FISH
Now roll it up! Roll it up, blond guy!
Not that way!
RAW FISH
RICE
Don't act surprised that it happened again!

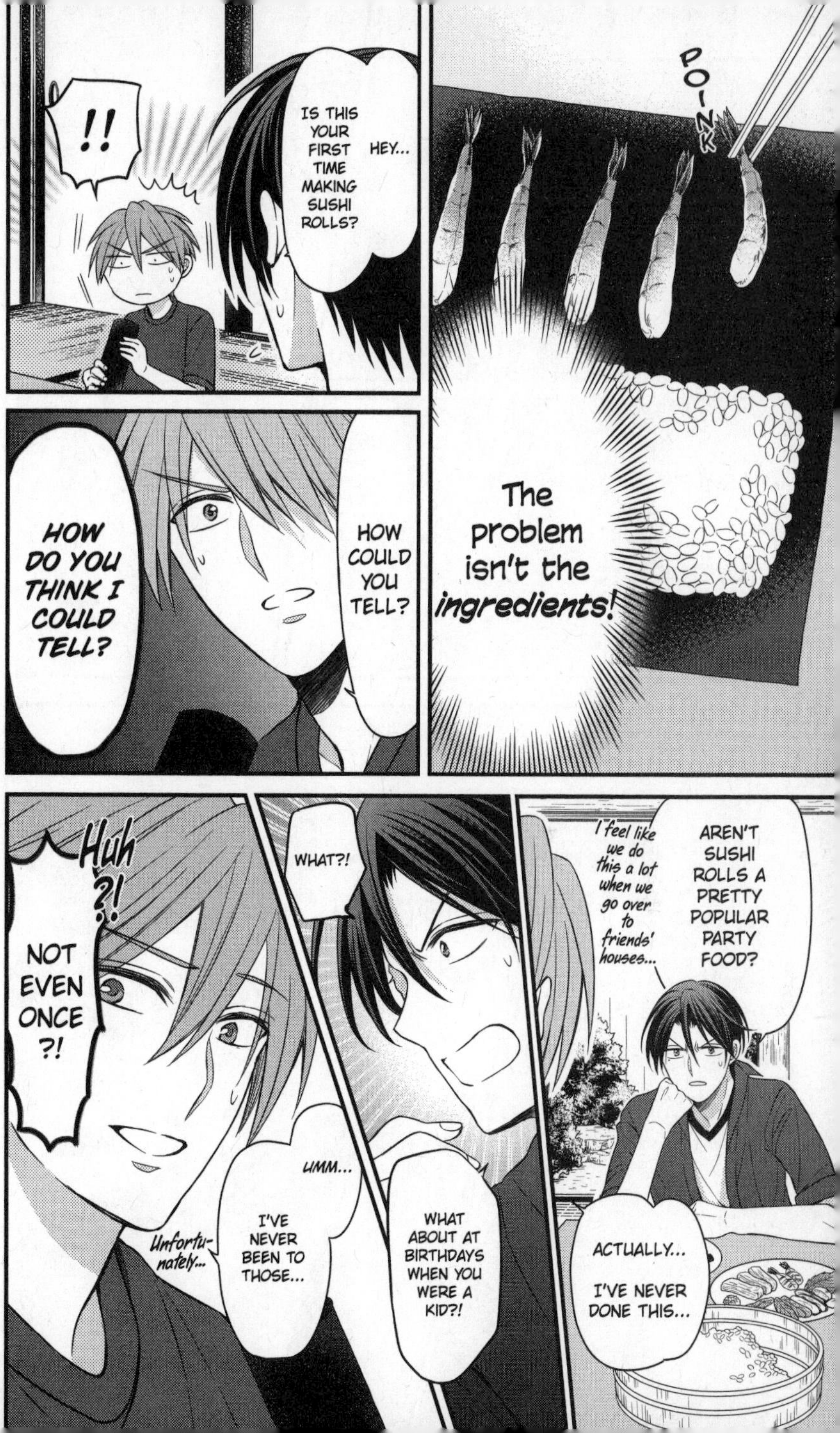
POINK
The problem isn't the *ingredients*!
HEY...
IS THIS YOUR FIRST TIME MAKING SUSHI ROLLS?
!!
HOW COULD YOU TELL?
HOW DO YOU THINK I COULD TELL?
AREN'T SUSHI ROLLS A PRETTY POPULAR PARTY FOOD?
I feel like we do this a lot when we go over to friends' houses...
ACTUALLY... I'VE NEVER DONE THIS...
WHAT?!
WHAT ABOUT AT BIRTHDAYS WHEN YOU WERE A KID?!
Huh ?!
NOT EVEN ONCE ?!
UMM...
I'VE NEVER BEEN TO THOSE...
Unfortu-nately...

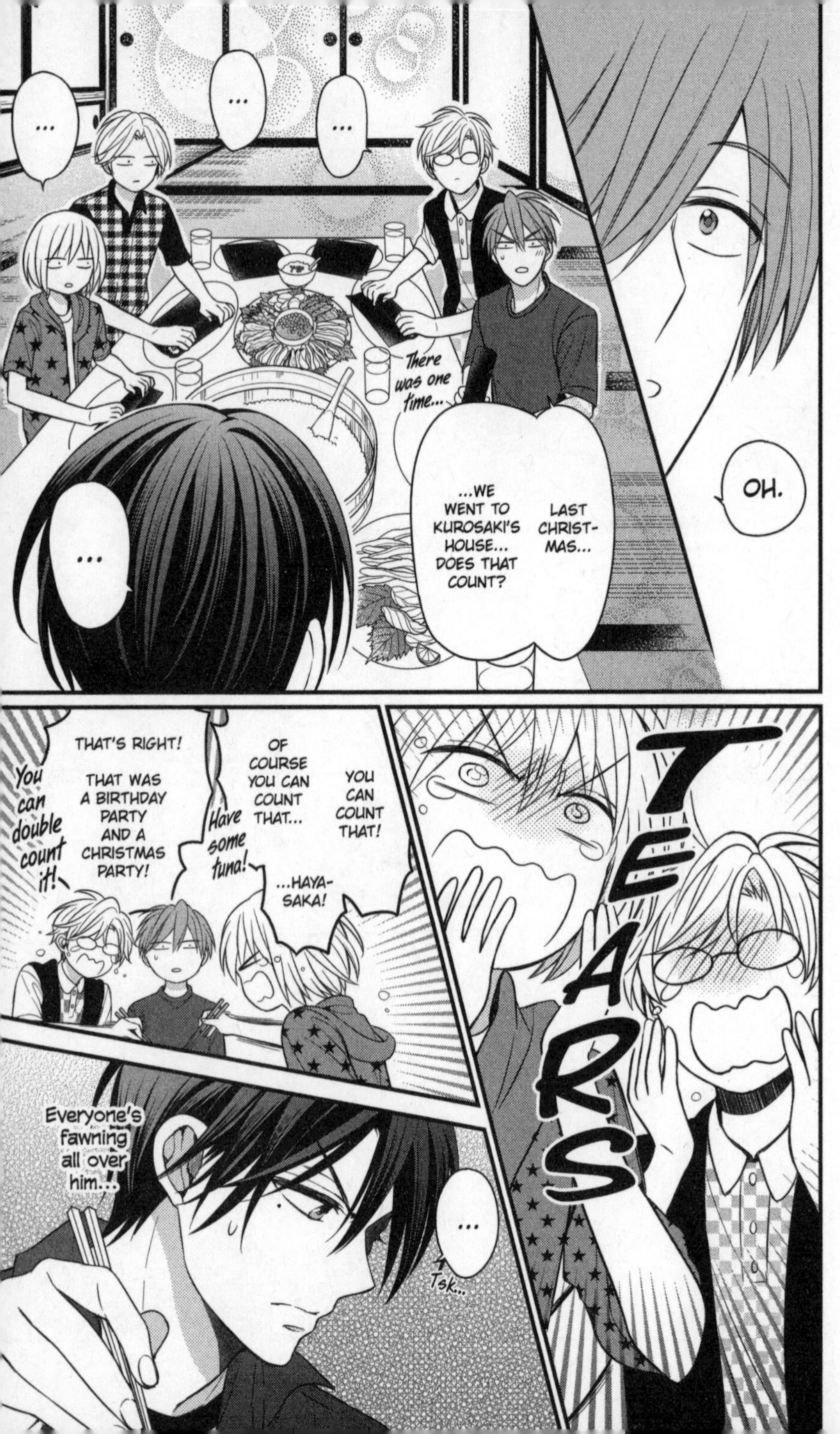
OH.
...
...
...
There was one time...
LAST CHRIST-MAS... ...WE WENT TO KUROSAKI'S HOUSE... DOES THAT COUNT?
...
TEARS
YOU CAN COUNT THAT!
OF COURSE YOU CAN COUNT THAT... ...HAYA-SAKA!
Have some tuna!
THAT'S RIGHT! THAT WAS A BIRTHDAY PARTY AND A CHRISTMAS PARTY!
You can double count it!
...
Tsk...
Everyone's fawning all over him...

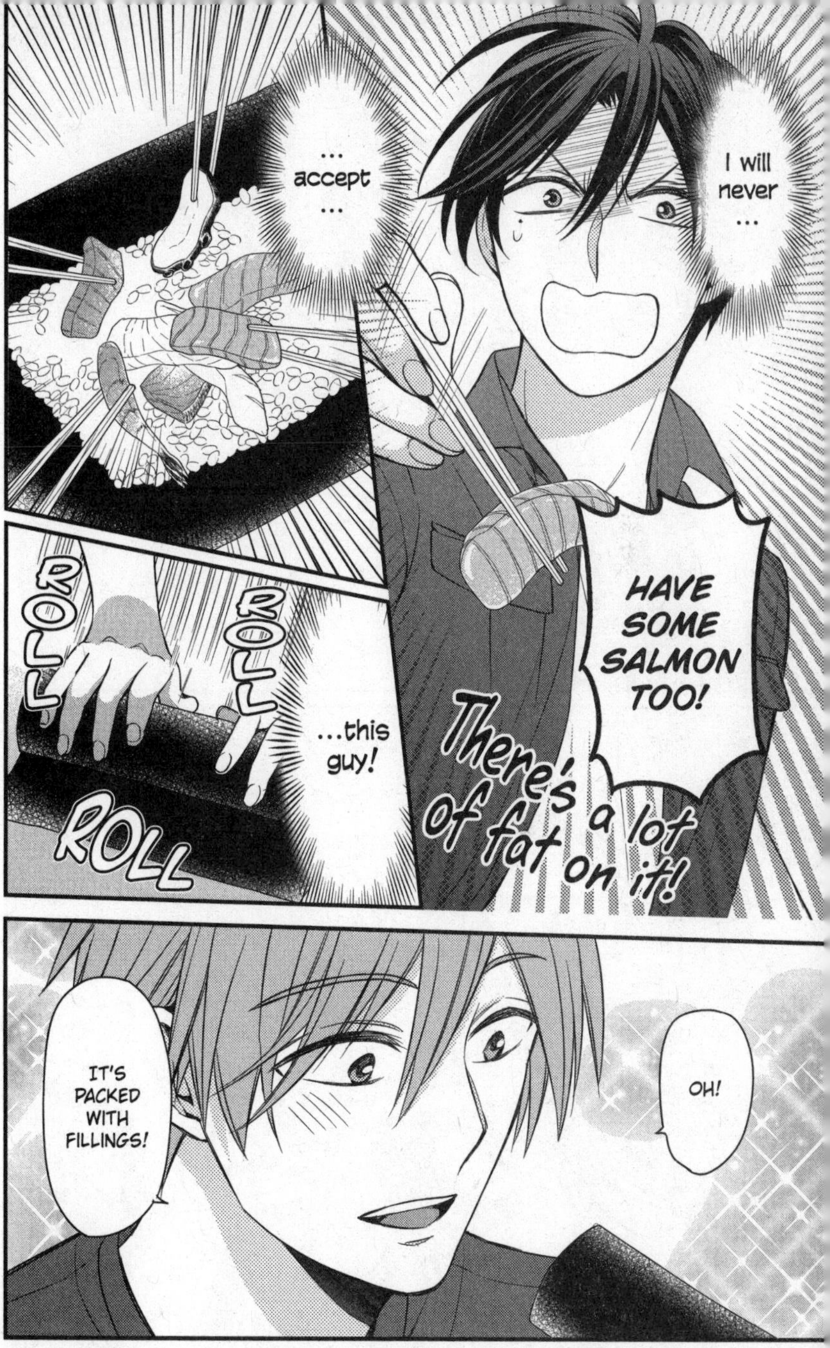
I will never ...
HAVE SOME SALMON TOO!
There's a lot of fat on it!
... accept ...
...this guy!
ROLL
ROLL
ROLL
OH!
IT'S PACKED WITH FILLINGS!

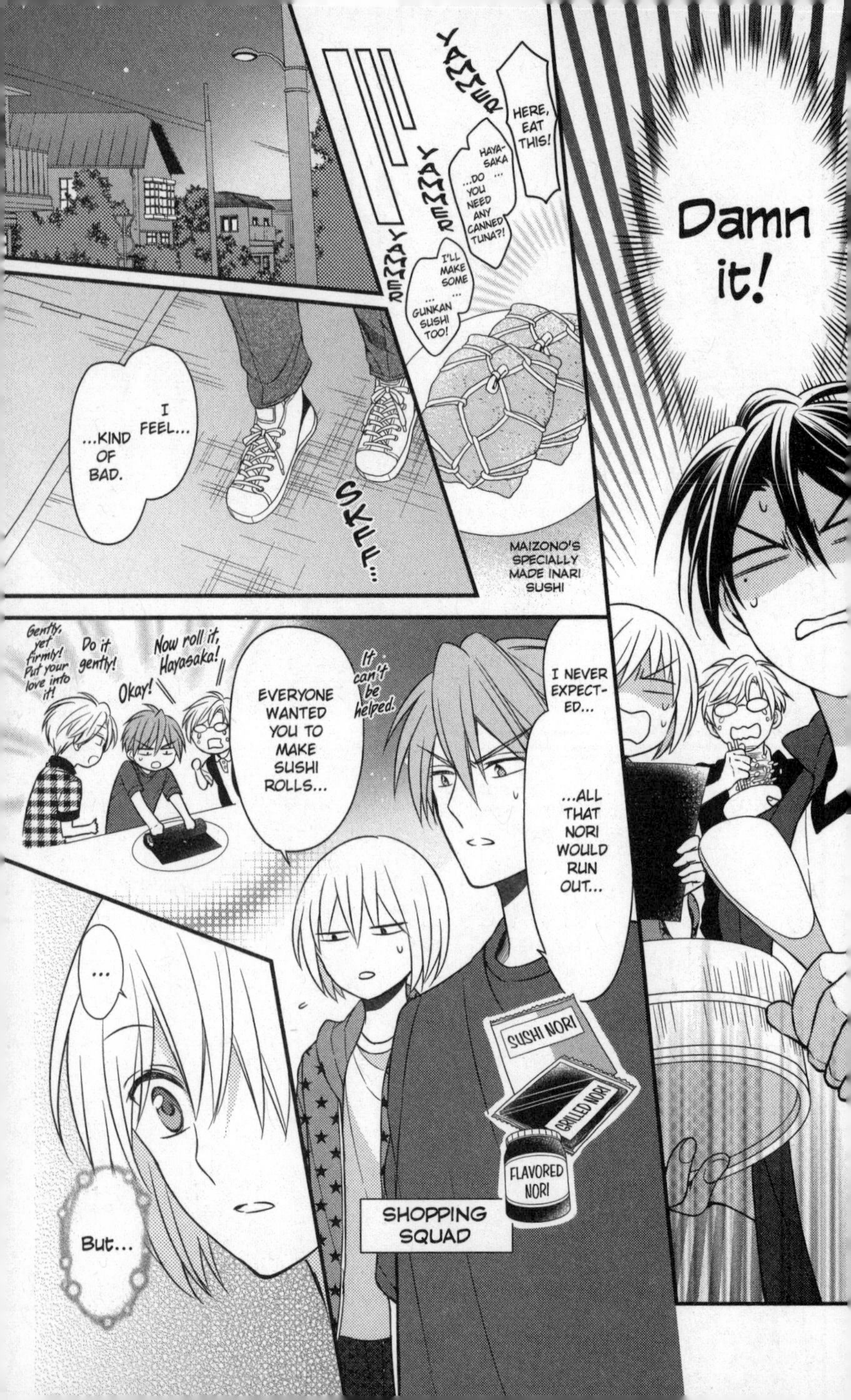

Damn it!
HERE, EAT THIS!
YAMMER
HAYA-SAKA... ...DO YOU NEED ANY CANNED TUNA?!
YAMMER
I'LL MAKE SOME... GUNKAN SUSHI TOO!
YAMMER
MAIZONO'S SPECIALLY MADE INARI SUSHI
I FEEL... ...KIND OF BAD.
SKFF...
I NEVER EXPECTED... ...ALL THAT NORI WOULD RUN OUT...
It can't be helped.
EVERYONE WANTED YOU TO MAKE SUSHI ROLLS...
Now roll it, Hayasaka!
Do it gently!
Gently, yet firmly! Put your love into it!
Okay!
SUSHI NORI
GRILLED NORI
FLAVORED NORI
SHOPPING SQUAD
...
But...

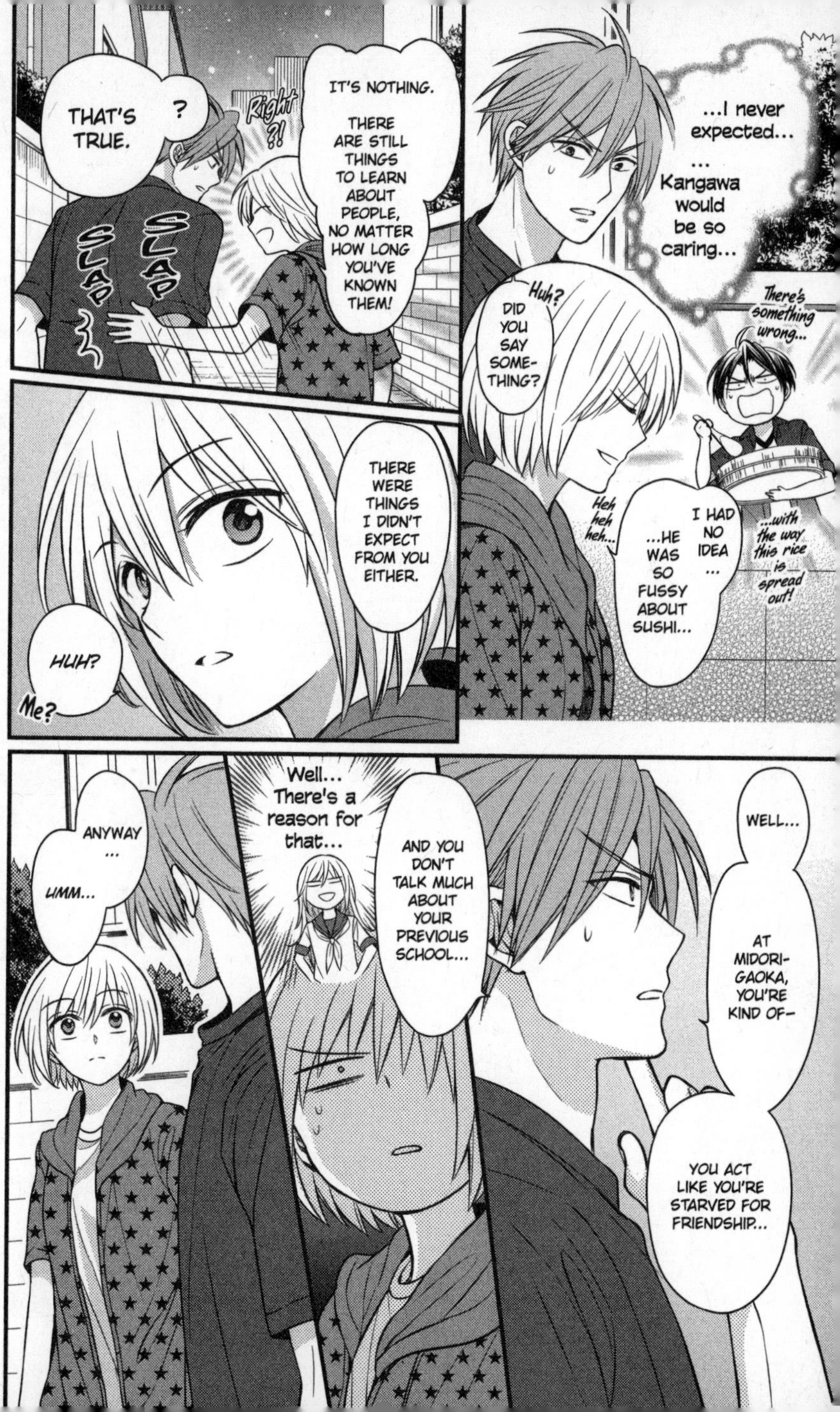

...I never expected... ... Kangawa would be so caring...
There's something wrong...
...with the way this rice is spread out!
Huh?
DID YOU SAY SOME-THING?
I HAD NO IDEA...
...HE WAS SO FUSSY ABOUT SUSHI...
Heh heh heh...
Right?!
IT'S NOTHING.
THERE ARE STILL THINGS TO LEARN ABOUT PEOPLE, NO MATTER HOW LONG YOU'VE KNOWN THEM!
?
THAT'S TRUE.
SLAP SLAP
THERE WERE THINGS I DIDN'T EXPECT FROM YOU EITHER.
HUH?
Me?
WELL...
AT MIDORI-GAOKA, YOU'RE KIND OF-
YOU ACT LIKE YOU'RE STARVED FOR FRIENDSHIP...
AND YOU DON'T TALK MUCH ABOUT YOUR PREVIOUS SCHOOL...
Well... There's a reason for that...
ANYWAY...
UMM...

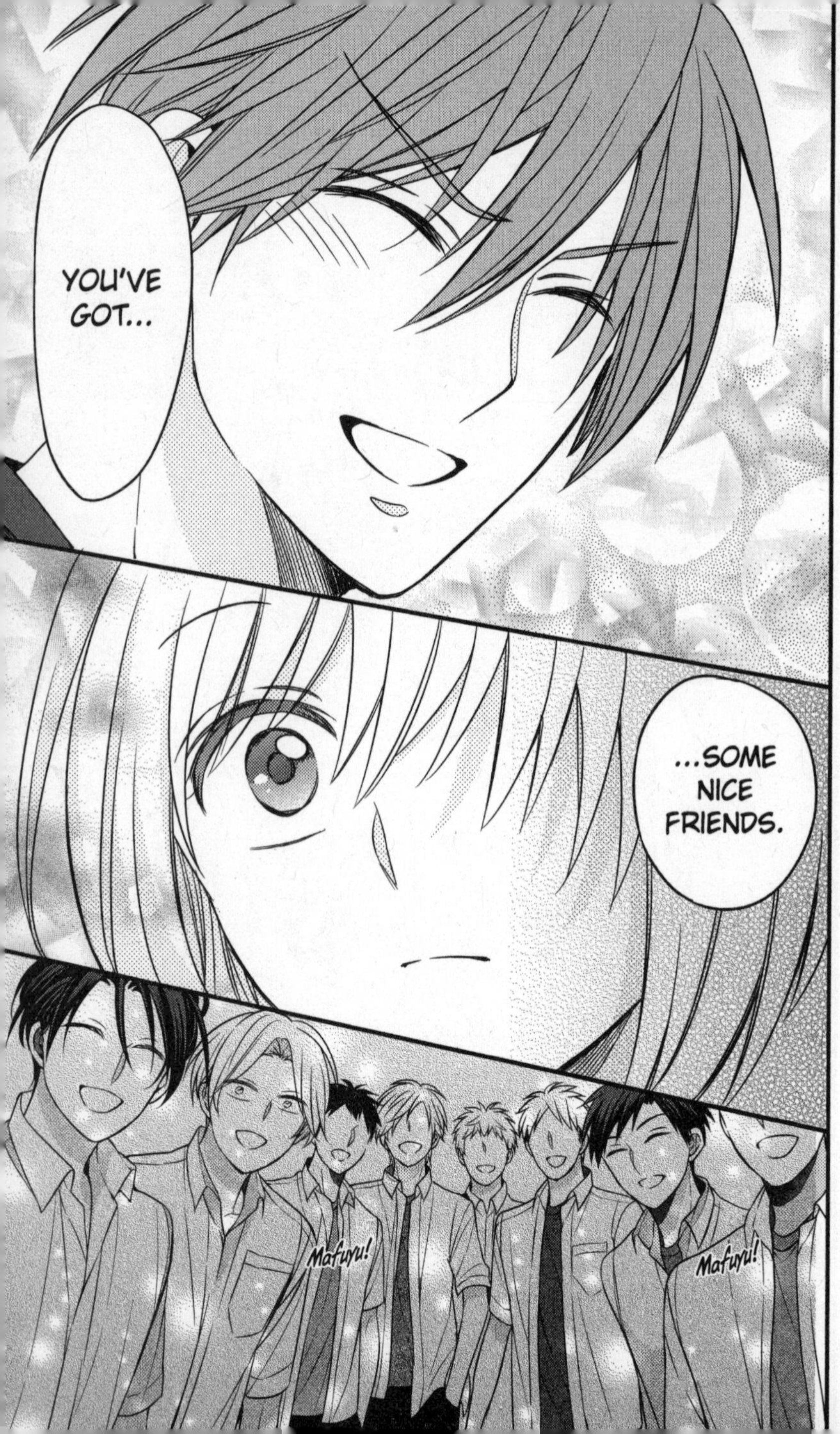
YOU'VE GOT...
...SOME NICE FRIENDS.
Mafuyu!
Mafuyu!

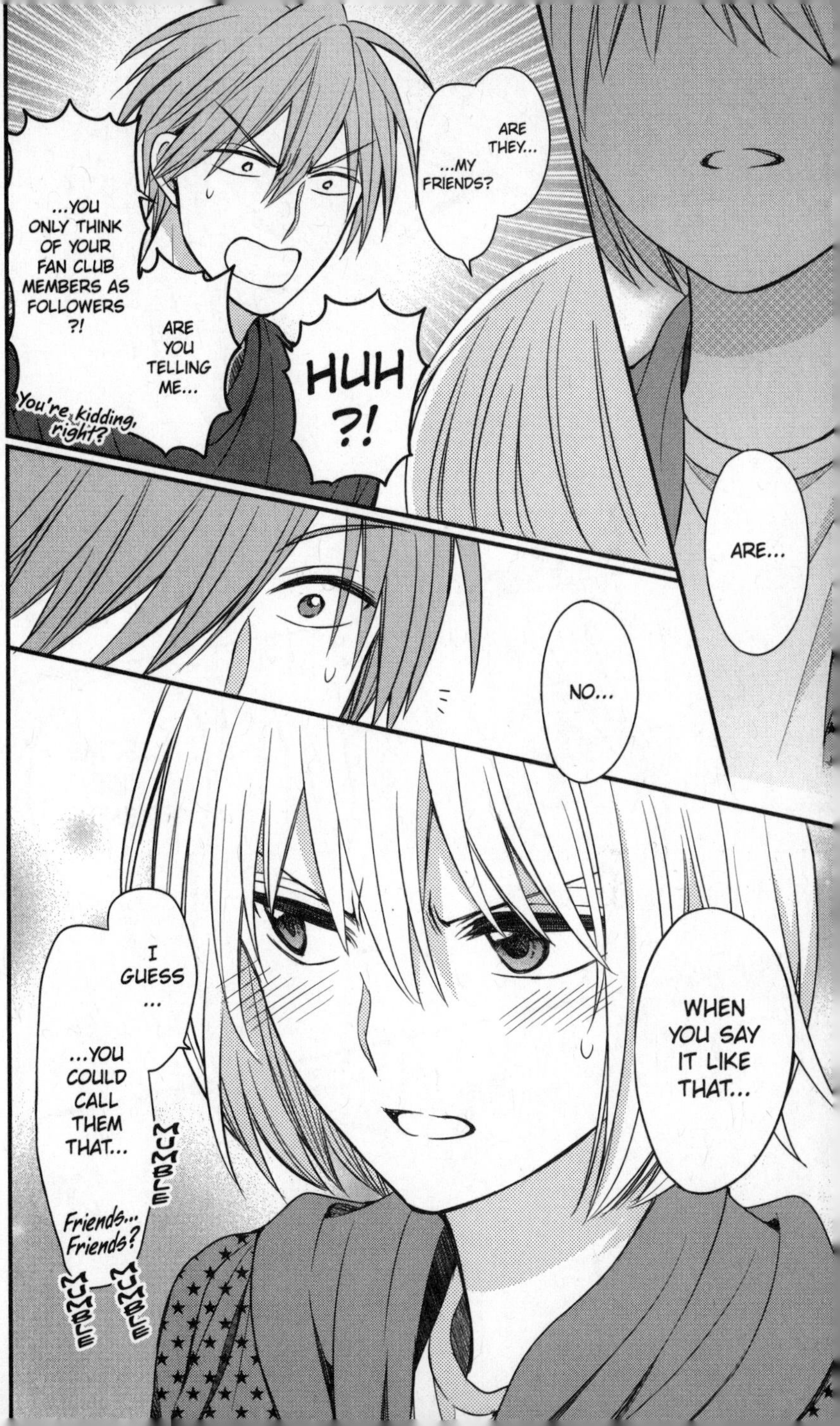
ARE...
ARE THEY...
...MY FRIENDS?
HUH ?!
ARE YOU TELLING ME...
...YOU ONLY THINK OF YOUR FAN CLUB MEMBERS AS FOLLOWERS ?!
You're kidding, right?
NO...
WHEN YOU SAY IT LIKE THAT...
I GUESS ...
...YOU COULD CALL THEM THAT...
MUMBLE
Friends... Friends?
MUMBLE
MUMBLE

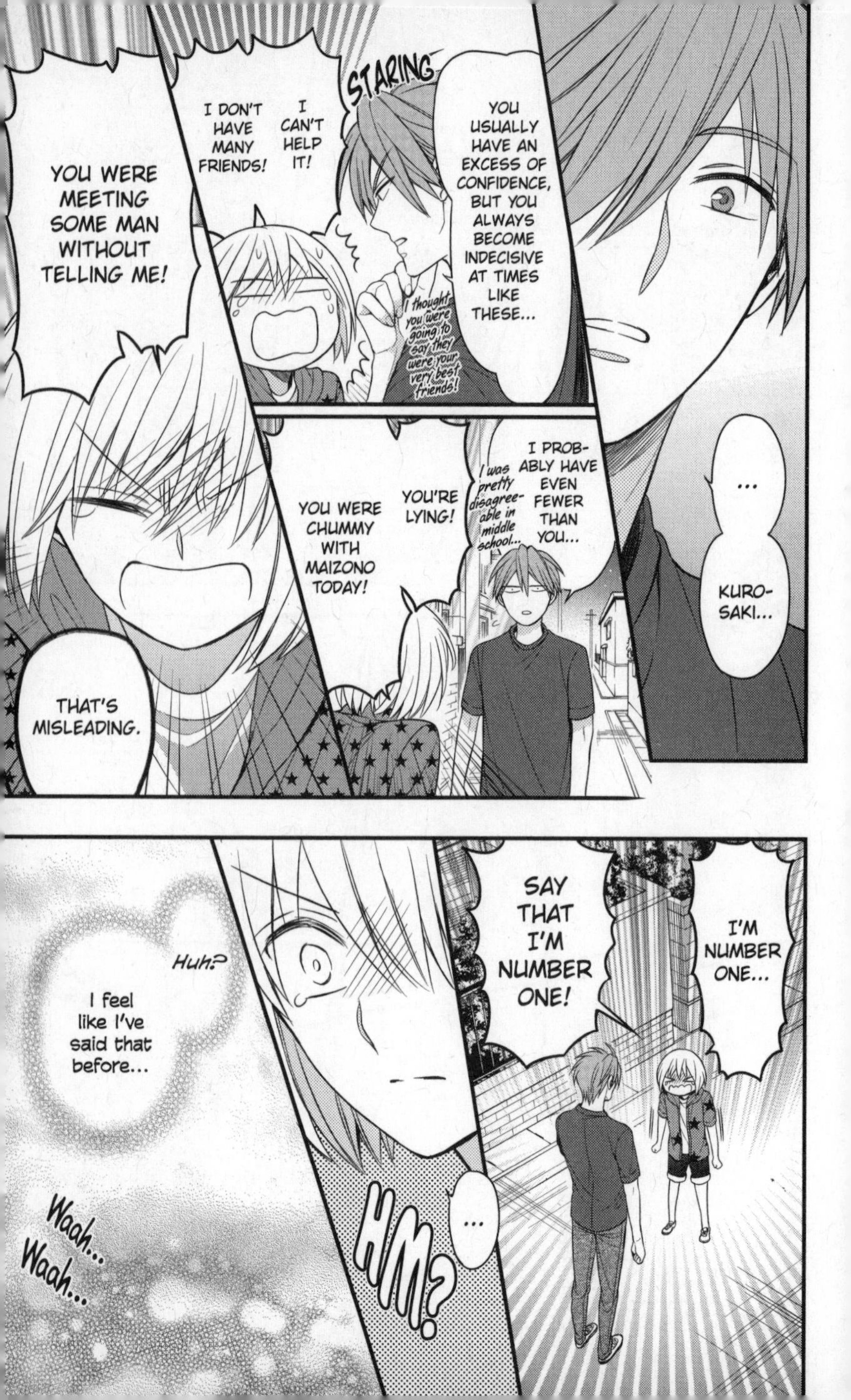
...
KURO-SAKI...
STARING
YOU USUALLY HAVE AN EXCESS OF CONFIDENCE, BUT YOU ALWAYS BECOME INDECISIVE AT TIMES LIKE THESE...
I CAN'T HELP IT!
I DON'T HAVE MANY FRIENDS!
I thought you were going to say they were your very best friends!
YOU WERE MEETING SOME MAN WITHOUT TELLING ME!
I PROB-ABLY HAVE EVEN FEWER THAN YOU...
I was pretty disagree-able in middle school...
YOU'RE LYING!
YOU WERE CHUMMY WITH MAIZONO TODAY!
THAT'S MISLEADING.
I'M NUMBER ONE...
SAY THAT I'M NUMBER ONE!
...
HM?
Huh?
I feel like I've said that before...
Waah... Waah...

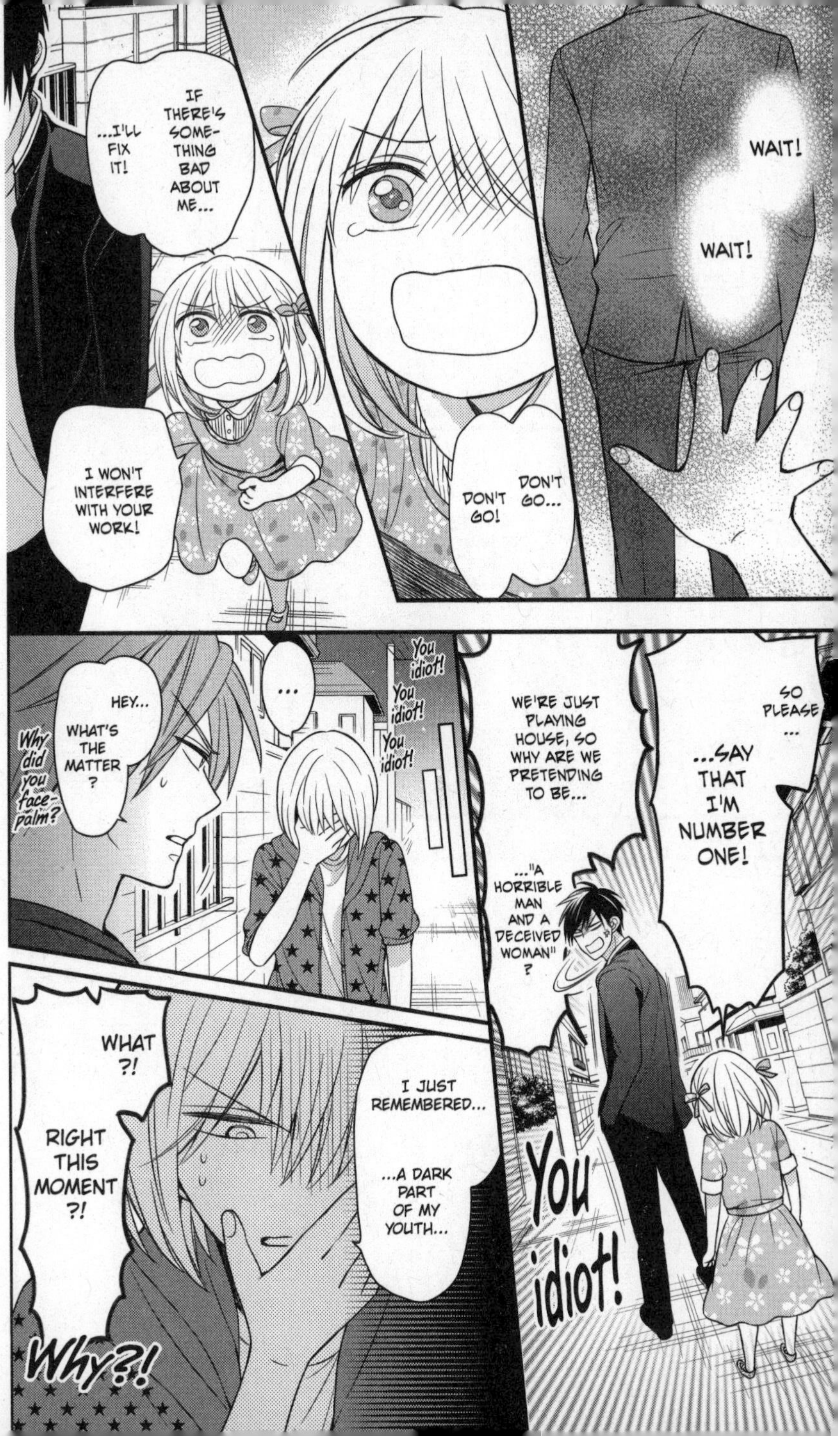
WAIT!
WAIT!
DON'T GO...
DON'T GO!
IF THERE'S SOMETHING BAD ABOUT ME...
...I'LL FIX IT!
I WON'T INTERFERE WITH YOUR WORK!
SO PLEASE...
...SAY THAT I'M NUMBER ONE!
WE'RE JUST PLAYING HOUSE, SO WHY ARE WE PRETENDING TO BE...
..."A HORRIBLE MAN AND A DECEIVED WOMAN"?
You idiot!
You idiot!
You idiot!
You idiot!
...
HEY... WHAT'S THE MATTER?
Why did you face-palm?
I JUST REMEMBERED...
...A DARK PART OF MY YOUTH...
WHAT?!
RIGHT THIS MOMENT?!
Why?!

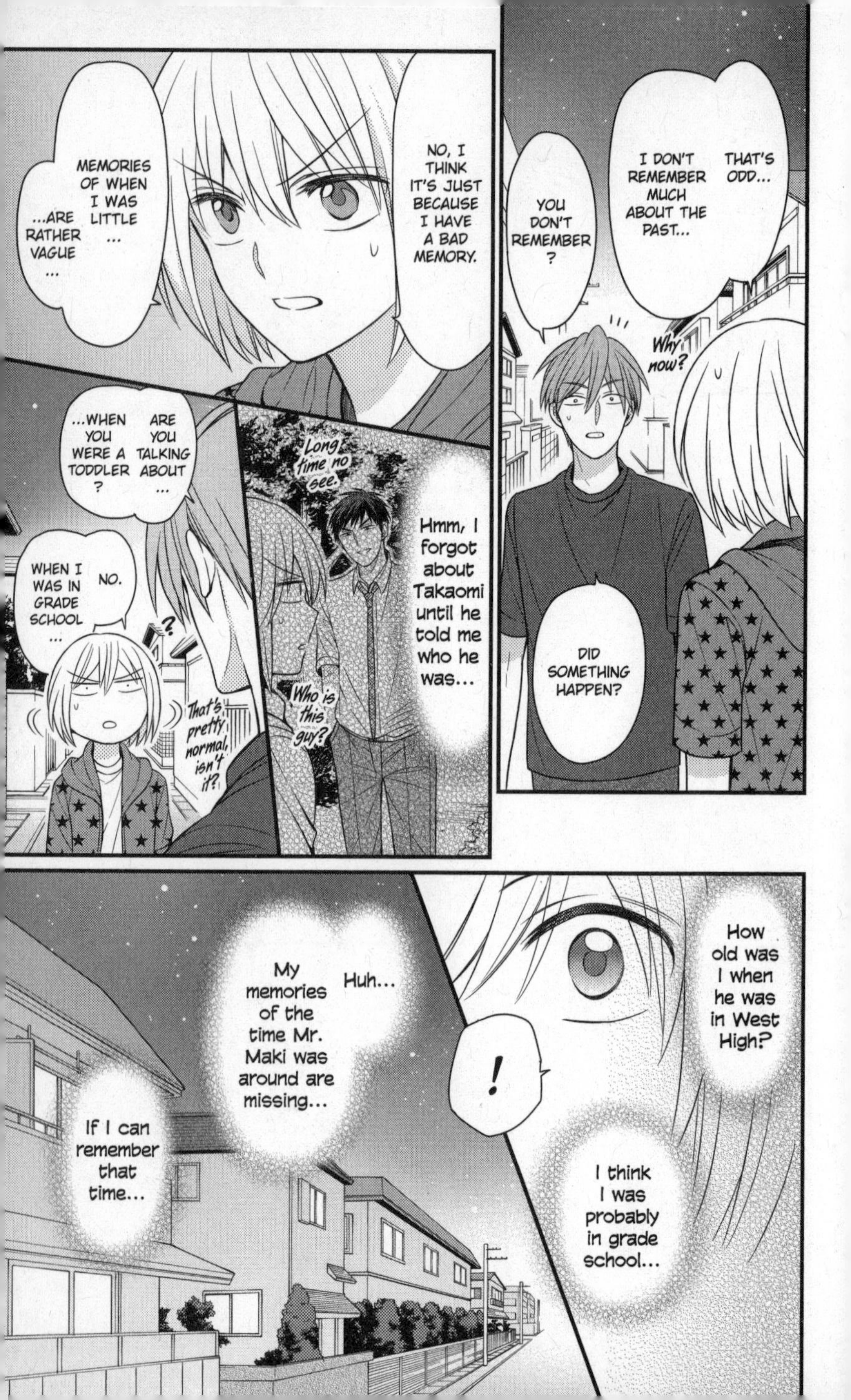
THAT'S ODD...
I DON'T REMEMBER MUCH ABOUT THE PAST...
YOU DON'T REMEMBER ?
Why now?
DID SOMETHING HAPPEN?
NO, I THINK IT'S JUST BECAUSE I HAVE A BAD MEMORY.
MEMORIES OF WHEN I WAS LITTLE ...
...ARE RATHER VAGUE ...
Long time no see.
Hmm, I forgot about Takaomi until he told me who he was...
Who is this guy?
ARE YOU TALKING ABOUT ...
...WHEN YOU WERE A TODDLER ?
NO.
WHEN I WAS IN GRADE SCHOOL ...
That's pretty normal, isn't it?
How old was I when he was in West High?
!
I think I was probably in grade school...
Huh...
My memories of the time Mr. Maki was around are missing...
If I can remember that time...

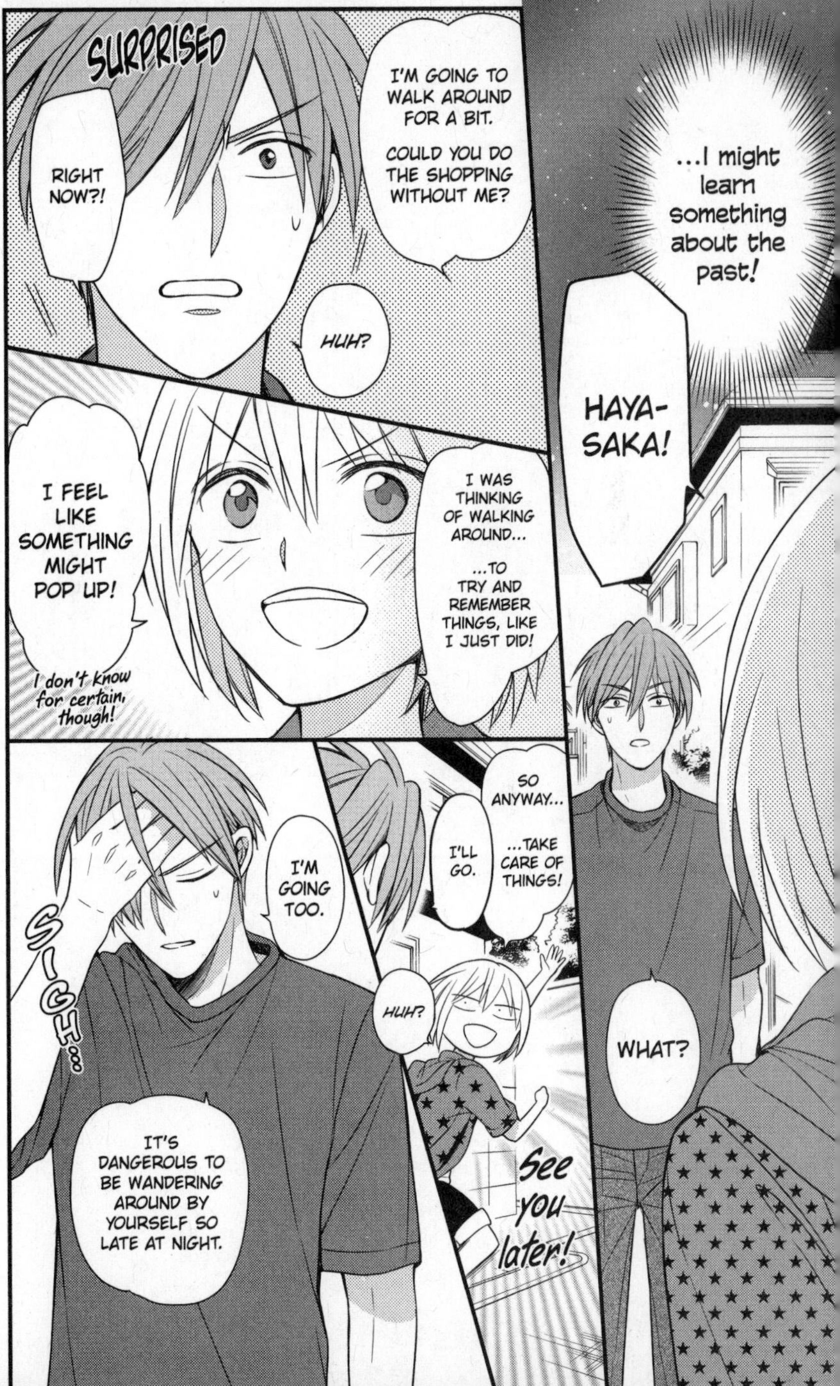
...I might learn something about the past!
HAYA-SAKA!
WHAT?
I'M GOING TO WALK AROUND FOR A BIT.
COULD YOU DO THE SHOPPING WITHOUT ME?
SURPRISED
RIGHT NOW?!
HUH?
I WAS THINKING OF WALKING AROUND...
...TO TRY AND REMEMBER THINGS, LIKE I JUST DID!
I FEEL LIKE SOMETHING MIGHT POP UP!
I don't know for certain, though!
SO ANYWAY...
...TAKE CARE OF THINGS!
I'LL GO.
HUH?
See you later!
I'M GOING TOO.
SIGH...
IT'S DANGEROUS TO BE WANDERING AROUND BY YOURSELF SO LATE AT NIGHT.

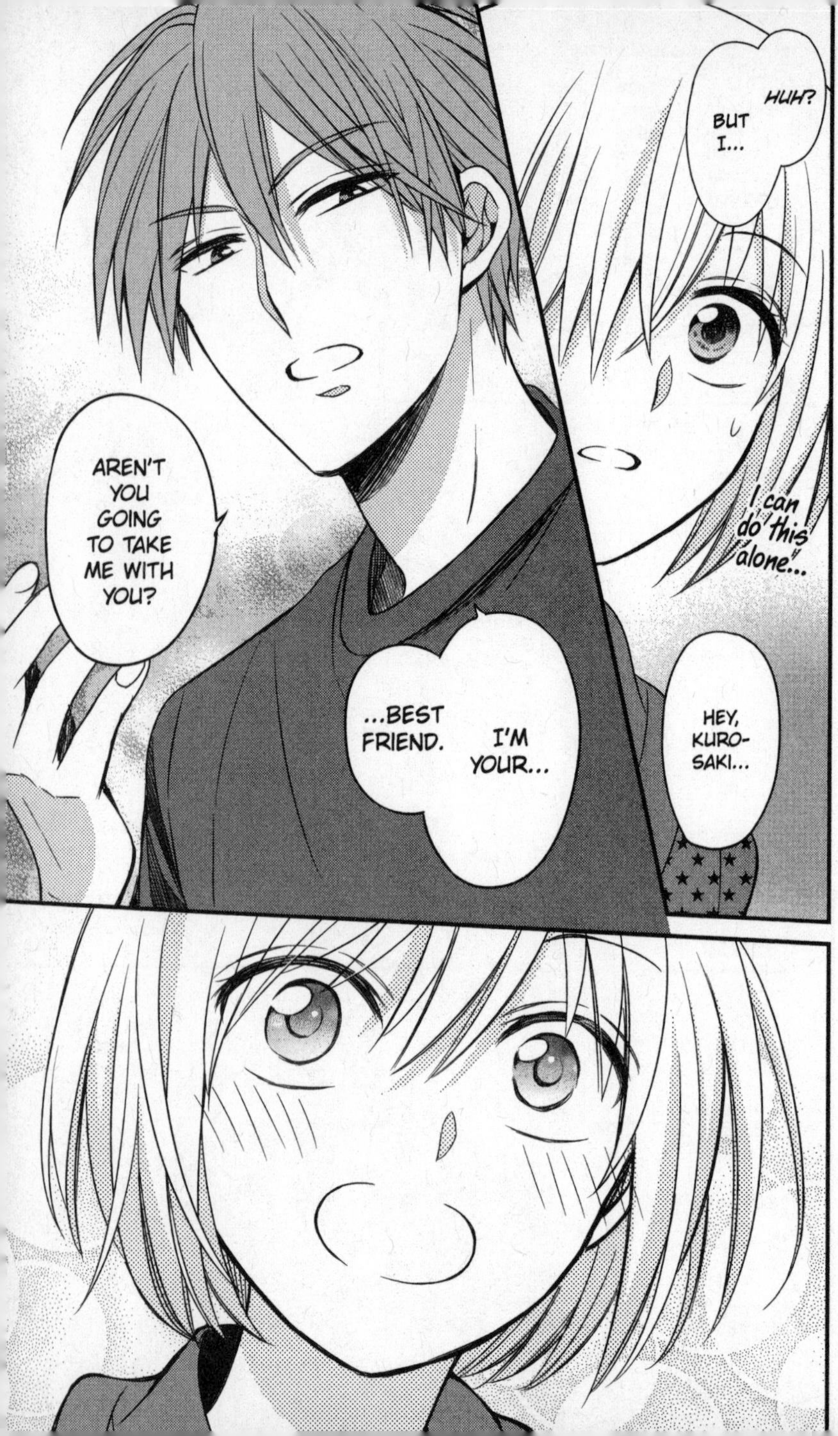
HUH? BUT I...
I can do this alone...
HEY, KURO-SAKI...
AREN'T YOU GOING TO TAKE ME WITH YOU?
I'M YOUR... ...BEST FRIEND.

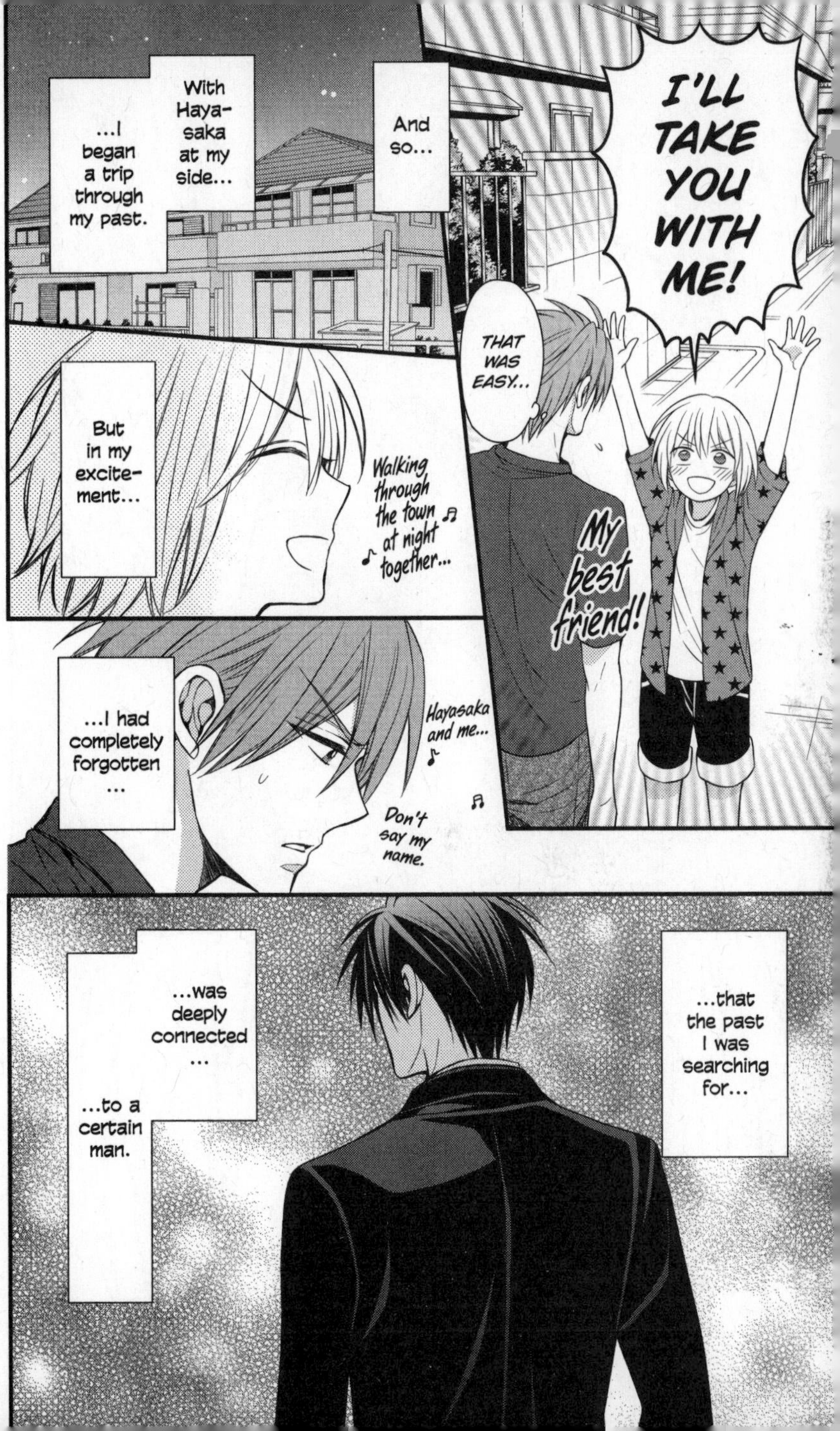
I'LL TAKE YOU WITH ME!
THAT WAS EASY...
My best friend!
And so...
With Haya-saka at my side...
...I began a trip through my past.
Walking through the town at night together...
But in my excite-ment...
Hayasaka and me...
Don't say my name.
...I had completely forgotten...
...that the past I was searching for...
...was deeply connected...
...to a certain man.

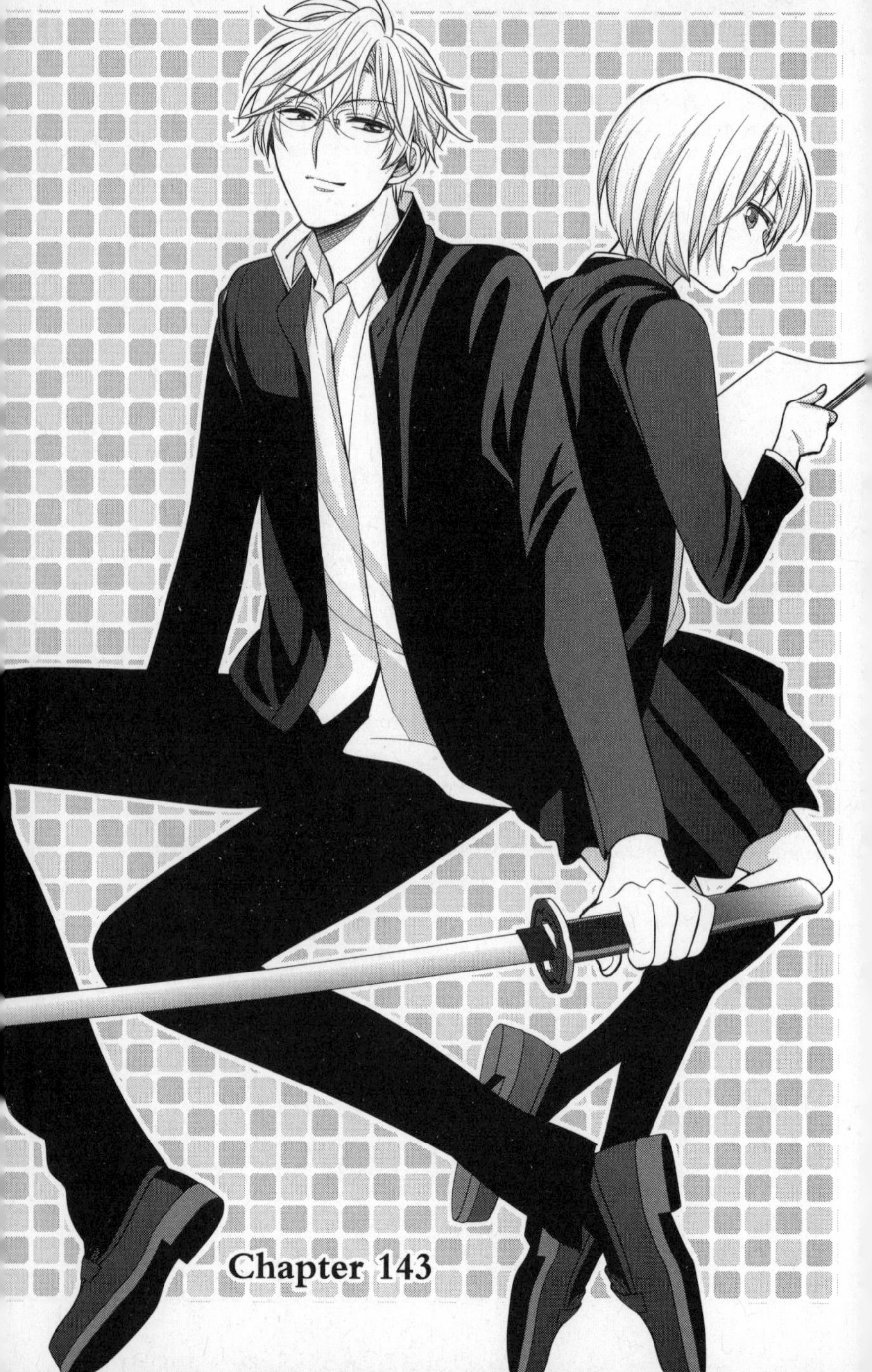
Chapter 143

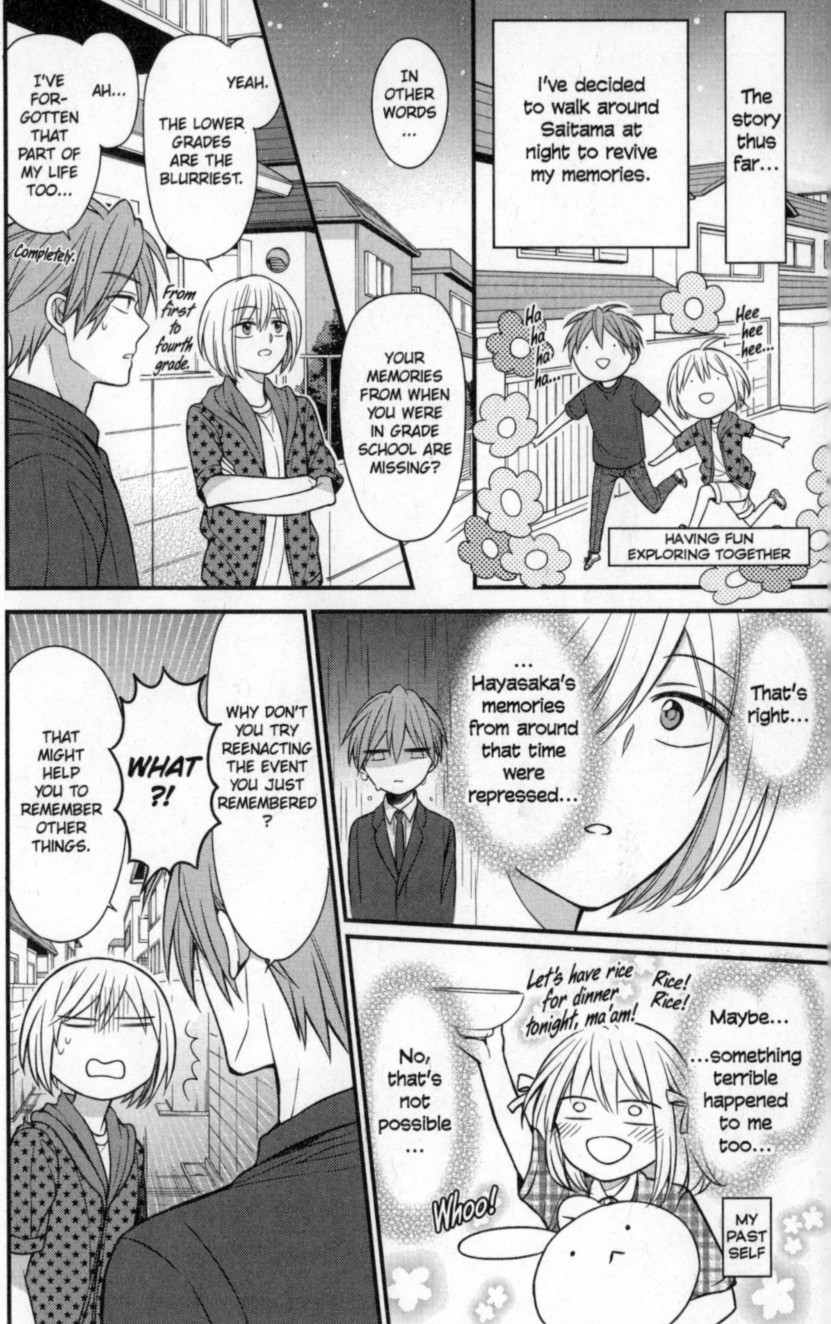
The story thus far...
I've decided to walk around Saitama at night to revive my memories.
Hee hee hee...
Ha ha ha ha...
HAVING FUN EXPLORING TOGETHER
IN OTHER WORDS...
YOUR MEMORIES FROM WHEN YOU WERE IN GRADE SCHOOL ARE MISSING?
YEAH.
THE LOWER GRADES ARE THE BLURRIEST.
From first to fourth grade.
AH...
I'VE FORGOTTEN THAT PART OF MY LIFE TOO...
Completely.
That's right...
...Hayasaka's memories from around that time were repressed...
Maybe...
...something terrible happened to me too...
Rice! Rice!
Let's have rice for dinner tonight, ma'am!
No, that's not possible...
MY PAST SELF
Whoo!
WHY DON'T YOU TRY REENACTING THE EVENT YOU JUST REMEMBERED?
WHAT?!
THAT MIGHT HELP YOU TO REMEMBER OTHER THINGS.

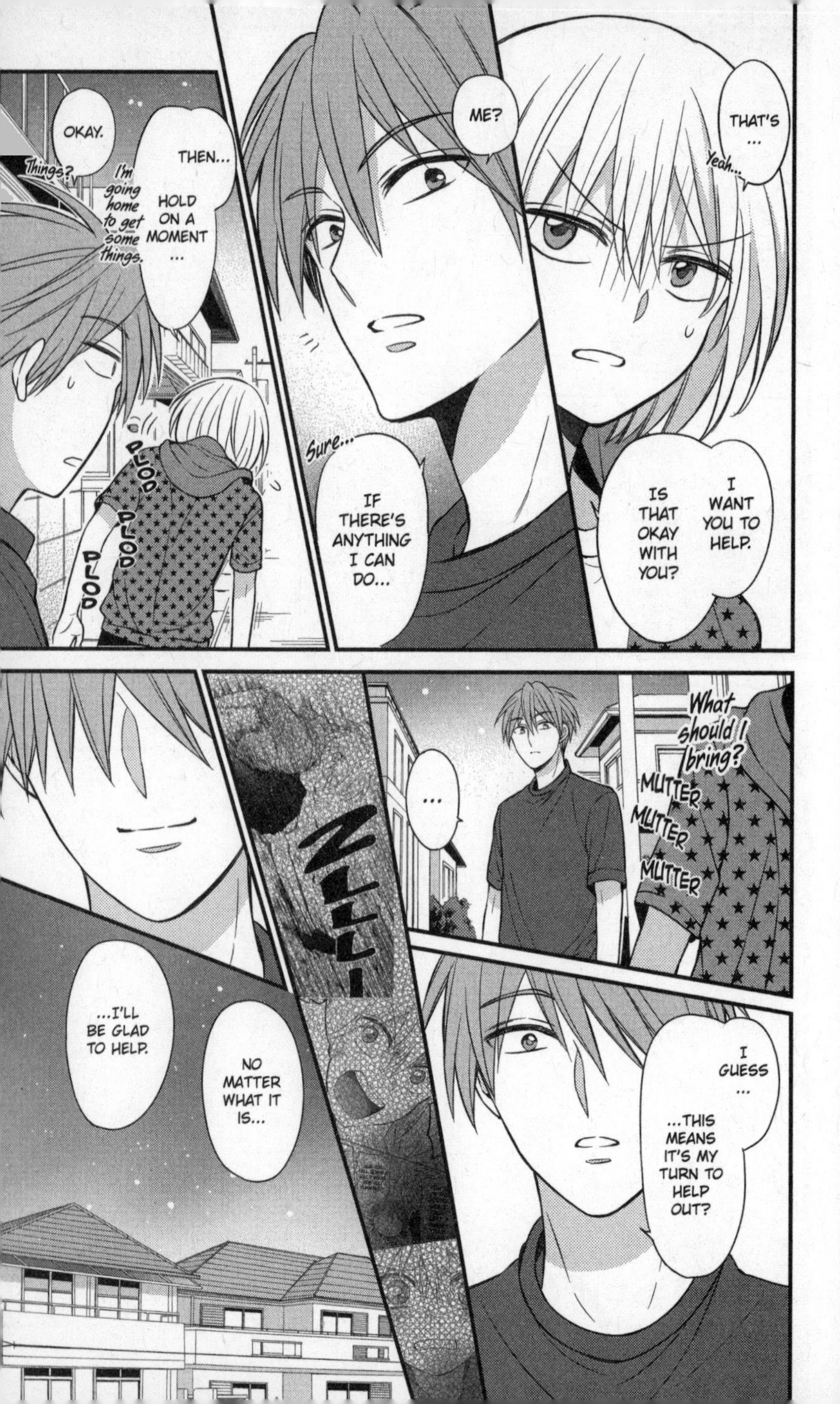
THAT'S...
Yeah...
I WANT YOU TO HELP.
IS THAT OKAY WITH YOU?
ME?
Sure...
IF THERE'S ANYTHING I CAN DO...
THEN...
HOLD ON A MOMENT...
OKAY.
I'm going home to get some things.
Things?
PLOD
PLOD
PLOD
What should I bring?
MUTTER
MUTTER
MUTTER
...
I GUESS...
...THIS MEANS IT'S MY TURN TO HELP OUT?
NO MATTER WHAT IT IS...
...I'LL BE GLAD TO HELP.

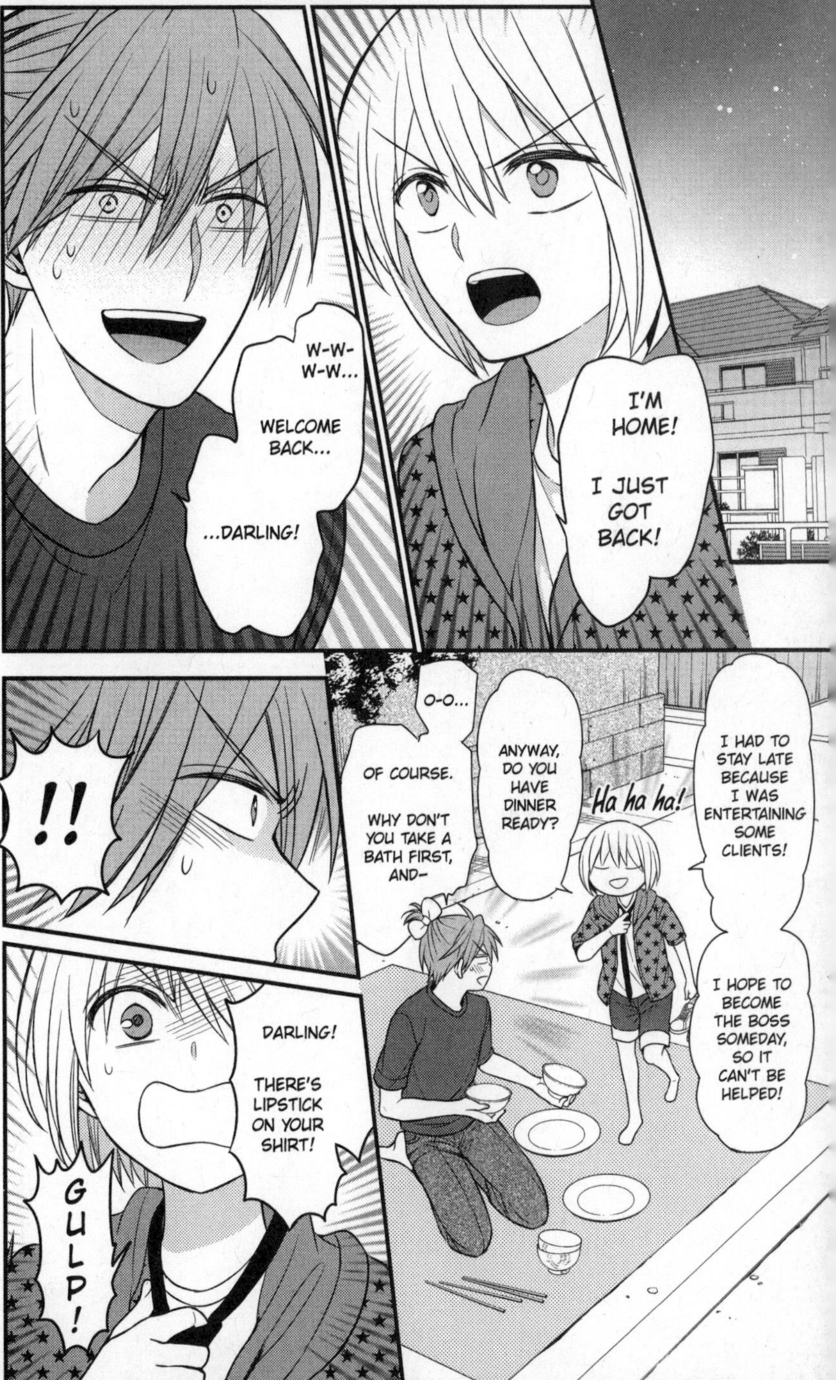
I'M HOME!
I JUST GOT BACK!
W-W-W-W...
WELCOME BACK...
...DARLING!
I HAD TO STAY LATE BECAUSE I WAS ENTERTAINING SOME CLIENTS!
I HOPE TO BECOME THE BOSS SOMEDAY, SO IT CAN'T BE HELPED!
Ha ha ha!
ANYWAY, DO YOU HAVE DINNER READY?
O-O-O...
OF COURSE.
WHY DON'T YOU TAKE A BATH FIRST, AND–
!!
DARLING!
THERE'S LIPSTICK ON YOUR SHIRT!
GULP!

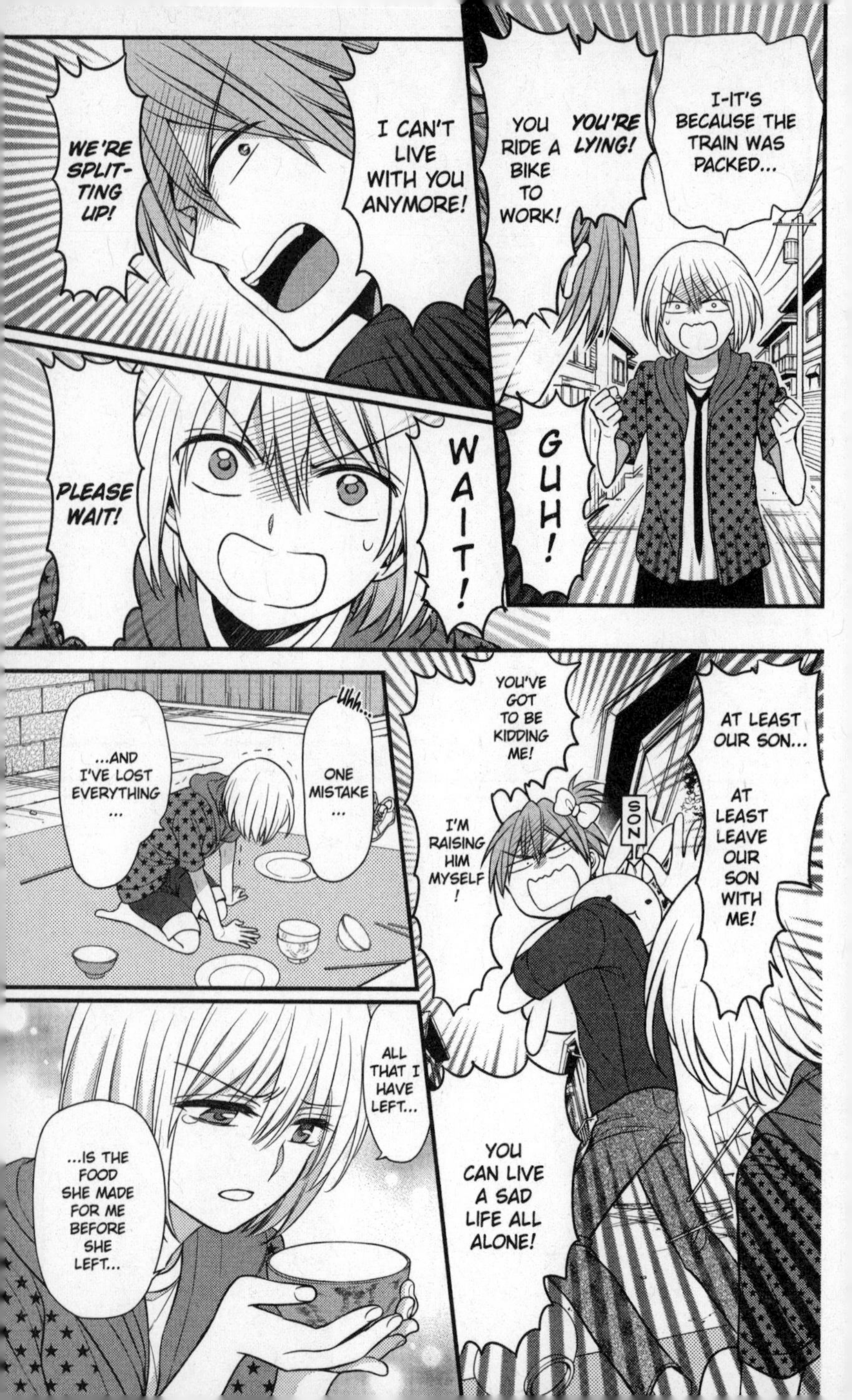
I-IT'S BECAUSE THE TRAIN WAS PACKED...
YOU'RE LYING!
YOU RIDE A BIKE TO WORK!
GUH!
I CAN'T LIVE WITH YOU ANYMORE!
WE'RE SPLIT-TING UP!
WAIT!
PLEASE WAIT!
AT LEAST OUR SON...
AT LEAST LEAVE OUR SON WITH ME!
YOU'VE GOT TO BE KIDDING ME!
I'M RAISING HIM MYSELF!
SON
YOU CAN LIVE A SAD LIFE ALL ALONE!
Uhh...
ONE MISTAKE...
...AND I'VE LOST EVERYTHING...
ALL THAT I HAVE LEFT...
...IS THE FOOD SHE MADE FOR ME BEFORE SHE LEFT...

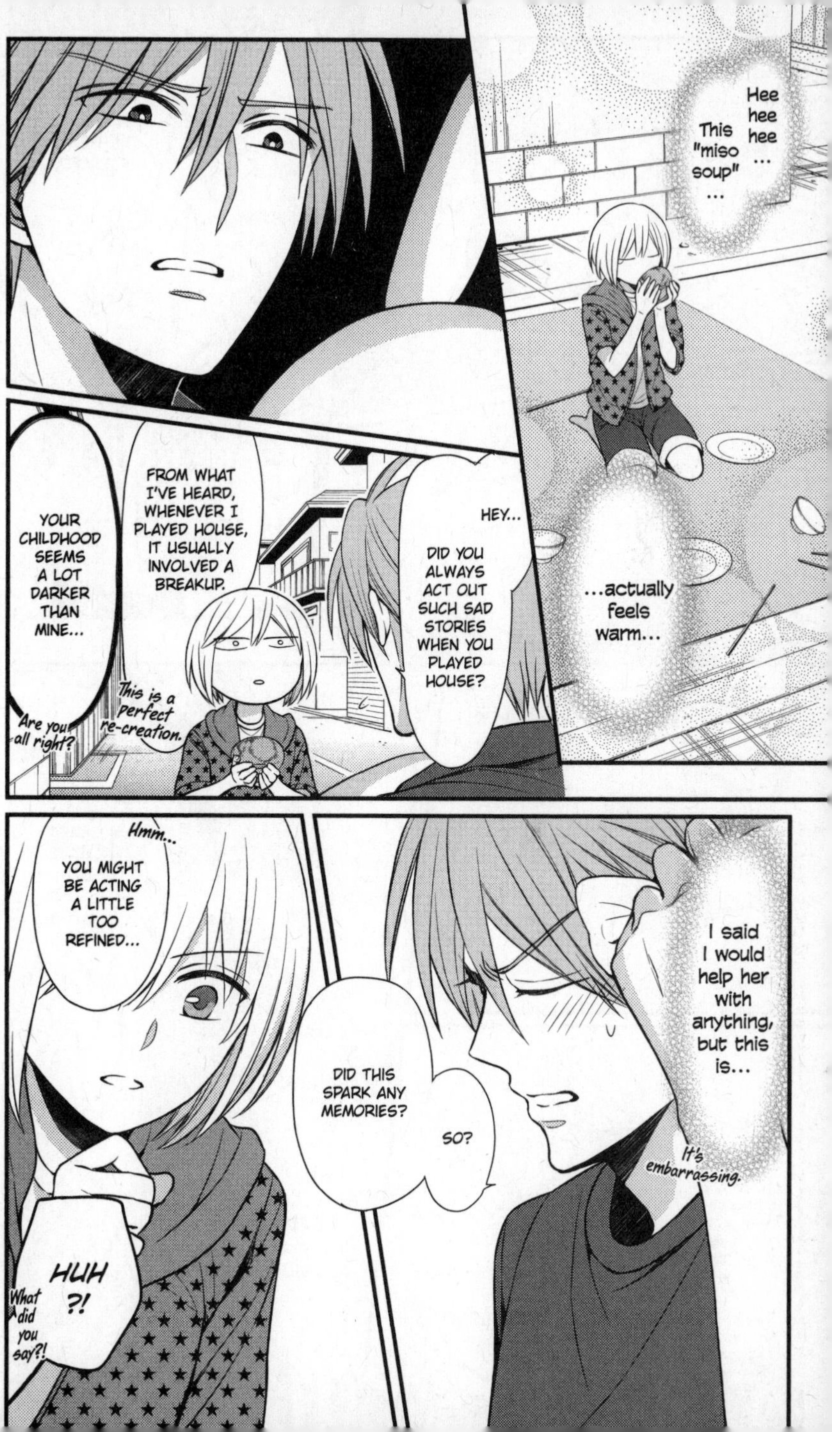
Hee hee hee...
This "miso soup"...
...actually feels warm...
HEY...
DID YOU ALWAYS ACT OUT SUCH SAD STORIES WHEN YOU PLAYED HOUSE?
This is a perfect re-creation.
FROM WHAT I'VE HEARD, WHENEVER I PLAYED HOUSE, IT USUALLY INVOLVED A BREAKUP.
YOUR CHILDHOOD SEEMS A LOT DARKER THAN MINE...
Are you all right?
I said I would help her with anything, but this is...
It's embarrassing.
SO?
DID THIS SPARK ANY MEMORIES?
Hmm...
YOU MIGHT BE ACTING A LITTLE TOO REFINED...
HUH?!
What did you say?!

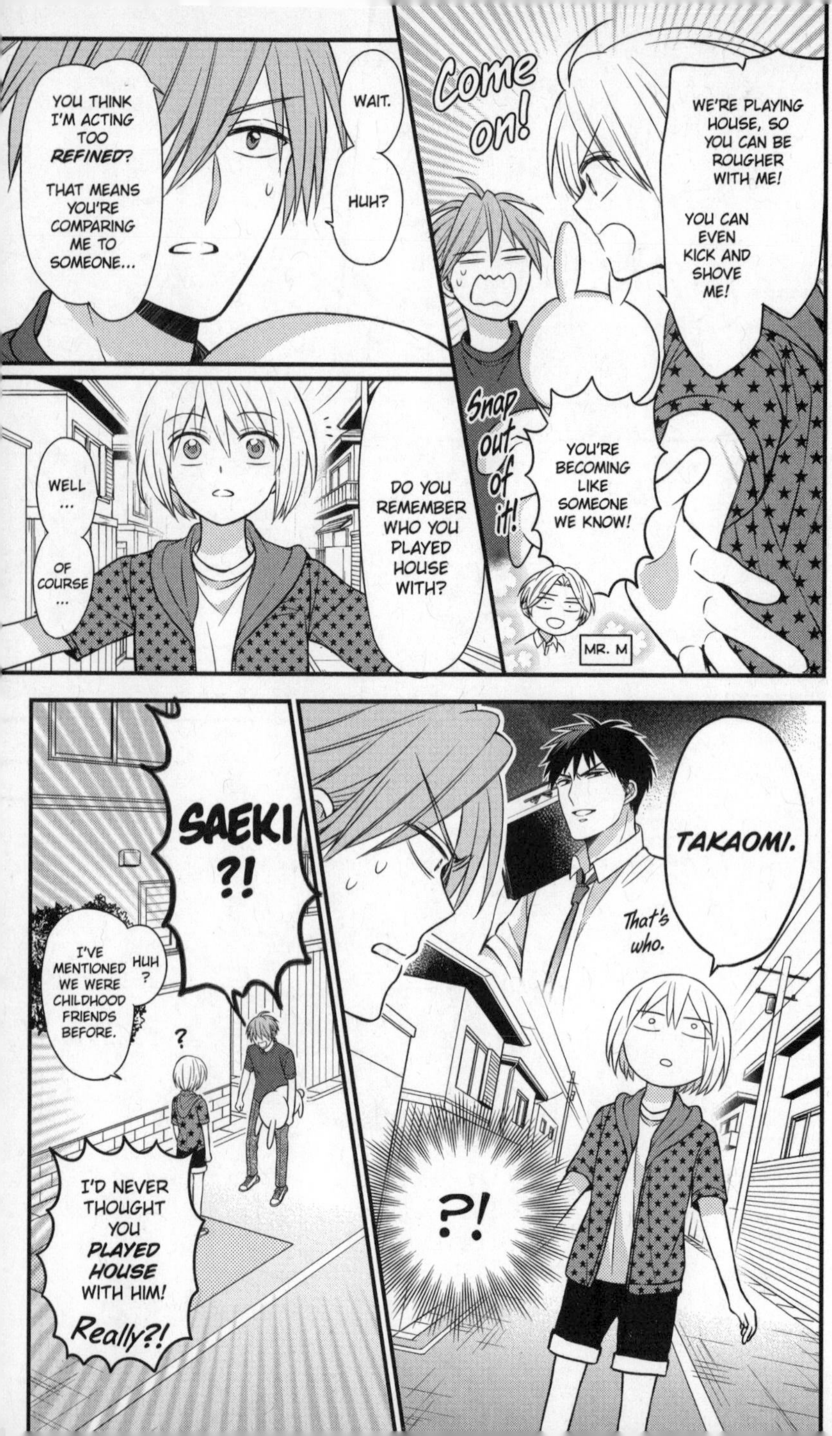

Come on!
WE'RE PLAYING HOUSE, SO YOU CAN BE ROUGHER WITH ME!
YOU CAN EVEN KICK AND SHOVE ME!
Snap out of it!
YOU'RE BECOMING LIKE SOMEONE WE KNOW!
MR. M
WAIT.
HUH?
YOU THINK I'M ACTING TOO REFINED?
THAT MEANS YOU'RE COMPARING ME TO SOMEONE...
DO YOU REMEMBER WHO YOU PLAYED HOUSE WITH?
WELL ...
OF COURSE ...
TAKAOMI.
That's who.
?!
SAEKI ?!
HUH ?
I'VE MENTIONED WE WERE CHILDHOOD FRIENDS BEFORE.
?
I'D NEVER THOUGHT YOU PLAYED HOUSE WITH HIM!
Really?!

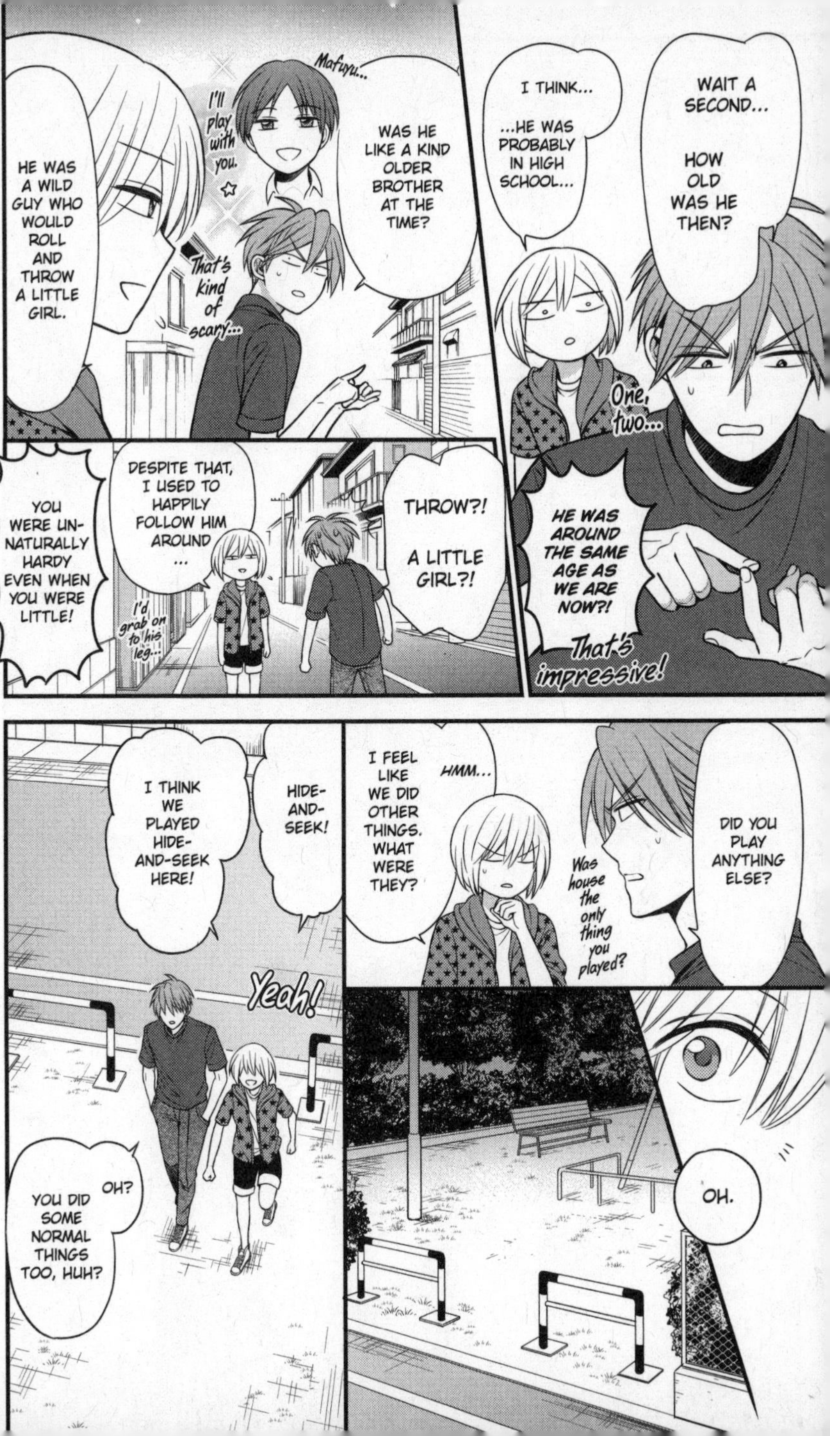
WAIT A SECOND... HOW OLD WAS HE THEN?
I THINK... ...HE WAS PROBABLY IN HIGH SCHOOL...
One, two...
HE WAS AROUND THE SAME AGE AS WE ARE NOW?!
That's impressive!
Mafuyu...
WAS HE LIKE A KIND OLDER BROTHER AT THE TIME?
I'll play with you.
That's kind of scary...
HE WAS A WILD GUY WHO WOULD ROLL AND THROW A LITTLE GIRL.
THROW?! A LITTLE GIRL?!
DESPITE THAT, I USED TO HAPPILY FOLLOW HIM AROUND...
I'd grab on to his leg...
YOU WERE UN-NATURALLY HARDY EVEN WHEN YOU WERE LITTLE!
DID YOU PLAY ANYTHING ELSE?
Was house the only thing you played?
HMM...
I FEEL LIKE WE DID OTHER THINGS. WHAT WERE THEY?
HIDE-AND-SEEK!
I THINK WE PLAYED HIDE-AND-SEEK HERE!
OH.
Yeah!
OH?
YOU DID SOME NORMAL THINGS TOO, HUH?

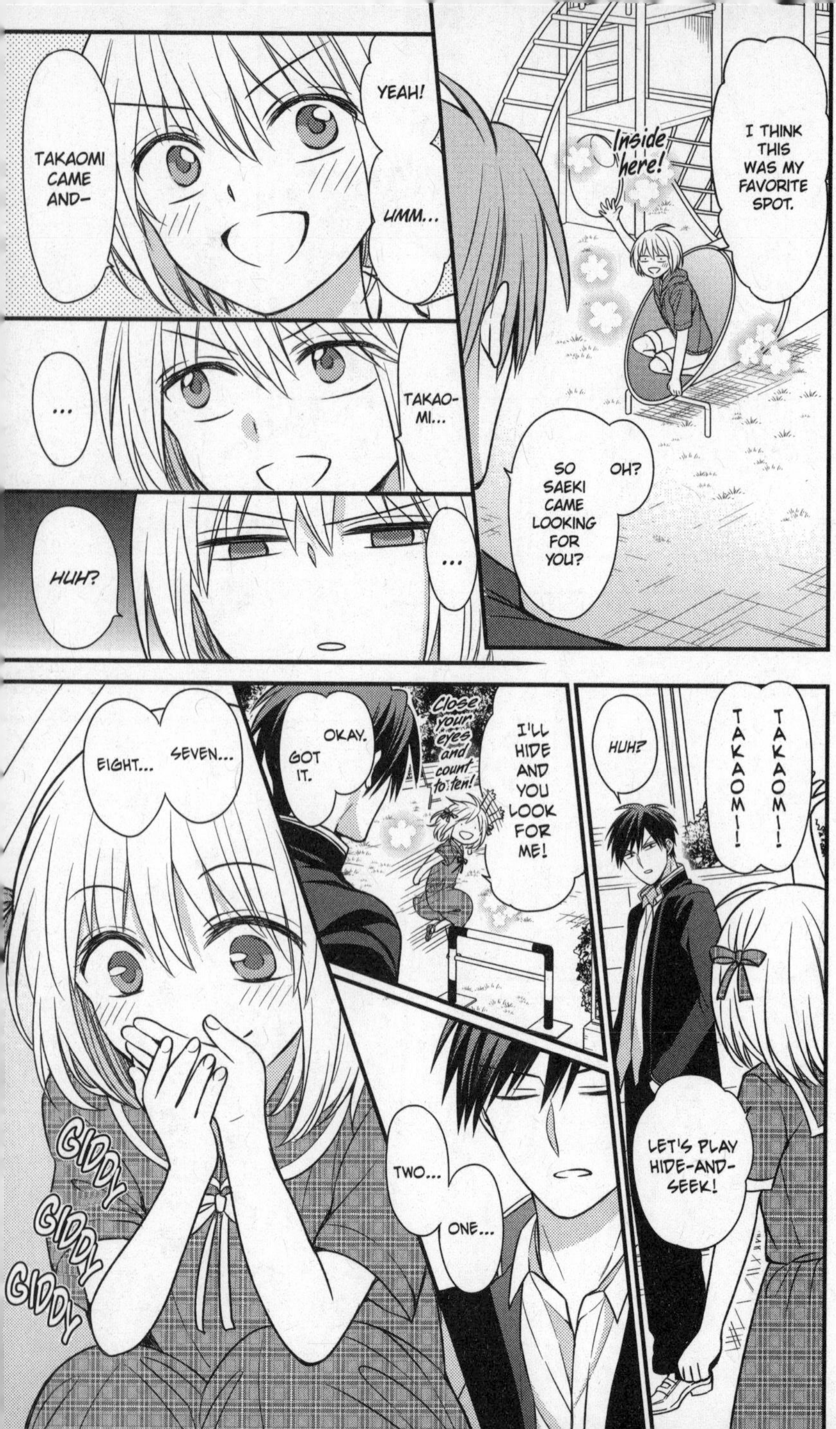
I THINK THIS WAS MY FAVORITE SPOT.
Inside here!
OH?
SO SAEKI CAME LOOKING FOR YOU?
YEAH!
UMM...
TAKAOMI CAME AND-
TAKAO-MI...
...
...
HUH?
TAKAOMI! TAKAOMI!
HUH?
LET'S PLAY HIDE-AND-SEEK!
I'LL HIDE AND YOU LOOK FOR ME!
Close your eyes and count to ten!
OKAY. GOT IT.
SEVEN...
EIGHT...
GIDDY GIDDY GIDDY
TWO...
ONE...

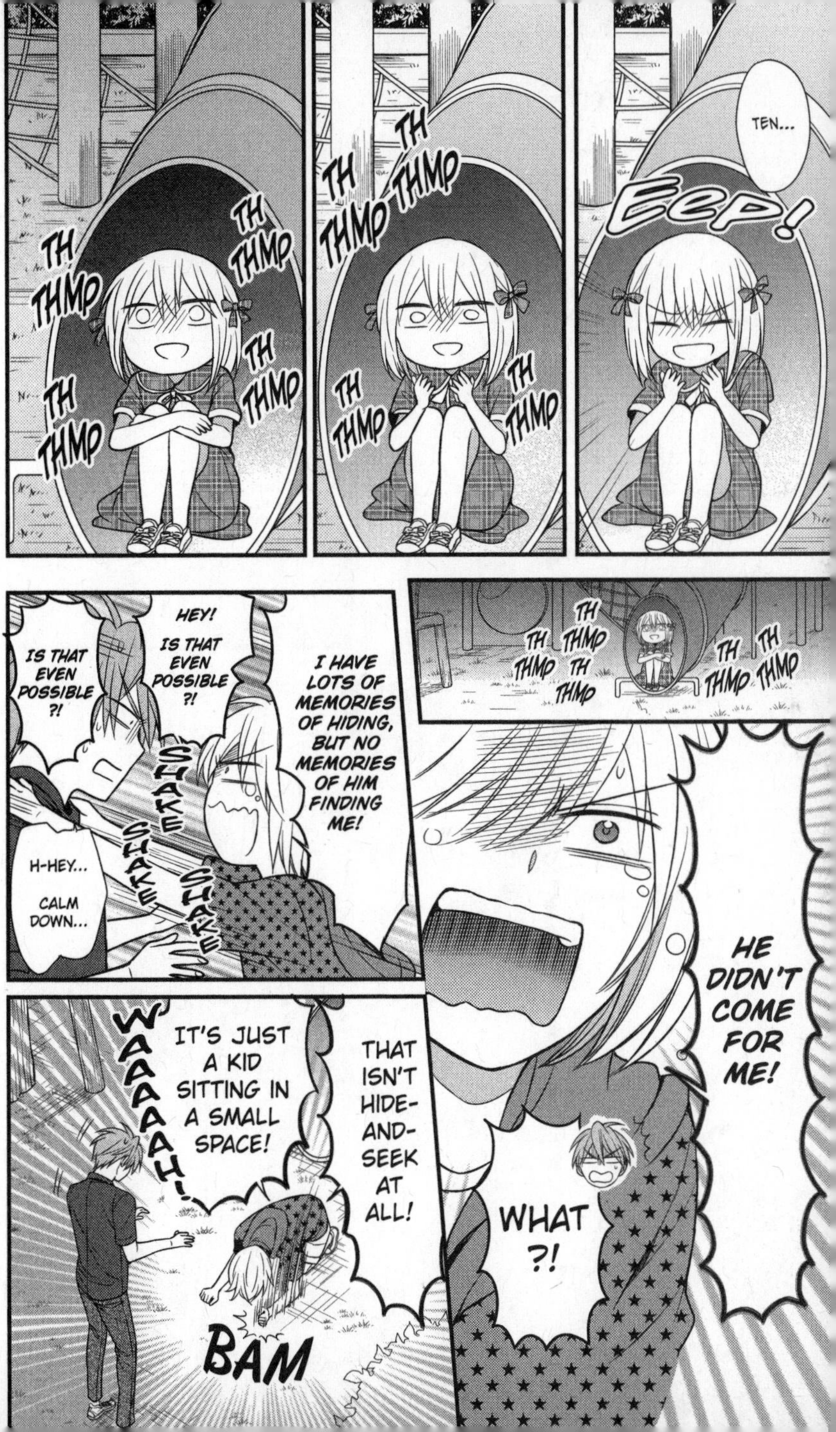

TEN...
Eep!
TH THMP
TH THMP
TH THMP
TH THMP
TH THMP
TH THMP
TH THMP
TH THMP
TH THMP
TH THMP
TH THMP
TH THMP
TH THMP
HE DIDN'T COME FOR ME!
WHAT ?!
I HAVE LOTS OF MEMORIES OF HIDING, BUT NO MEMORIES OF HIM FINDING ME!
HEY! IS THAT EVEN POSSIBLE ?!
IS THAT EVEN POSSIBLE ?!
SHAKE SHAKE SHAKE SHAKE
H-HEY... CALM DOWN...
THAT ISN'T HIDE-AND-SEEK AT ALL!
IT'S JUST A KID SITTING IN A SMALL SPACE!
WAAAAAH!
BAM

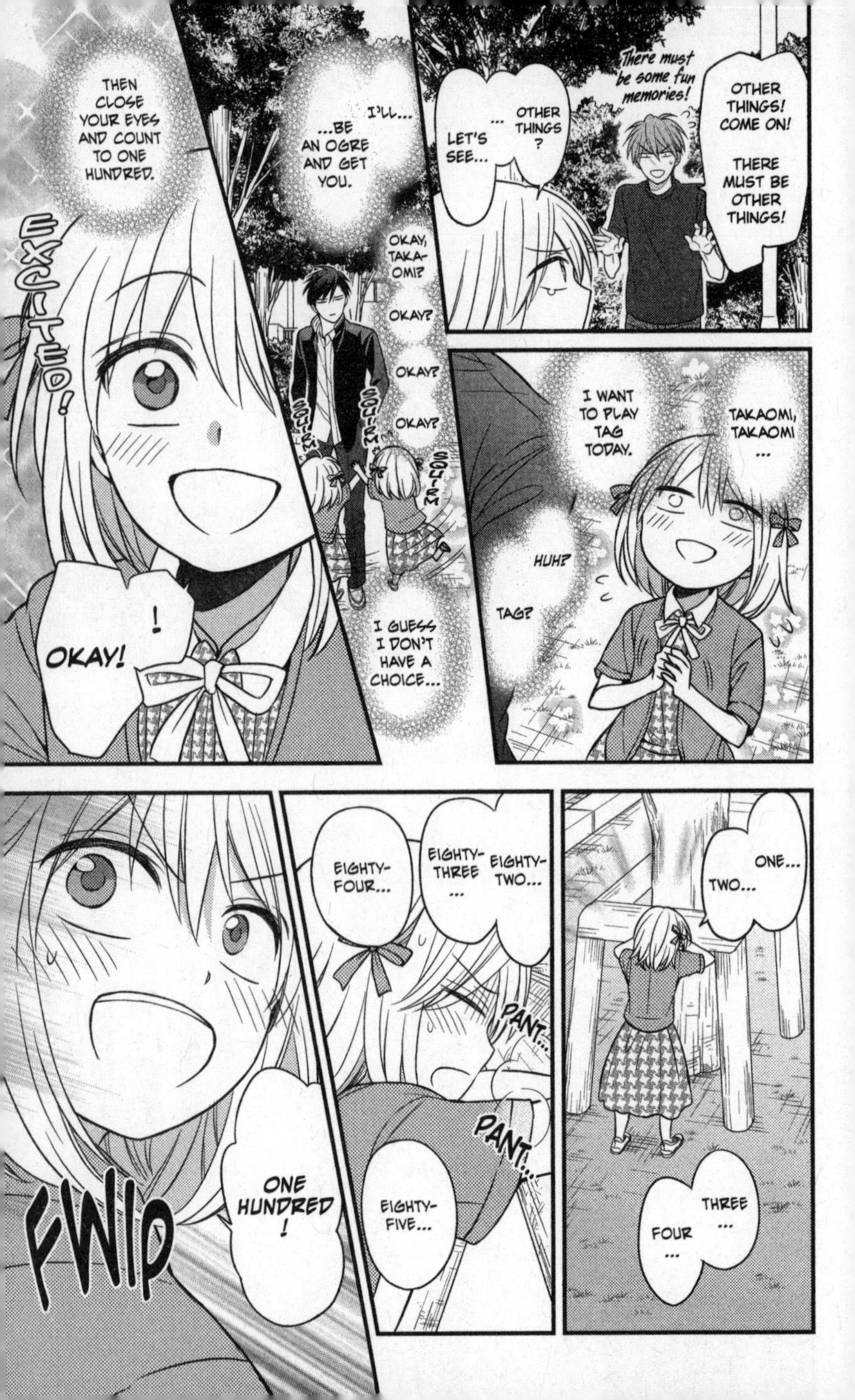
OTHER THINGS! COME ON!
THERE MUST BE OTHER THINGS!
There must be some fun memories!
... OTHER THINGS ?
LET'S SEE...
TAKAOMI, TAKAOMI ...
I WANT TO PLAY TAG TODAY.
HUH?
TAG?
OKAY, TAKAOMI?
OKAY?
OKAY?
OKAY?
SQUIRM
SQUIRM
SQUIRM
I GUESS I DON'T HAVE A CHOICE...
I'LL...
...BE AN OGRE AND GET YOU.
THEN CLOSE YOUR EYES AND COUNT TO ONE HUNDRED.
EXCITED!
!
OKAY!
ONE...
TWO...
THREE ...
FOUR ...
EIGHTY-TWO...
EIGHTY-THREE ...
EIGHTY-FOUR...
PANT...
PANT...
EIGHTY-FIVE...
ONE HUNDRED !
FWIP

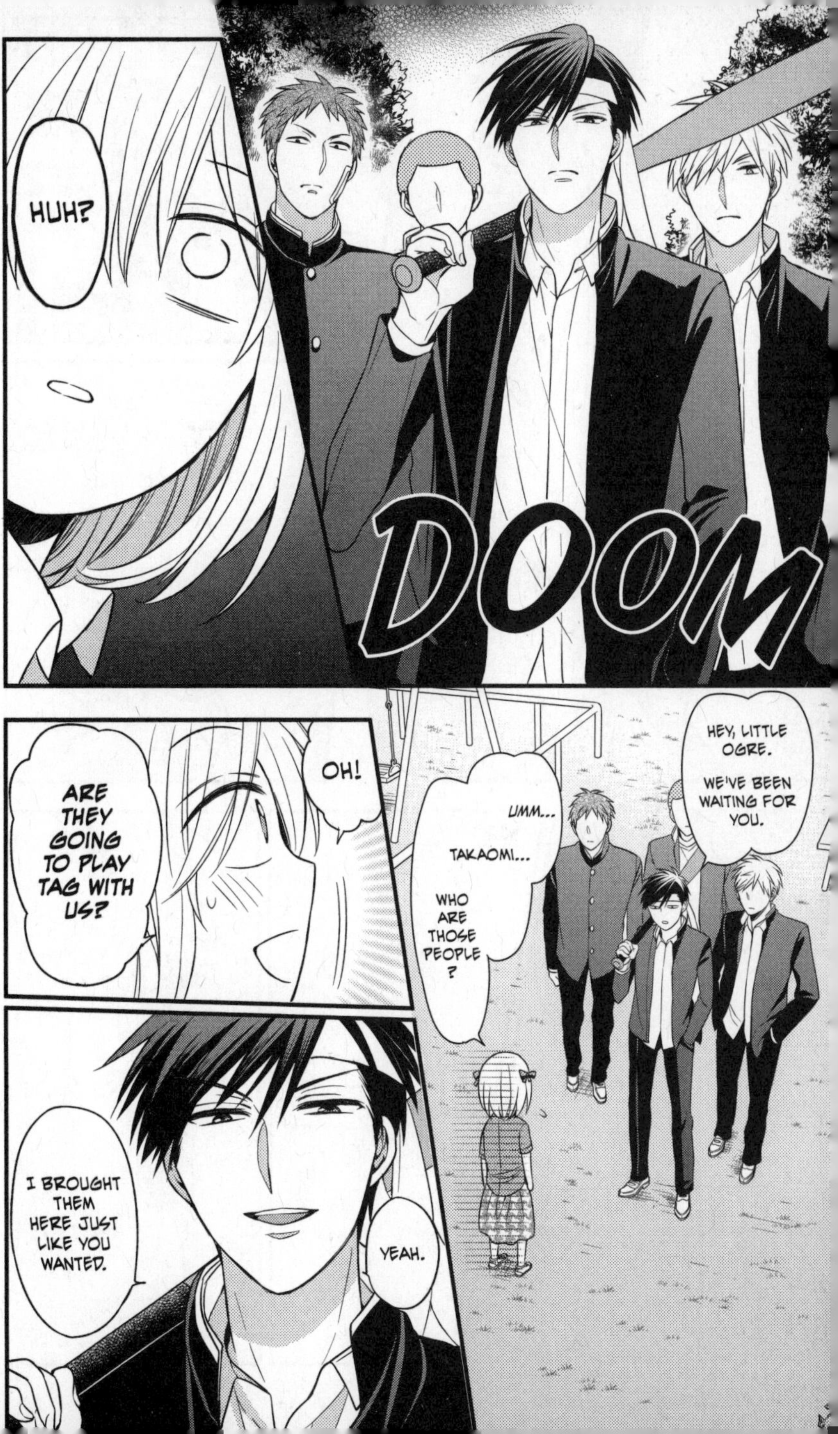
DOOM
HUH?
HEY, LITTLE OGRE. WE'VE BEEN WAITING FOR YOU.
UMM... TAKAOMI... WHO ARE THOSE PEOPLE?
OH!
ARE THEY GOING TO PLAY TAG WITH US?
YEAH.
I BROUGHT THEM HERE JUST LIKE YOU WANTED.

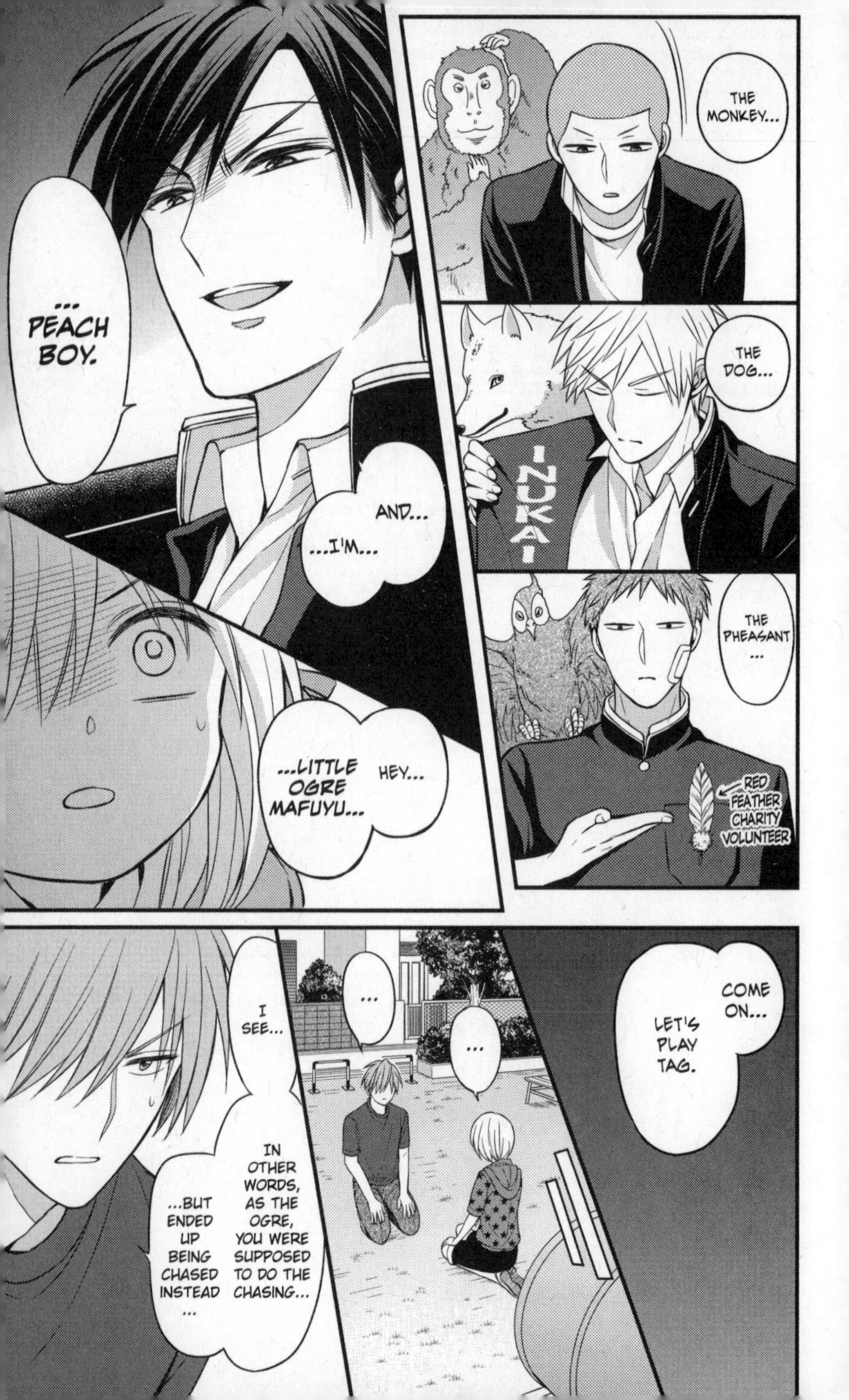
THE MONKEY...
THE DOG...
INUKAI
THE PHEASANT...
RED FEATHER CHARITY VOLUNTEER
...PEACH BOY.
AND... ...I'M...
HEY... ...LITTLE OGRE MAFUYU...
COME ON... LET'S PLAY TAG.
...
...
I SEE...
IN OTHER WORDS, AS THE OGRE, YOU WERE SUPPOSED TO DO THE CHASING...
...BUT ENDED UP BEING CHASED INSTEAD...

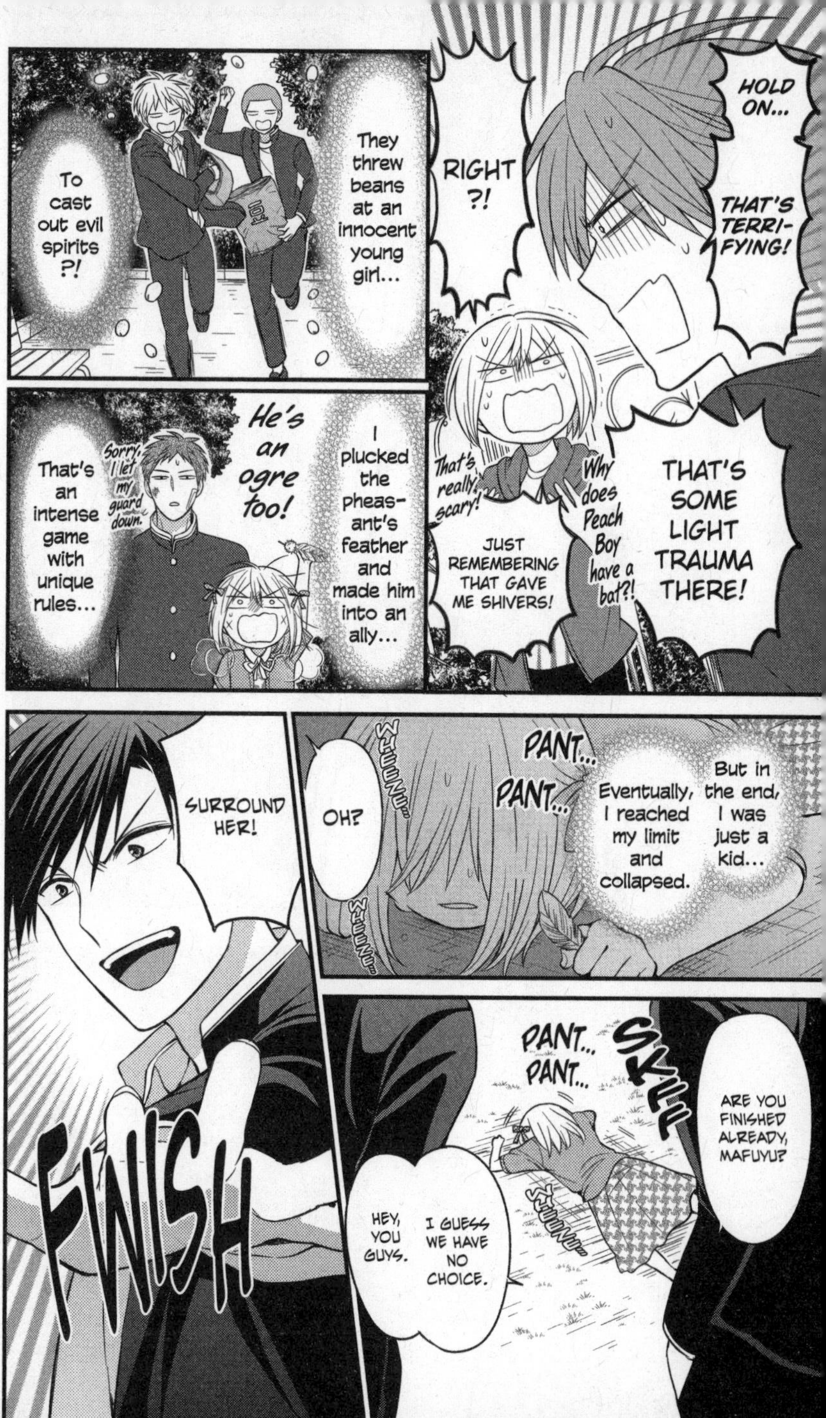
HOLD ON...
THAT'S TERRIFYING!
RIGHT?!
THAT'S SOME LIGHT TRAUMA THERE!
Why does Peach Boy have a bat?!
That's really scary!
JUST REMEMBERING THAT GAVE ME SHIVERS!
They threw beans at an innocent young girl...
To cast out evil spirits?!
I plucked the pheasant's feather and made him into an ally...
He's an ogre too!
Sorry, I let my guard down.
That's an intense game with unique rules...
PANT...
PANT...
But in the end, I was just a kid...
Eventually, I reached my limit and collapsed.
OH?
WHEEZE...
WHEEZE...
ARE YOU FINISHED ALREADY, MAFUYU?
SKFF
PANT... PANT...
I GUESS WE HAVE NO CHOICE.
HEY, YOU GUYS.
SURROUND HER!
FINISH

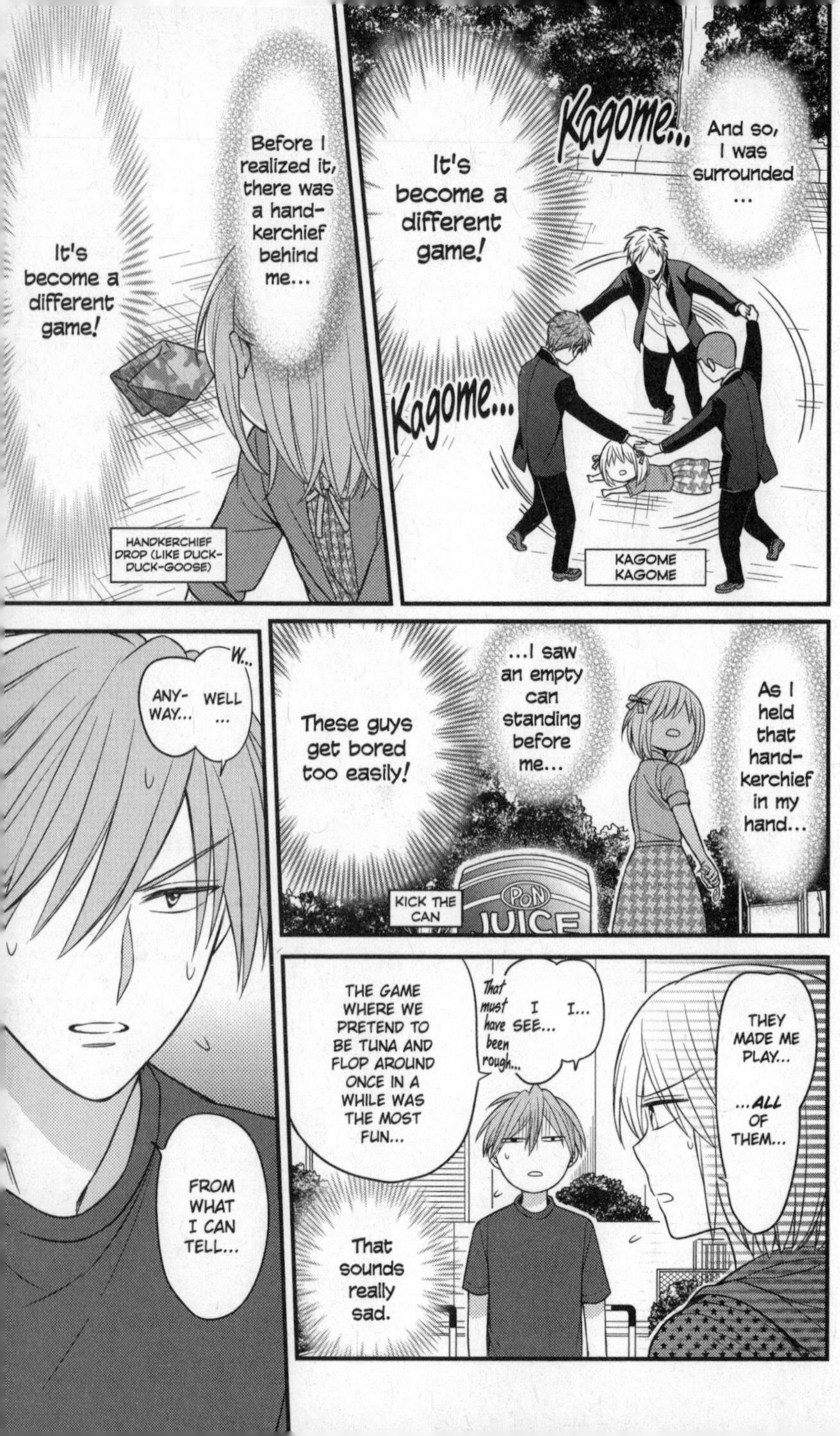
And so, I was surrounded...
Kagome...
It's become a different game!
Kagome...
KAGOME KAGOME
Before I realized it, there was a handkerchief behind me...
It's become a different game!
HANDKERCHIEF DROP (LIKE DUCK-DUCK-GOOSE)
As I held that handkerchief in my hand...
...I saw an empty can standing before me...
These guys get bored too easily!
KICK THE CAN
PON JUICE
THEY MADE ME PLAY...
...ALL OF THEM...
I... I SEE...
That must have been rough...
THE GAME WHERE WE PRETEND TO BE TUNA AND FLOP AROUND ONCE IN A WHILE WAS THE MOST FUN...
That sounds really sad.
W... WELL...
ANYWAY...
FROM WHAT I CAN TELL...

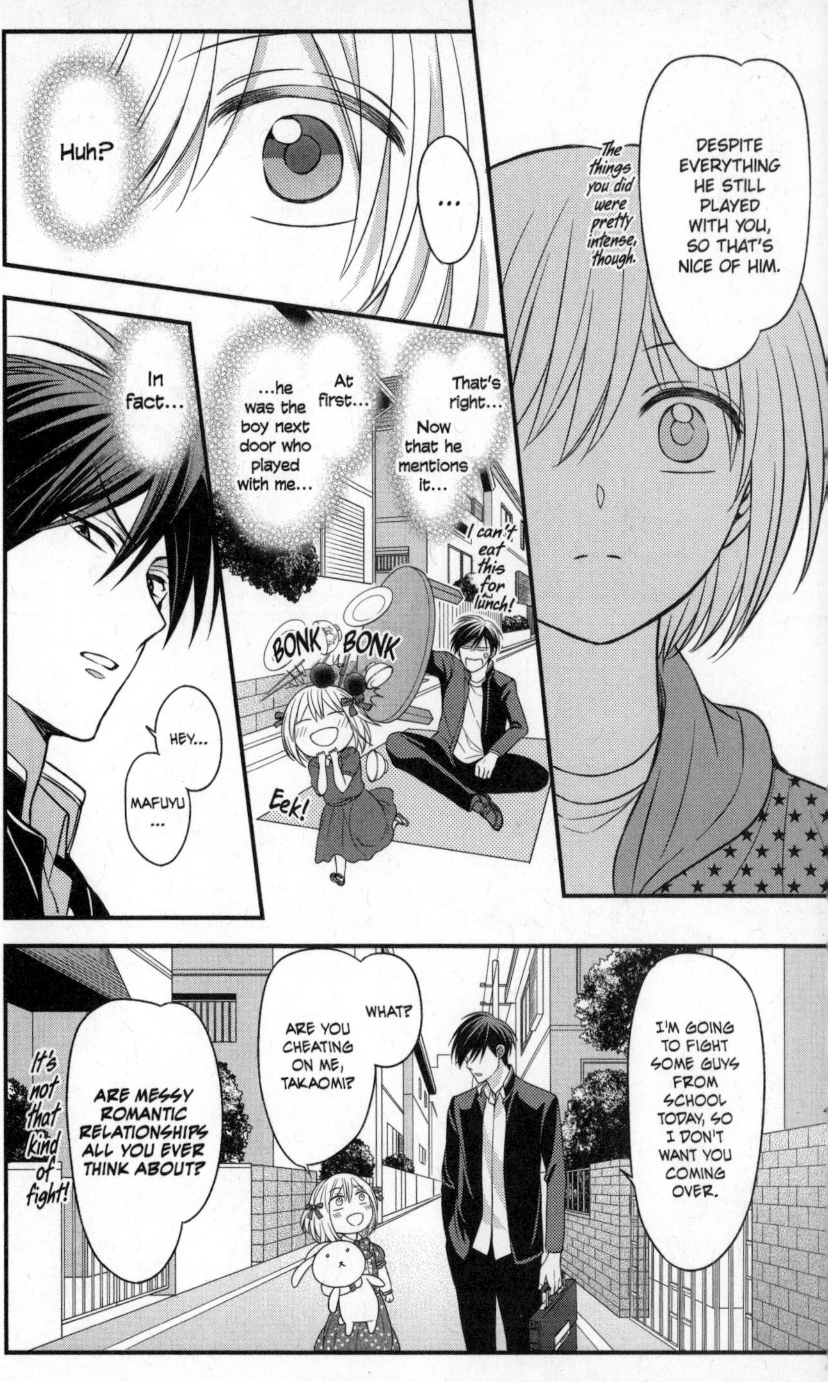
DESPITE EVERYTHING HE STILL PLAYED WITH YOU, SO THAT'S NICE OF HIM.
The things you did were pretty intense, though.
...
Huh?
That's right... Now that he mentions it...
At first... ...he was the boy next door who played with me...
In fact...
I can't eat this for lunch!
BONK BONK
Eek!
HEY...
MAFUYU...
I'M GOING TO FIGHT SOME GUYS FROM SCHOOL TODAY, SO I DON'T WANT YOU COMING OVER.
WHAT?
ARE YOU CHEATING ON ME, TAKAOMI?
ARE MESSY ROMANTIC RELATIONSHIPS ALL YOU EVER THINK ABOUT?
It's not that kind of fight!

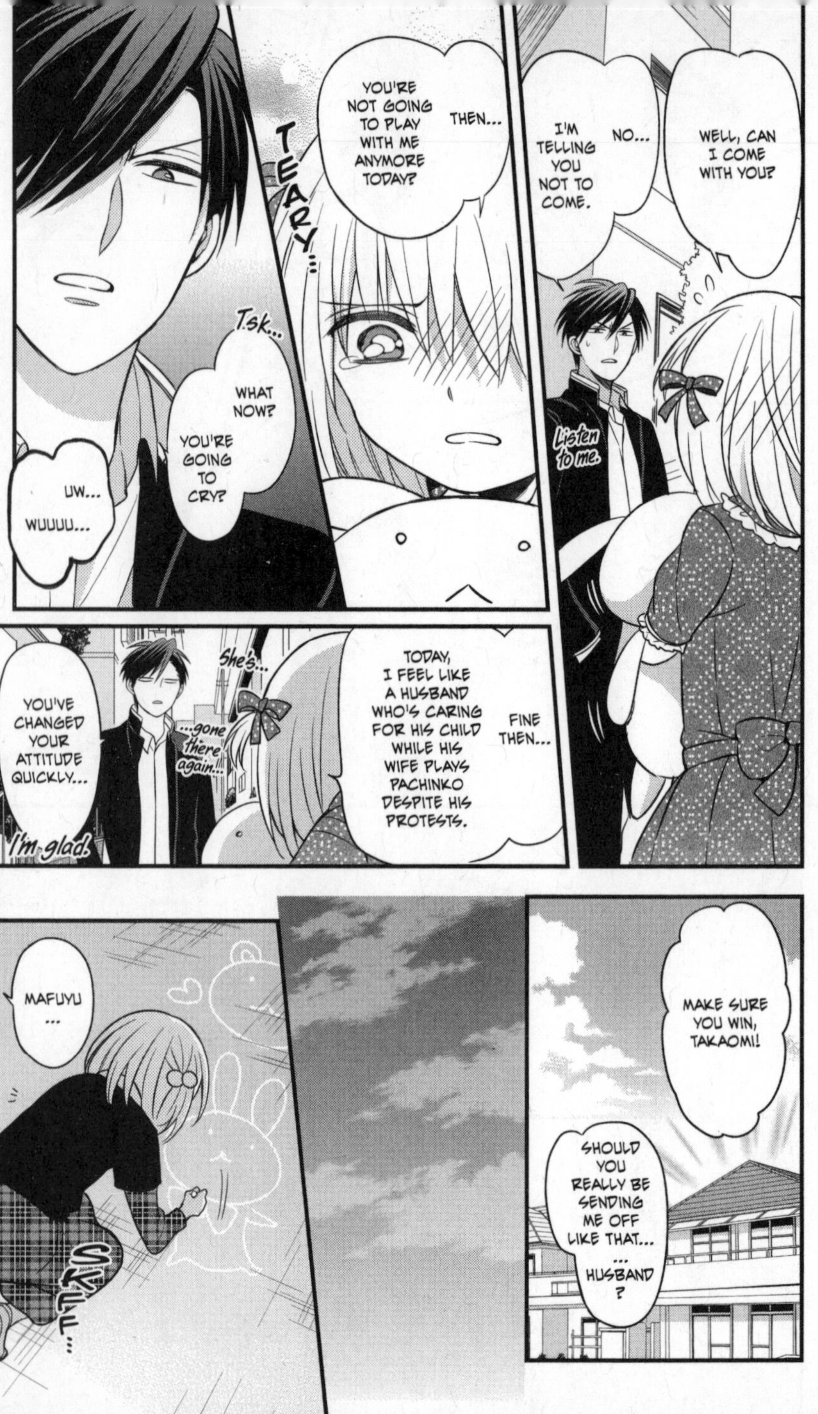
WELL, CAN I COME WITH YOU?
NO...
I'M TELLING YOU NOT TO COME.
Listen to me.
THEN...
YOU'RE NOT GOING TO PLAY WITH ME ANYMORE TODAY?
TEARY...
Tsk...
WHAT NOW?
YOU'RE GOING TO CRY?
UW... WUUUU...
FINE THEN...
TODAY, I FEEL LIKE A HUSBAND WHO'S CARING FOR HIS CHILD WHILE HIS WIFE PLAYS PACHINKO DESPITE HIS PROTESTS.
She's...
...gone there again...
YOU'VE CHANGED YOUR ATTITUDE QUICKLY...
I'm glad.
MAKE SURE YOU WIN, TAKAOMI!
SHOULD YOU REALLY BE SENDING ME OFF LIKE THAT... ...HUSBAND?
MAFUYU ...
SKFF...

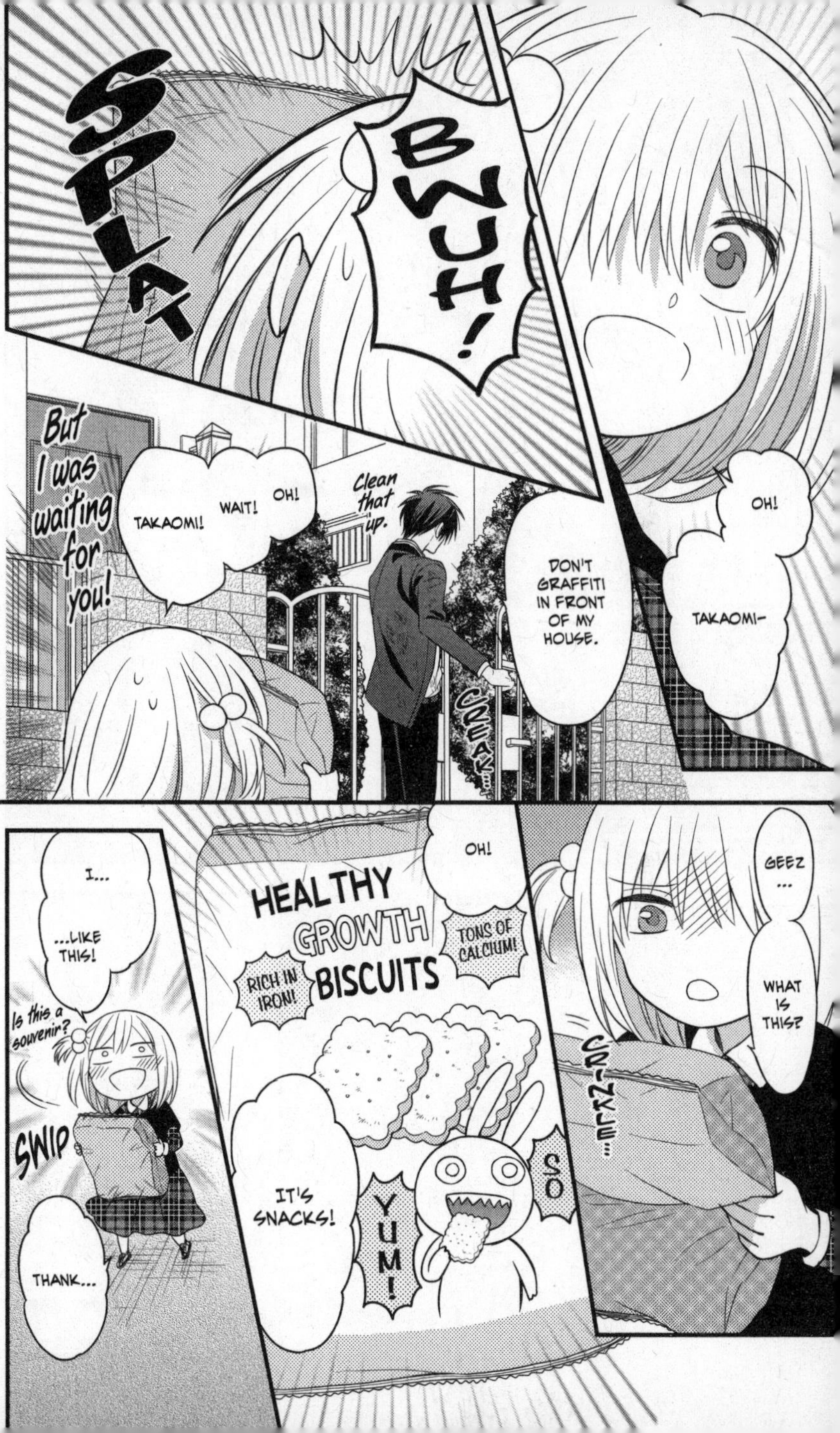
SPLAT
BWUH!
OH!
TAKAOMI-
DON'T GRAFFITI IN FRONT OF MY HOUSE.
CREAK...
Clean that up.
OH!
WAIT!
TAKAOMI!
But I was waiting for you!
GEEZ...
WHAT IS THIS?
CRINKLE...
OH!
HEALTHY GROWTH BISCUITS
TONS OF CALCIUM!
RICH IN IRON!
SO YUM!
IT'S SNACKS!
I...
...LIKE THIS!
Is this a souvenir?
SWIP
THANK...

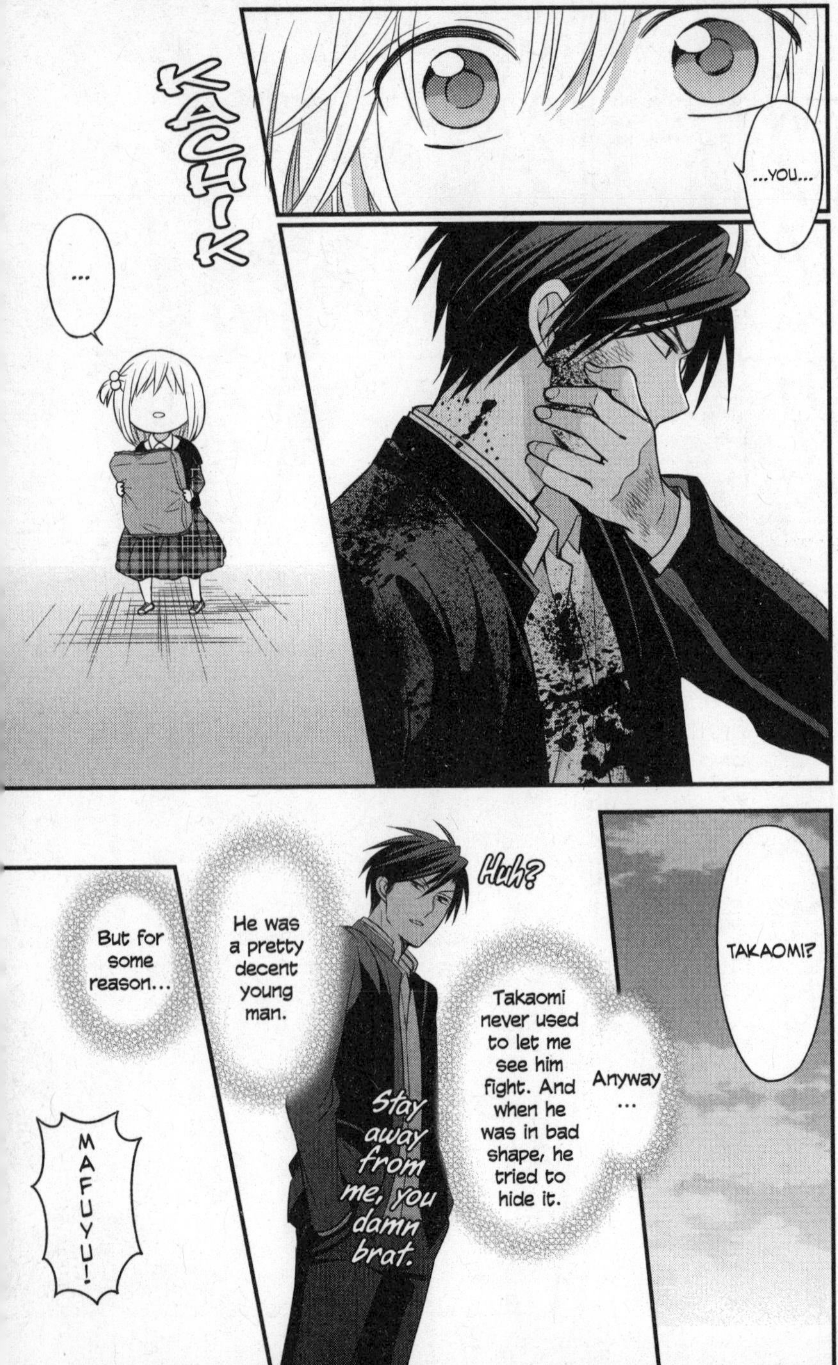
...YOU...
KACHIK
...
TAKAOMI?
Huh?
Anyway...
Takaomi never used to let me see him fight. And when he was in bad shape, he tried to hide it.
Stay away from me, you damn brat.
He was a pretty decent young man.
But for some reason...
MAFUYU!

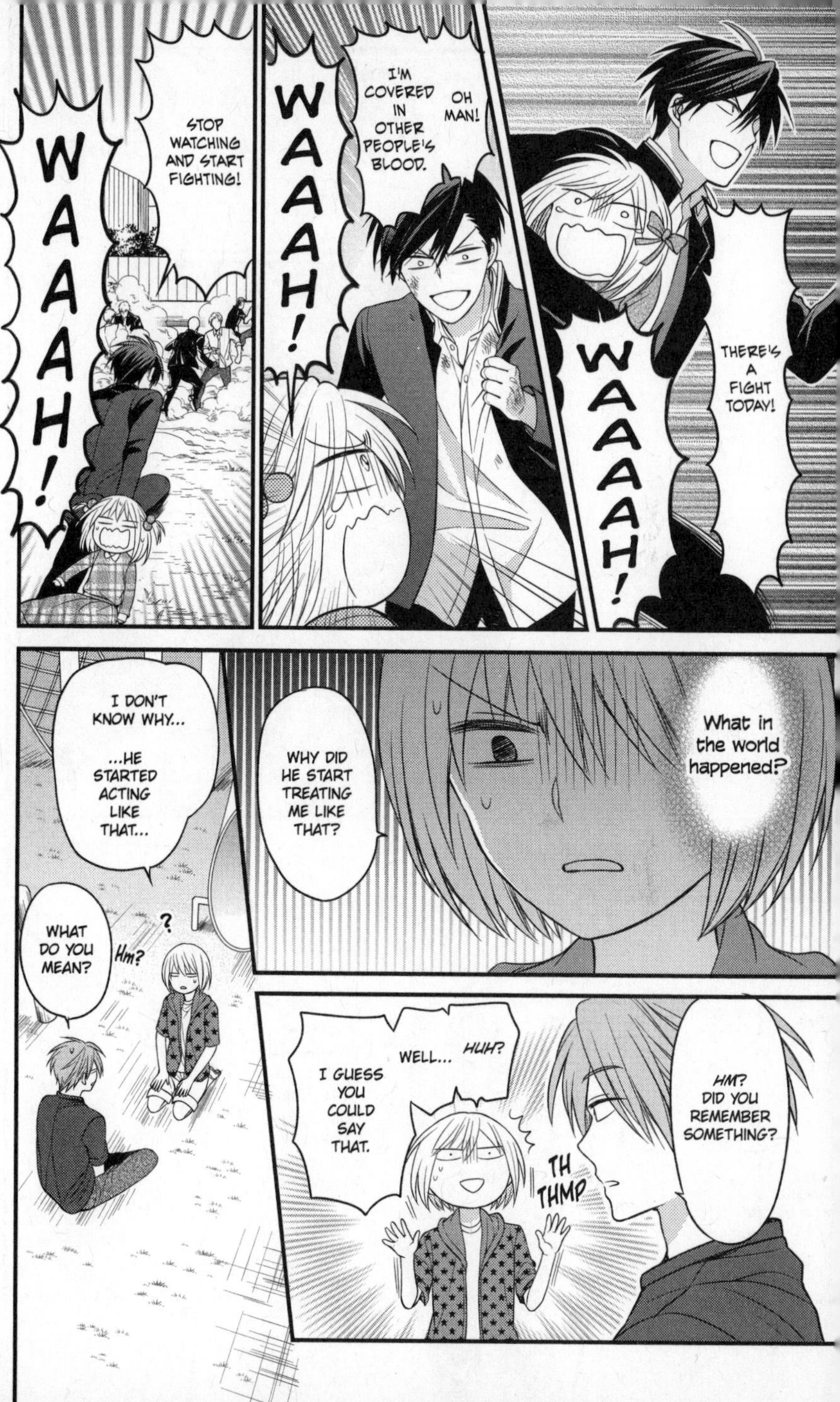
THERE'S A FIGHT TODAY!
WAAAAAH!
OH MAN!
I'M COVERED IN OTHER PEOPLE'S BLOOD.
WAAAH!
STOP WATCHING AND START FIGHTING!
WAAAH!
What in the world happened?
WHY DID HE START TREATING ME LIKE THAT?
HM? DID YOU REMEMBER SOMETHING?
HUH?
TH THMP
WELL...
I GUESS YOU COULD SAY THAT.
I DON'T KNOW WHY...
...HE STARTED ACTING LIKE THAT...
?
Hm?
WHAT DO YOU MEAN?

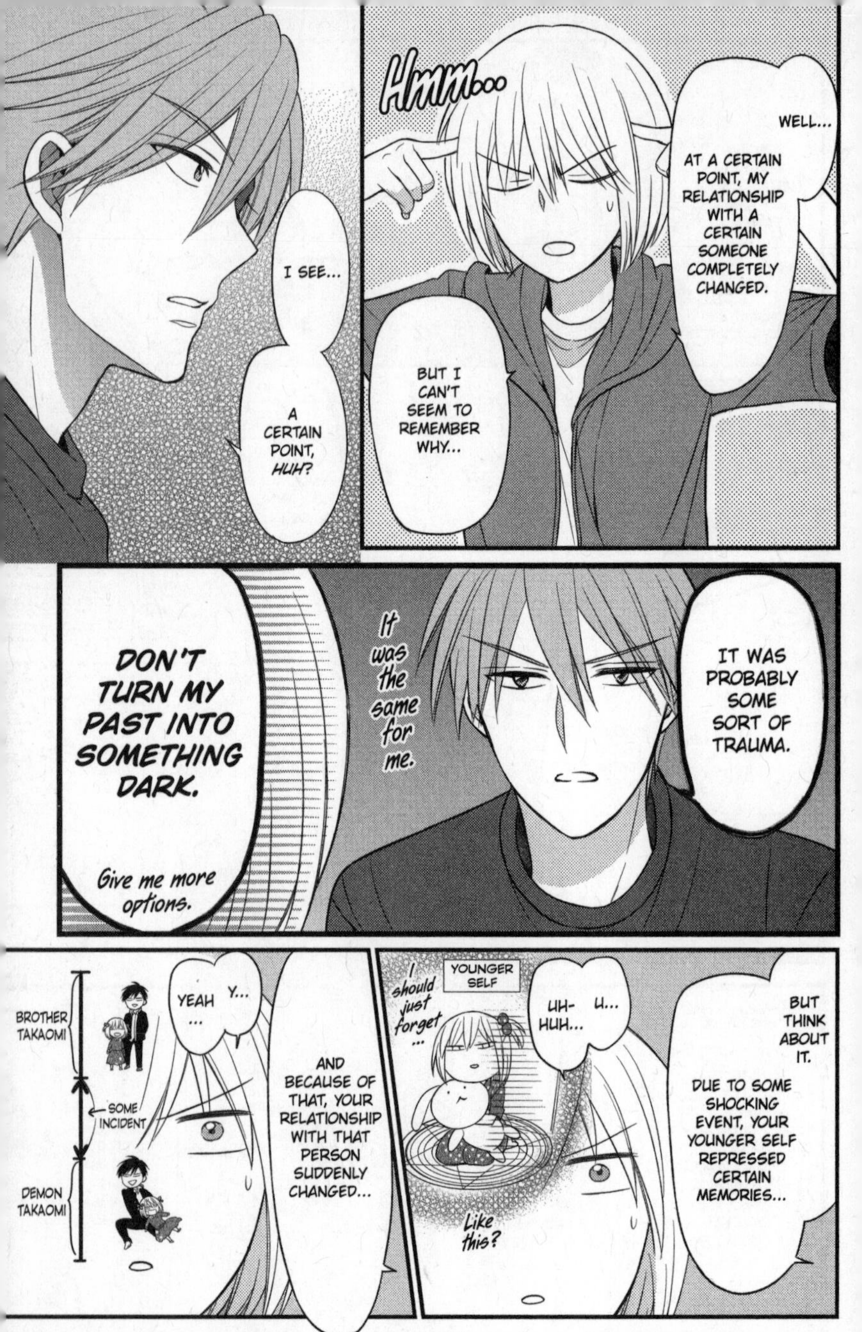
Hmm...
WELL...
AT A CERTAIN POINT, MY RELATIONSHIP WITH A CERTAIN SOMEONE COMPLETELY CHANGED.
BUT I CAN'T SEEM TO REMEMBER WHY...
I SEE...
A CERTAIN POINT, *HUH?*
IT WAS PROBABLY SOME SORT OF TRAUMA.
It was the same for me.
DON'T TURN MY PAST INTO SOMETHING DARK.
Give me more options.
BUT THINK ABOUT IT.
DUE TO SOME SHOCKING EVENT, YOUR YOUNGER SELF REPRESSED CERTAIN MEMORIES...
UH-HUH... U...
YOUNGER SELF
I should just forget...
Like this?
AND BECAUSE OF THAT, YOUR RELATIONSHIP WITH THAT PERSON SUDDENLY CHANGED...
YEAH... Y...
BROTHER TAKAOMI
SOME INCIDENT
DEMON TAKAOMI

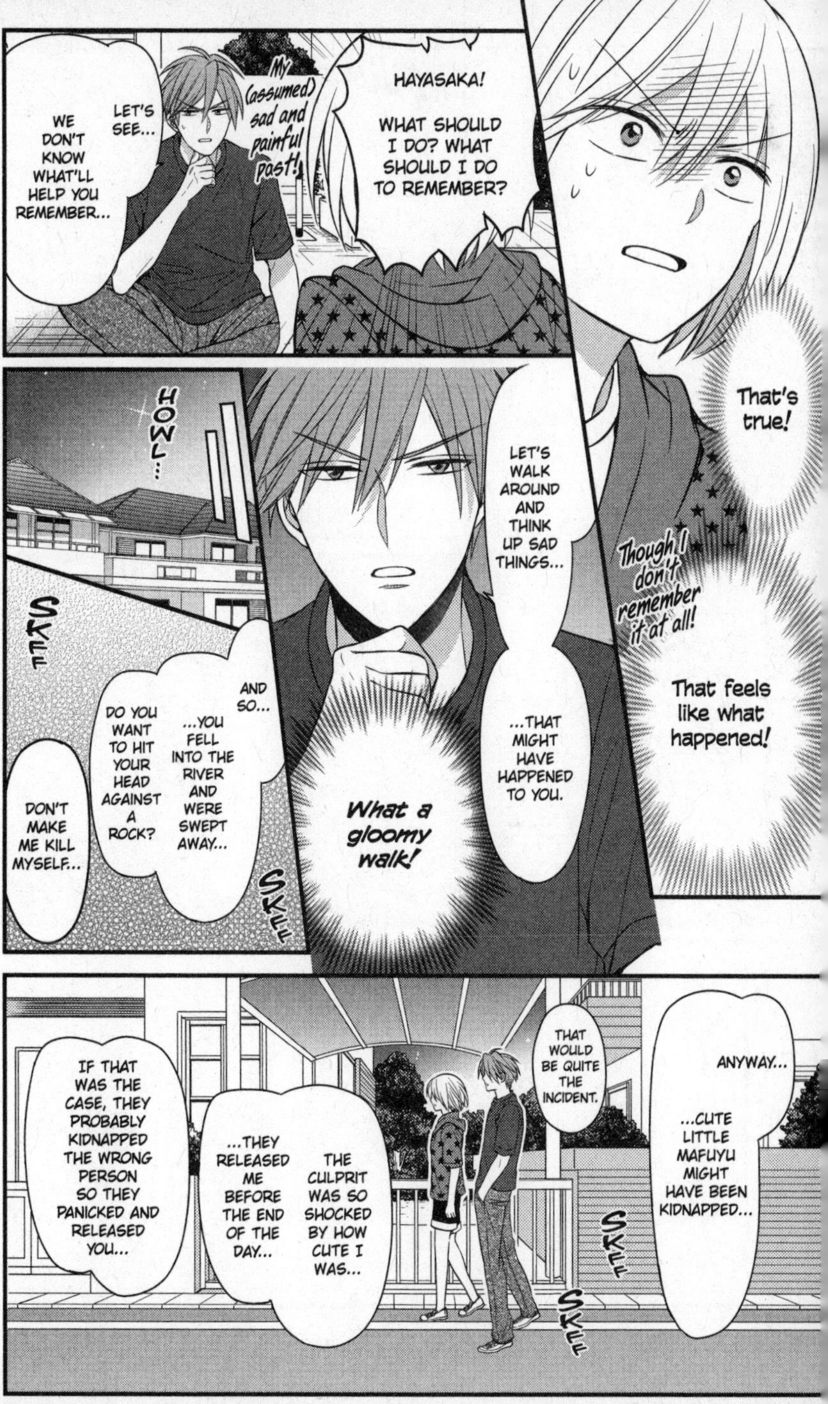
That's true!
Though I don't remember it at all!
That feels like what happened!
My (assumed) sad and painful past!
HAYASAKA!
WHAT SHOULD I DO? WHAT SHOULD I DO TO REMEMBER?
LET'S SEE...
WE DON'T KNOW WHAT'LL HELP YOU REMEMBER...
LET'S WALK AROUND AND THINK UP SAD THINGS...
...THAT MIGHT HAVE HAPPENED TO YOU.
What a gloomy walk!
HOWL...
AND SO...
...YOU FELL INTO THE RIVER AND WERE SWEPT AWAY...
DO YOU WANT TO HIT YOUR HEAD AGAINST A ROCK?
DON'T MAKE ME KILL MYSELF...
SKFF
SKFF
ANYWAY...
...CUTE LITTLE MAFUYU MIGHT HAVE BEEN KIDNAPPED...
THAT WOULD BE QUITE THE INCIDENT.
SKFF
SKFF
THE CULPRIT WAS SO SHOCKED BY HOW CUTE I WAS...
...THEY RELEASED ME BEFORE THE END OF THE DAY...
IF THAT WAS THE CASE, THEY PROBABLY KIDNAPPED THE WRONG PERSON SO THEY PANICKED AND RELEASED YOU...

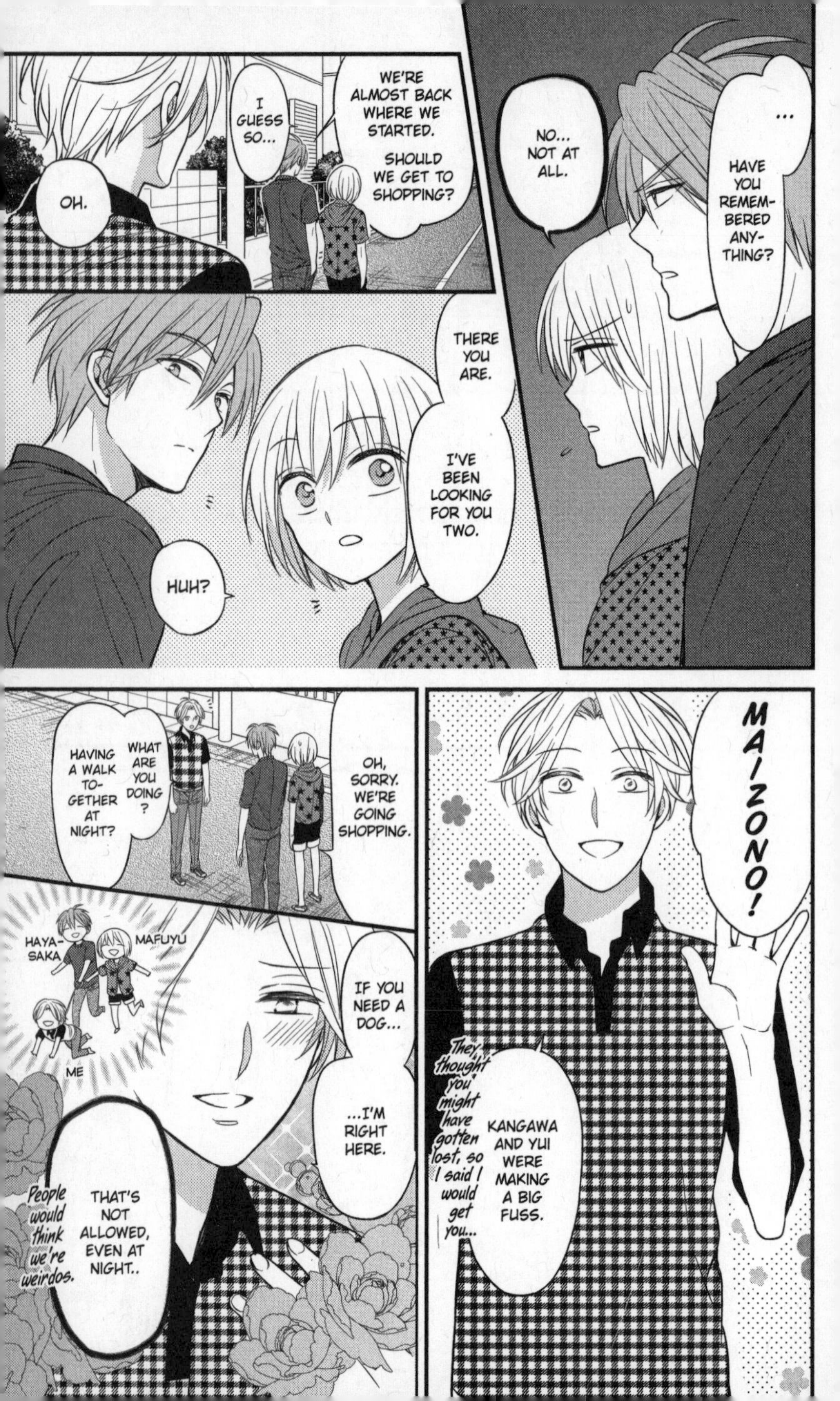
...
HAVE YOU REMEMBERED ANYTHING?
NO... NOT AT ALL.
WE'RE ALMOST BACK WHERE WE STARTED.
SHOULD WE GET TO SHOPPING?
I GUESS SO...
OH.
THERE YOU ARE.
I'VE BEEN LOOKING FOR YOU TWO.
HUH?
MAIZONO!
KANGAWA AND YUI WERE MAKING A BIG FUSS.
They thought you might have gotten lost, so I said I would get you...
OH, SORRY. WE'RE GOING SHOPPING.
WHAT ARE YOU DOING?
HAVING A WALK TOGETHER AT NIGHT?
IF YOU NEED A DOG...
...I'M RIGHT HERE.
HAYASAKA
MAFUYU
ME
THAT'S NOT ALLOWED, EVEN AT NIGHT..
People would think we're weirdos.

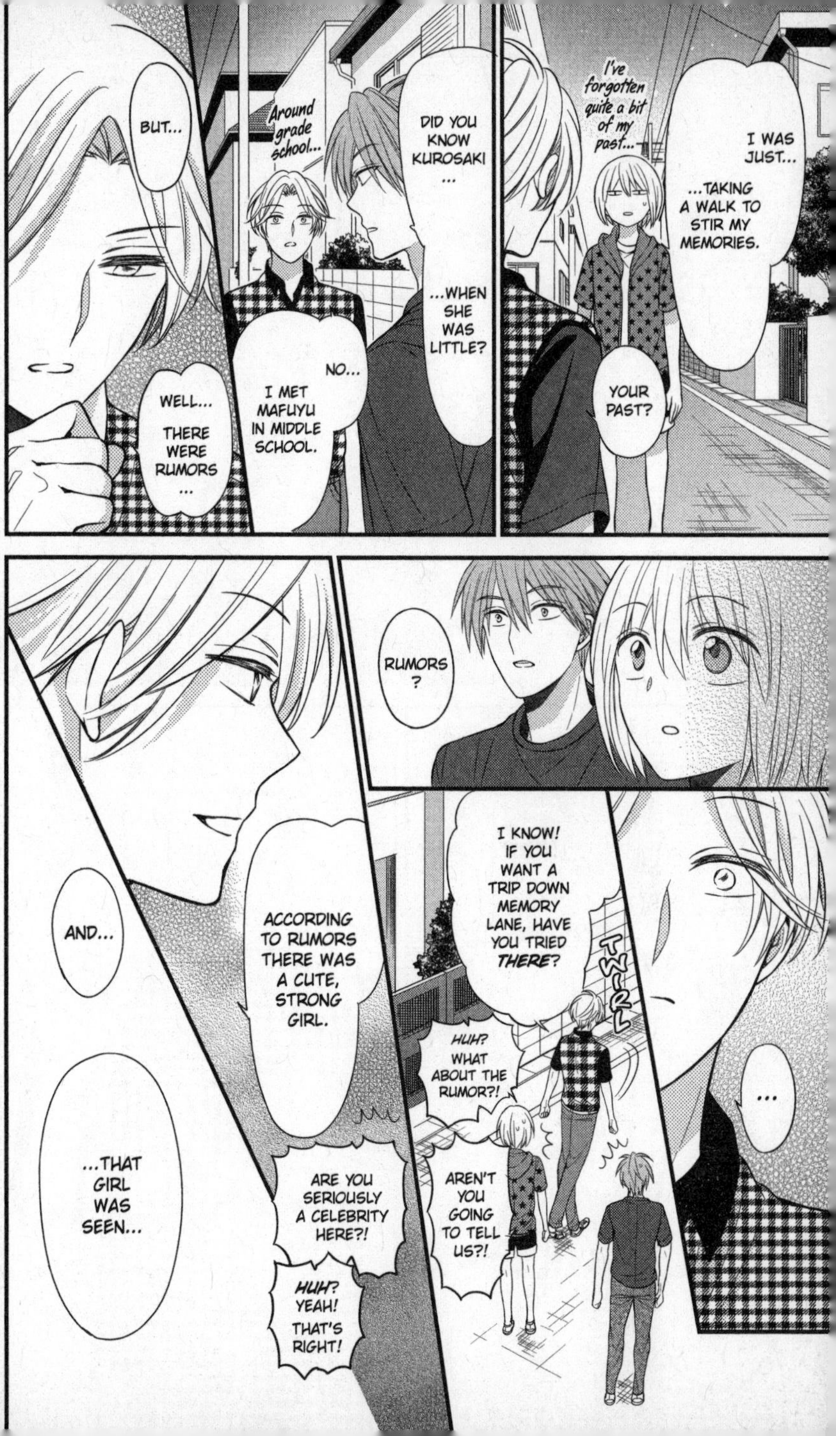
I WAS JUST...
...TAKING A WALK TO STIR MY MEMORIES.
I've forgotten quite a bit of my past...
YOUR PAST?
DID YOU KNOW KUROSAKI ...
...WHEN SHE WAS LITTLE?
Around grade school...
NO...
I MET MAFUYU IN MIDDLE SCHOOL.
BUT...
WELL...
THERE WERE RUMORS ...
RUMORS?
ACCORDING TO RUMORS THERE WAS A CUTE, STRONG GIRL.
AND...
...THAT GIRL WAS SEEN...
...
I KNOW! IF YOU WANT A TRIP DOWN MEMORY LANE, HAVE YOU TRIED *THERE*?
TWIRL
HUH? WHAT ABOUT THE RUMOR?!
AREN'T YOU GOING TO TELL US?!
ARE YOU SERIOUSLY A CELEBRITY HERE?!
HUH? YEAH!
THAT'S RIGHT!

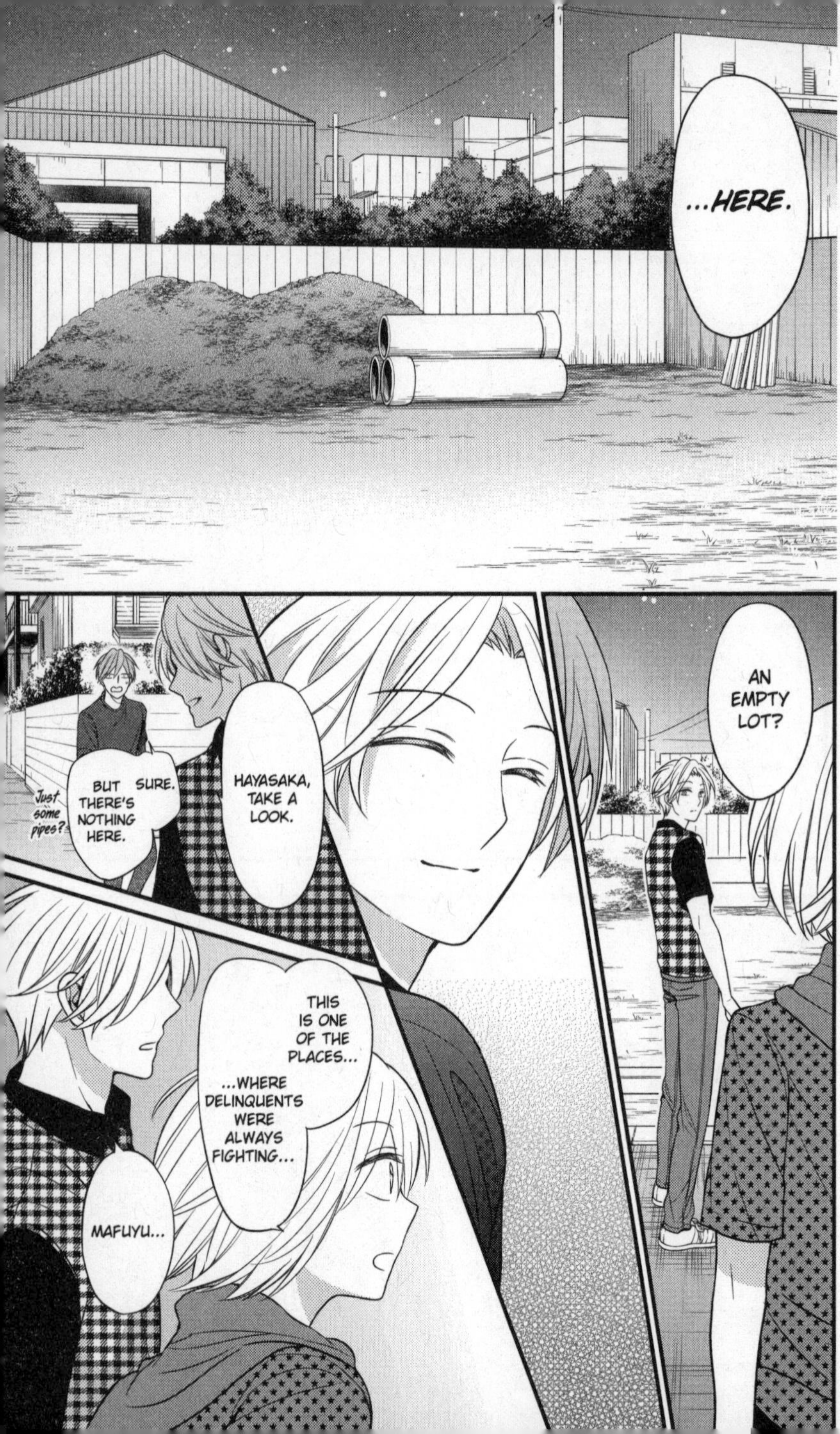
...HERE.
AN EMPTY LOT?
HAYASAKA, TAKE A LOOK.
SURE.
BUT THERE'S NOTHING HERE.
Just some pipes?
THIS IS ONE OF THE PLACES...
...WHERE DELINQUENTS WERE ALWAYS FIGHTING...
MAFUYU...

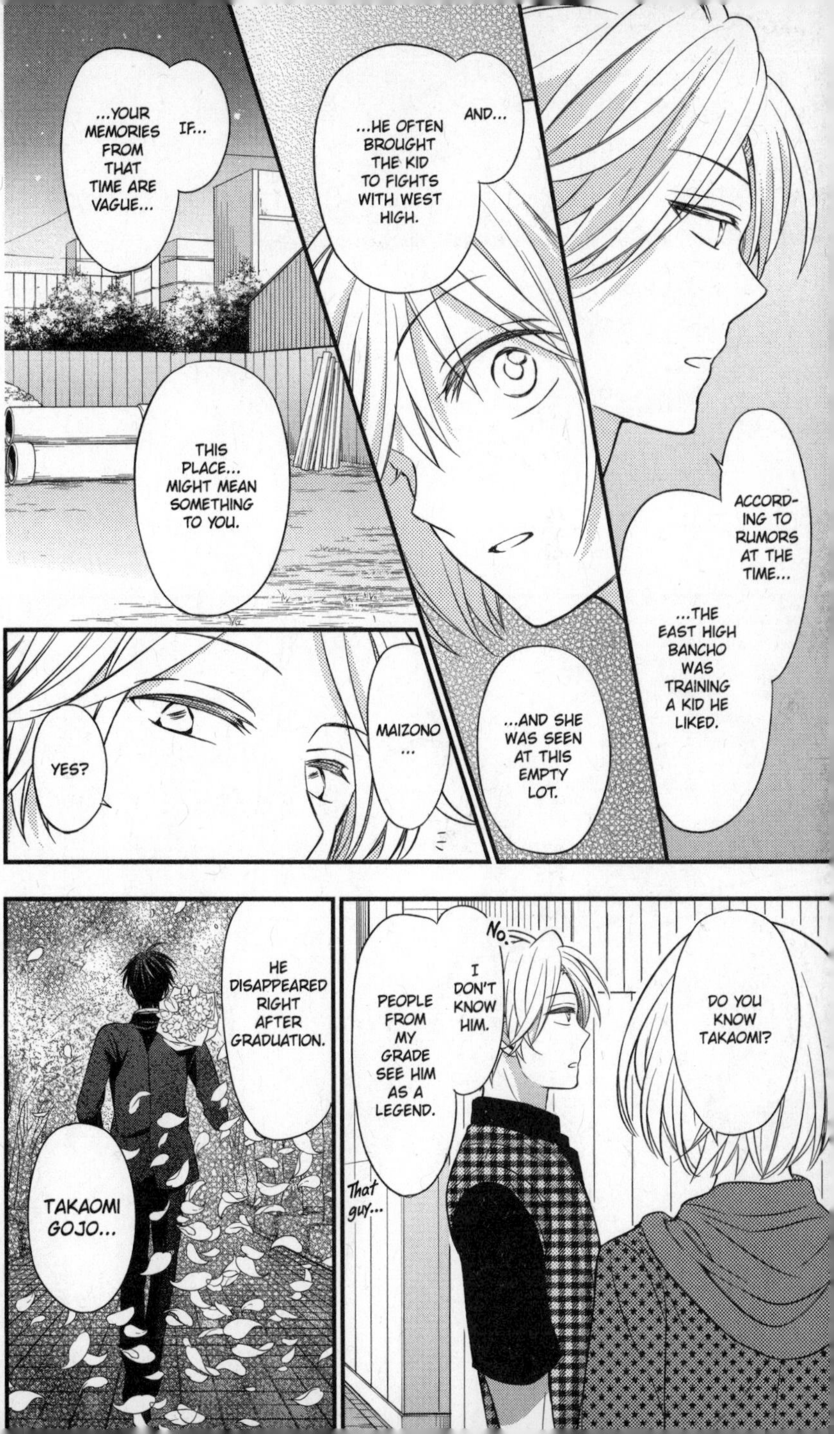
ACCORDING TO RUMORS AT THE TIME...
...THE EAST HIGH BANCHO WAS TRAINING A KID HE LIKED.
...AND SHE WAS SEEN AT THIS EMPTY LOT.
AND...
...HE OFTEN BROUGHT THE KID TO FIGHTS WITH WEST HIGH.
IF...
...YOUR MEMORIES FROM THAT TIME ARE VAGUE...
THIS PLACE... MIGHT MEAN SOMETHING TO YOU.
MAIZONO...
YES?
DO YOU KNOW TAKAOMI?
No.
I DON'T KNOW HIM.
PEOPLE FROM MY GRADE SEE HIM AS A LEGEND.
That guy...
HE DISAPPEARED RIGHT AFTER GRADUATION.
TAKAOMI GOJO...

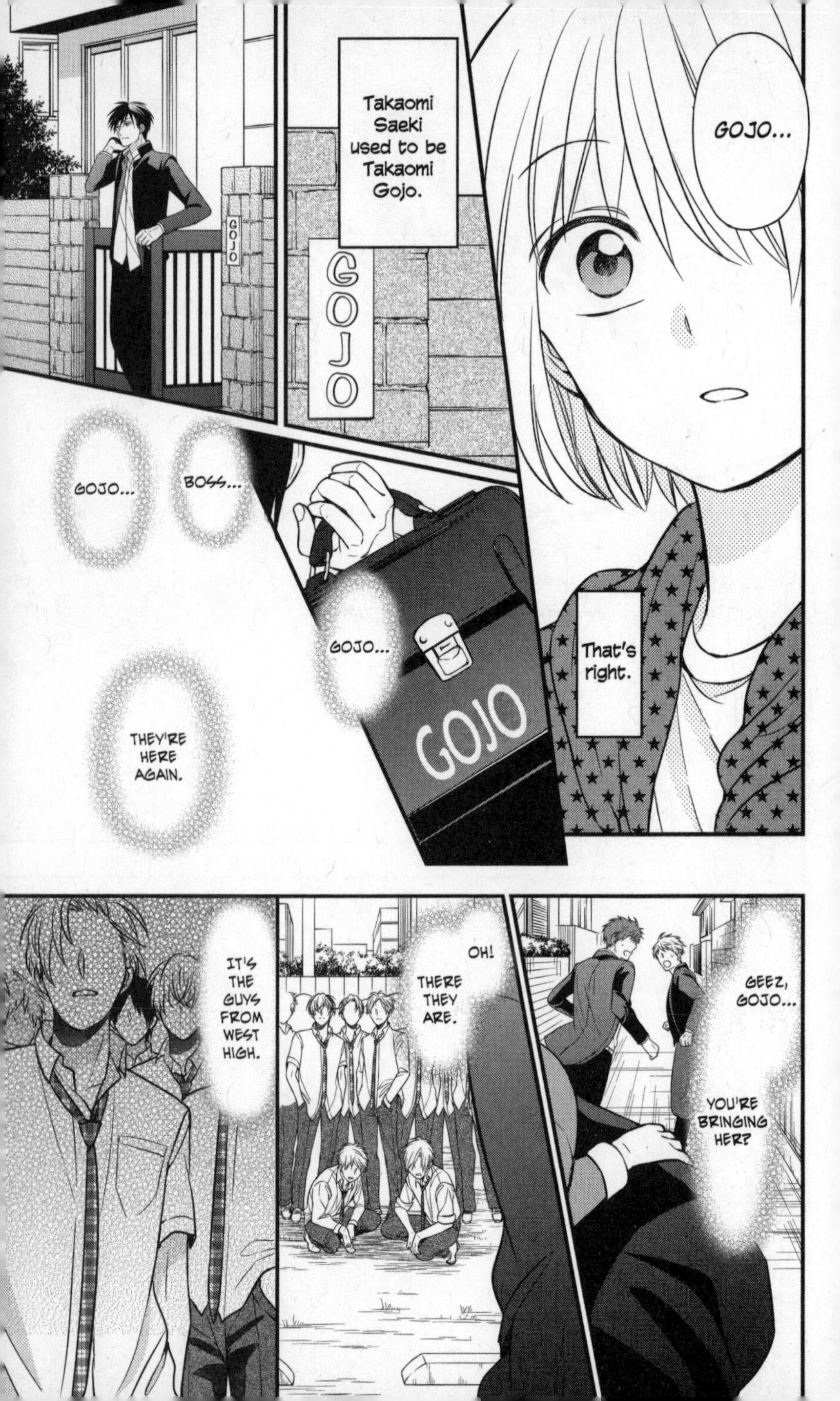
GOJO...
That's right.
Takaomi Saeki used to be Takaomi Gojo.
GOJO
GOJO
GOJO...
BOSS...
GOJO...
GOJO
THEY'RE HERE AGAIN.
GEEZ, GOJO...
YOU'RE BRINGING HER?
OH!
THERE THEY ARE.
IT'S THE GUYS FROM WEST HIGH.

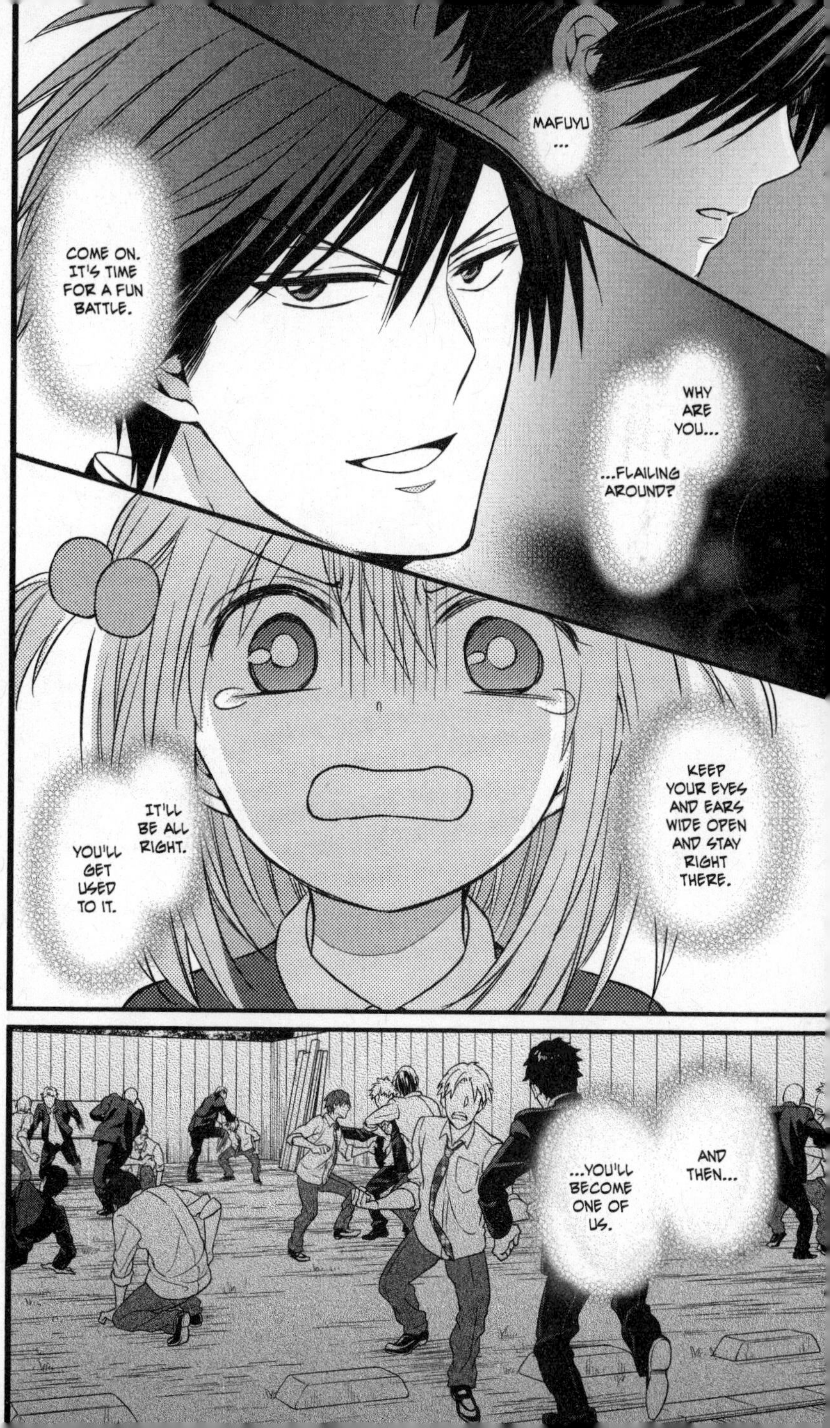
MAFUYU...
WHY ARE YOU...
...FLAILING AROUND?
COME ON. IT'S TIME FOR A FUN BATTLE.
KEEP YOUR EYES AND EARS WIDE OPEN AND STAY RIGHT THERE.
IT'LL BE ALL RIGHT.
YOU'LL GET USED TO IT.
AND THEN...
...YOU'LL BECOME ONE OF US.

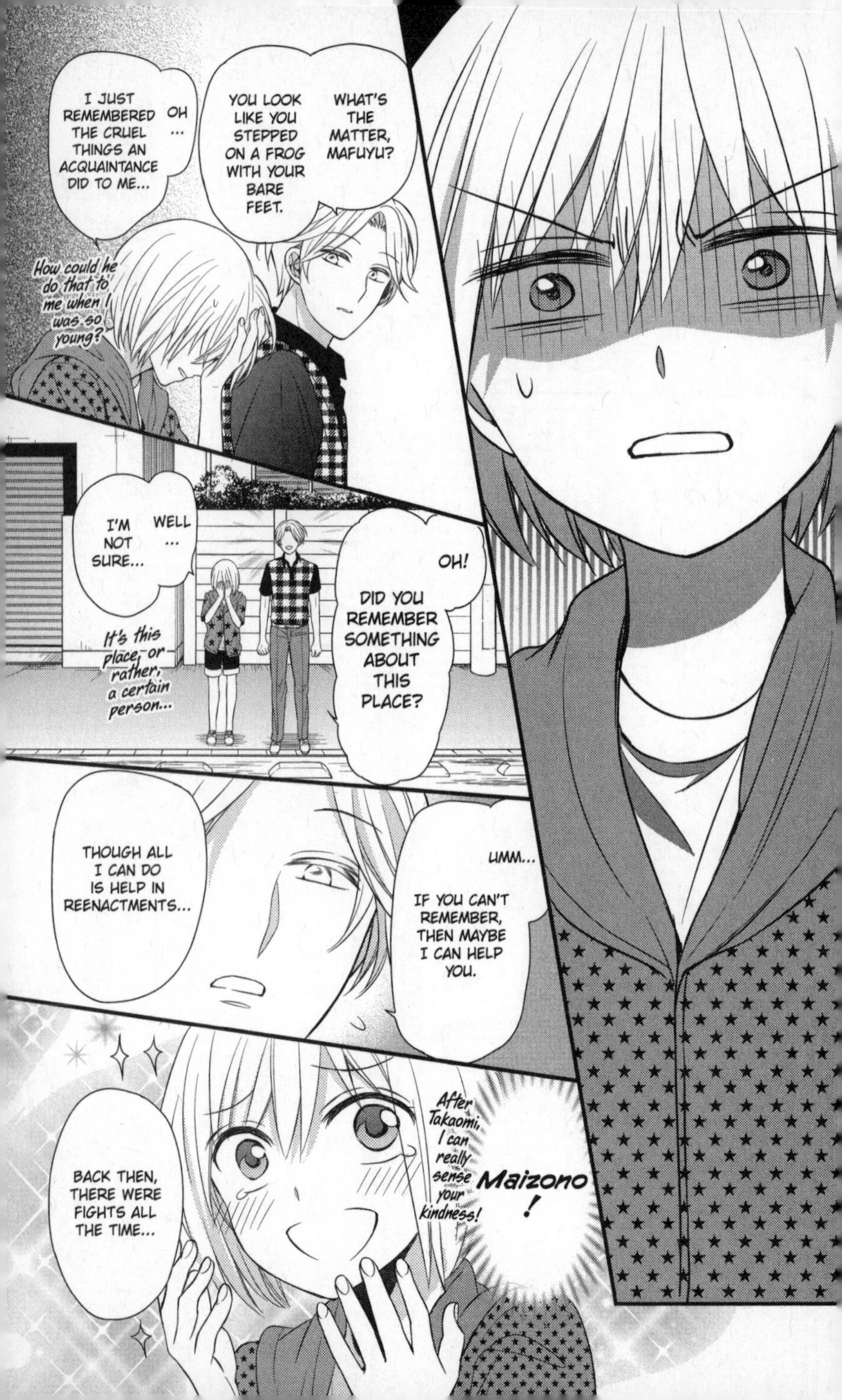
WHAT'S THE MATTER, MAFUYU?
YOU LOOK LIKE YOU STEPPED ON A FROG WITH YOUR BARE FEET.
OH ...
I JUST REMEMBERED THE CRUEL THINGS AN ACQUAINTANCE DID TO ME...
How could he do that to me when I was so young?
OH!
DID YOU REMEMBER SOMETHING ABOUT THIS PLACE?
WELL ...
I'M NOT SURE...
It's this place, or rather, a certain person...
UMM...
IF YOU CAN'T REMEMBER, THEN MAYBE I CAN HELP YOU.
THOUGH ALL I CAN DO IS HELP IN REENACTMENTS...
Maizono!
After Takaomi, I can really sense your kindness!
BACK THEN, THERE WERE FIGHTS ALL THE TIME...

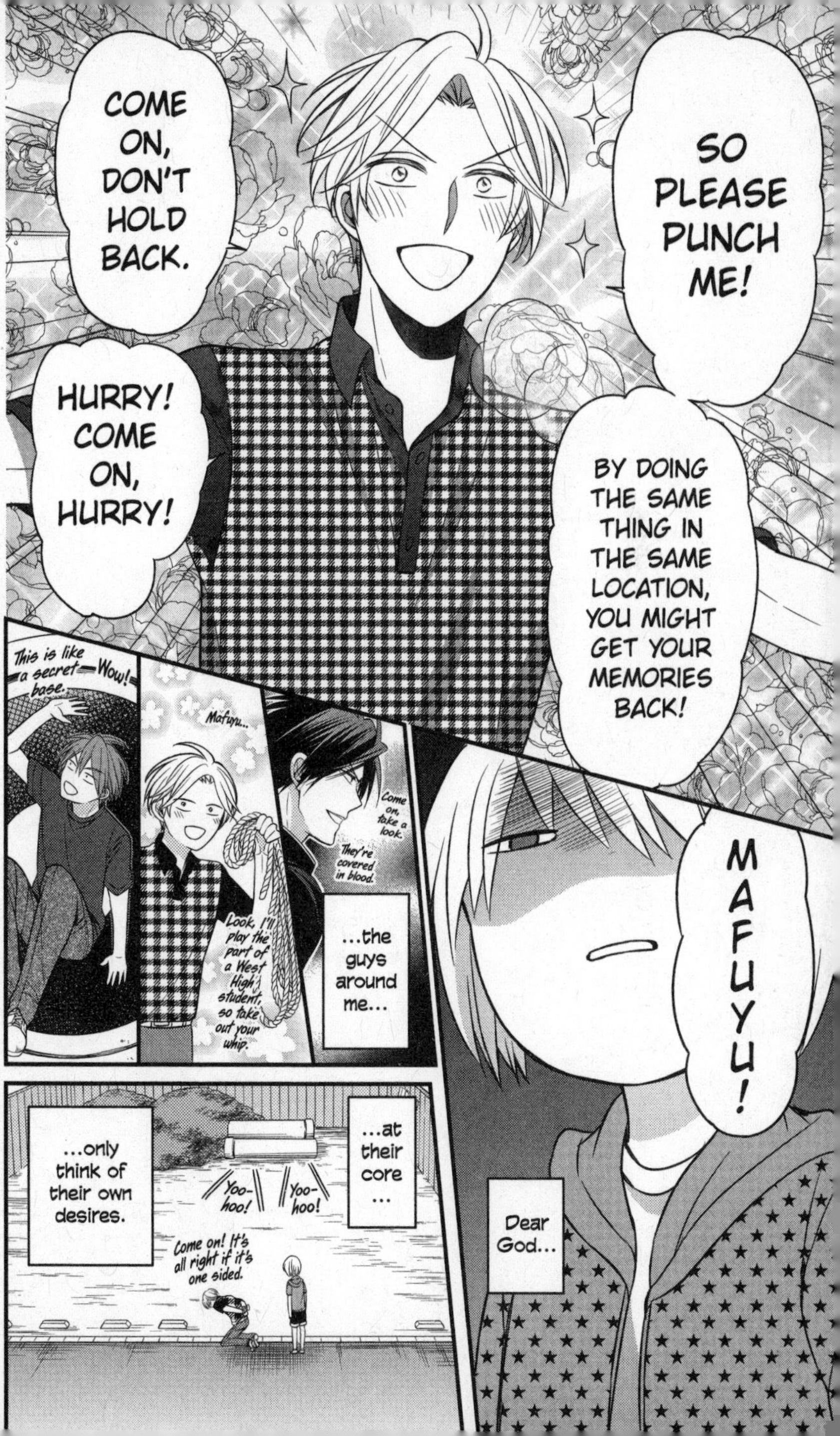

SO PLEASE PUNCH ME!
COME ON, DON'T HOLD BACK.
BY DOING THE SAME THING IN THE SAME LOCATION, YOU MIGHT GET YOUR MEMORIES BACK!
HURRY! COME ON, HURRY!
MAFUYU!
Dear God...
Come on, take a look.
They're covered in blood.
...the guys around me...
Mafuyu...
Look, I'll play the part of a West High student, so take out your whip.
This is like a secret base.
Wow!
...at their core...
Yoo-hoo!
Yoo-hoo!
...only think of their own desires.
Come on! It's all right if it's one sided.

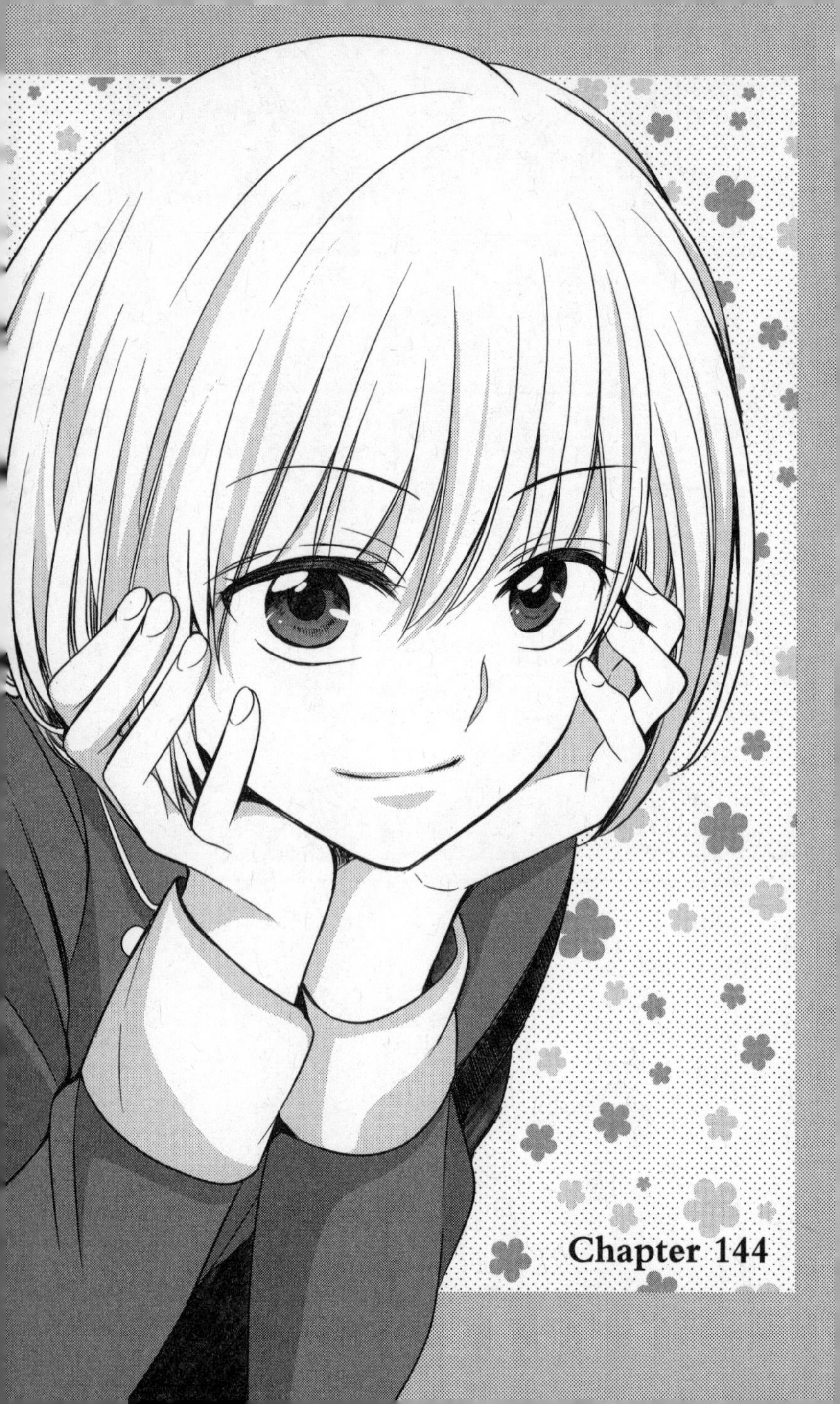

Chapter 144

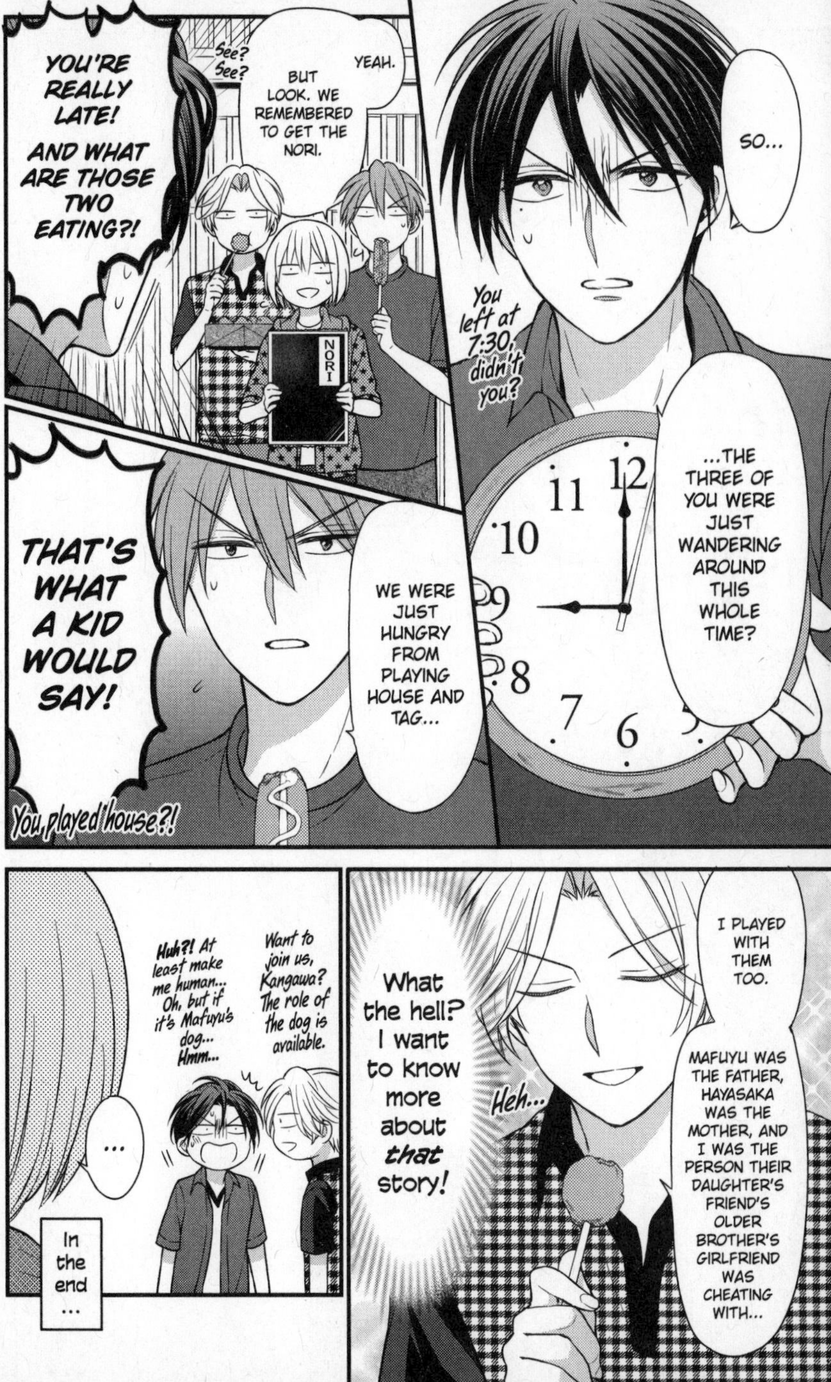
SO...
You left at 7:30, didn't you?
...THE THREE OF YOU WERE JUST WANDERING AROUND THIS WHOLE TIME?
YEAH.
See? See?
BUT LOOK. WE REMEMBERED TO GET THE NORI.
YOU'RE REALLY LATE!
AND WHAT ARE THOSE TWO EATING?!
NORI
WE WERE JUST HUNGRY FROM PLAYING HOUSE AND TAG...
THAT'S WHAT A KID WOULD SAY!
You played house?!
I PLAYED WITH THEM TOO.
MAFUYU WAS THE FATHER, HAYASAKA WAS THE MOTHER, AND I WAS THE PERSON THEIR DAUGHTER'S FRIEND'S OLDER BROTHER'S GIRLFRIEND WAS CHEATING WITH...
Heh...
What the hell? I want to know more about *that* story!
Want to join us, Kangawa? The role of the dog is available.
Huh?! At least make me human... Oh, but if it's Mafuyu's dog... Hmm...
...
In the end ...

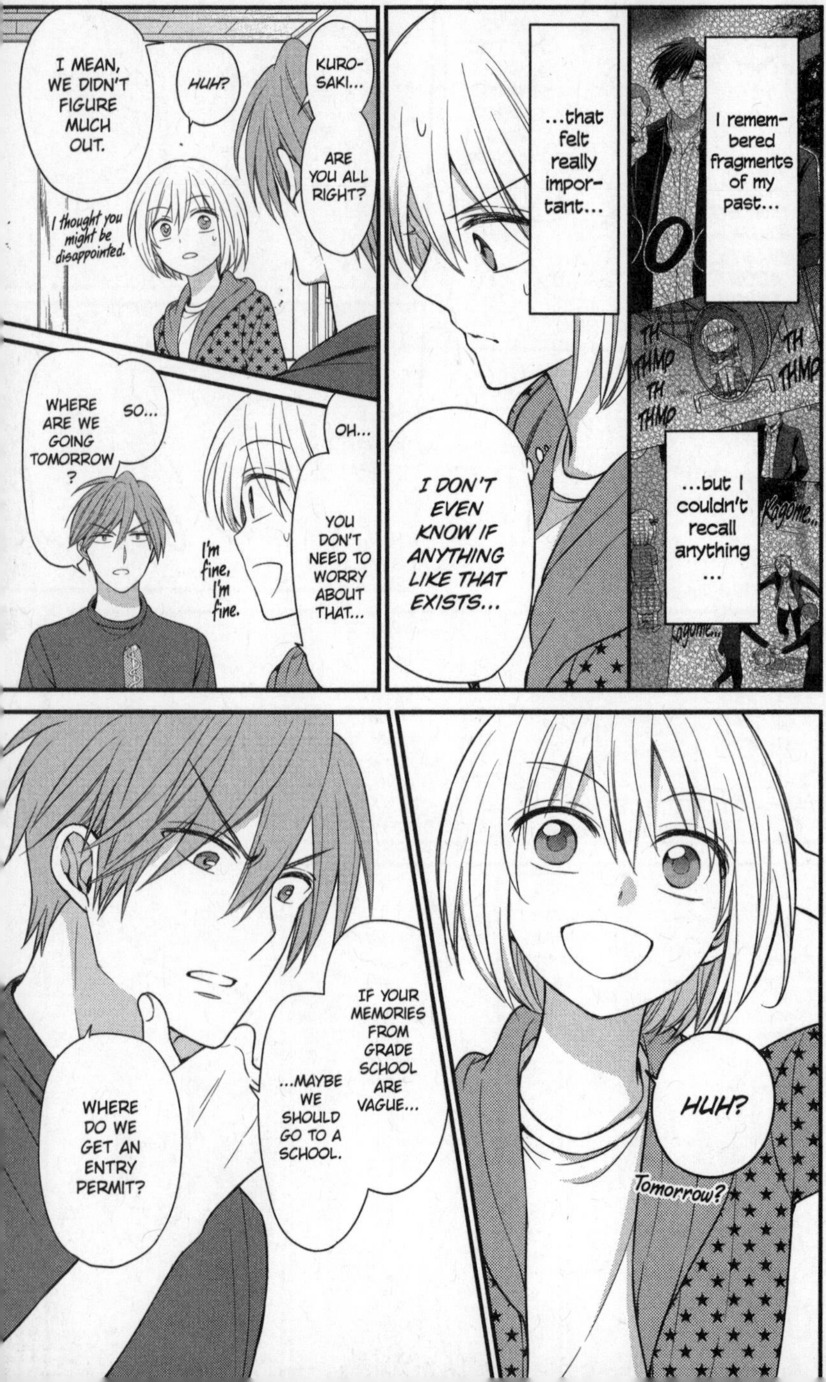
I remembered fragments of my past...
...that felt really important...
TH THMP TH THMP
TH THMP
Kagome...
...but I couldn't recall anything...
Kagome...
I DON'T EVEN KNOW IF ANYTHING LIKE THAT EXISTS...
KUROSAKI...
ARE YOU ALL RIGHT?
HUH?
I MEAN, WE DIDN'T FIGURE MUCH OUT.
I thought you might be disappointed.
OH...
YOU DON'T NEED TO WORRY ABOUT THAT...
I'm fine, I'm fine.
SO...
WHERE ARE WE GOING TOMORROW?
HUH?
Tomorrow?
IF YOUR MEMORIES FROM GRADE SCHOOL ARE VAGUE...
...MAYBE WE SHOULD GO TO A SCHOOL.
WHERE DO WE GET AN ENTRY PERMIT?

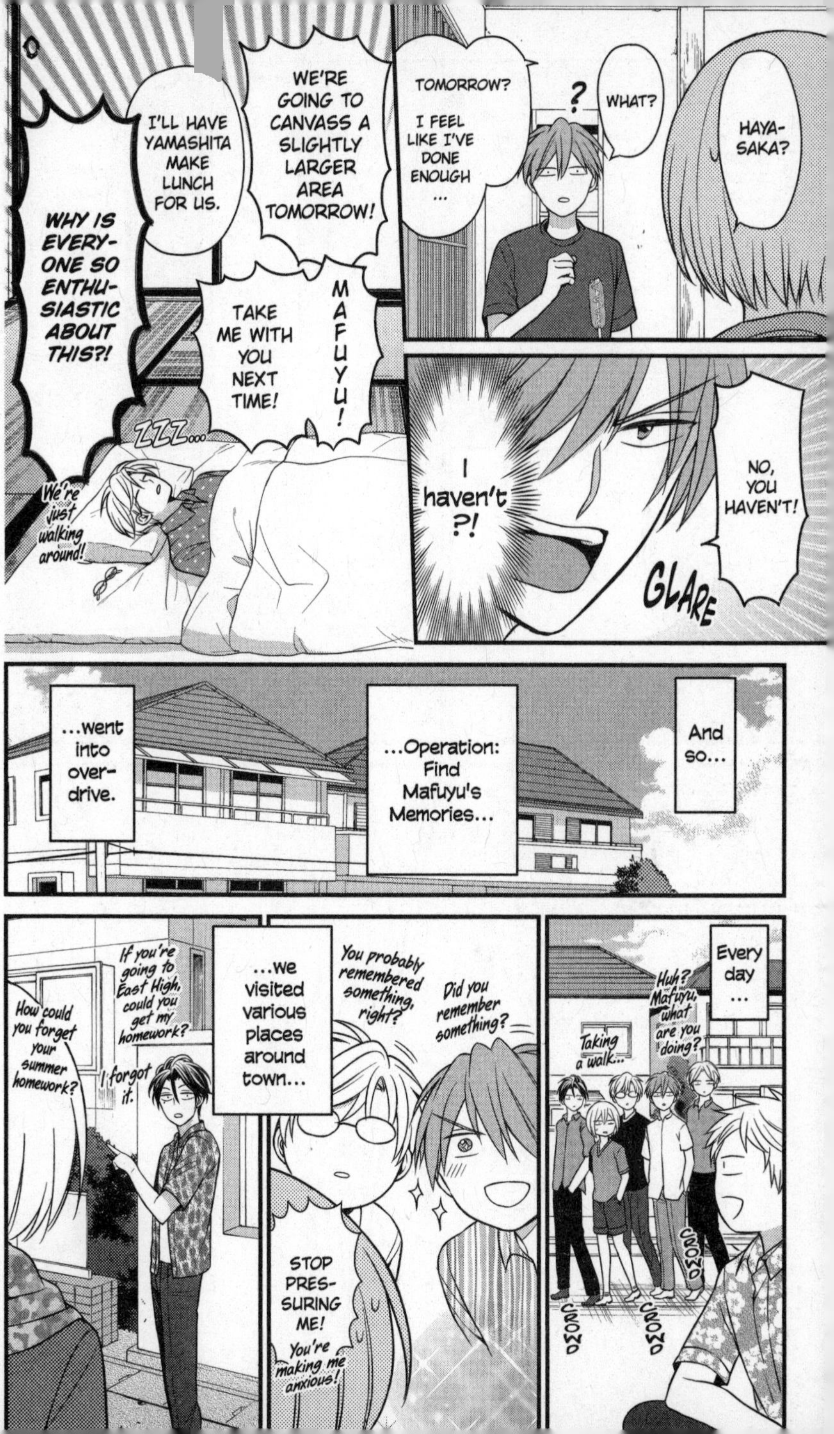
HAYA-SAKA?
WHAT?
?
TOMORROW?
I FEEL LIKE I'VE DONE ENOUGH...
NO, YOU HAVEN'T!
GLARE
I haven't?!
WE'RE GOING TO CANVASS A SLIGHTLY LARGER AREA TOMORROW!
I'LL HAVE YAMASHITA MAKE LUNCH FOR US.
MAFUYU!
TAKE ME WITH YOU NEXT TIME!
WHY IS EVERYONE SO ENTHUSIASTIC ABOUT THIS?!
ZZZ...
We're just walking around!
And so...
...Operation: Find Mafuyu's Memories...
...went into overdrive.
Every day...
Huh? Mafuyu, what are you doing?
Taking a walk...
CROWD
CROWD
CROWD
Did you remember something?
You probably remembered something, right?
...we visited various places around town...
STOP PRESSURING ME!
You're making me anxious!
If you're going to East High, could you get my homework?
I forgot it.
How could you forget your summer homework?

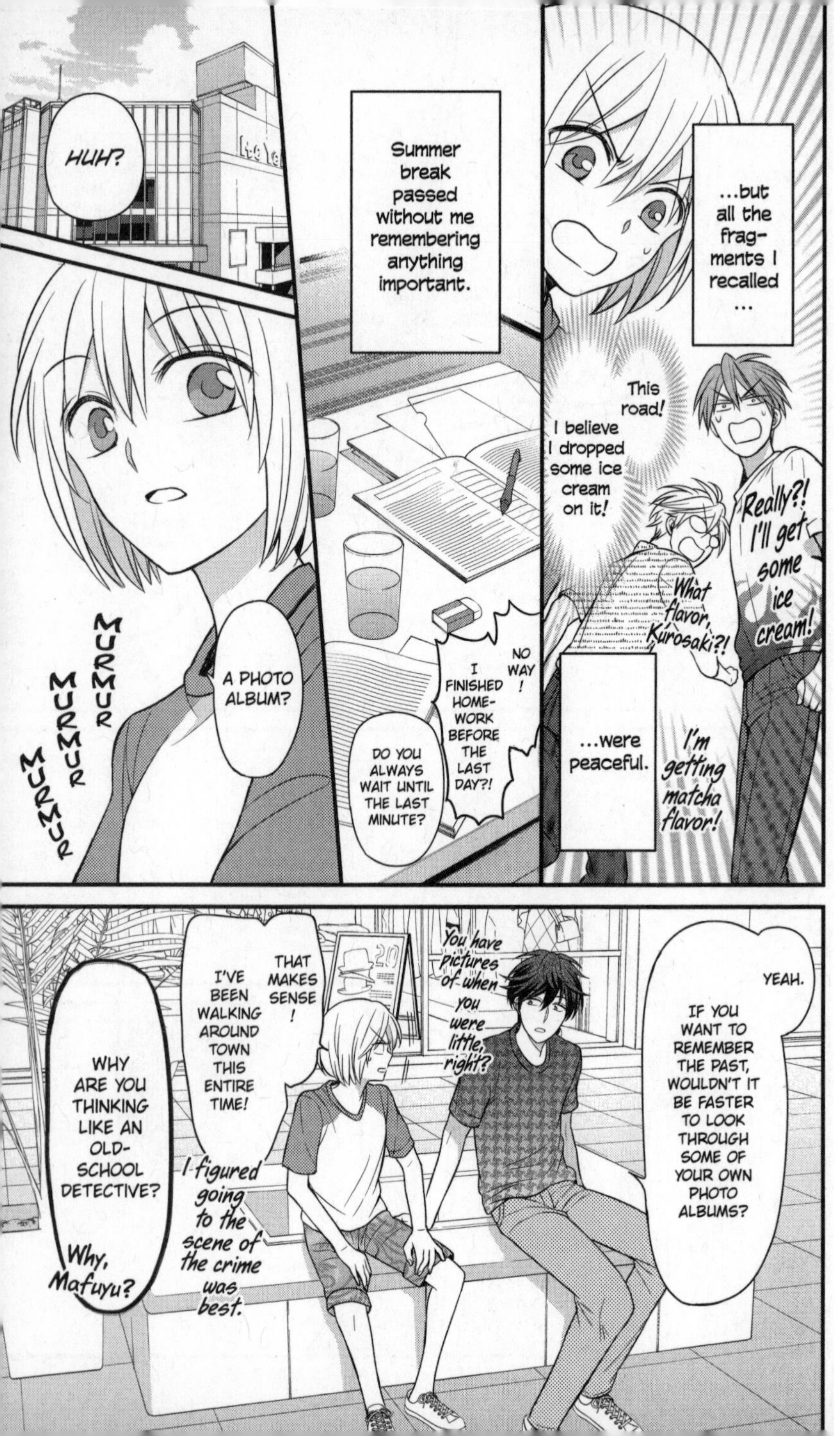
...but all the frag-ments I recalled ...
This road! I believe I dropped some ice cream on it!
Really?! I'll get some ice cream!
What flavor, Kurosaki?!
...were peaceful.
I'm getting matcha flavor!
Summer break passed without me remembering anything important.
NO WAY! I FINISHED HOME-WORK BEFORE THE LAST DAY?!
DO YOU ALWAYS WAIT UNTIL THE LAST MINUTE?
HUH?
A PHOTO ALBUM?
MURMUR MURMUR MURMUR
YEAH.
IF YOU WANT TO REMEMBER THE PAST, WOULDN'T IT BE FASTER TO LOOK THROUGH SOME OF YOUR OWN PHOTO ALBUMS?
You have pictures of when you were little, right?
THAT MAKES SENSE!
I'VE BEEN WALKING AROUND TOWN THIS ENTIRE TIME!
I figured going to the scene of the crime was best.
WHY ARE YOU THINKING LIKE AN OLD-SCHOOL DETECTIVE?
Why, Mafuyu?

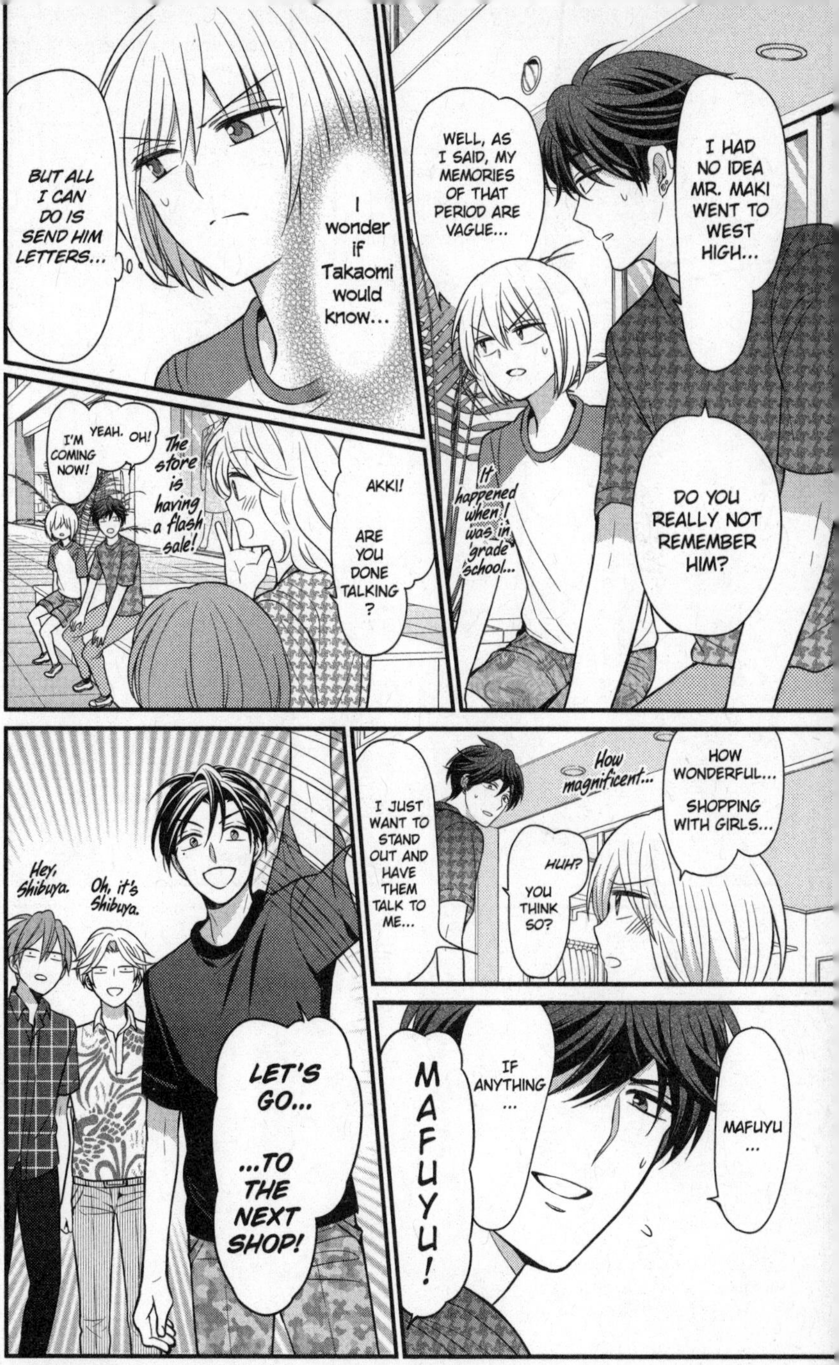
I HAD NO IDEA MR. MAKI WENT TO WEST HIGH...
WELL, AS I SAID, MY MEMORIES OF THAT PERIOD ARE VAGUE...
DO YOU REALLY NOT REMEMBER HIM?
It happened when I was in grade school...
I wonder if Takaomi would know...
BUT ALL I CAN DO IS SEND HIM LETTERS...
AKKI!
ARE YOU DONE TALKING?
The store is having a flash sale!
YEAH. OH!
I'M COMING NOW!
HOW WONDERFUL...
SHOPPING WITH GIRLS...
How magnificent...
HUH?
YOU THINK SO?
I JUST WANT TO STAND OUT AND HAVE THEM TALK TO ME...
MAFUYU...
IF ANYTHING...
MAFUYU!
LET'S GO...
...TO THE NEXT SHOP!
Oh, it's Shibuya.
Hey, Shibuya.

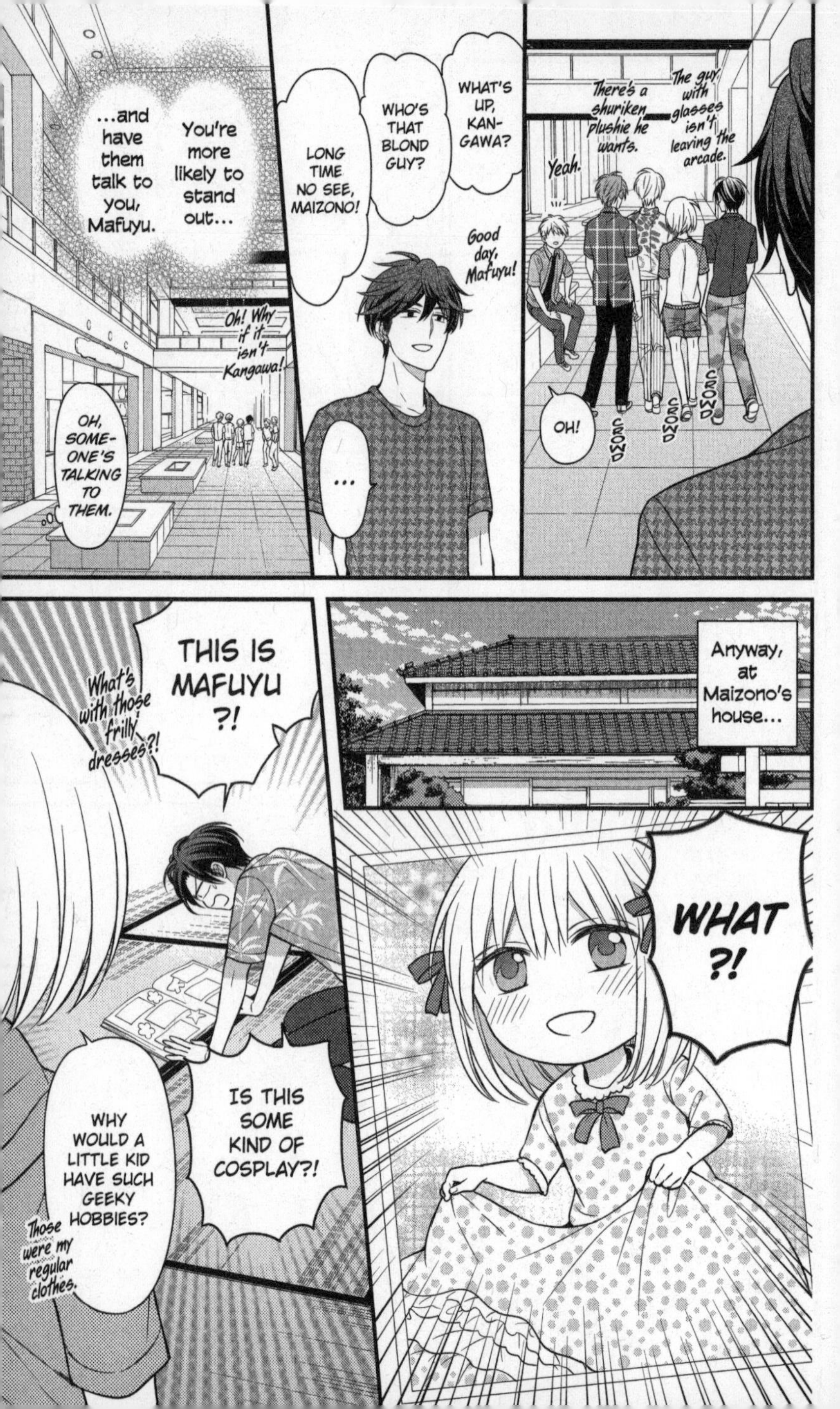
The guy with glasses isn't leaving the arcade.
There's a shuriken plushie he wants.
Yeah.
OH!
CROWD
CROWD
CROWD
WHAT'S UP, KAN-GAWA?
WHO'S THAT BLOND GUY?
LONG TIME NO SEE, MAIZONO!
Good day, Mafuyu!
...
You're more likely to stand out...
...and have them talk to you, Mafuyu.
Oh! Why if it isn't Kangawa!
OH, SOMEONE'S TALKING TO THEM.
Anyway, at Maizono's house...
WHAT ?!
THIS IS MAFUYU ?!
What's with those frilly dresses?!
IS THIS SOME KIND OF COSPLAY?!
WHY WOULD A LITTLE KID HAVE SUCH GEEKY HOBBIES?
Those were my regular clothes.

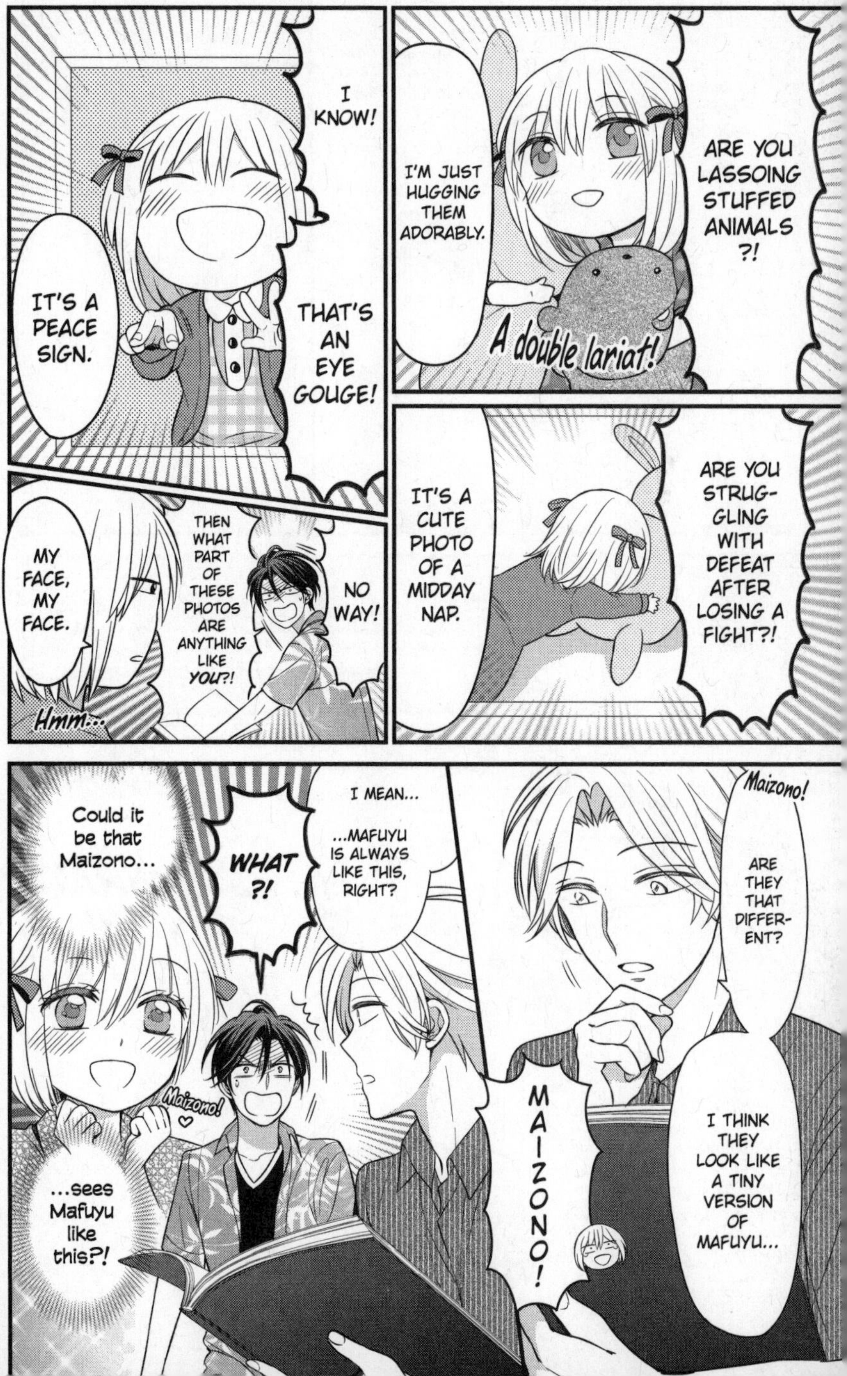

ARE YOU LASSOING STUFFED ANIMALS?!
I'M JUST HUGGING THEM ADORABLY.
A double lariat!
I KNOW!
THAT'S AN EYE GOUGE!
IT'S A PEACE SIGN.
ARE YOU STRUGGLING WITH DEFEAT AFTER LOSING A FIGHT?!
IT'S A CUTE PHOTO OF A MIDDAY NAP.
NO WAY!
THEN WHAT PART OF THESE PHOTOS ARE ANYTHING LIKE YOU?!
MY FACE, MY FACE.
Hmm...
Maizono!
ARE THEY THAT DIFFERENT?
I THINK THEY LOOK LIKE A TINY VERSION OF MAFUYU...
MAIZONO!
I MEAN...
...MAFUYU IS ALWAYS LIKE THIS, RIGHT?
WHAT?!
Could it be that Maizono...
Maizono! ♡
...sees Mafuyu like this?!

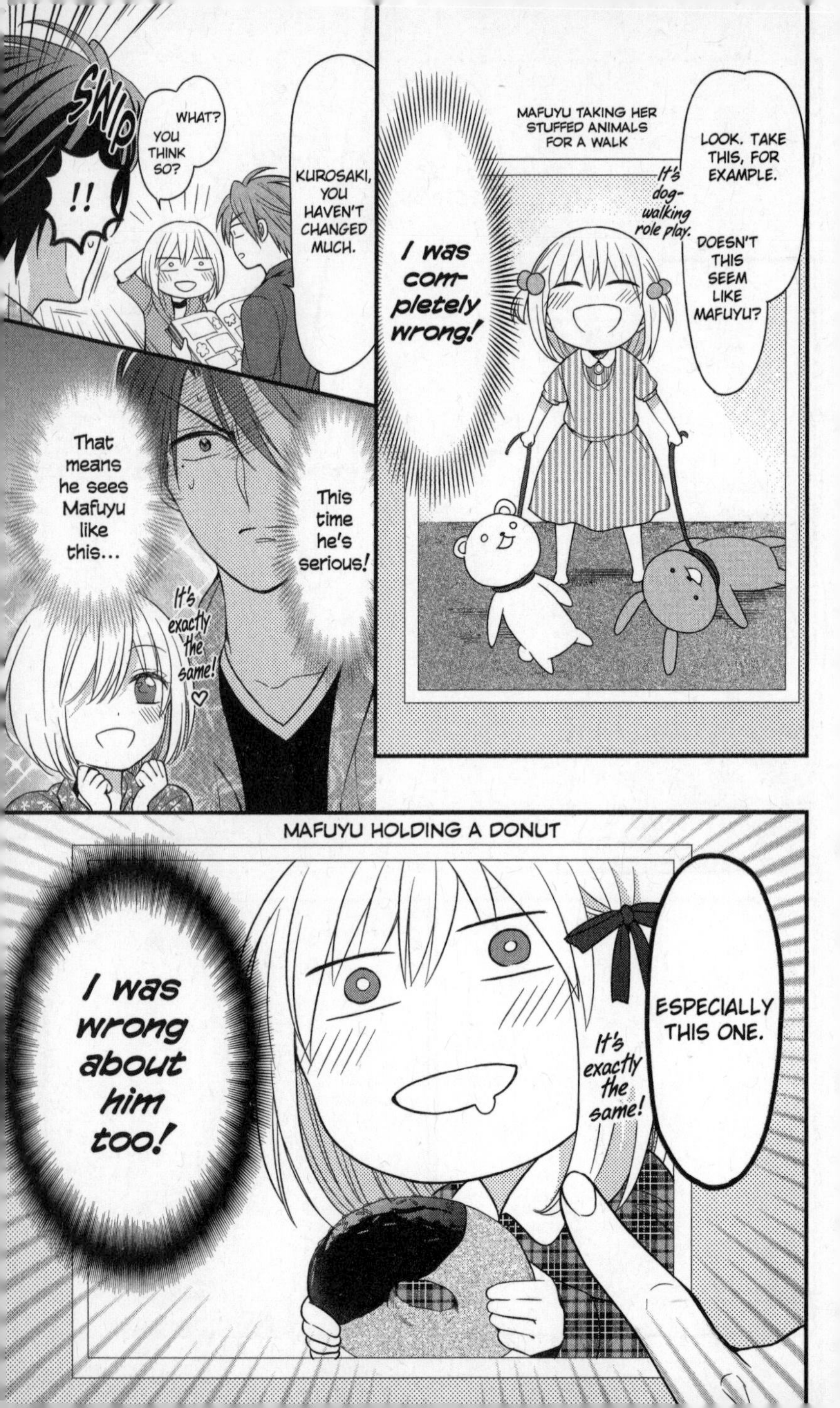
MAFUYU TAKING HER STUFFED ANIMALS FOR A WALK
LOOK. TAKE THIS, FOR EXAMPLE.
It's dog-walking role play.
DOESN'T THIS SEEM LIKE MAFUYU?
I was completely wrong!
KUROSAKI, YOU HAVEN'T CHANGED MUCH.
WHAT? YOU THINK SO?
SWIP
!!
This time he's serious!
That means he sees Mafuyu like this...
It's exactly the same! ♡
MAFUYU HOLDING A DONUT
ESPECIALLY THIS ONE.
It's exactly the same!
I was wrong about him too!

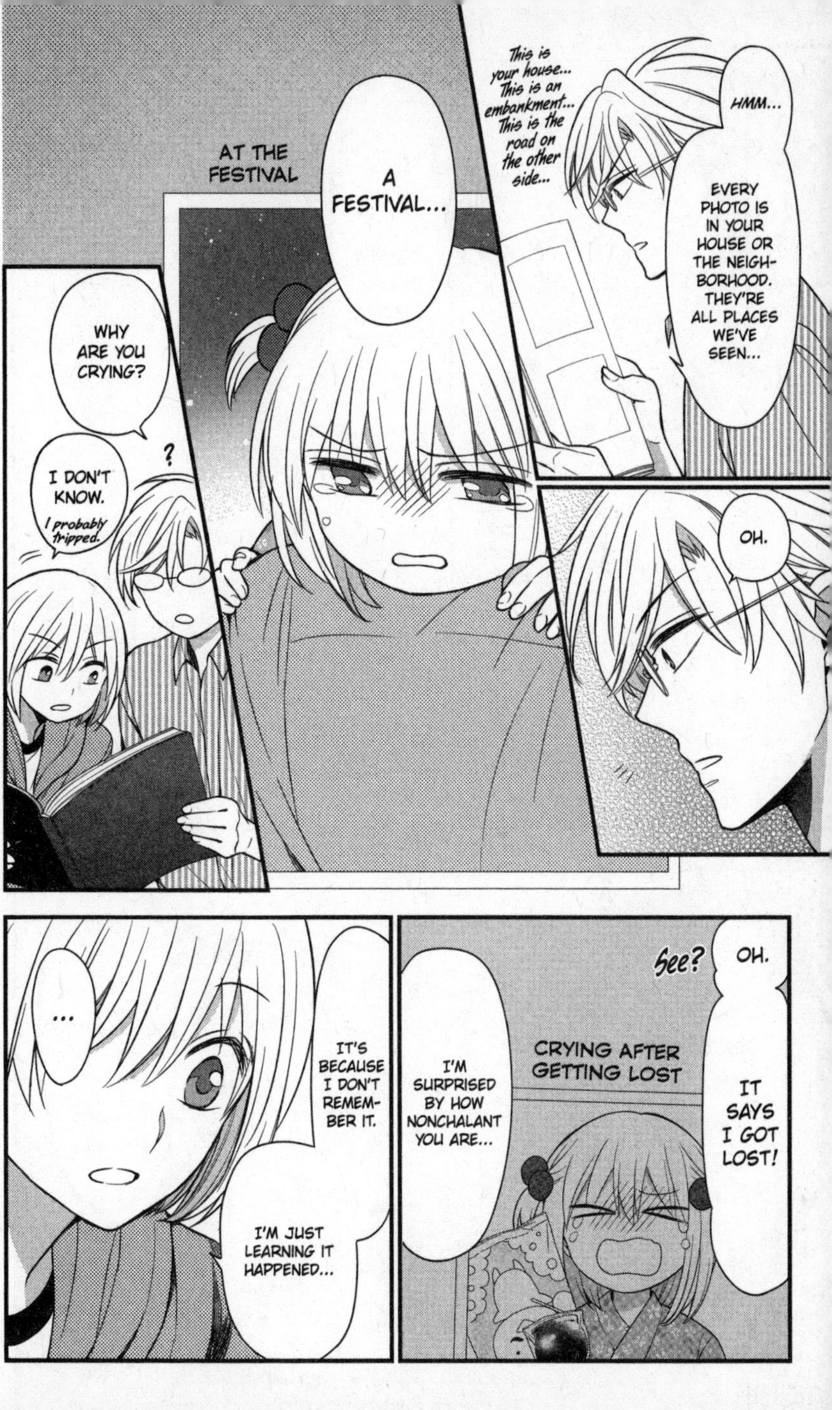
HMM...
EVERY PHOTO IS IN YOUR HOUSE OR THE NEIGH-BORHOOD. THEY'RE ALL PLACES WE'VE SEEN...
This is your house... This is an embankment... This is the road on the other side...
A FESTIVAL...
AT THE FESTIVAL
OH.
WHY ARE YOU CRYING?
?
I DON'T KNOW.
I probably tripped.
OH.
See?
IT SAYS I GOT LOST!
CRYING AFTER GETTING LOST
I'M SURPRISED BY HOW NONCHALANT YOU ARE...
IT'S BECAUSE I DON'T REMEM-BER IT.
...
I'M JUST LEARNING IT HAPPENED...

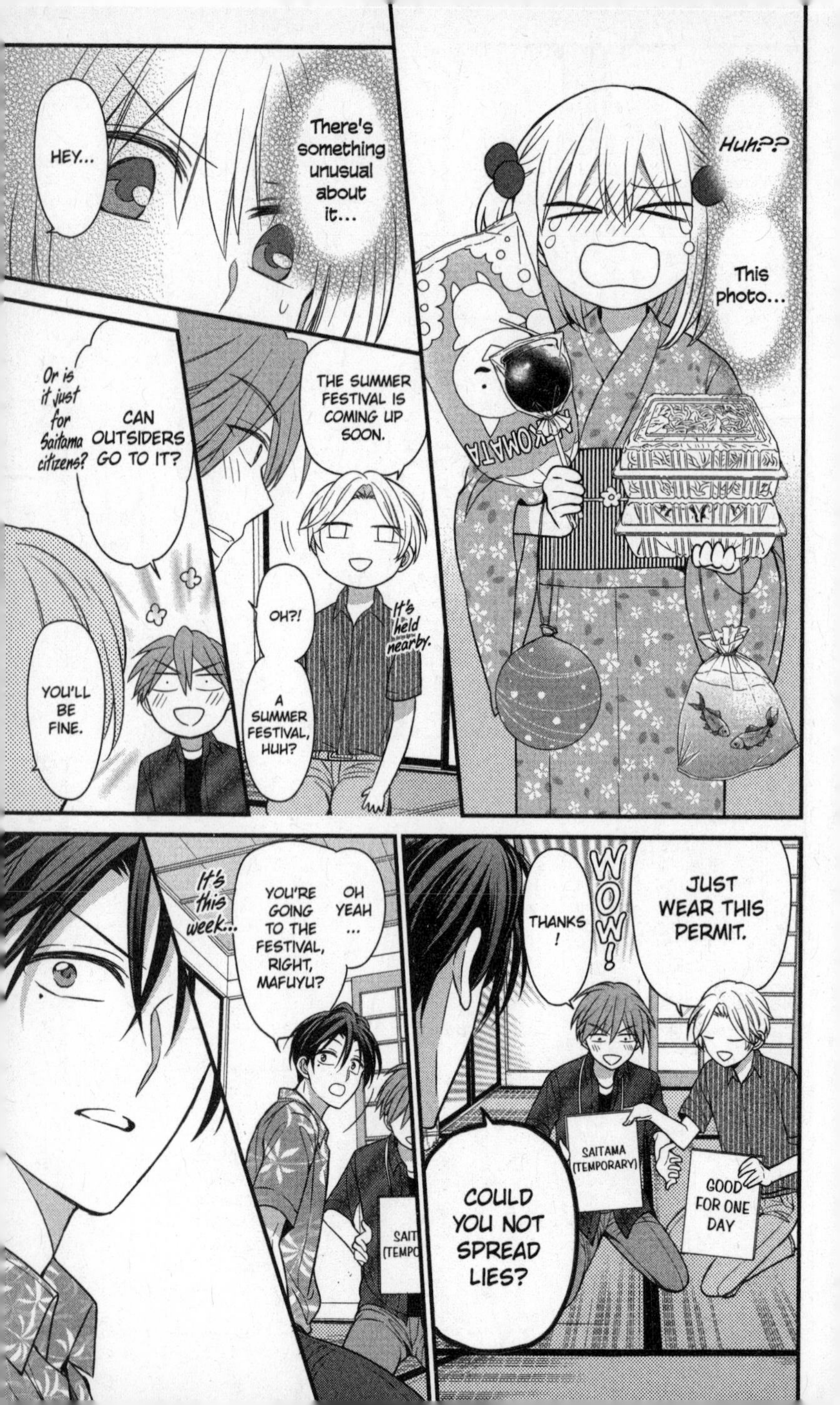
Huh??
This photo...
There's something unusual about it...
HEY...
THE SUMMER FESTIVAL IS COMING UP SOON.
It's held nearby.
OH?!
A SUMMER FESTIVAL, HUH?
CAN OUTSIDERS GO TO IT?
Or is it just for Saitama citizens?
YOU'LL BE FINE.
JUST WEAR THIS PERMIT.
WOW!
THANKS!
SAITAMA (TEMPORARY)
GOOD FOR ONE DAY
COULD YOU NOT SPREAD LIES?
OH YEAH ...
YOU'RE GOING TO THE FESTIVAL, RIGHT, MAFUYU?
It's this week...

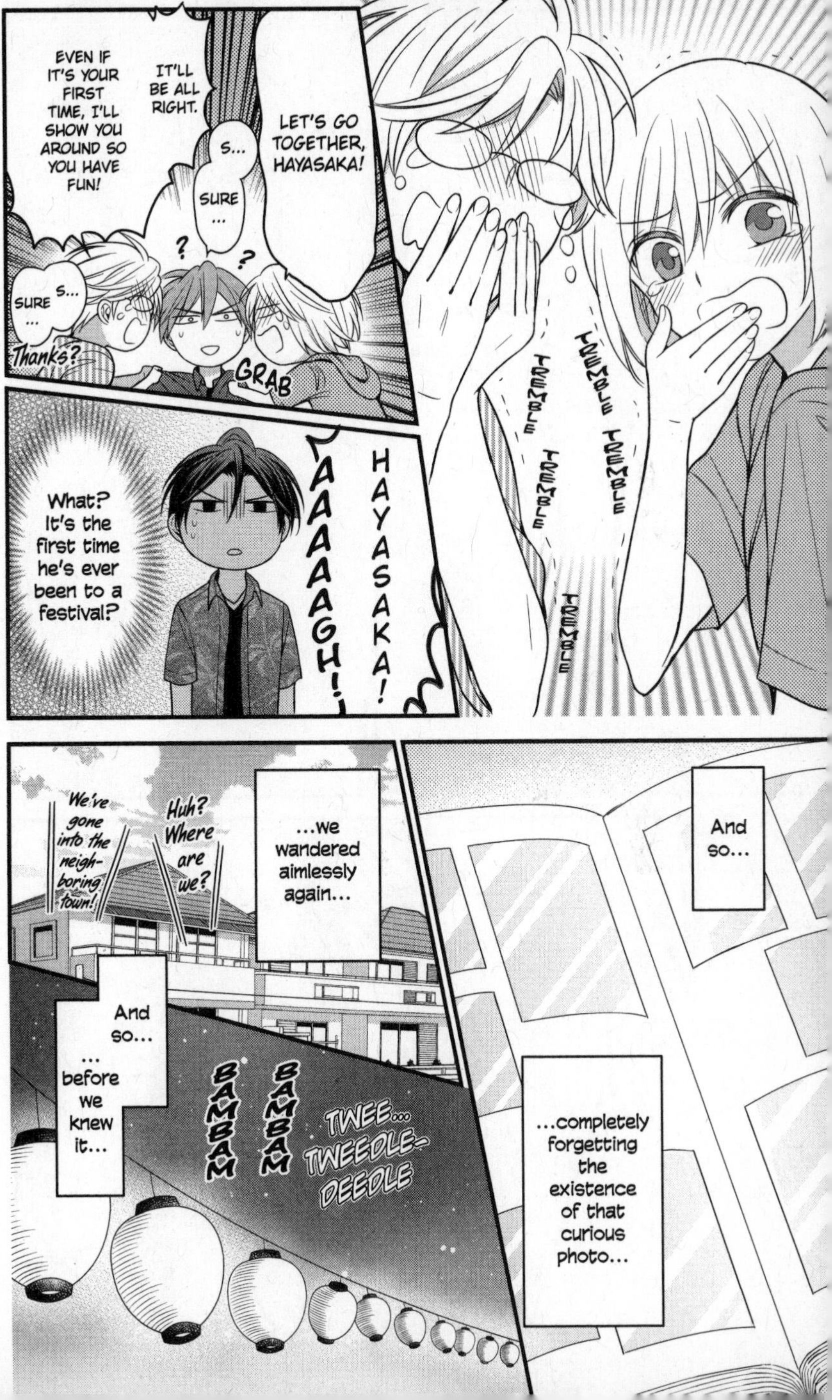
TREMBLE TREMBLE
TREMBLE TREMBLE
TREMBLE
LET'S GO TOGETHER, HAYASAKA!
IT'LL BE ALL RIGHT.
EVEN IF IT'S YOUR FIRST TIME, I'LL SHOW YOU AROUND SO YOU HAVE FUN!
S... SURE...
?
?
S... SURE...
Thanks?
GRAB
HAYASAKA!
AAAAAAGH!
What? It's the first time he's ever been to a festival?
And so...
...completely forgetting the existence of that curious photo...
...we wandered aimlessly again...
Huh? Where are we?
We've gone into the neigh-boring town!
And so... ...before we knew it...
BAMBAM
BAMBAM
TWEE... TWEEDLE-DEEDLE

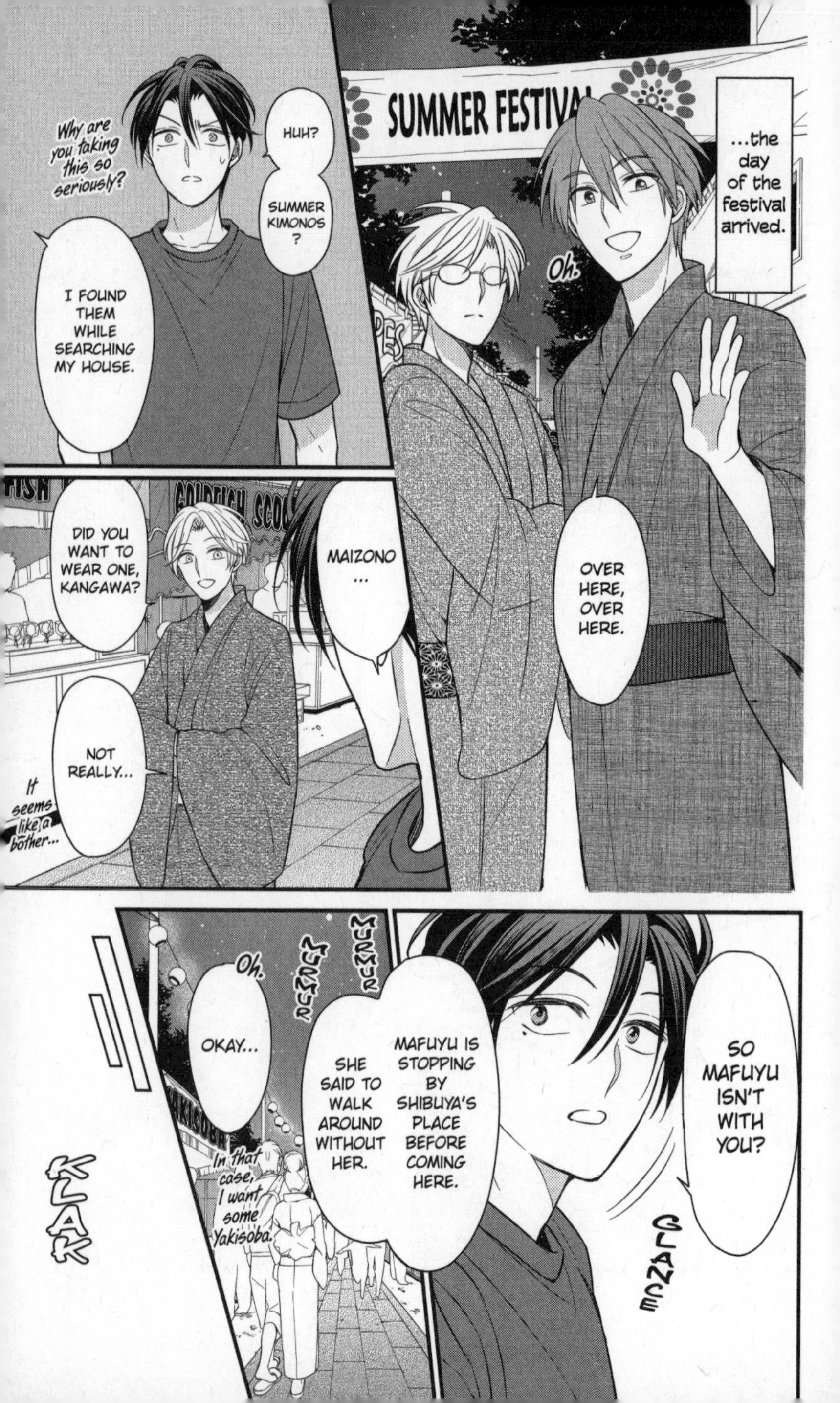

...the day of the festival arrived.
SUMMER FESTIVAL
Oh.
OVER HERE, OVER HERE.
HUH?
SUMMER KIMONOS?
Why are you taking this so seriously?
I FOUND THEM WHILE SEARCHING MY HOUSE.
MAIZONO...
DID YOU WANT TO WEAR ONE, KANGAWA?
NOT REALLY...
It seems like a bother...
SO MAFUYU ISN'T WITH YOU?
GLANCE
MAFUYU IS STOPPING BY SHIBUYA'S PLACE BEFORE COMING HERE.
SHE SAID TO WALK AROUND WITHOUT HER.
MURMUR MURMUR
Oh.
OKAY...
In that case, I want some Yakisoba.
KLAK

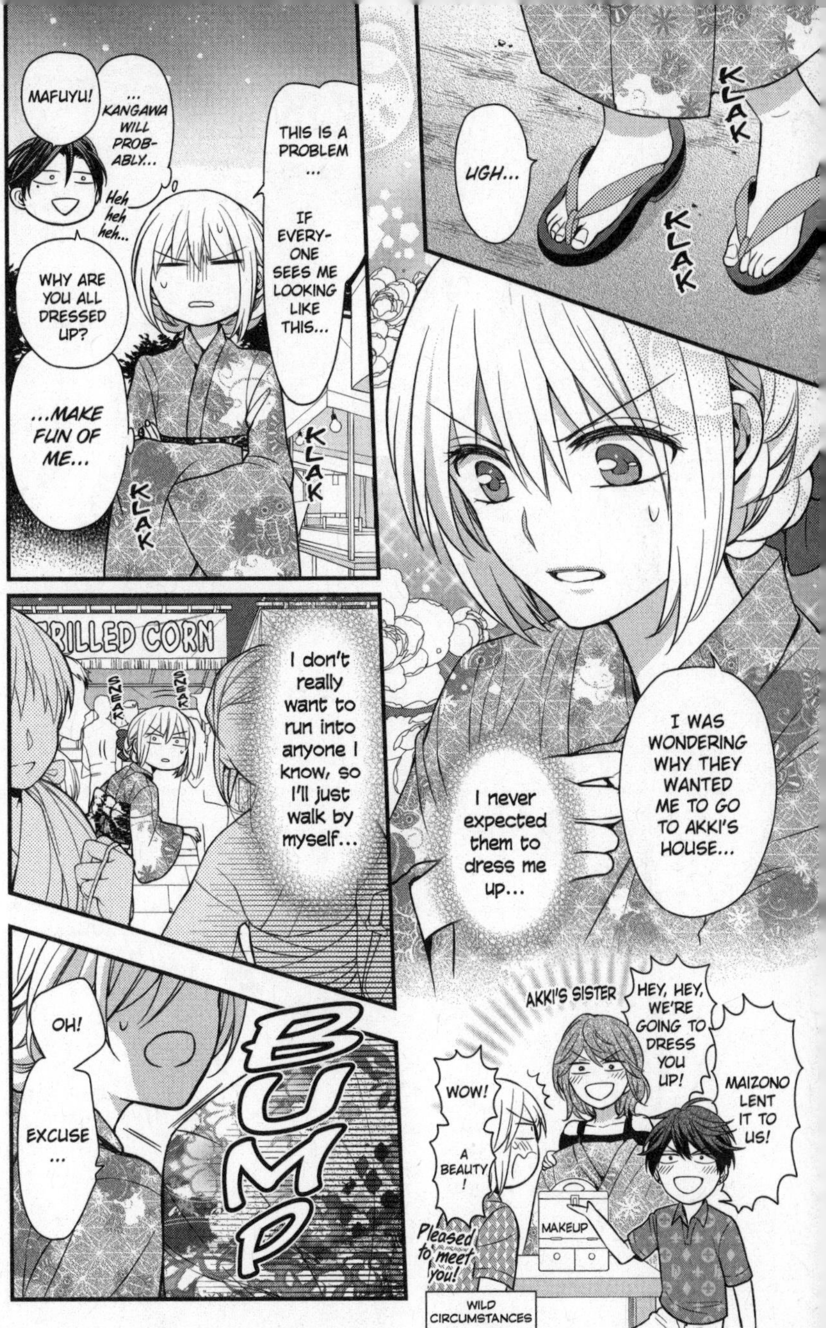
UGH...
KLAK
KLAK
KLAK
THIS IS A PROBLEM ...
IF EVERYONE SEES ME LOOKING LIKE THIS...
... KANGAWA WILL PROBABLY...
MAFUYU!
Heh heh heh...
WHY ARE YOU ALL DRESSED UP?
...MAKE FUN OF ME...
KLAK
KLAK
I WAS WONDERING WHY THEY WANTED ME TO GO TO AKKI'S HOUSE...
I never expected them to dress me up...
HEY, HEY, WE'RE GOING TO DRESS YOU UP!
MAIZONO LENT IT TO US!
AKKI'S SISTER
WOW!
A BEAUTY!
MAKEUP
Pleased to meet you!
WILD CIRCUMSTANCES
I don't really want to run into anyone I know, so I'll just walk by myself...
GRILLED CORN
SNEAK
SNEAK
BUMP
OH!
EXCUSE ...

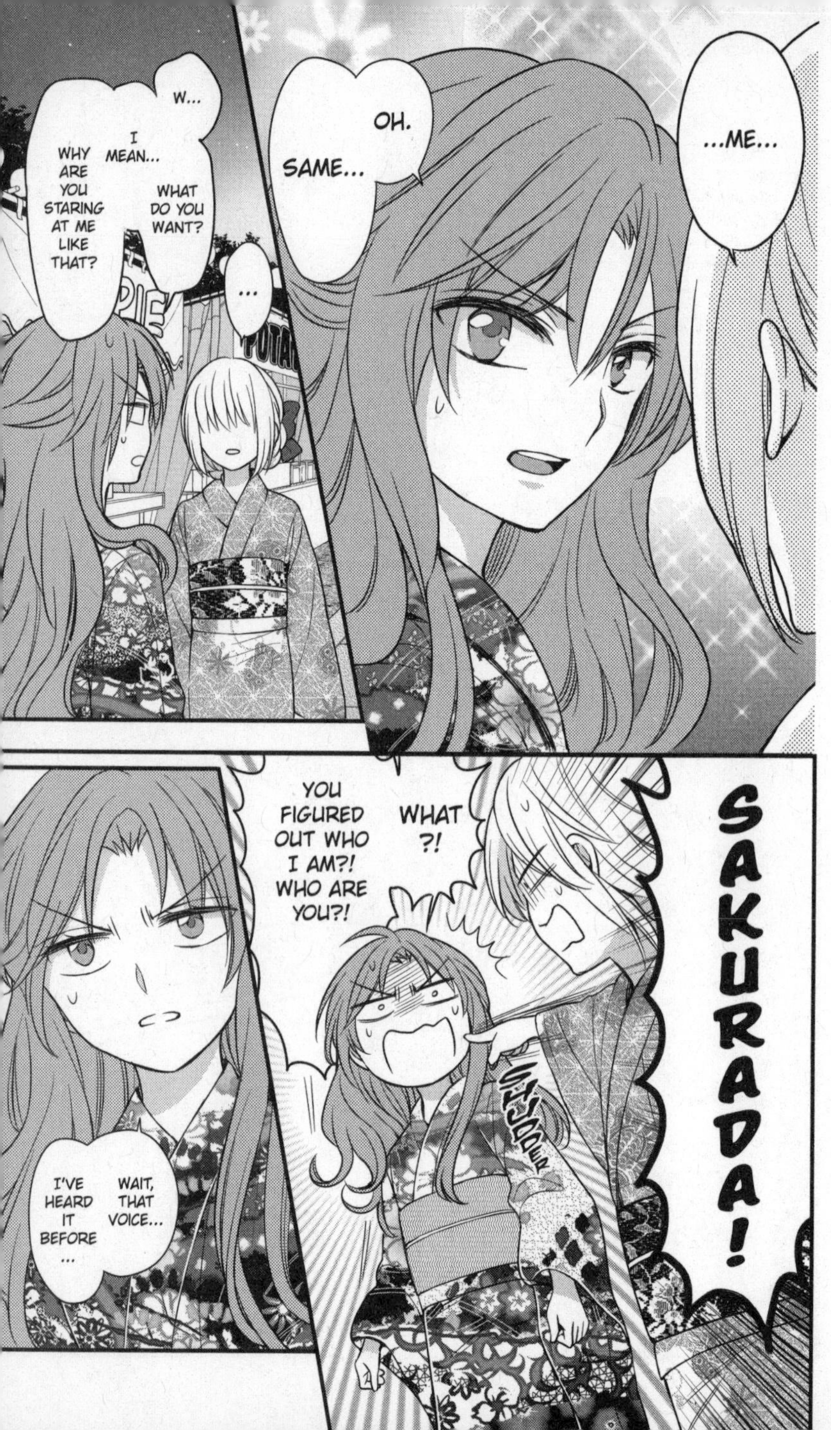
...ME...
OH.
SAME...
W...
I MEAN...
WHY ARE YOU STARING AT ME LIKE THAT?
WHAT DO YOU WANT?
...
SAKURADA!
WHAT?!
YOU FIGURED OUT WHO I AM?! WHO ARE YOU?!
SHUDDER
WAIT, THAT VOICE...
I'VE HEARD IT BEFORE...

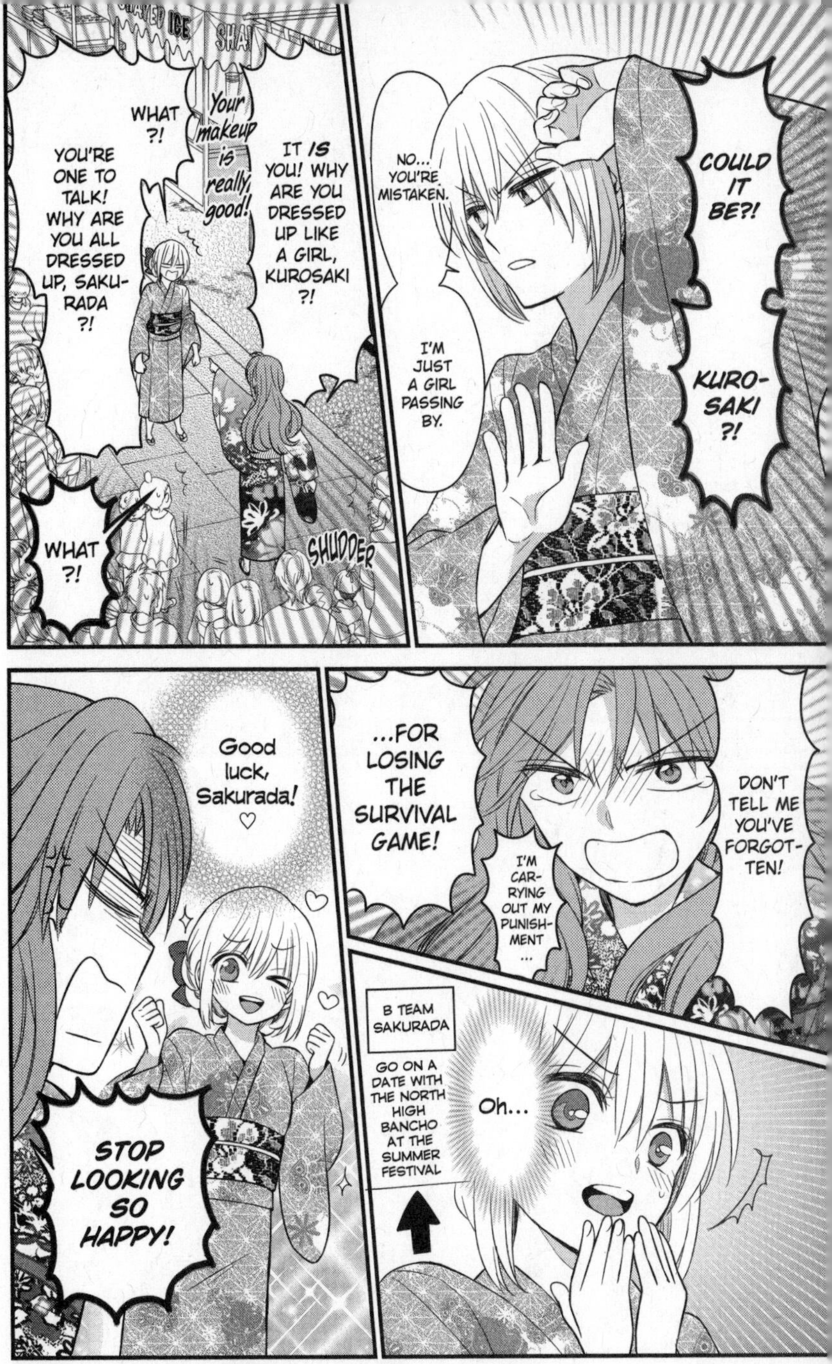
COULD IT BE?!
KURO-SAKI?!
NO... YOU'RE MISTAKEN.
I'M JUST A GIRL PASSING BY.
SHAVED ICE
IT *IS* YOU! WHY ARE YOU DRESSED UP LIKE A GIRL, KUROSAKI?!
Your makeup is really good!
WHAT?!
YOU'RE ONE TO TALK! WHY ARE YOU ALL DRESSED UP, SAKU-RADA?!
SHUDDER
WHAT?!
DON'T TELL ME YOU'VE FORGOT-TEN!
I'M CAR-RYING OUT MY PUNISH-MENT...
...FOR LOSING THE SURVIVAL GAME!
B TEAM SAKURADA
GO ON A DATE WITH THE NORTH HIGH BANCHO AT THE SUMMER FESTIVAL
Oh...
Good luck, Sakurada! ♡
STOP LOOKING SO HAPPY!

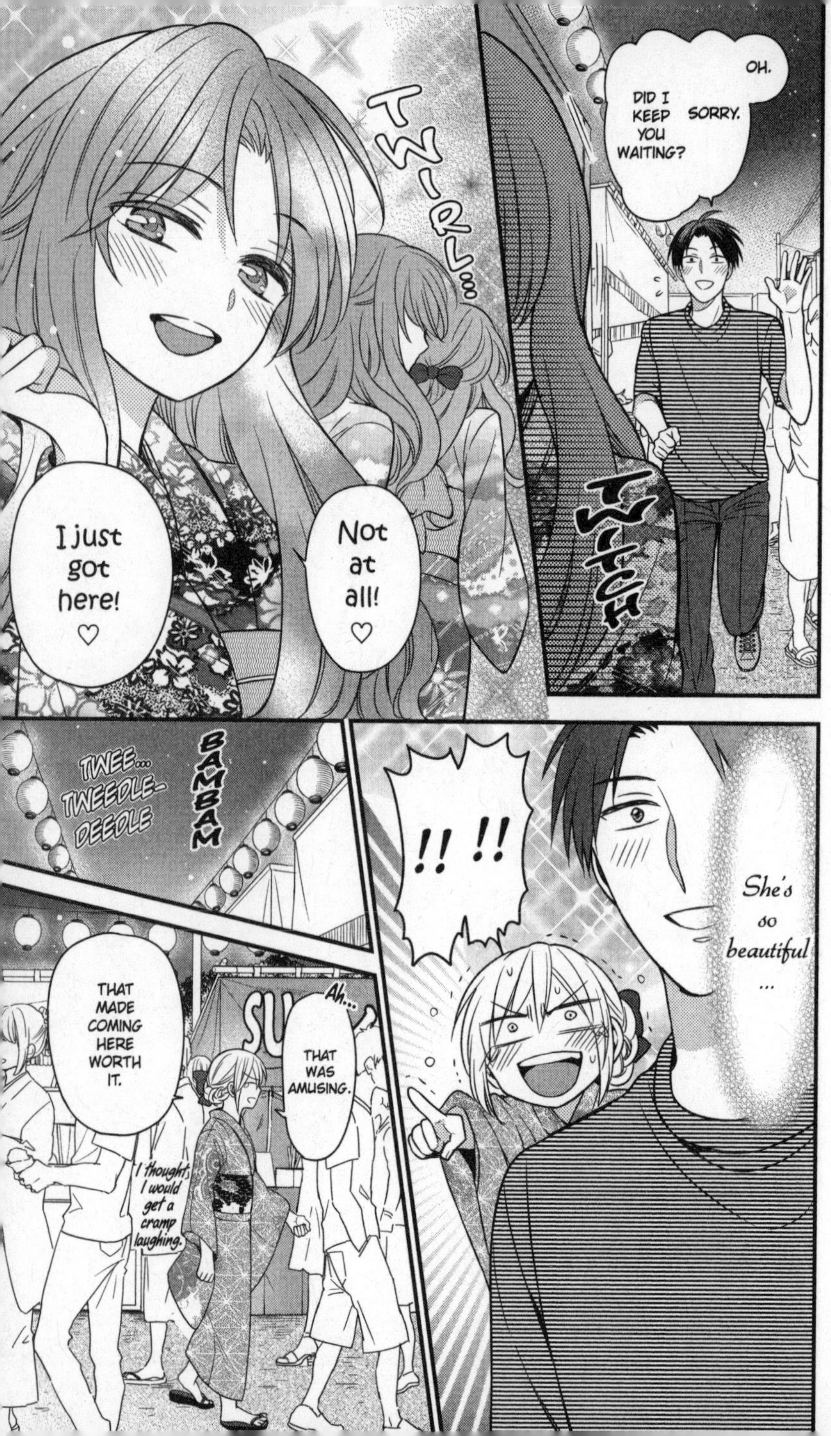
OH.
SORRY.
DID I KEEP YOU WAITING?
TWITCH
TWIRL...
Not at all! ♡
I just got here! ♡
!! !!
She's so beautiful...
BAMBAM
TWEE... TWEEDLE-DEEDLE
Ah...
THAT WAS AMUSING.
THAT MADE COMING HERE WORTH IT.
I thought I would get a cramp laughing.

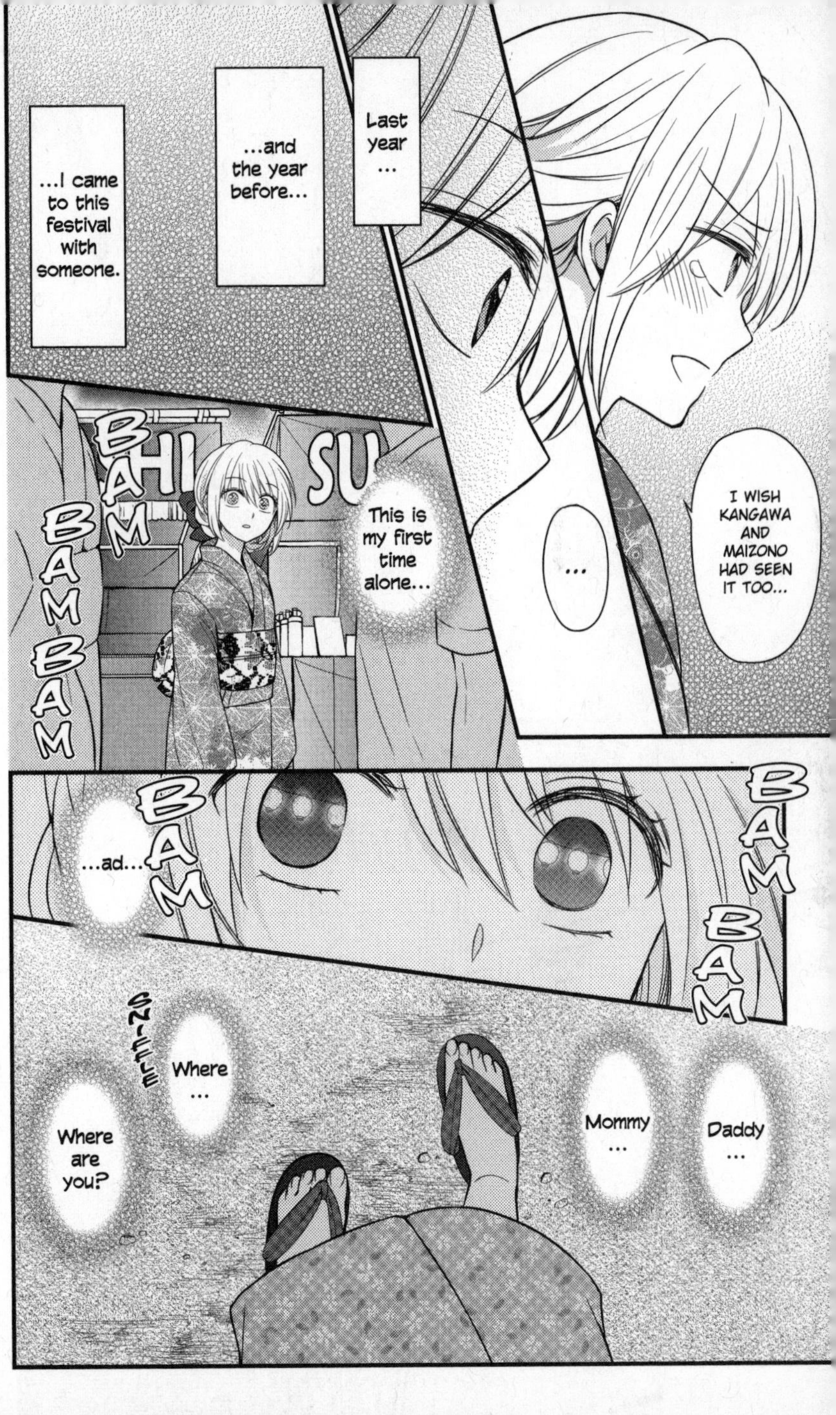
Last year...
...and the year before...
...I came to this festival with someone.
I WISH KANGAWA AND MAIZONO HAD SEEN IT TOO...
...
BAM
BAM BAM BAM BAM
SU
HI
This is my first time alone...
BAM BAM
BAM
...ad...
Daddy...
Mommy...
Where...
SNIFFLE
Where are you?

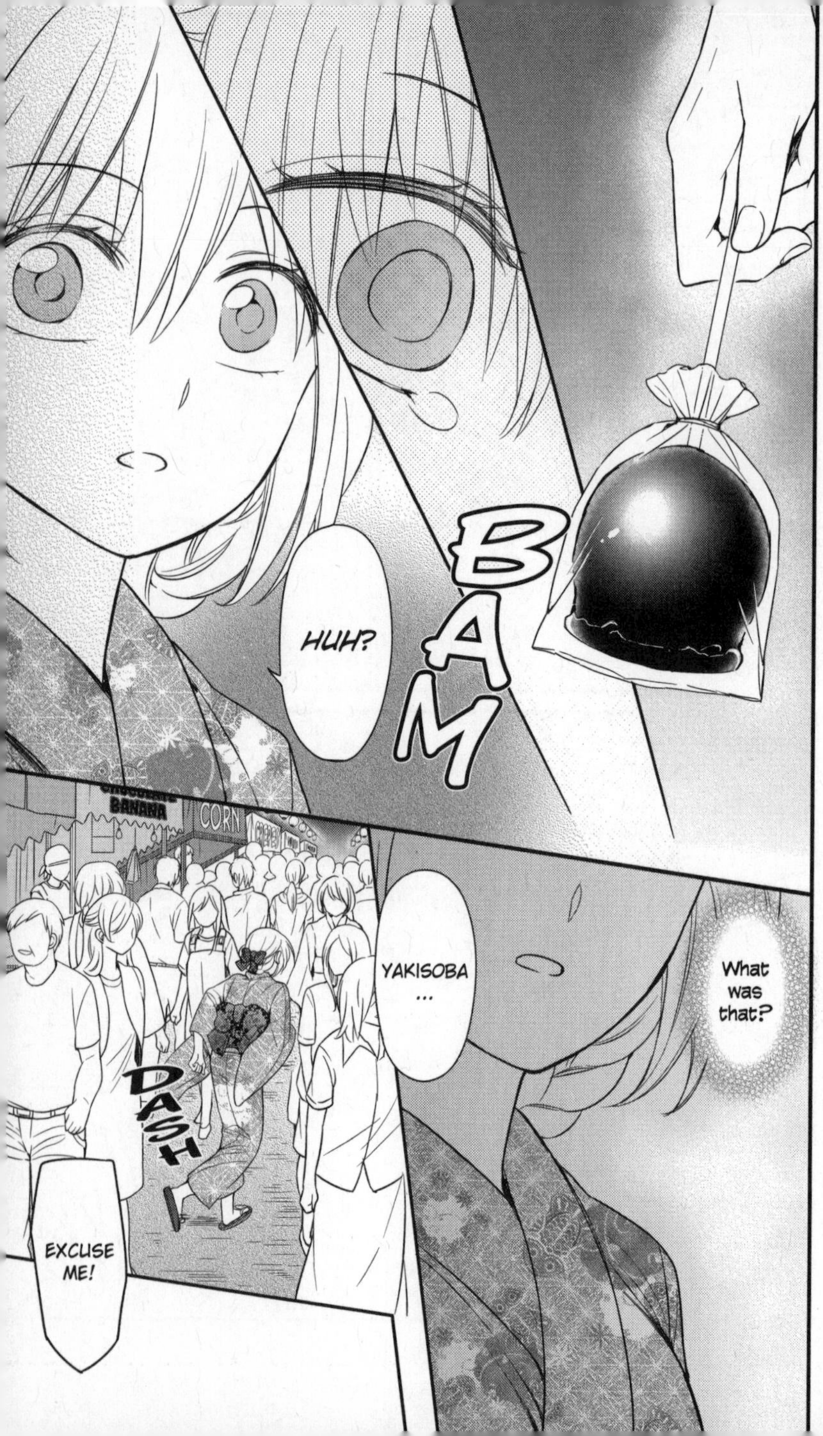
BAM
HUH?
BANANA
CORN
YAKISOBA ...
What was that?
DASH
EXCUSE ME!

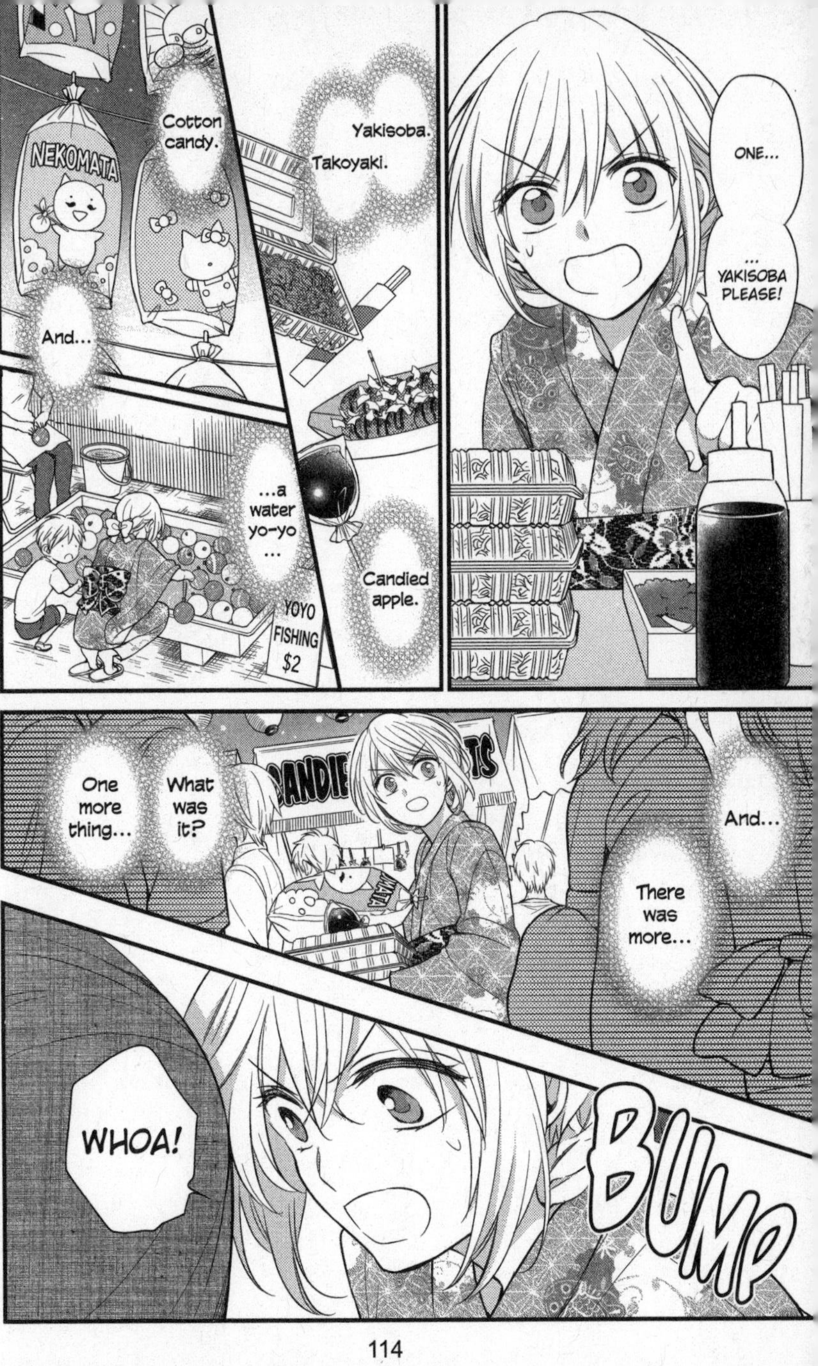

ONE...
...YAKISOBA PLEASE!
Yakisoba.
Takoyaki.
Candied apple.
Cotton candy.
NEKOMATA
And...
...a water yo-yo ...
YOYO FISHING $2
And...
There was more...
What was it?
One more thing...
BUMP
WHOA!

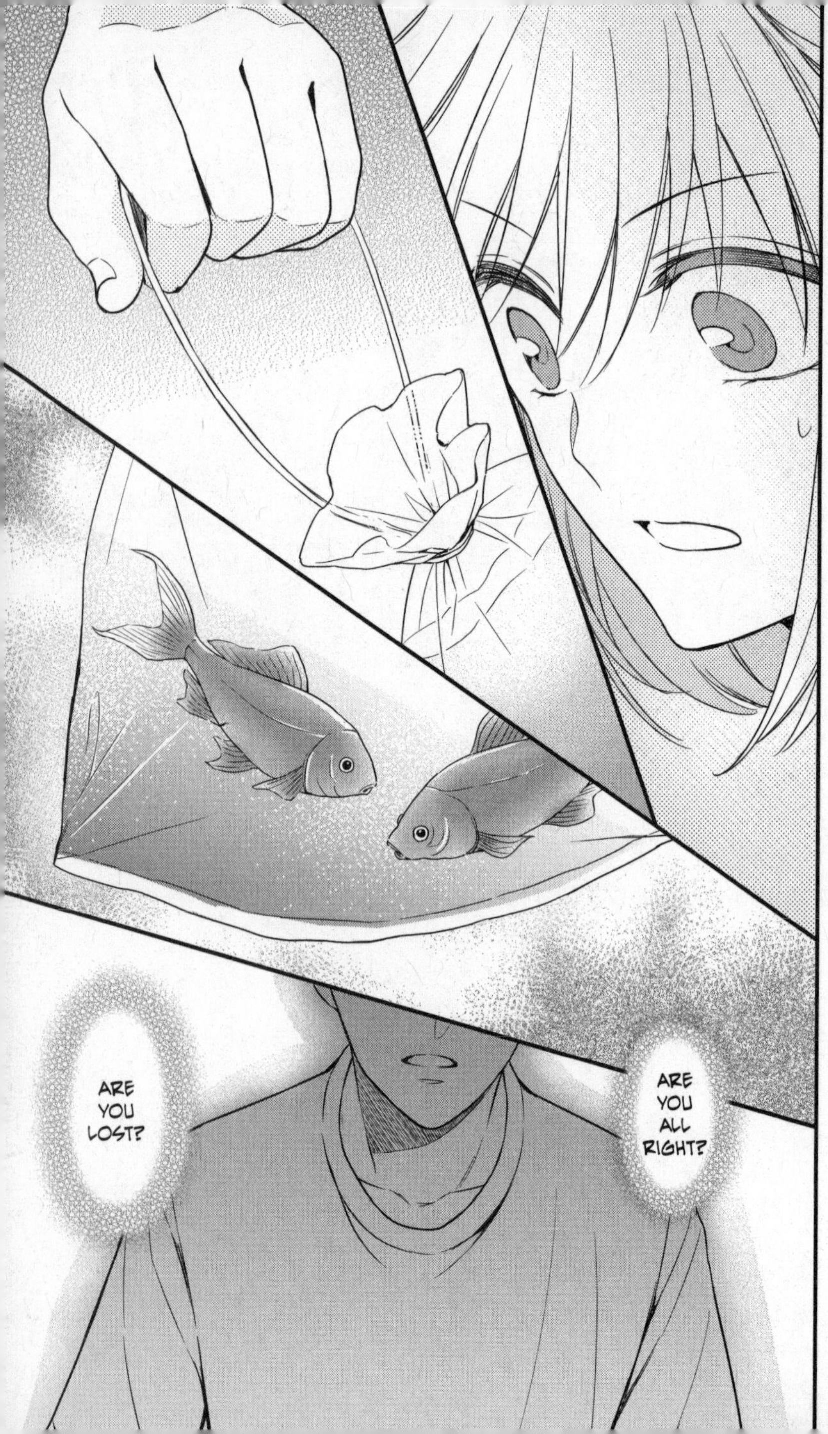
ARE YOU ALL RIGHT?
ARE YOU LOST?

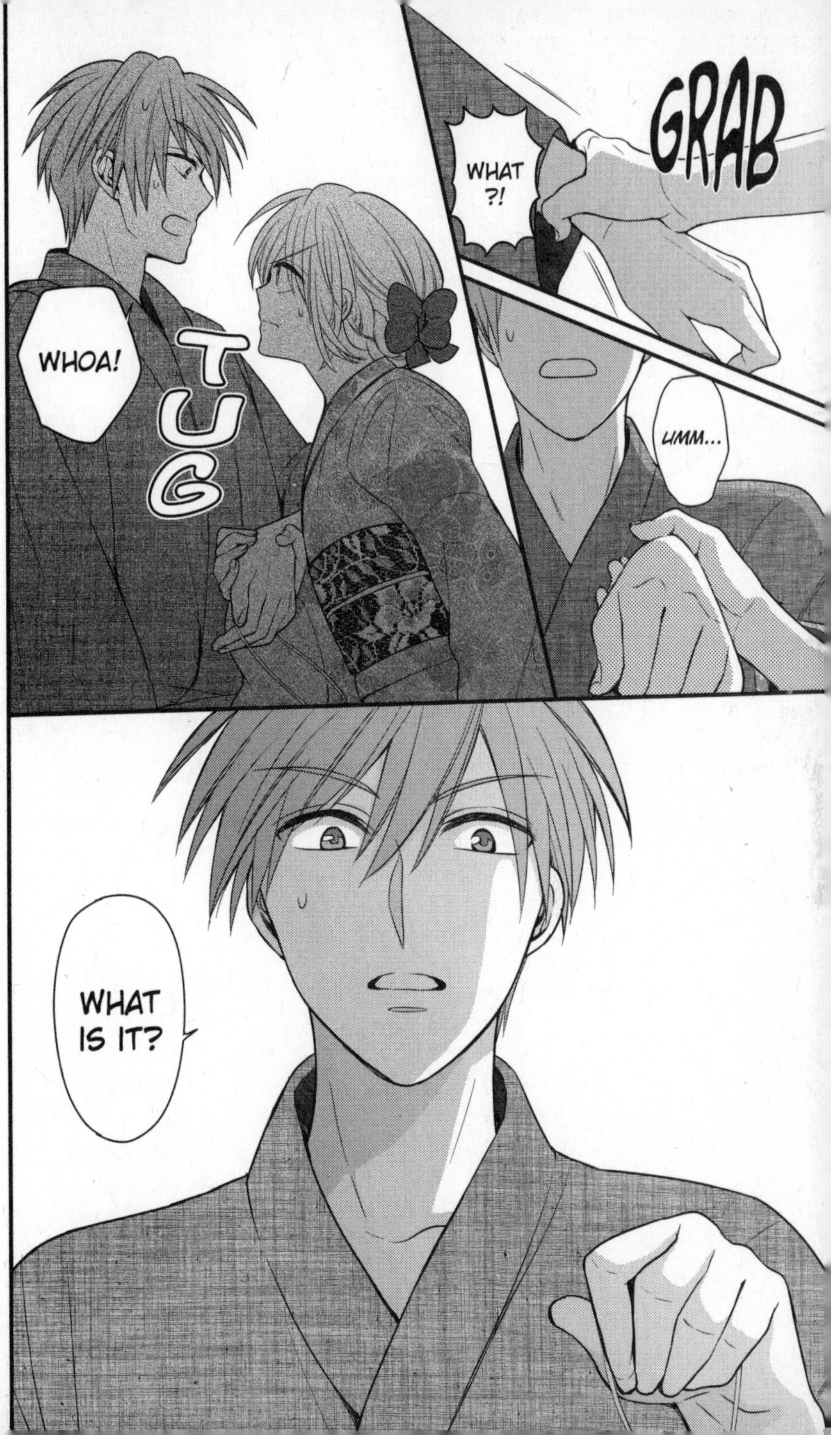
GRAB
WHAT ?!
UMM...
WHOA!
TUG
WHAT IS IT?

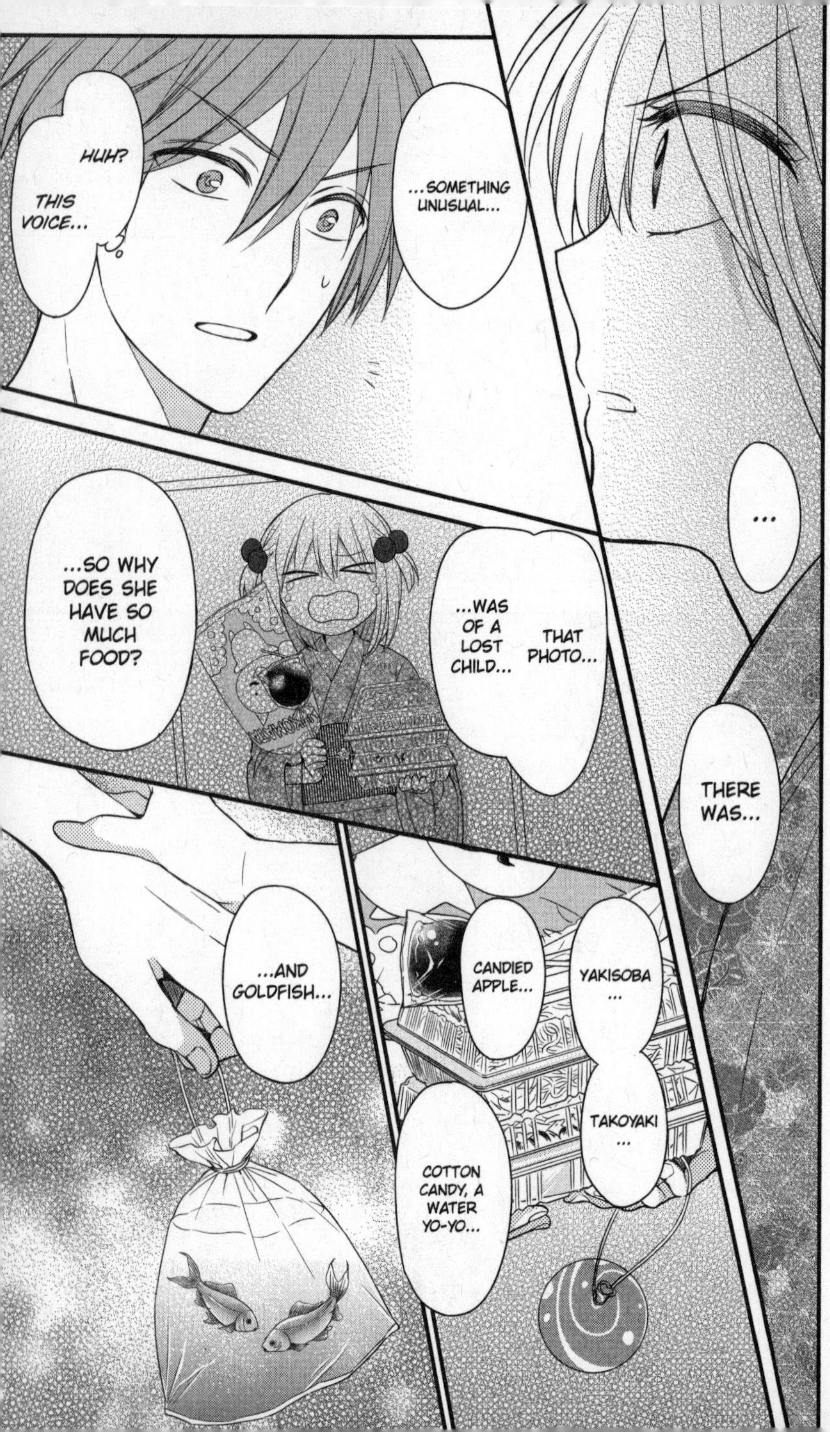
...
...SOMETHING UNUSUAL...
HUH? THIS VOICE...
THAT PHOTO...
...WAS OF A LOST CHILD...
...SO WHY DOES SHE HAVE SO MUCH FOOD?
THERE WAS...
YAKISOBA...
TAKOYAKI...
CANDIED APPLE...
COTTON CANDY, A WATER YO-YO...
...AND GOLDFISH...

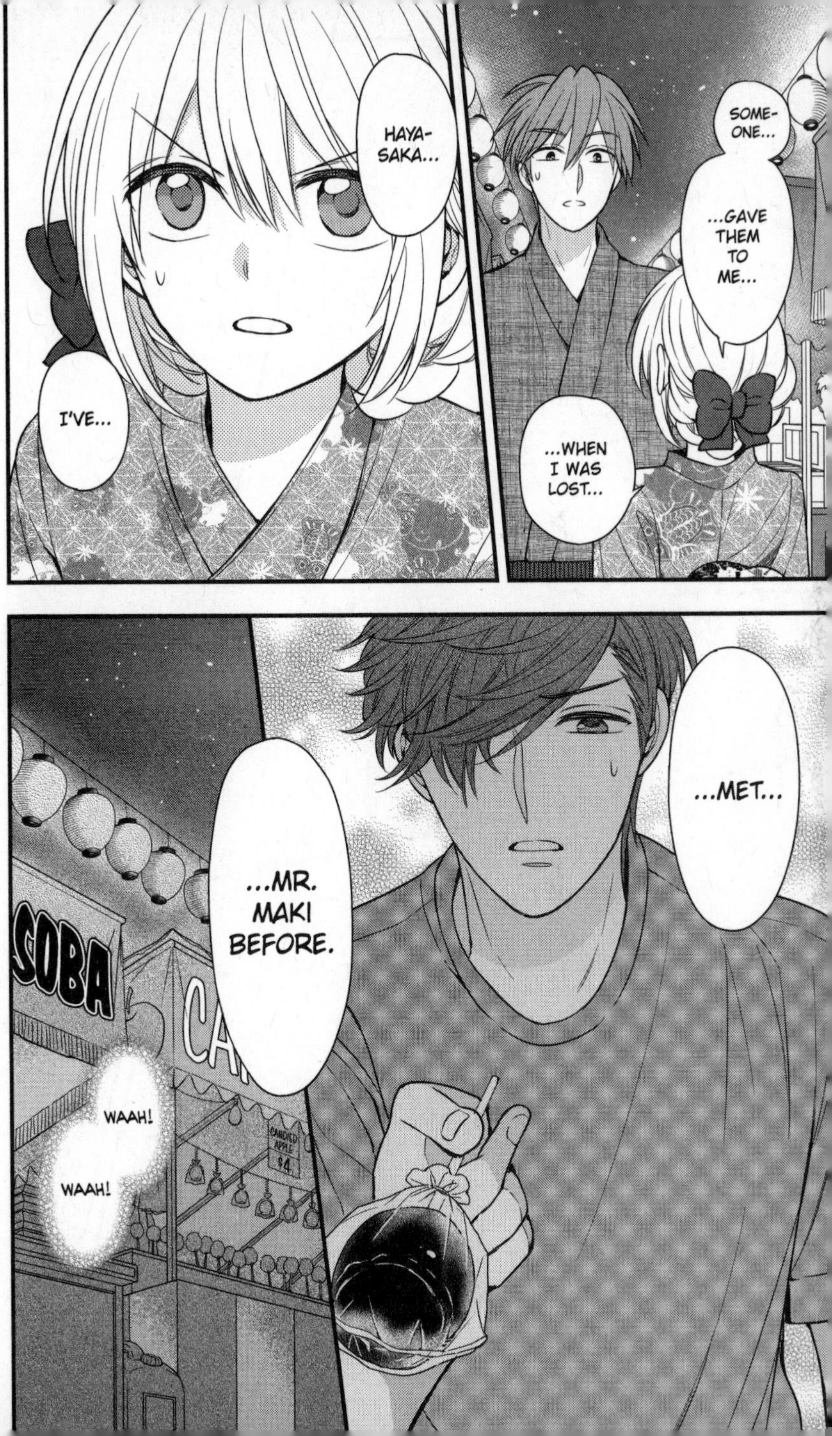
SOME-ONE...
...GAVE THEM TO ME...
...WHEN I WAS LOST...
HAYA-SAKA...
I'VE...
...MET...
...MR. MAKI BEFORE.
SOBA
CANDIED APPLE $4
WAAH!
WAAH!

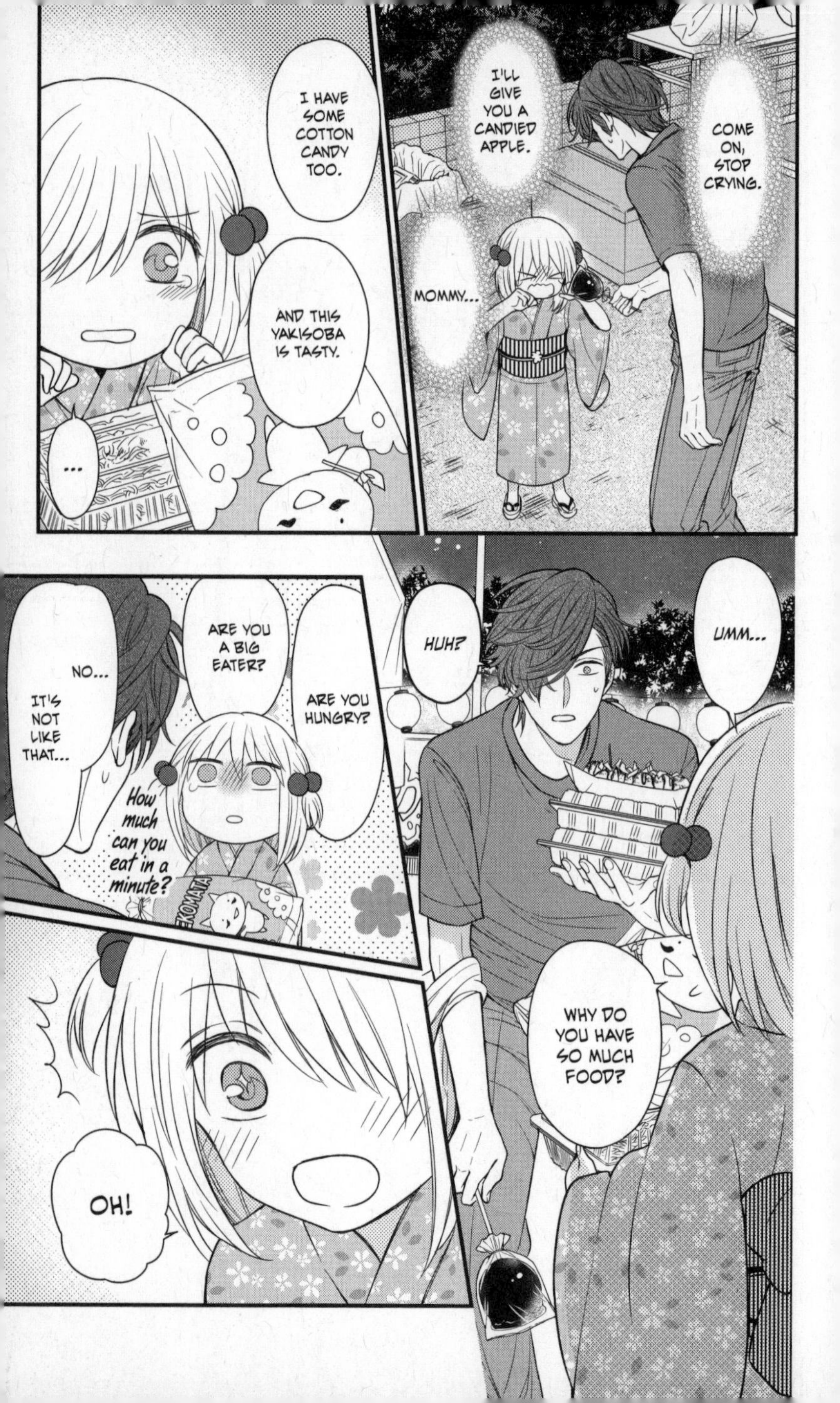
COME ON, STOP CRYING.
I'LL GIVE YOU A CANDIED APPLE.
MOMMY...
I HAVE SOME COTTON CANDY TOO.
AND THIS YAKISOBA IS TASTY.
...
UMM...
HUH?
WHY DO YOU HAVE SO MUCH FOOD?
ARE YOU HUNGRY?
ARE YOU A BIG EATER?
How much can you eat in a minute?
NO... IT'S NOT LIKE THAT...
OH!

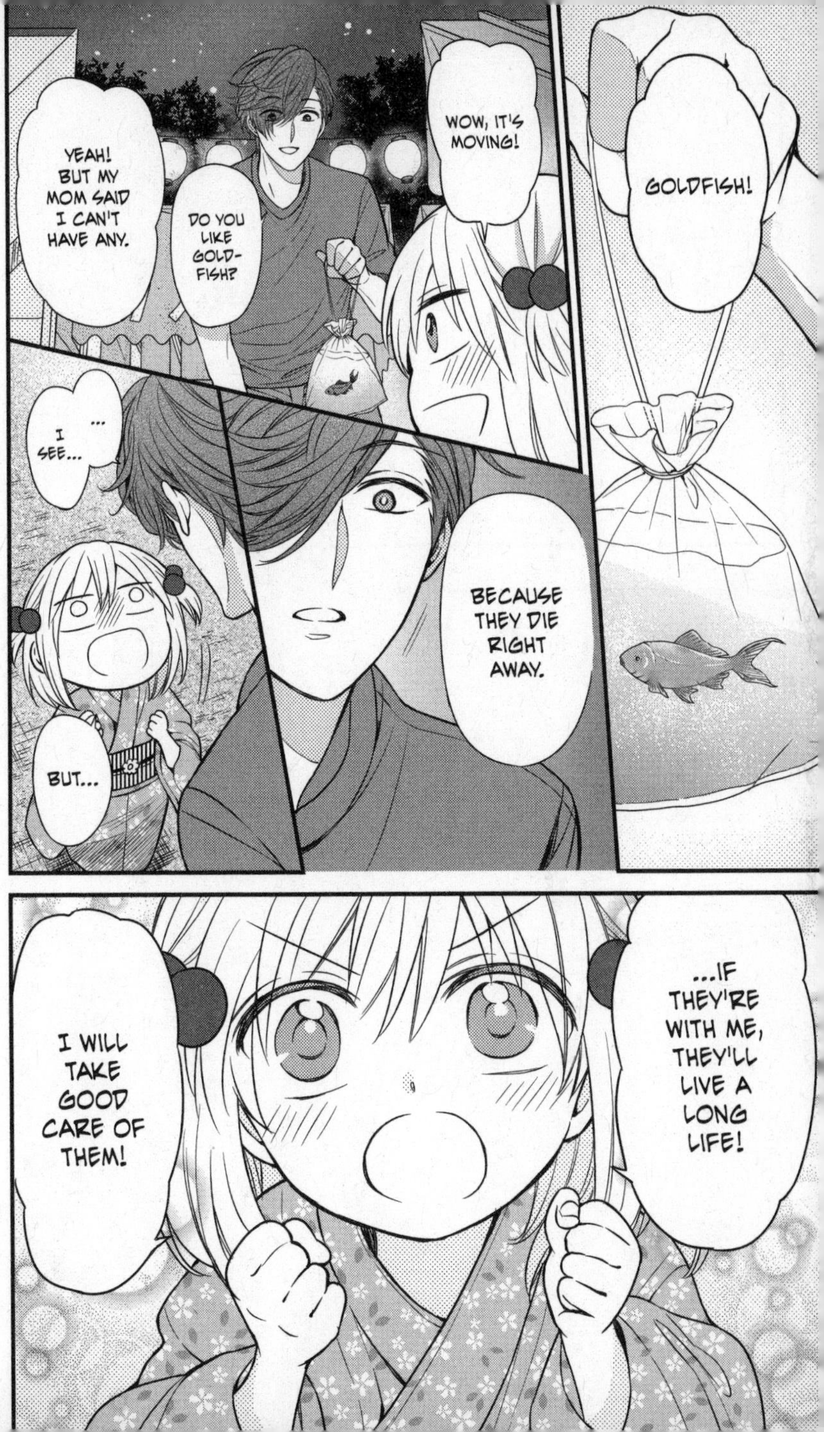
GOLDFISH!
WOW, IT'S MOVING!
DO YOU LIKE GOLDFISH?
YEAH! BUT MY MOM SAID I CAN'T HAVE ANY.
BECAUSE THEY DIE RIGHT AWAY.
... I SEE...
BUT...
...IF THEY'RE WITH ME, THEY'LL LIVE A LONG LIFE!
I WILL TAKE GOOD CARE OF THEM!

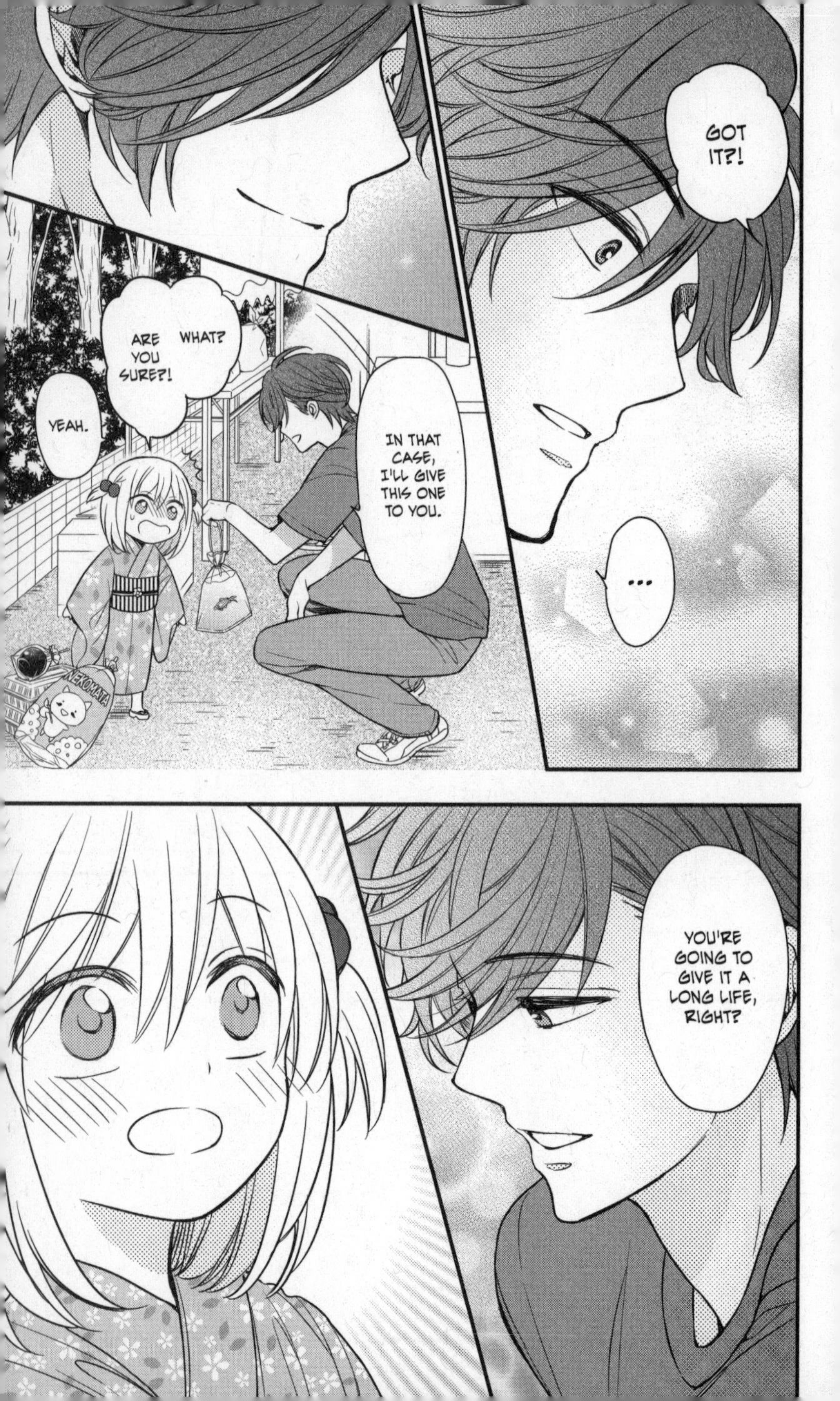
GOT IT?!
...
IN THAT CASE, I'LL GIVE THIS ONE TO YOU.
WHAT? ARE YOU SURE?!
YEAH.
NEKOMATA
YOU'RE GOING TO GIVE IT A LONG LIFE, RIGHT?

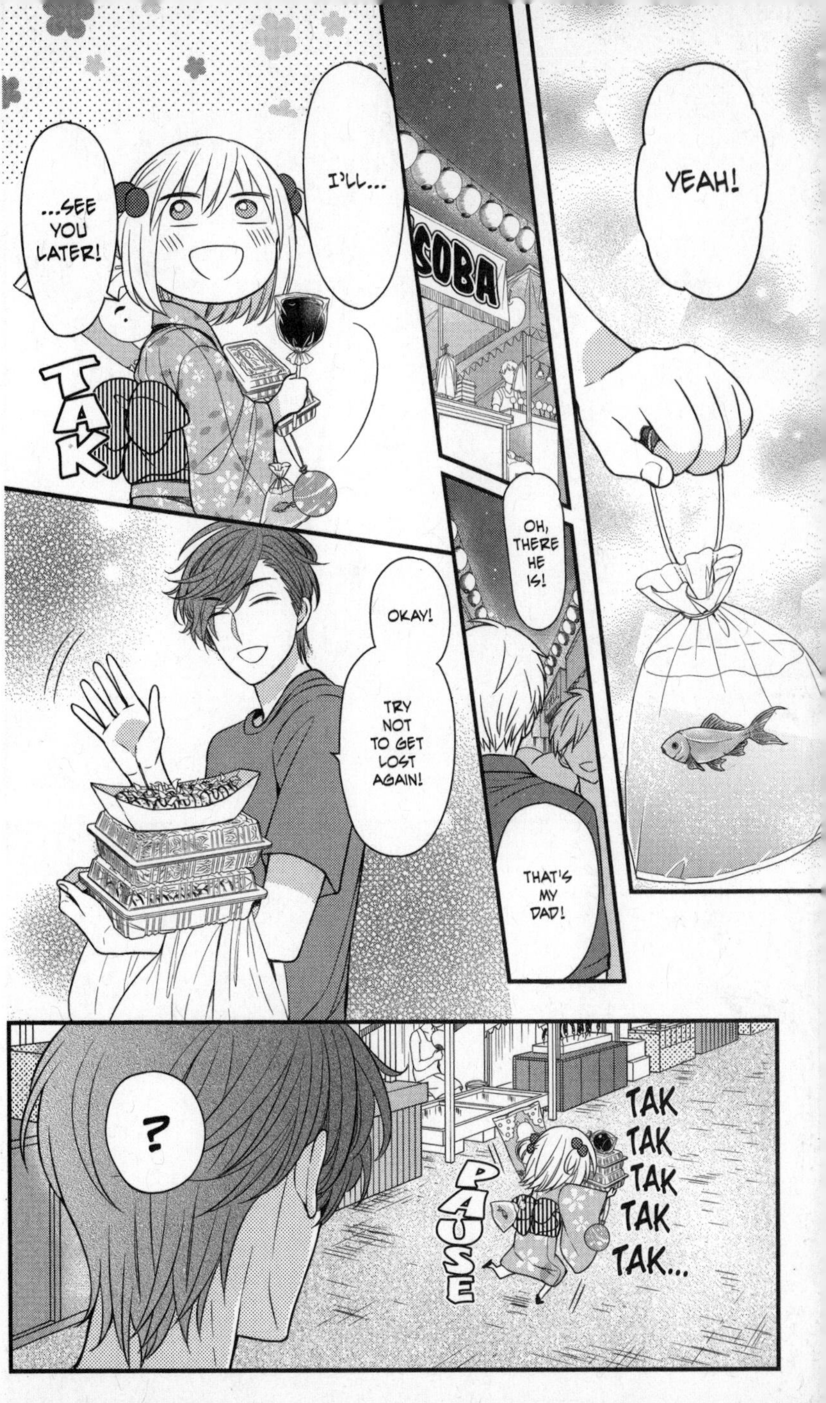

YEAH!
SOBA
OH, THERE HE IS!
THAT'S MY DAD!
I'LL...
...SEE YOU LATER!
TAK
OKAY!
TRY NOT TO GET LOST AGAIN!
TAK TAK TAK TAK TAK...
PAUSE
?

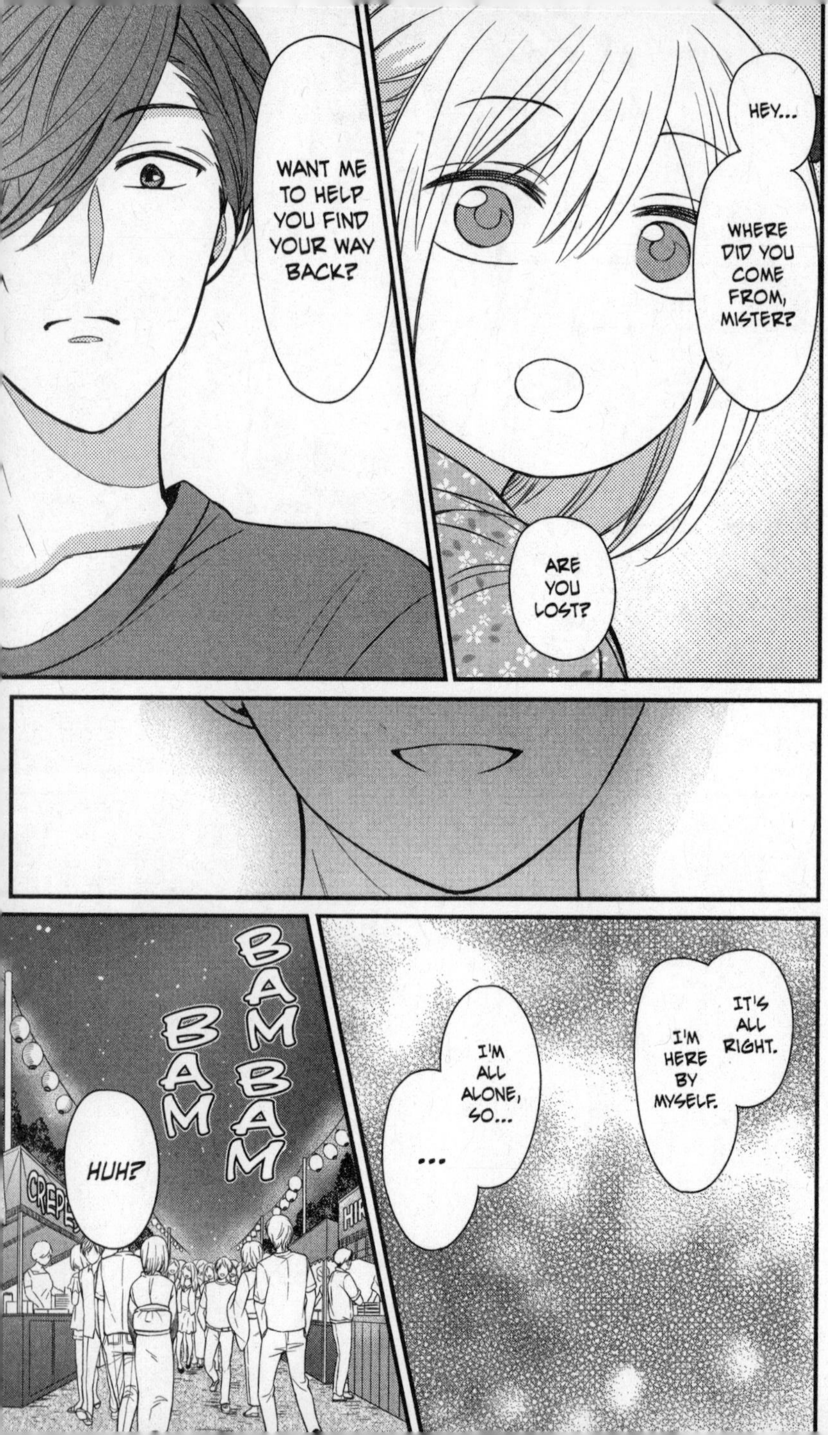
HEY...
WHERE DID YOU COME FROM, MISTER?
ARE YOU LOST?
WANT ME TO HELP YOU FIND YOUR WAY BACK?
IT'S ALL RIGHT.
I'M HERE BY MYSELF.
I'M ALL ALONE, SO...
...
BAM
BAM BAM
BAM
HUH?

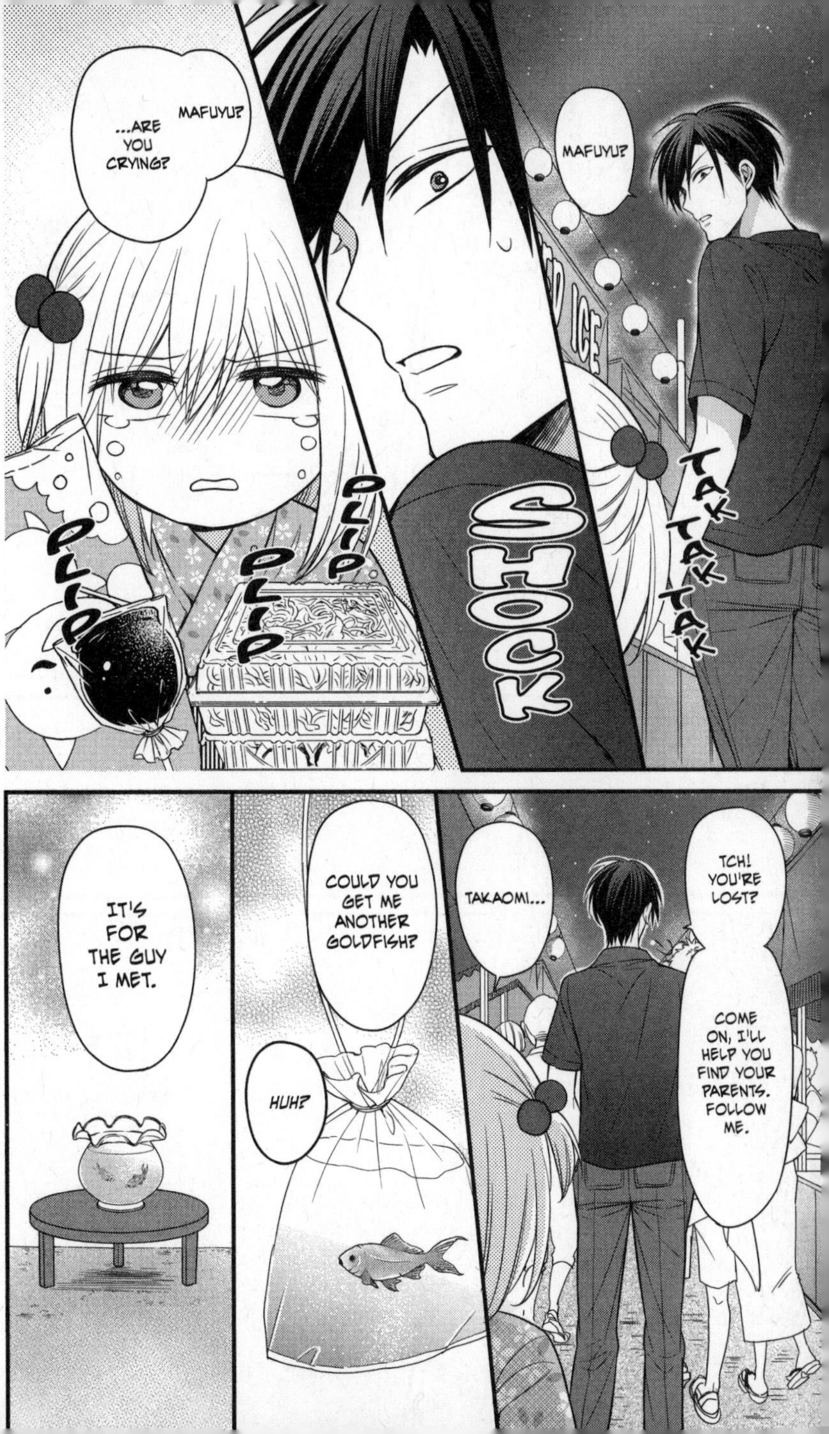

MAFUYU?
TAK TAK TAK TAK
SHOCK
MAFUYU? ...ARE YOU CRYING?
PLIP PLIP PLIP PLIP
TCH! YOU'RE LOST?
COME ON, I'LL HELP YOU FIND YOUR PARENTS. FOLLOW ME.
TAKAOMI...
COULD YOU GET ME ANOTHER GOLDFISH?
HUH?
IT'S FOR THE GUY I MET.

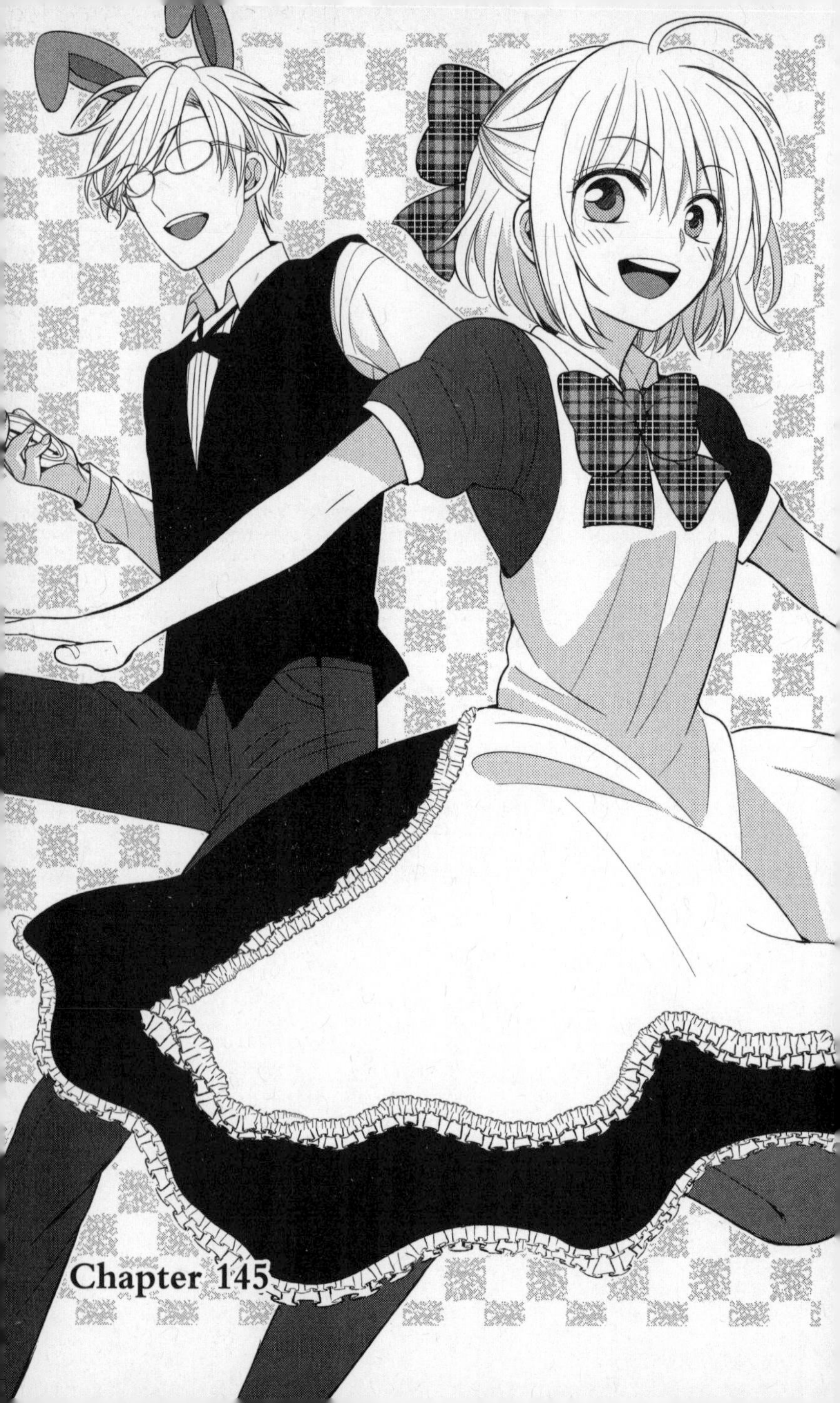
Chapter 145

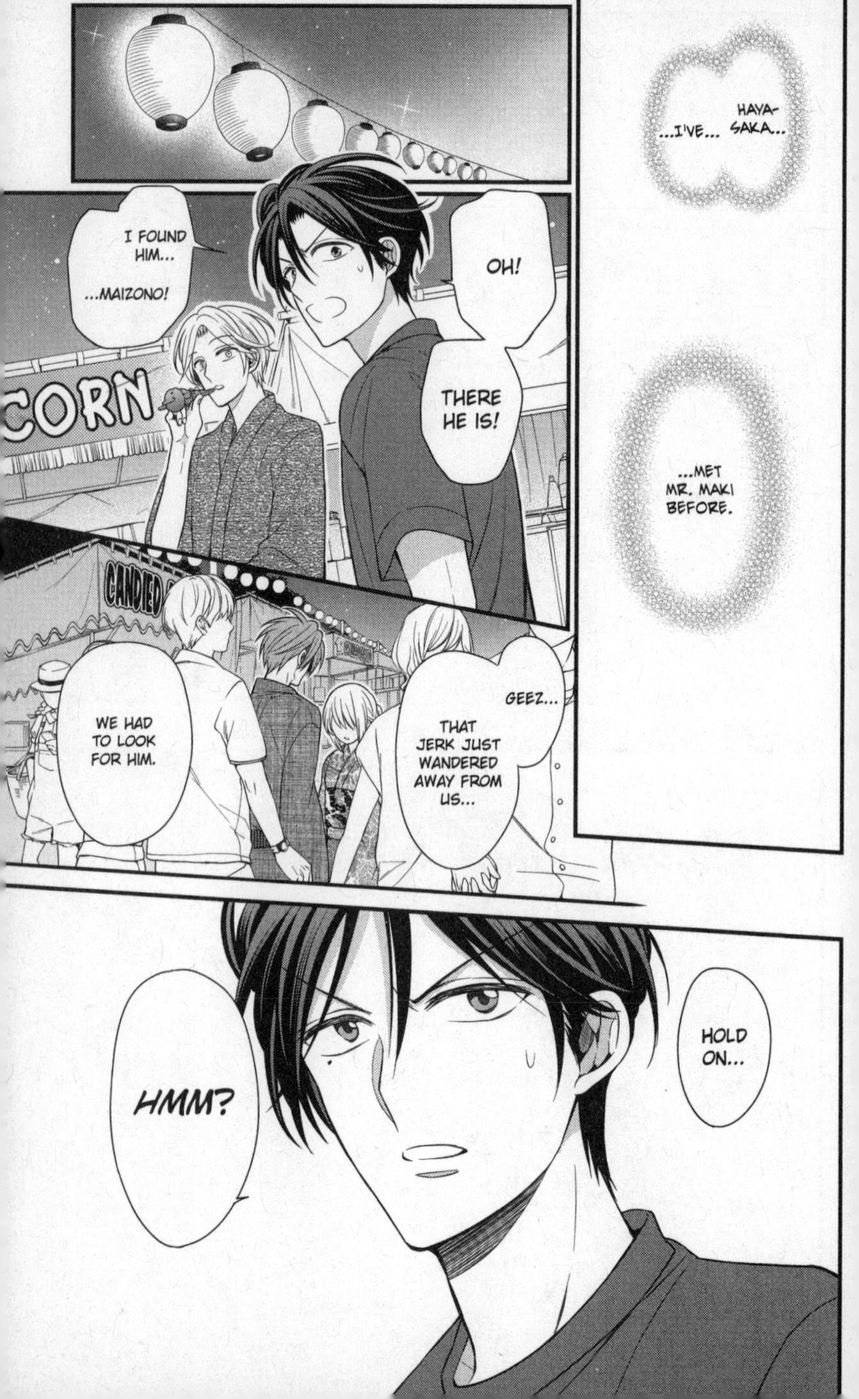
HAYA-SAKA...
...I'VE...
...MET MR. MAKI BEFORE.
OH!
THERE HE IS!
I FOUND HIM...
...MAIZONO!
CORN
CANDIED
GEEZ...
THAT JERK JUST WANDERED AWAY FROM US...
WE HAD TO LOOK FOR HIM.
HOLD ON...
HMM?

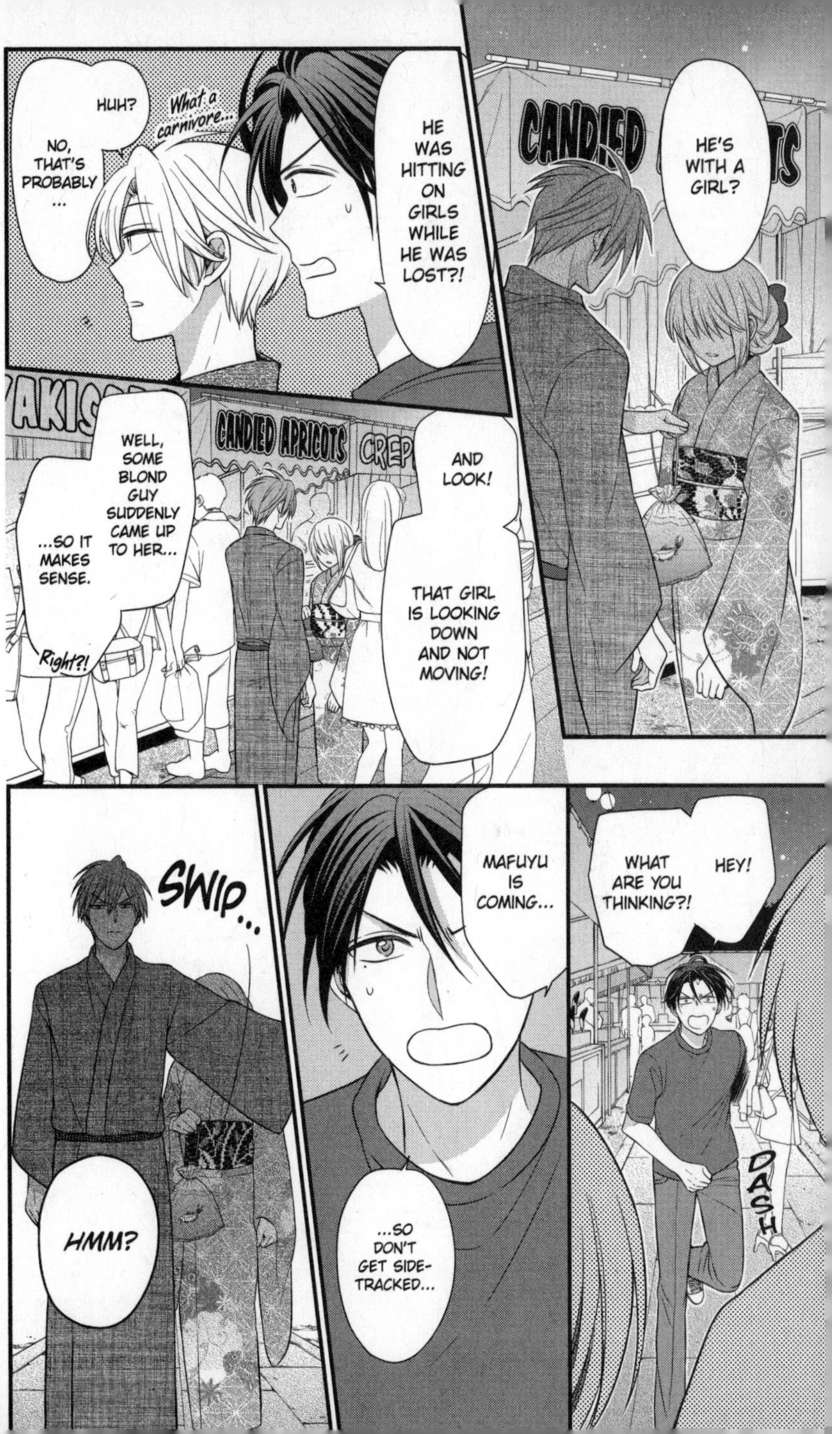
HE'S WITH A GIRL?
HE WAS HITTING ON GIRLS WHILE HE WAS LOST?!
What a carnivore...
HUH?
NO, THAT'S PROBABLY ...
CANDIED APRICOTS
CREP
AND LOOK!
THAT GIRL IS LOOKING DOWN AND NOT MOVING!
WELL, SOME BLOND GUY SUDDENLY CAME UP TO HER...
...SO IT MAKES SENSE.
Right?!
HEY!
WHAT ARE YOU THINKING?!
DASH
MAFUYU IS COMING...
...SO DON'T GET SIDE-TRACKED...
SWIP...
HMM?

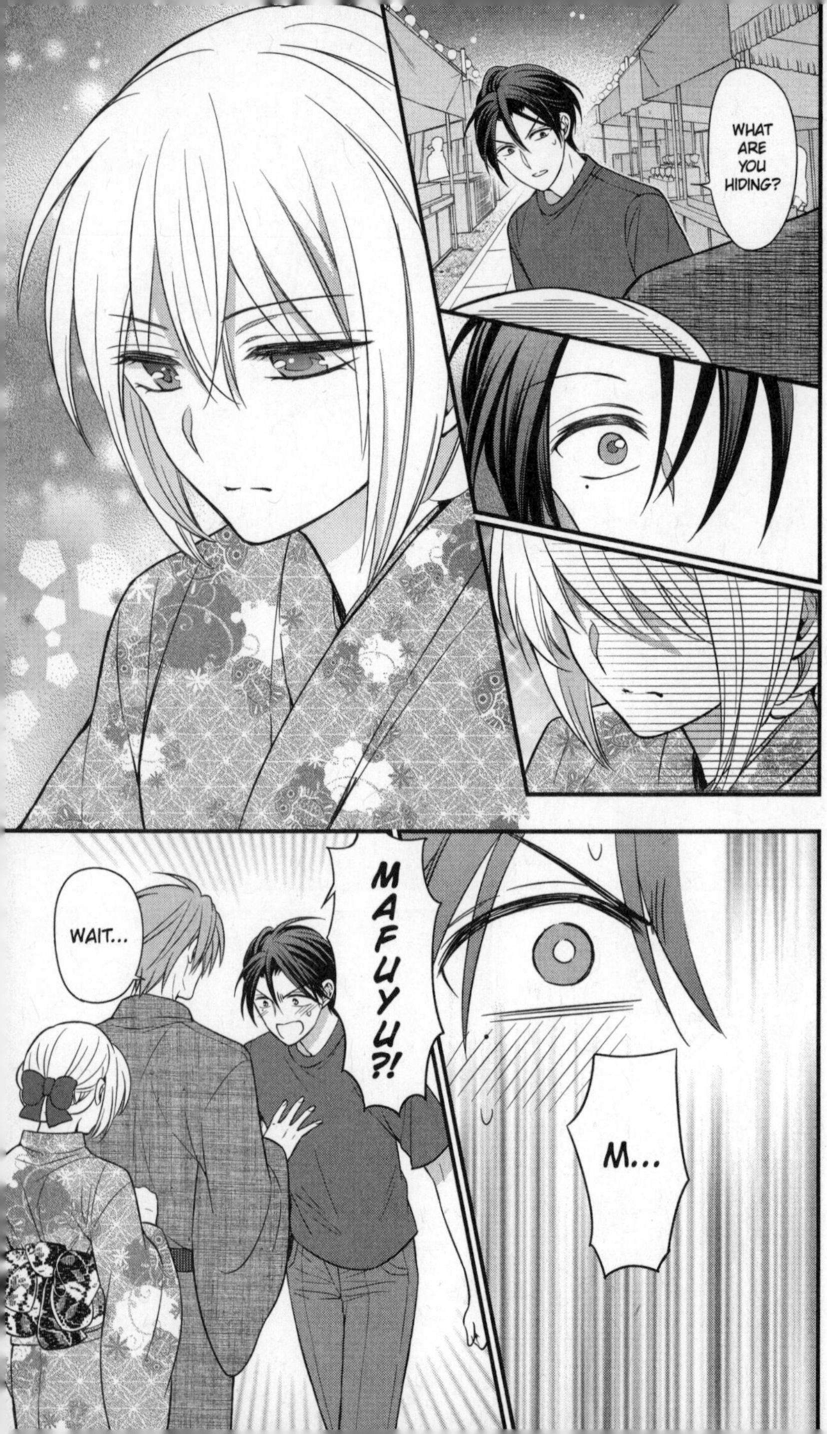
WHAT ARE YOU HIDING?
M...
MAFUYU?!
WAIT...

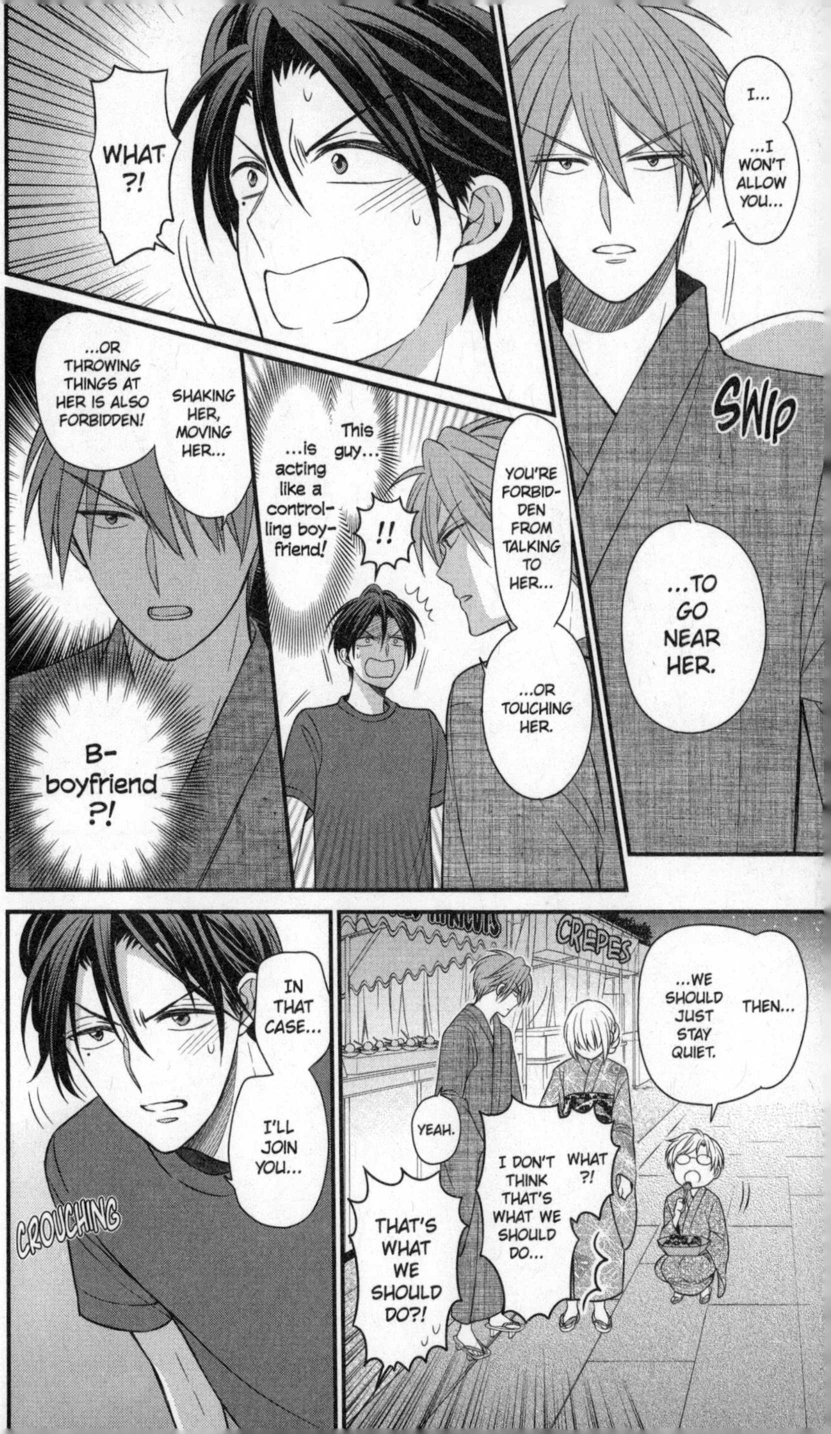
I...
...I WON'T ALLOW YOU...
WHAT ?!
SWIP
...TO GO NEAR HER.
YOU'RE FORBID-DEN FROM TALKING TO HER...
...OR TOUCHING HER.
SHAKING HER, MOVING HER...
...OR THROWING THINGS AT HER IS ALSO FORBIDDEN!
!!
This guy...
...is acting like a control-ling boy-friend!
B-boyfriend ?!
CREPES
THEN...
...WE SHOULD JUST STAY QUIET.
YEAH.
WHAT ?!
I DON'T THINK THAT'S WHAT WE SHOULD DO...
THAT'S WHAT WE SHOULD DO?!
IN THAT CASE...
I'LL JOIN YOU...
CROUCHING

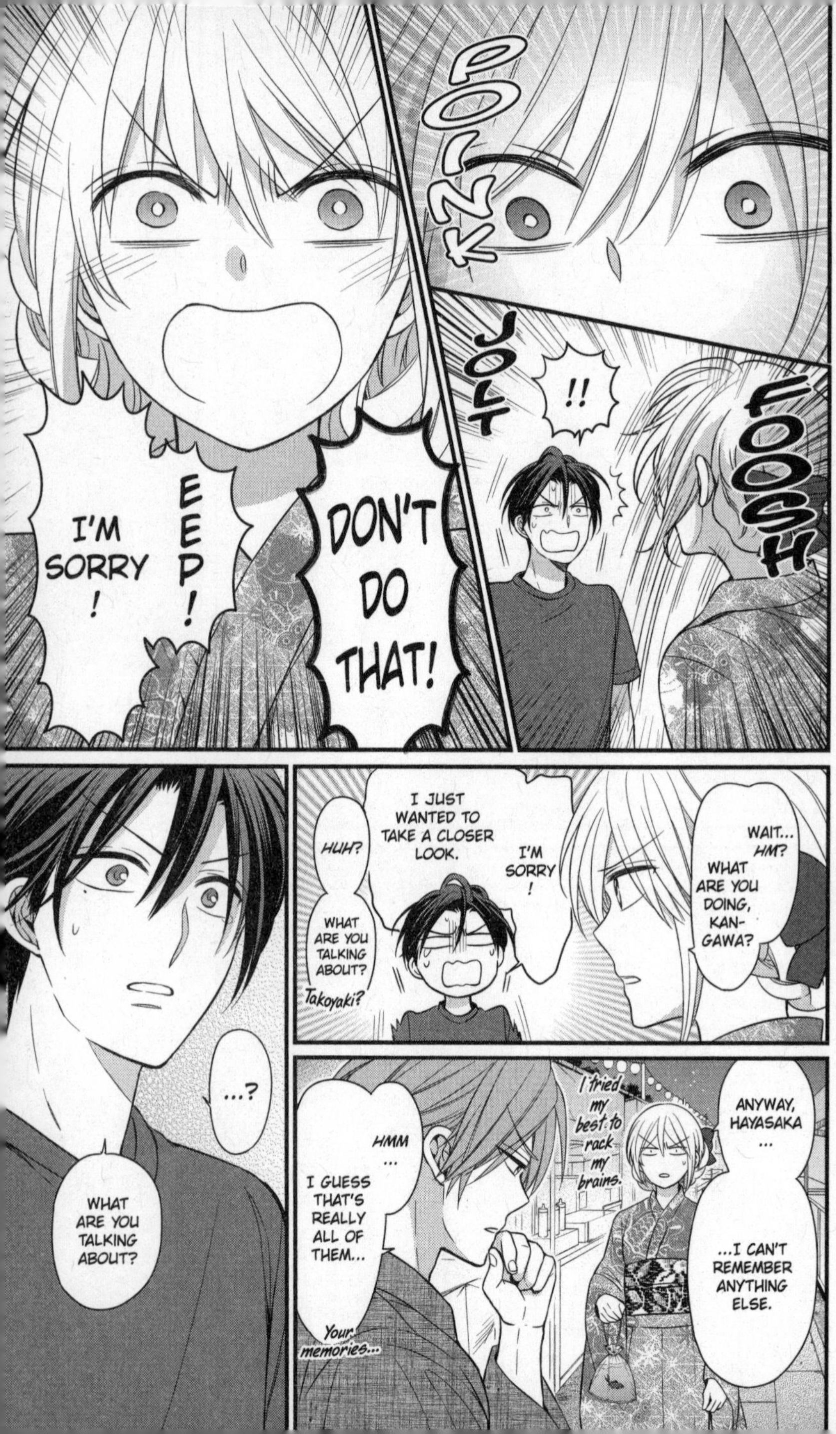
POINK
JOLT
!!
FOOSH
DON'T DO THAT!
EEP!
I'M SORRY!
WAIT... HM?
WHAT ARE YOU DOING, KAN-GAWA?
I'M SORRY!
I JUST WANTED TO TAKE A CLOSER LOOK.
HUH?
WHAT ARE YOU TALKING ABOUT?
Takoyaki?
ANYWAY, HAYASAKA ...
...I CAN'T REMEMBER ANYTHING ELSE.
I tried my best to rack my brains.
HMM ...
I GUESS THAT'S REALLY ALL OF THEM...
Your memories...
...?
WHAT ARE YOU TALKING ABOUT?

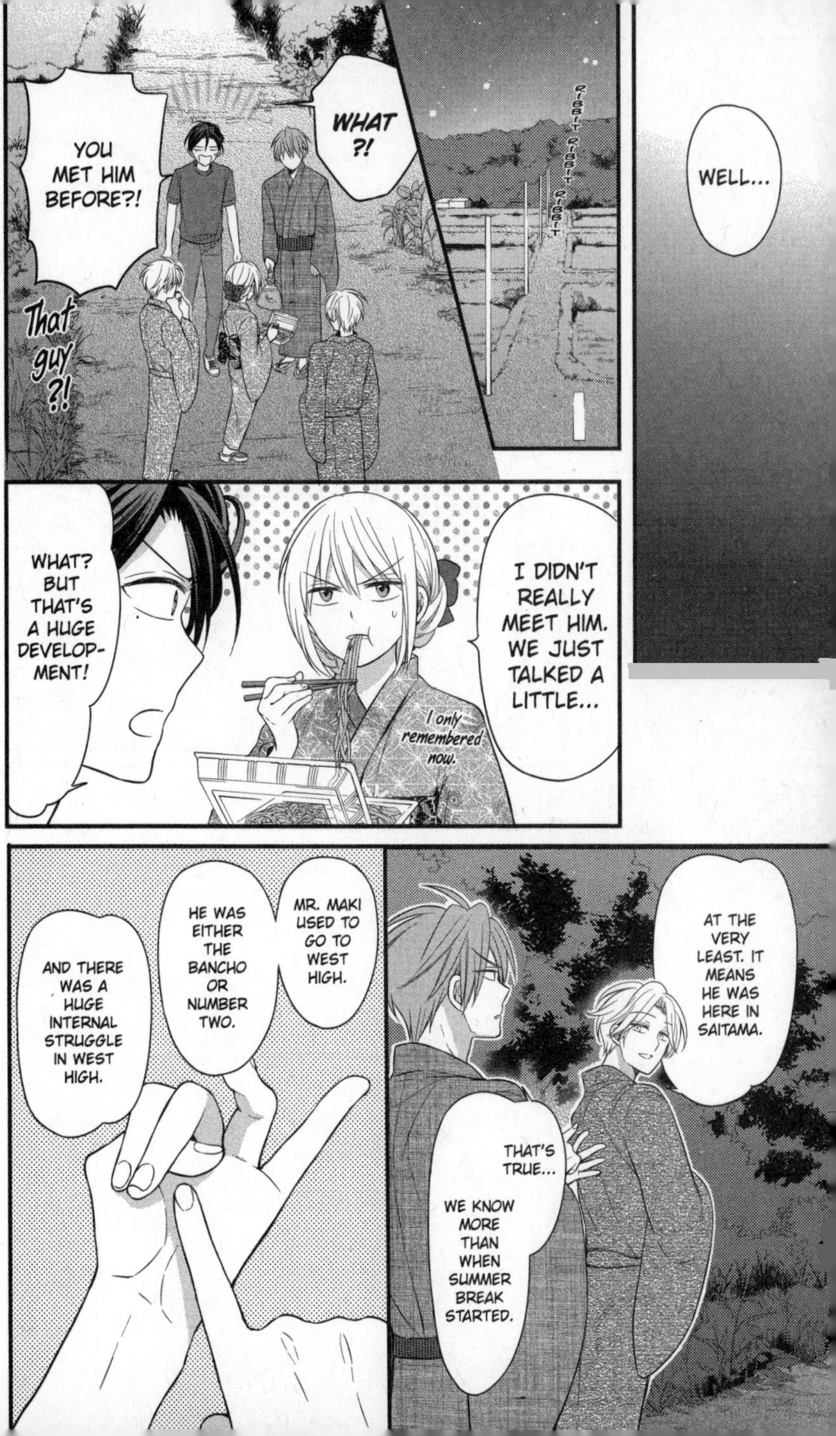
WELL...
RIBBIT RIBBIT RIBBIT
WHAT ?!
YOU MET HIM BEFORE?!
That guy ?!
I DIDN'T REALLY MEET HIM. WE JUST TALKED A LITTLE...
I only remembered now.
WHAT? BUT THAT'S A HUGE DEVELOPMENT!
AT THE VERY LEAST. IT MEANS HE WAS HERE IN SAITAMA.
THAT'S TRUE...
WE KNOW MORE THAN WHEN SUMMER BREAK STARTED.
MR. MAKI USED TO GO TO WEST HIGH.
HE WAS EITHER THE BANCHO OR NUMBER TWO.
AND THERE WAS A HUGE INTERNAL STRUGGLE IN WEST HIGH.

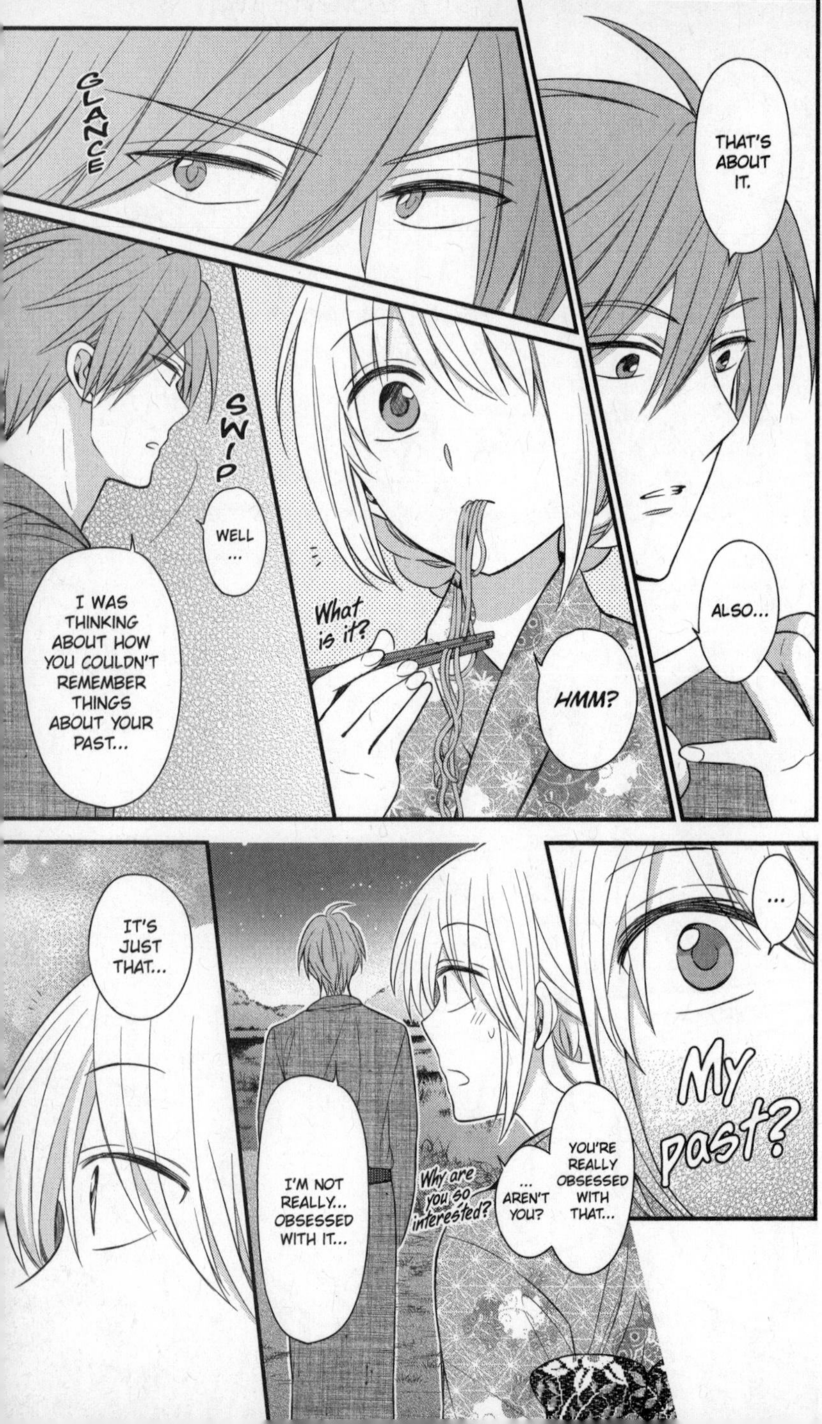
THAT'S ABOUT IT.
GLANCE
ALSO...
HMM?
What is it?
SWIP
WELL...
I WAS THINKING ABOUT HOW YOU COULDN'T REMEMBER THINGS ABOUT YOUR PAST...
...
My past?
YOU'RE REALLY OBSESSED WITH THAT...
... AREN'T YOU?
Why are you so interested?
I'M NOT REALLY... OBSESSED WITH IT...
IT'S JUST THAT...

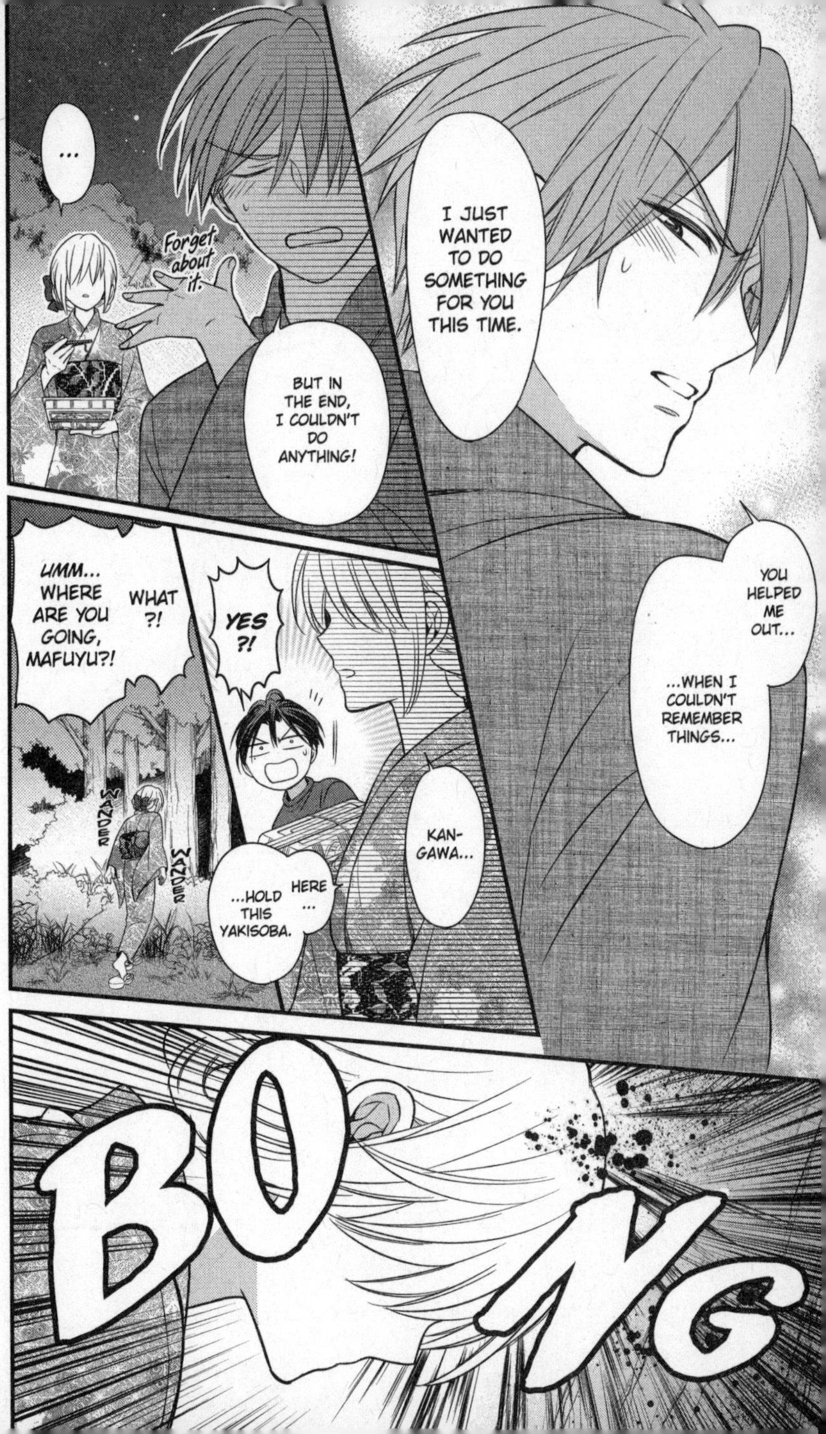
I JUST WANTED TO DO SOMETHING FOR YOU THIS TIME.
YOU HELPED ME OUT...
...WHEN I COULDN'T REMEMBER THINGS...
BUT IN THE END, I COULDN'T DO ANYTHING!
Forget about it.
...
KAN-GAWA...
HERE...
...HOLD THIS YAKISOBA.
YES?!
WHAT?!
UMM... WHERE ARE YOU GOING, MAFUYU?!
WANDER
WANDER
BOING

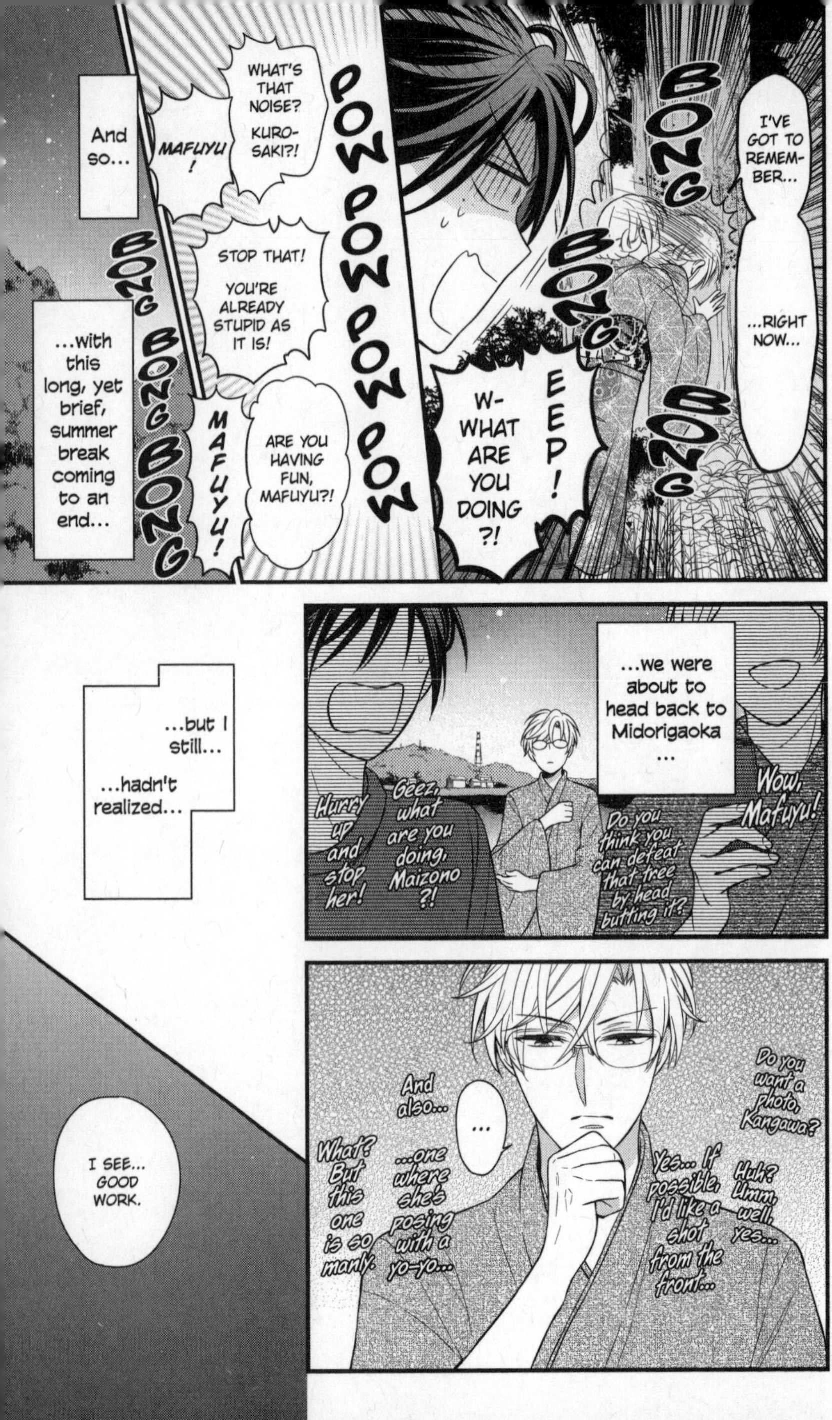
I'VE GOT TO REMEMBER...
...RIGHT NOW...
BONG BONG BONG
EEP!
W-WHAT ARE YOU DOING?!
POW POW POW POW
WHAT'S THAT NOISE? KURO-SAKI?!
MAFUYU!
STOP THAT! YOU'RE ALREADY STUPID AS IT IS!
ARE YOU HAVING FUN, MAFUYU?!
MAFUYU!
BONG BONG BONG
And so...
...with this long, yet brief, summer break coming to an end...
...we were about to head back to Midorigaoka...
Wow, Mafuyu!
Do you think you can defeat that tree by head butting it?
Geez, what are you doing, Maizono?!
Hurry up and stop her!
...but I still...
...hadn't realized...
Do you want a photo, Kangawa?
Huh? Umm, well, yes...
Yes... If possible, I'd like a shot from the front...
...
And also...
...one where she's posing with a yo-yo...
What? But this one is so manly.
I SEE... GOOD WORK.

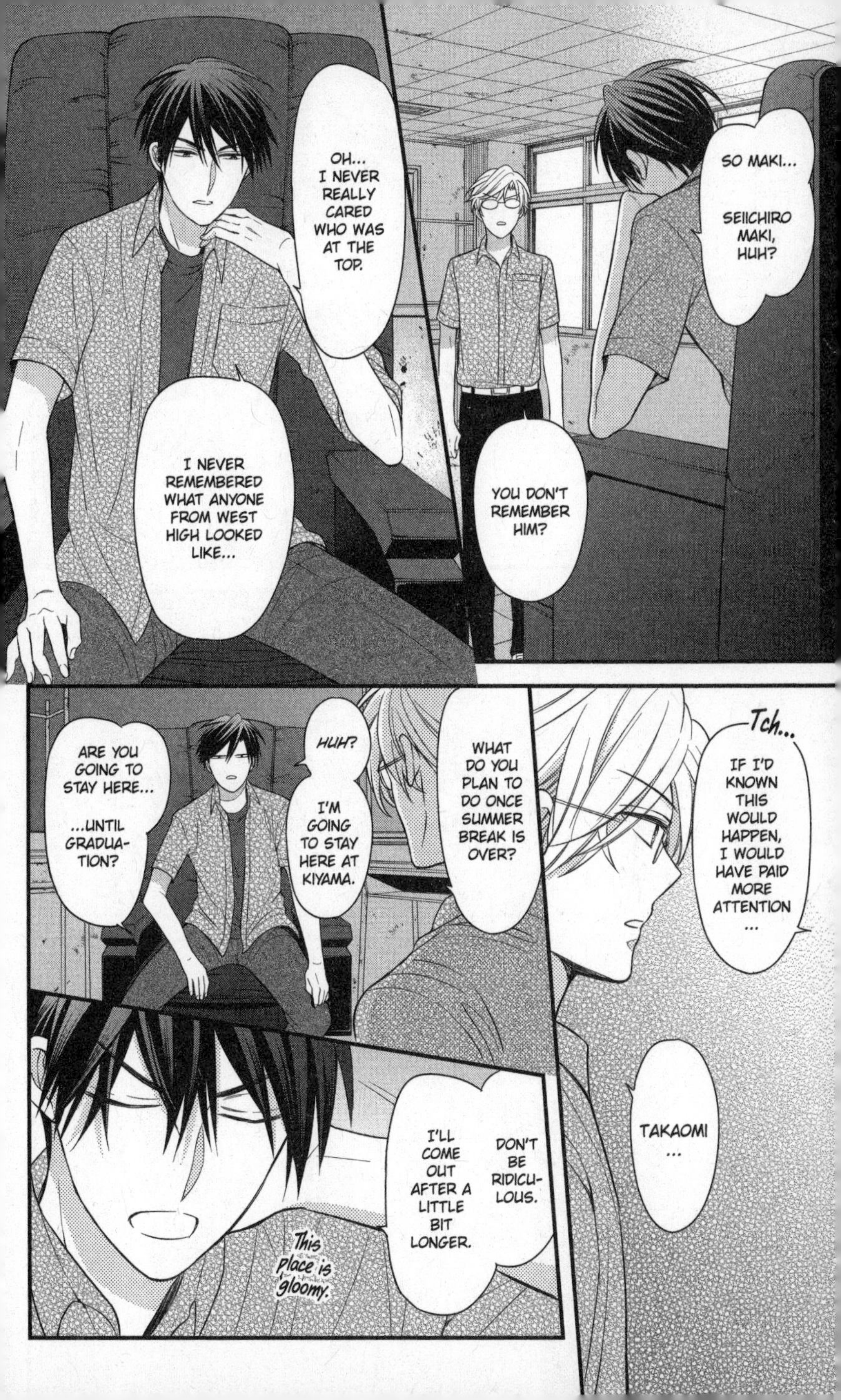
SO MAKI...
SEIICHIRO MAKI, HUH?
YOU DON'T REMEMBER HIM?
OH... I NEVER REALLY CARED WHO WAS AT THE TOP.
I NEVER REMEMBERED WHAT ANYONE FROM WEST HIGH LOOKED LIKE...
Tch...
IF I'D KNOWN THIS WOULD HAPPEN, I WOULD HAVE PAID MORE ATTENTION...
TAKAOMI...
WHAT DO YOU PLAN TO DO ONCE SUMMER BREAK IS OVER?
HUH?
I'M GOING TO STAY HERE AT KIYAMA.
ARE YOU GOING TO STAY HERE...
...UNTIL GRADUA-TION?
DON'T BE RIDICU-LOUS.
I'LL COME OUT AFTER A LITTLE BIT LONGER.
This place is gloomy.

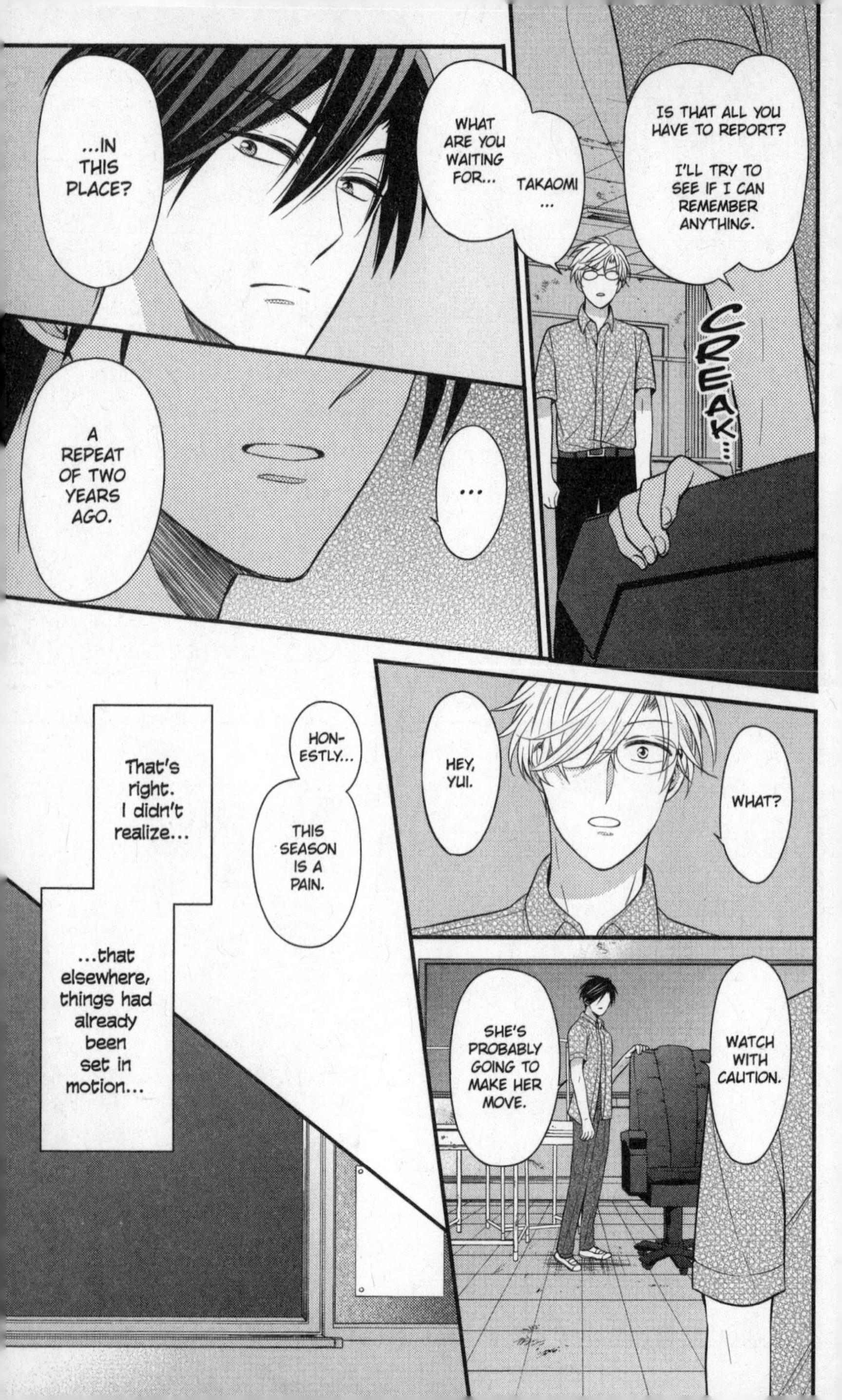
IS THAT ALL YOU HAVE TO REPORT?
I'LL TRY TO SEE IF I CAN REMEMBER ANYTHING.
CREAK...
WHAT ARE YOU WAITING FOR...
TAKAOMI...
...IN THIS PLACE?
...
A REPEAT OF TWO YEARS AGO.
WHAT?
HEY, YUI.
HON-ESTLY...
THIS SEASON IS A PAIN.
WATCH WITH CAUTION.
SHE'S PROBABLY GOING TO MAKE HER MOVE.
That's right. I didn't realize...
...that elsewhere, things had already been set in motion...

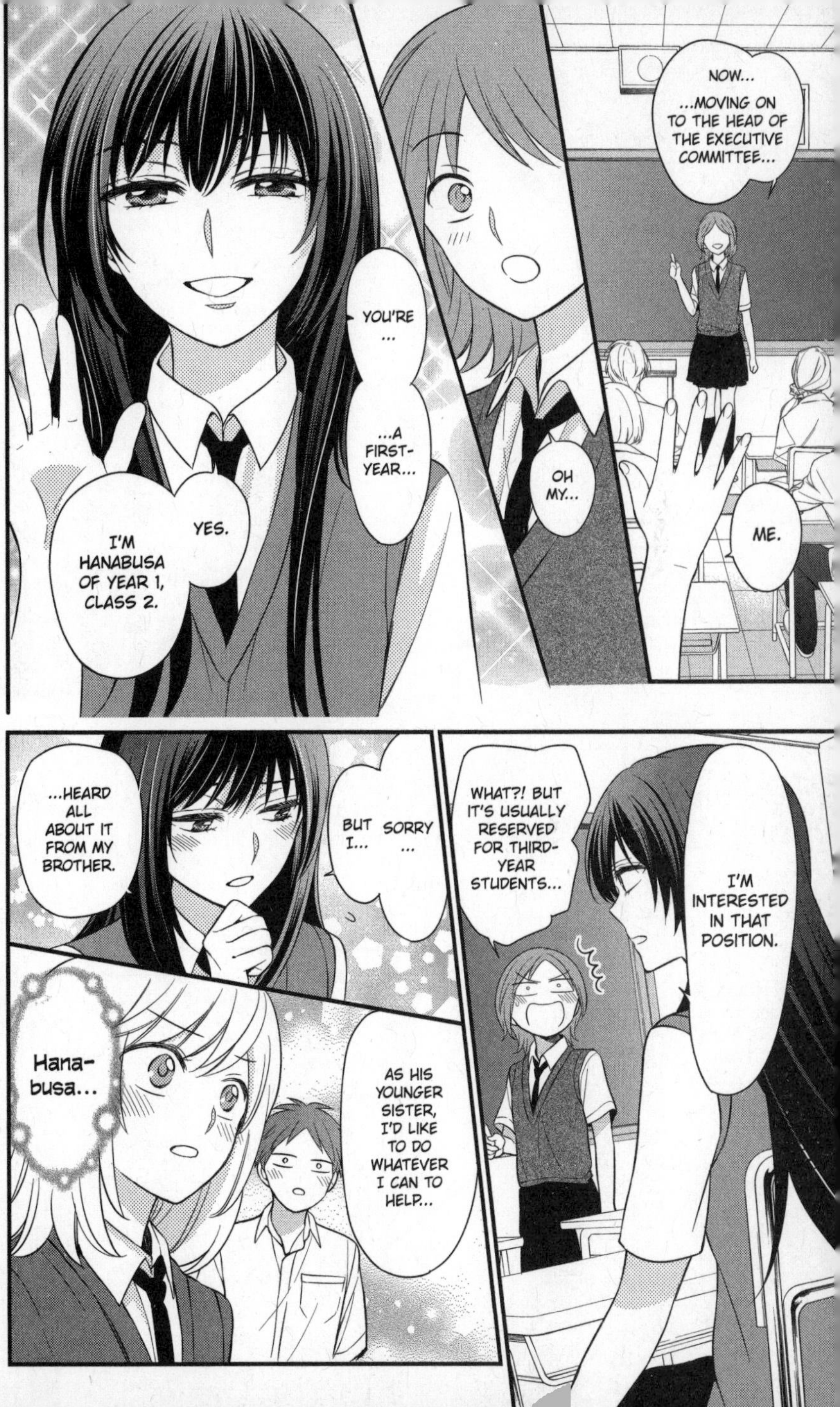
NOW...
...MOVING ON TO THE HEAD OF THE EXECUTIVE COMMITTEE...
ME.
OH MY...
YOU'RE ...
...A FIRST-YEAR...
YES.
I'M HANABUSA OF YEAR 1, CLASS 2.
I'M INTERESTED IN THAT POSITION.
WHAT?! BUT IT'S USUALLY RESERVED FOR THIRD-YEAR STUDENTS...
SORRY ...
BUT I...
...HEARD ALL ABOUT IT FROM MY BROTHER.
AS HIS YOUNGER SISTER, I'D LIKE TO DO WHATEVER I CAN TO HELP...
Hana-busa...

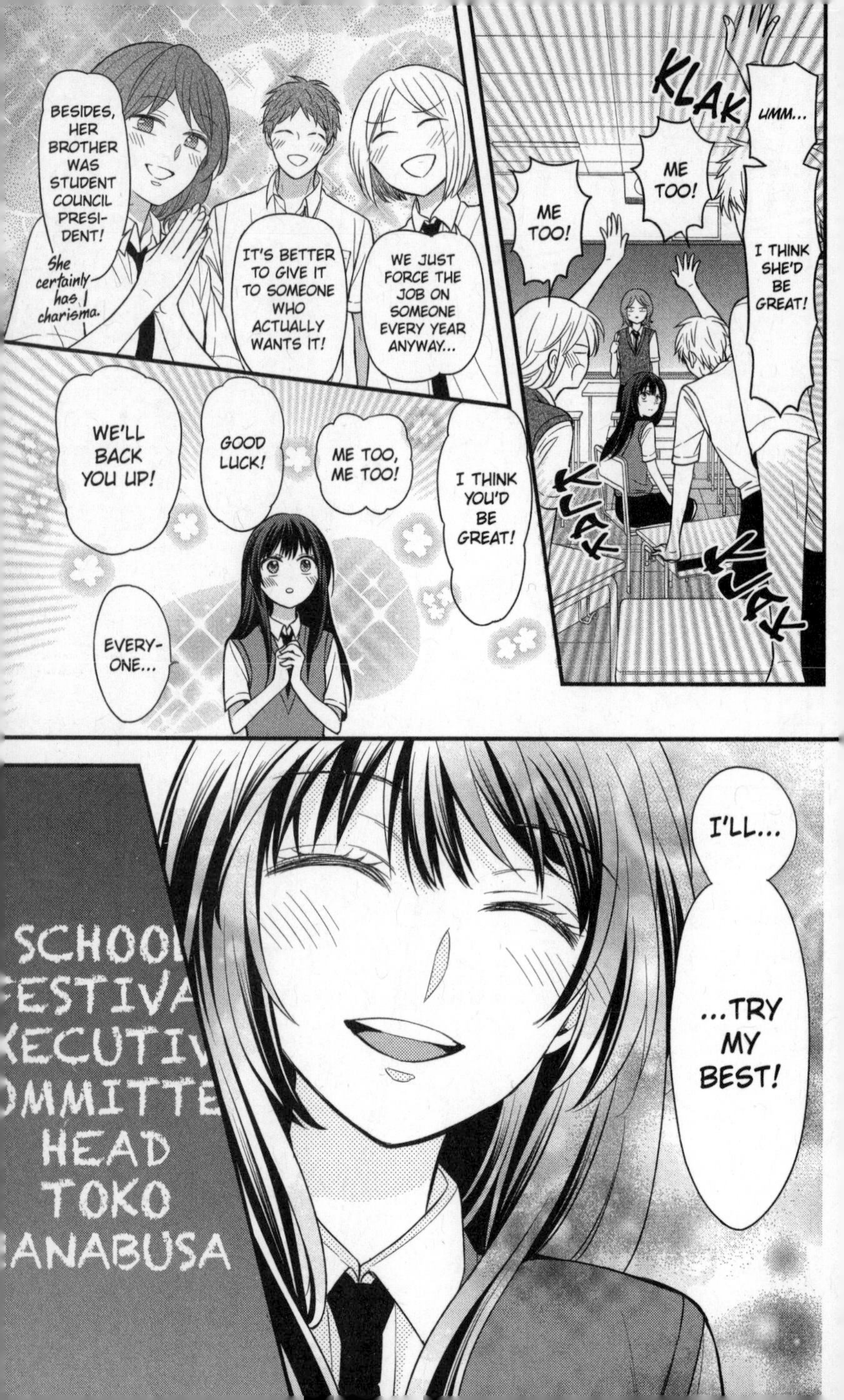

KLAK
UMM...
I THINK SHE'D BE GREAT!
ME TOO!
ME TOO!
KLAK
KLAK
WE JUST FORCE THE JOB ON SOMEONE EVERY YEAR ANYWAY...
IT'S BETTER TO GIVE IT TO SOMEONE WHO ACTUALLY WANTS IT!
BESIDES, HER BROTHER WAS STUDENT COUNCIL PRESI-DENT!
She certainly has charisma.
I THINK YOU'D BE GREAT!
ME TOO, ME TOO!
GOOD LUCK!
WE'LL BACK YOU UP!
EVERY-ONE...
I'LL...
...TRY MY BEST!
SCHOO
ESTIVA
ECUTIV
OMMITTE
HEAD
TOKO
ANABUSA

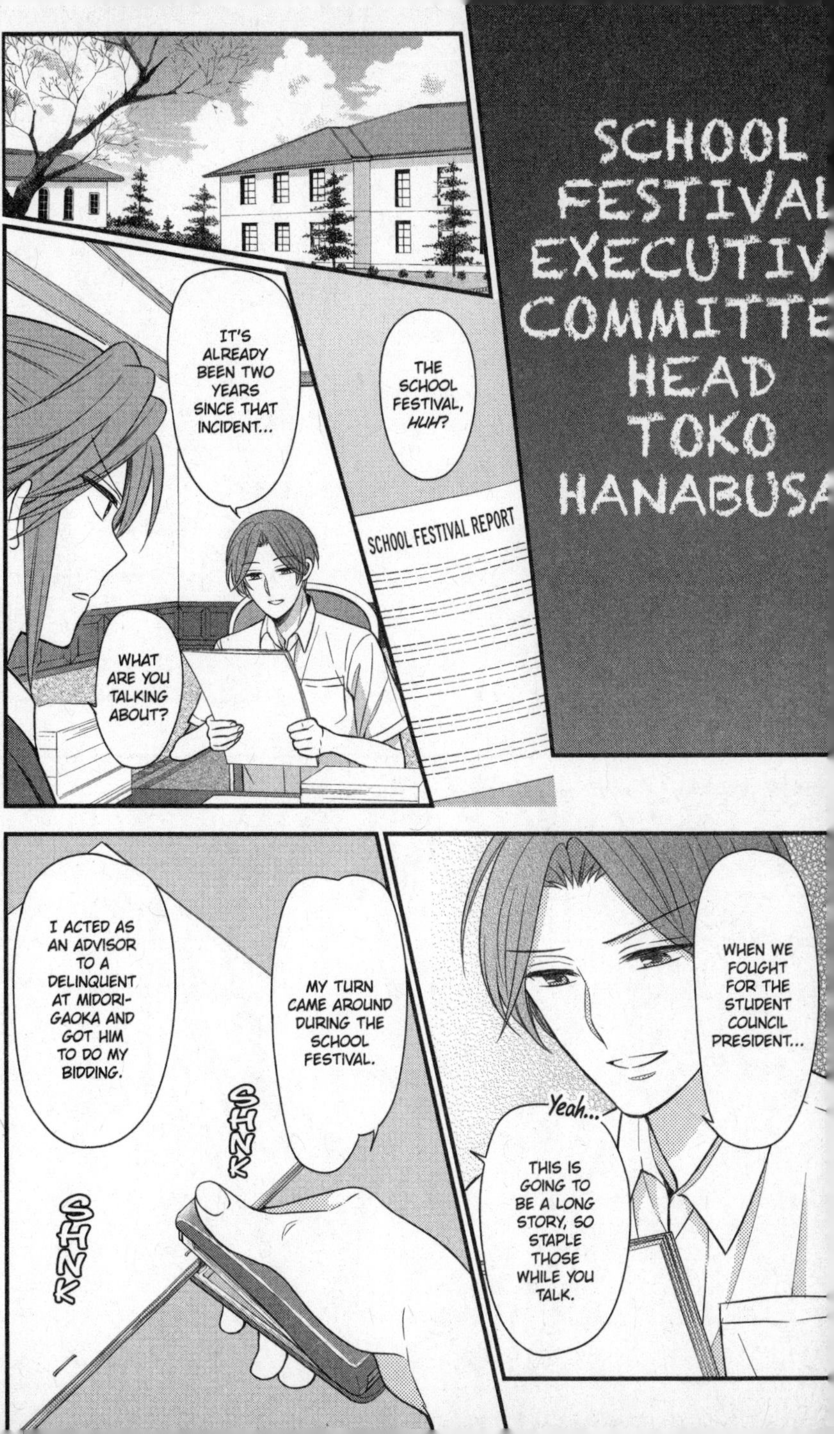
SCHOOL FESTIVAL EXECUTIV COMMITTE HEAD TOKO HANABUSA
THE SCHOOL FESTIVAL, *HUH?*
IT'S ALREADY BEEN TWO YEARS SINCE THAT INCIDENT...
SCHOOL FESTIVAL REPORT
WHAT ARE YOU TALKING ABOUT?
WHEN WE FOUGHT FOR THE STUDENT COUNCIL PRESIDENT...
Yeah...
THIS IS GOING TO BE A LONG STORY, SO STAPLE THOSE WHILE YOU TALK.
MY TURN CAME AROUND DURING THE SCHOOL FESTIVAL.
I ACTED AS AN ADVISOR TO A DELINQUENT AT MIDORI-GAOKA AND GOT HIM TO DO MY BIDDING.
SHNK
SHNK

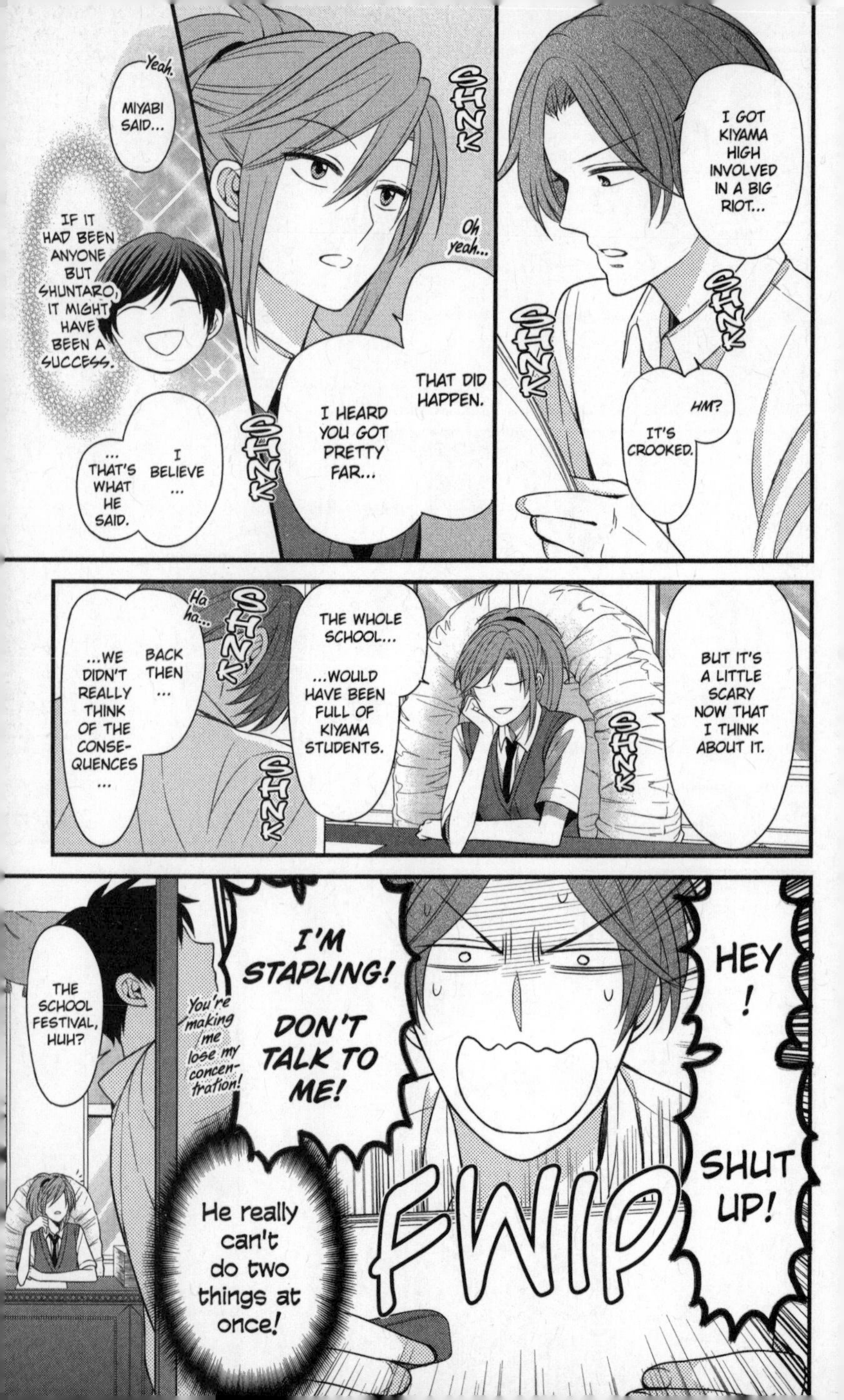
I GOT KIYAMA HIGH INVOLVED IN A BIG RIOT...
SHNK
SHNK
HM?
IT'S CROOKED.
SHNK
Oh yeah...
THAT DID HAPPEN.
I HEARD YOU GOT PRETTY FAR...
SHNK
Yeah.
MIYABI SAID...
IF IT HAD BEEN ANYONE BUT SHUNTARO, IT MIGHT HAVE BEEN A SUCCESS.
I BELIEVE...
...THAT'S WHAT HE SAID.
BUT IT'S A LITTLE SCARY NOW THAT I THINK ABOUT IT.
SHNK
THE WHOLE SCHOOL...
...WOULD HAVE BEEN FULL OF KIYAMA STUDENTS.
SHNK
Ha ha...
BACK THEN...
...WE DIDN'T REALLY THINK OF THE CONSEQUENCES...
SHNK
HEY!
SHUT UP!
I'M STAPLING!
DON'T TALK TO ME!
You're making me lose my concentration!
FWIP
He really can't do two things at once!
THE SCHOOL FESTIVAL, HUH?

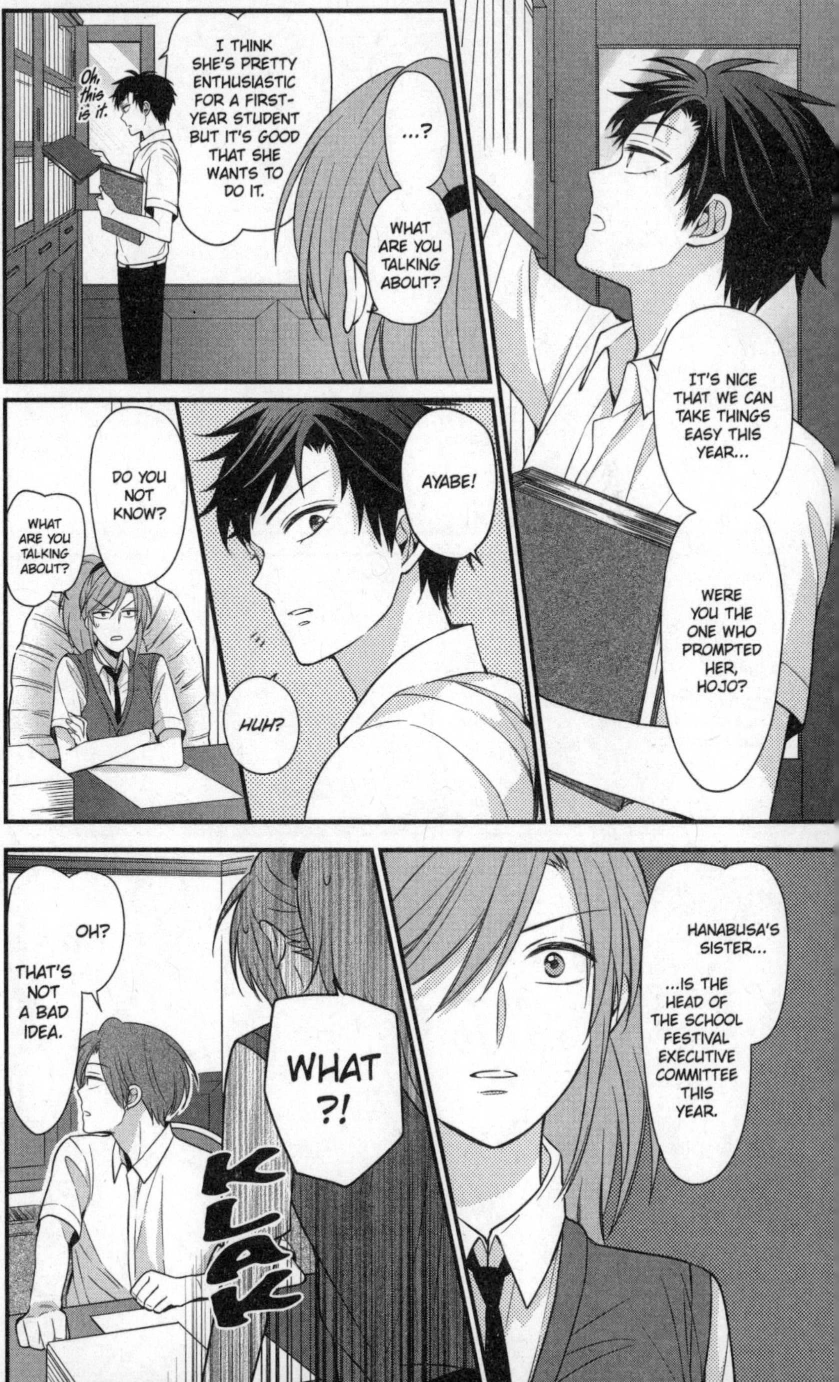
IT'S NICE THAT WE CAN TAKE THINGS EASY THIS YEAR...
WERE YOU THE ONE WHO PROMPTED HER, HOJO?
...?
WHAT ARE YOU TALKING ABOUT?
Oh, this is it.
I THINK SHE'S PRETTY ENTHUSIASTIC FOR A FIRST-YEAR STUDENT BUT IT'S GOOD THAT SHE WANTS TO DO IT.
AYABE!
HUH?
DO YOU NOT KNOW?
WHAT ARE YOU TALKING ABOUT?
HANABUSA'S SISTER...
...IS THE HEAD OF THE SCHOOL FESTIVAL EXECUTIVE COMMITTEE THIS YEAR.
WHAT ?!
KLAK
OH?
THAT'S NOT A BAD IDEA.

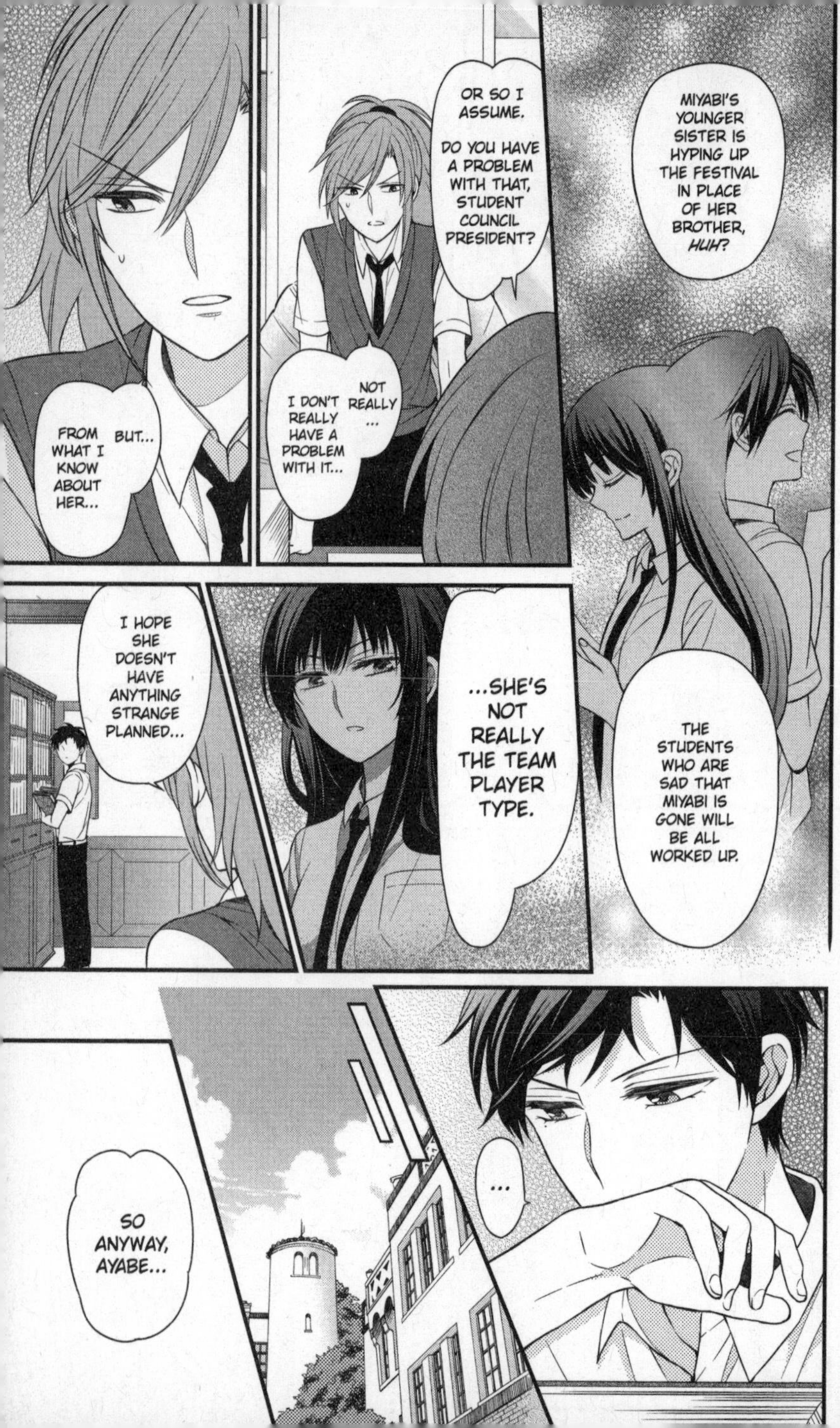
MIYABI'S YOUNGER SISTER IS HYPING UP THE FESTIVAL IN PLACE OF HER BROTHER, *HUH?*
THE STUDENTS WHO ARE SAD THAT MIYABI IS GONE WILL BE ALL WORKED UP.
OR SO I ASSUME.
DO YOU HAVE A PROBLEM WITH THAT, STUDENT COUNCIL PRESIDENT?
NOT REALLY...
I DON'T REALLY HAVE A PROBLEM WITH IT...
BUT...
FROM WHAT I KNOW ABOUT HER...
...SHE'S NOT REALLY THE TEAM PLAYER TYPE.
I HOPE SHE DOESN'T HAVE ANYTHING STRANGE PLANNED...
...
SO ANYWAY, AYABE...

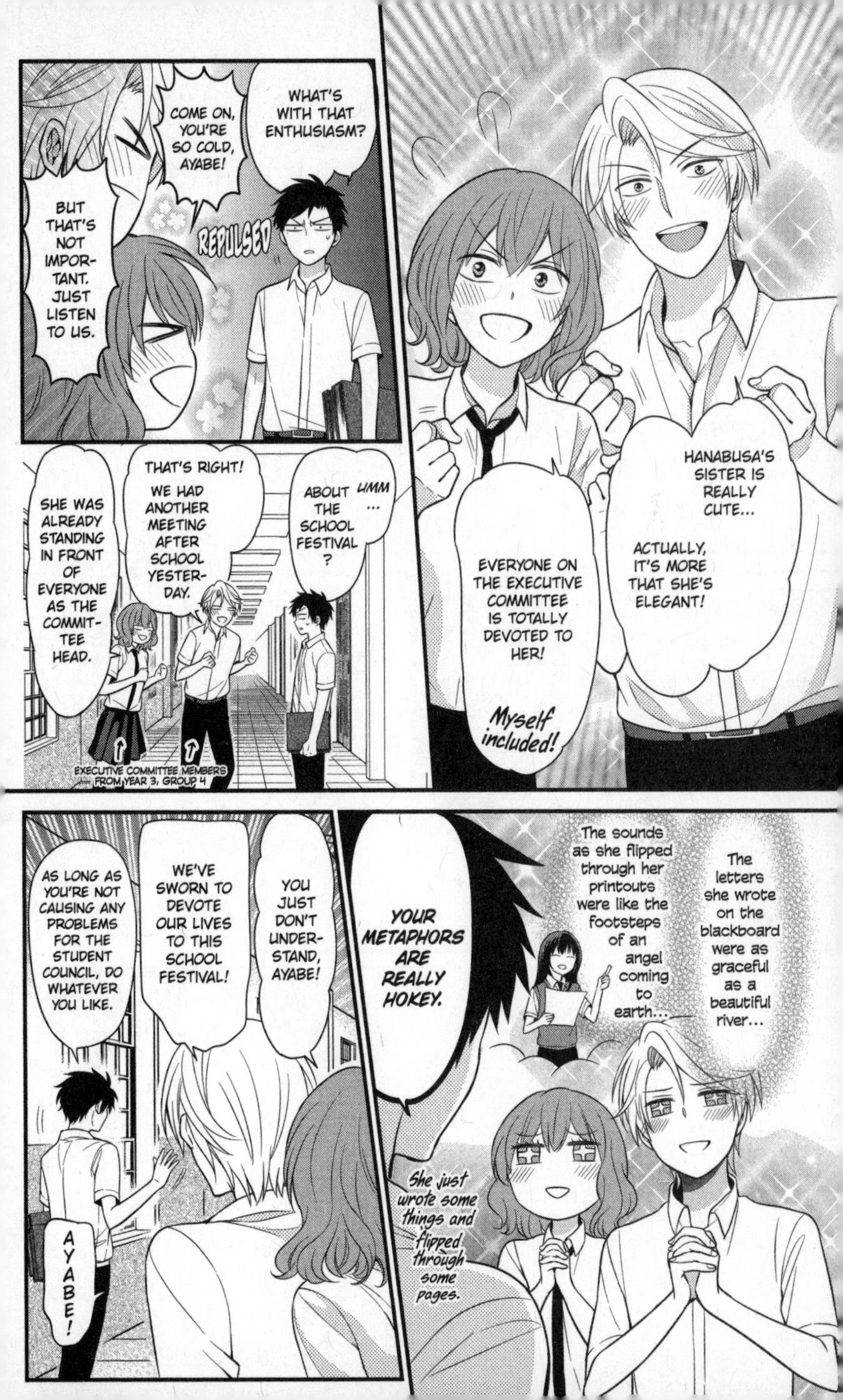
HANABUSA'S SISTER IS REALLY CUTE...
ACTUALLY, IT'S MORE THAT SHE'S ELEGANT!
EVERYONE ON THE EXECUTIVE COMMITTEE IS TOTALLY DEVOTED TO HER!
Myself included!
WHAT'S WITH THAT ENTHUSIASM?
COME ON, YOU'RE SO COLD, AYABE!
REPULSED
BUT THAT'S NOT IMPOR-TANT. JUST LISTEN TO US.
UMM ...
ABOUT THE SCHOOL FESTIVAL?
THAT'S RIGHT!
WE HAD ANOTHER MEETING AFTER SCHOOL YESTER-DAY.
SHE WAS ALREADY STANDING IN FRONT OF EVERYONE AS THE COMMIT-TEE HEAD.
EXECUTIVE COMMITTEE MEMBERS FROM YEAR 3, GROUP 4
The letters she wrote on the blackboard were as graceful as a beautiful river...
The sounds as she flipped through her printouts were like the footsteps of an angel coming to earth...
YOUR METAPHORS ARE REALLY HOKEY.
She just wrote some things and flipped through some pages.
YOU JUST DON'T UNDER-STAND, AYABE!
WE'VE SWORN TO DEVOTE OUR LIVES TO THIS SCHOOL FESTIVAL!
AS LONG AS YOU'RE NOT CAUSING ANY PROBLEMS FOR THE STUDENT COUNCIL, DO WHATEVER YOU LIKE.
AYABE!

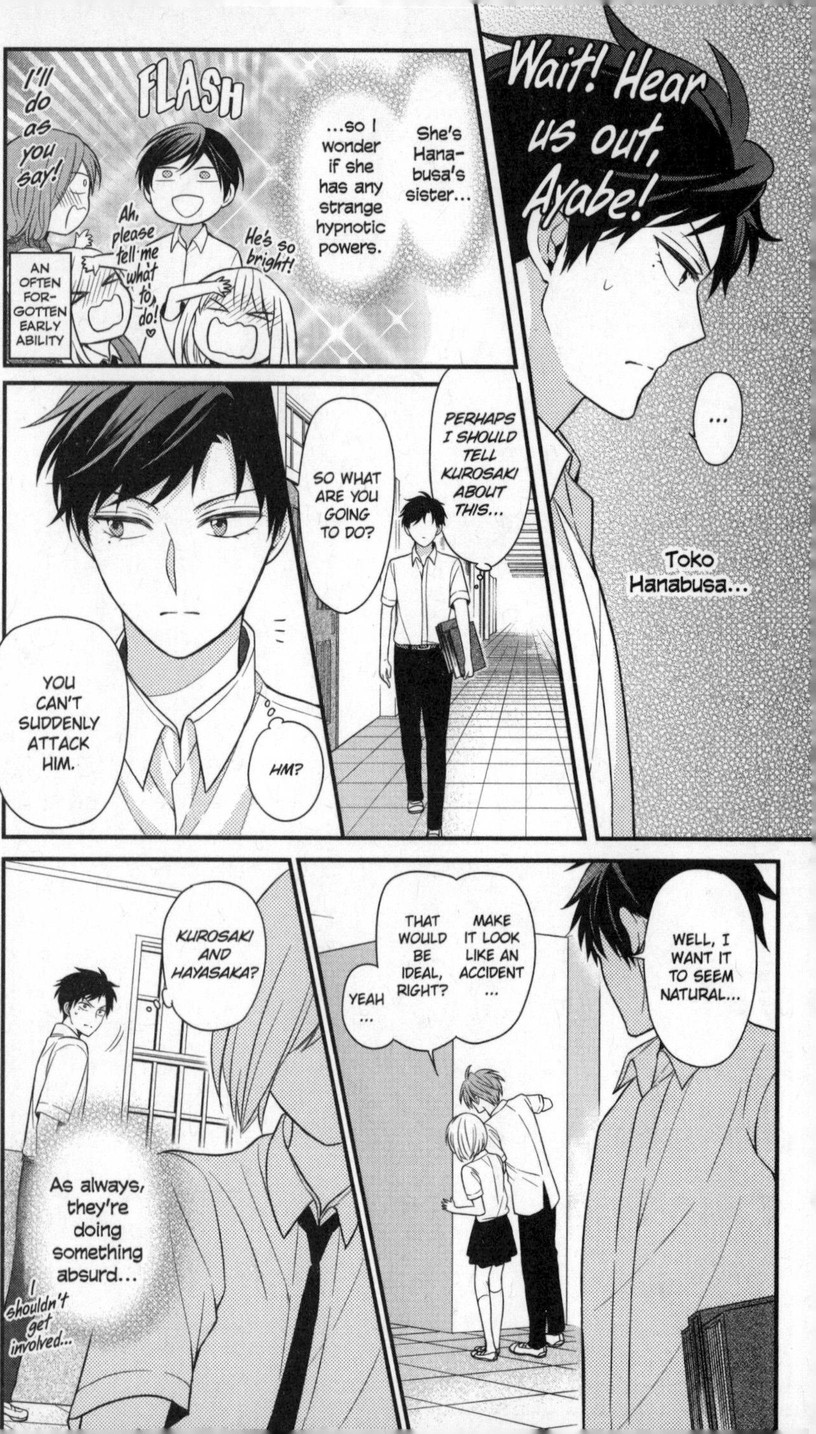
Wait! Hear us out, Ayabe!
...
Toko Hanabusa...
She's Hanabusa's sister...
...so I wonder if she has any strange hypnotic powers.
FLASH
He's so bright!
Ah, please tell me what to do!
I'll do as you say!
AN OFTEN FORGOTTEN EARLY ABILITY
PERHAPS I SHOULD TELL KUROSAKI ABOUT THIS...
SO WHAT ARE YOU GOING TO DO?
HM?
YOU CAN'T SUDDENLY ATTACK HIM.
WELL, I WANT IT TO SEEM NATURAL...
MAKE IT LOOK LIKE AN ACCIDENT...
THAT WOULD BE IDEAL, RIGHT?
YEAH...
KUROSAKI AND HAYASAKA?
As always, they're doing something absurd...
I shouldn't get involved...

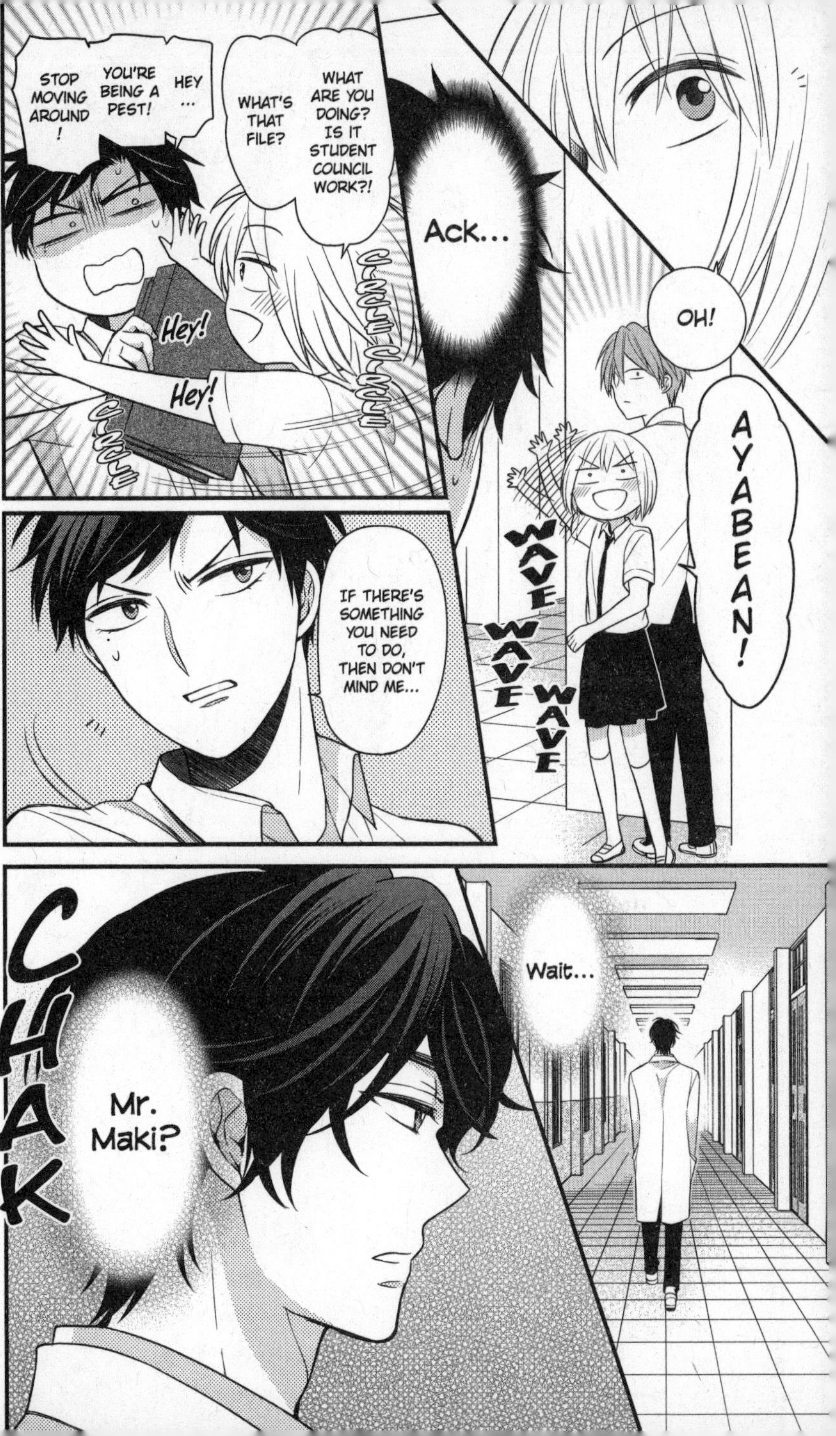
OH!
AYABEAN!
WAVE WAVE WAVE WAVE
Ack...
WHAT ARE YOU DOING? IS IT STUDENT COUNCIL WORK?!
WHAT'S THAT FILE?
HEY ...
YOU'RE BEING A PEST!
STOP MOVING AROUND!
CIRCLE CIRCLE
Hey!
Hey!
CIRCLE
IF THERE'S SOMETHING YOU NEED TO DO, THEN DON'T MIND ME...
Wait...
Mr. Maki?
CHAK

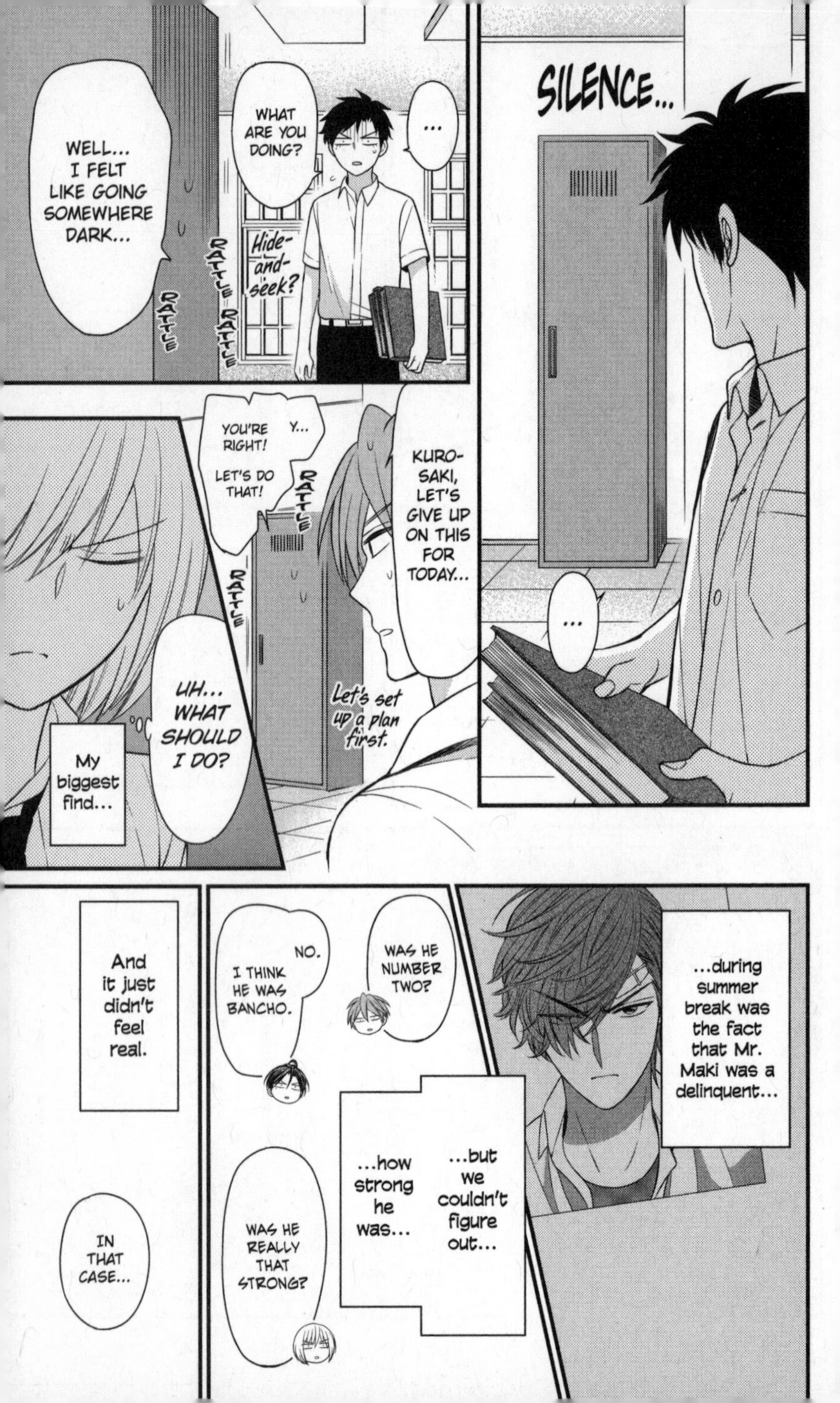
SILENCE...
...
...
WHAT ARE YOU DOING?
Hide-and-seek?
RATTLE RATTLE
RATTLE
WELL... I FELT LIKE GOING SOMEWHERE DARK...
KURO-SAKI, LET'S GIVE UP ON THIS FOR TODAY...
Let's set up a plan first.
Y...
YOU'RE RIGHT!
LET'S DO THAT!
RATTLE
RATTLE
UH... WHAT SHOULD I DO?
My biggest find...
...during summer break was the fact that Mr. Maki was a delinquent...
...but we couldn't figure out...
...how strong he was...
WAS HE NUMBER TWO?
NO.
I THINK HE WAS BANCHO.
WAS HE REALLY THAT STRONG?
And it just didn't feel real.
IN THAT CASE...

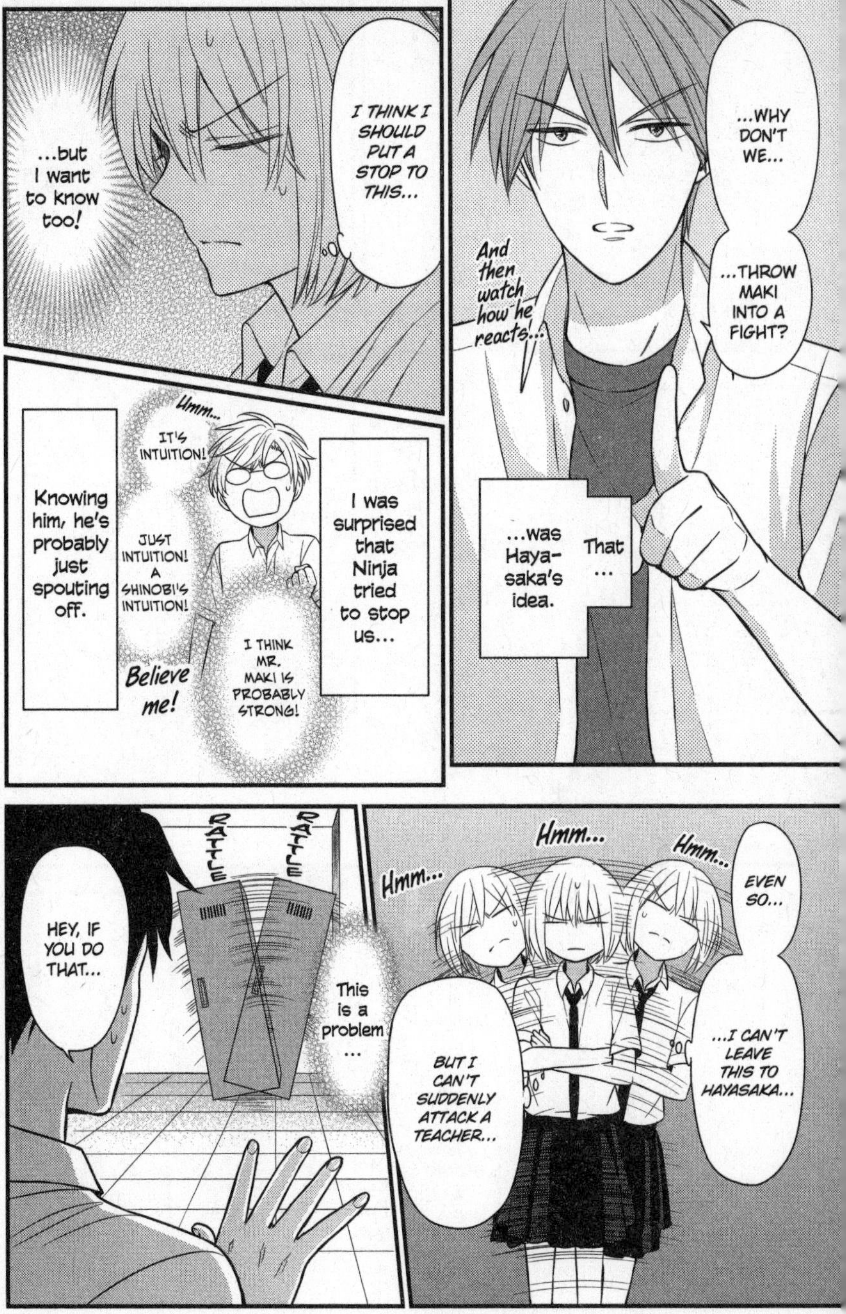
...WHY DON'T WE...
...THROW MAKI INTO A FIGHT?
And then watch how he reacts!...
That...
...was Haya-saka's idea.
I THINK I SHOULD PUT A STOP TO THIS...
...but I want to know too!
I was surprised that Ninja tried to stop us...
Umm...
IT'S INTUITION!
JUST INTUITION! A SHINOBI'S INTUITION!
I THINK MR. MAKI IS PROBABLY STRONG!
Believe me!
Knowing him, he's probably just spouting off.
Hmm...
Hmm...
Hmm...
EVEN SO...
...I CAN'T LEAVE THIS TO HAYASAKA...
BUT I CAN'T SUDDENLY ATTACK A TEACHER...
RATTLE
RATTLE
This is a problem...
HEY, IF YOU DO THAT...

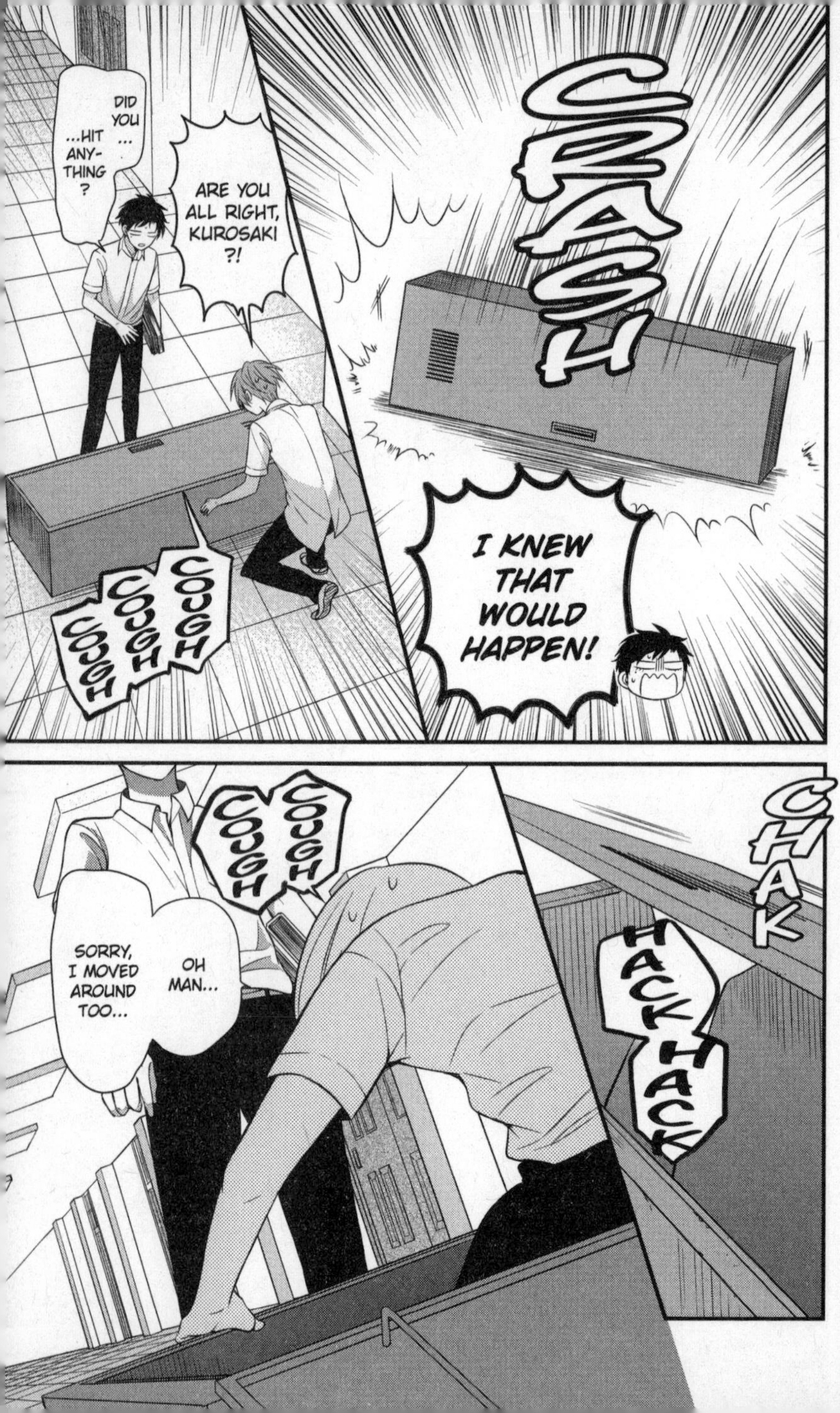
CRASH
I KNEW THAT WOULD HAPPEN!
ARE YOU ALL RIGHT, KUROSAKI?!
DID YOU... ...HIT ANYTHING?
COUGH COUGH COUGH
CHAK
HACK HACK HACK
COUGH COUGH
OH MAN...
SORRY, I MOVED AROUND TOO...

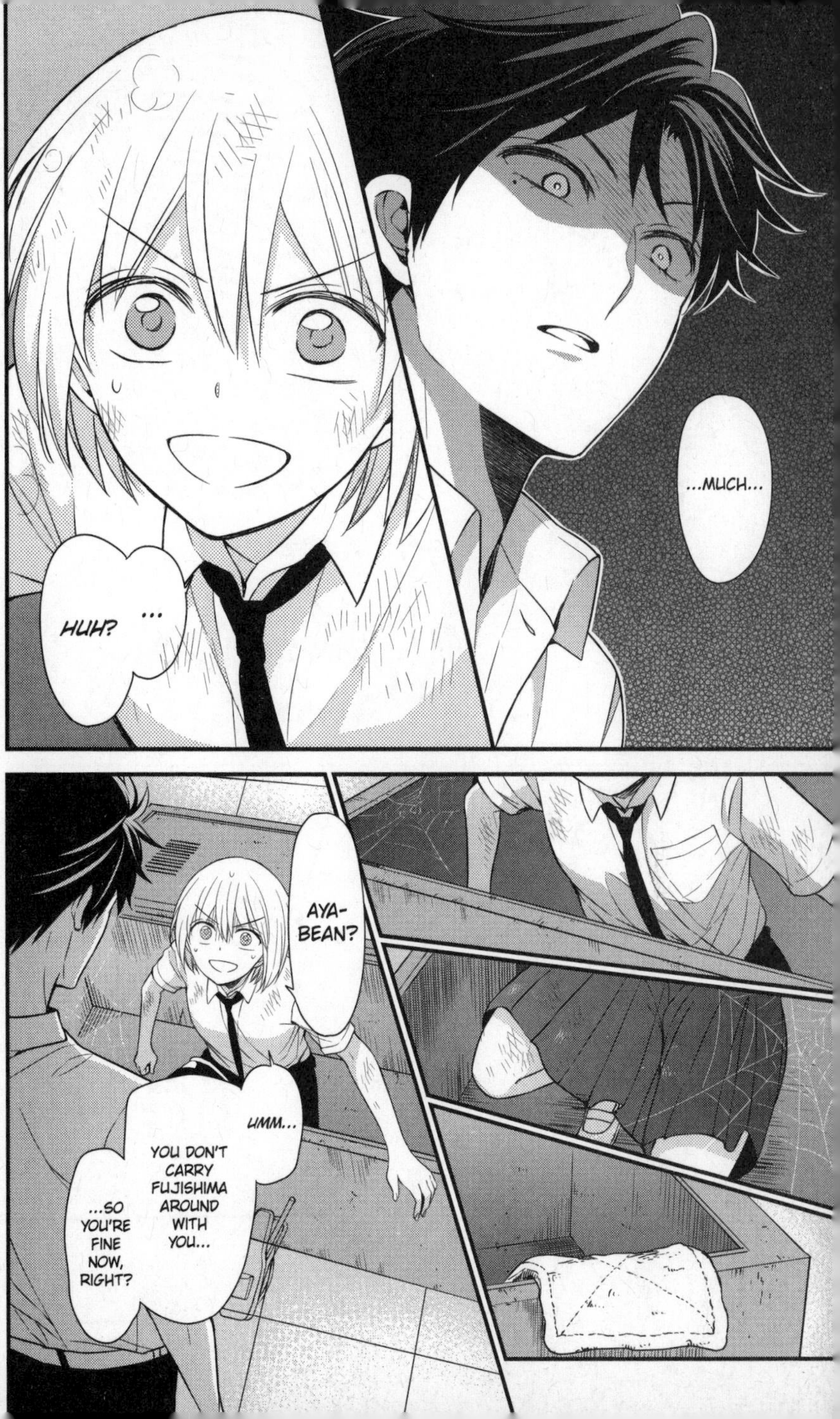
...MUCH...
... HUH?
AYA-BEAN?
UMM...
YOU DON'T CARRY FUJISHIMA AROUND WITH YOU...
...SO YOU'RE FINE NOW, RIGHT?

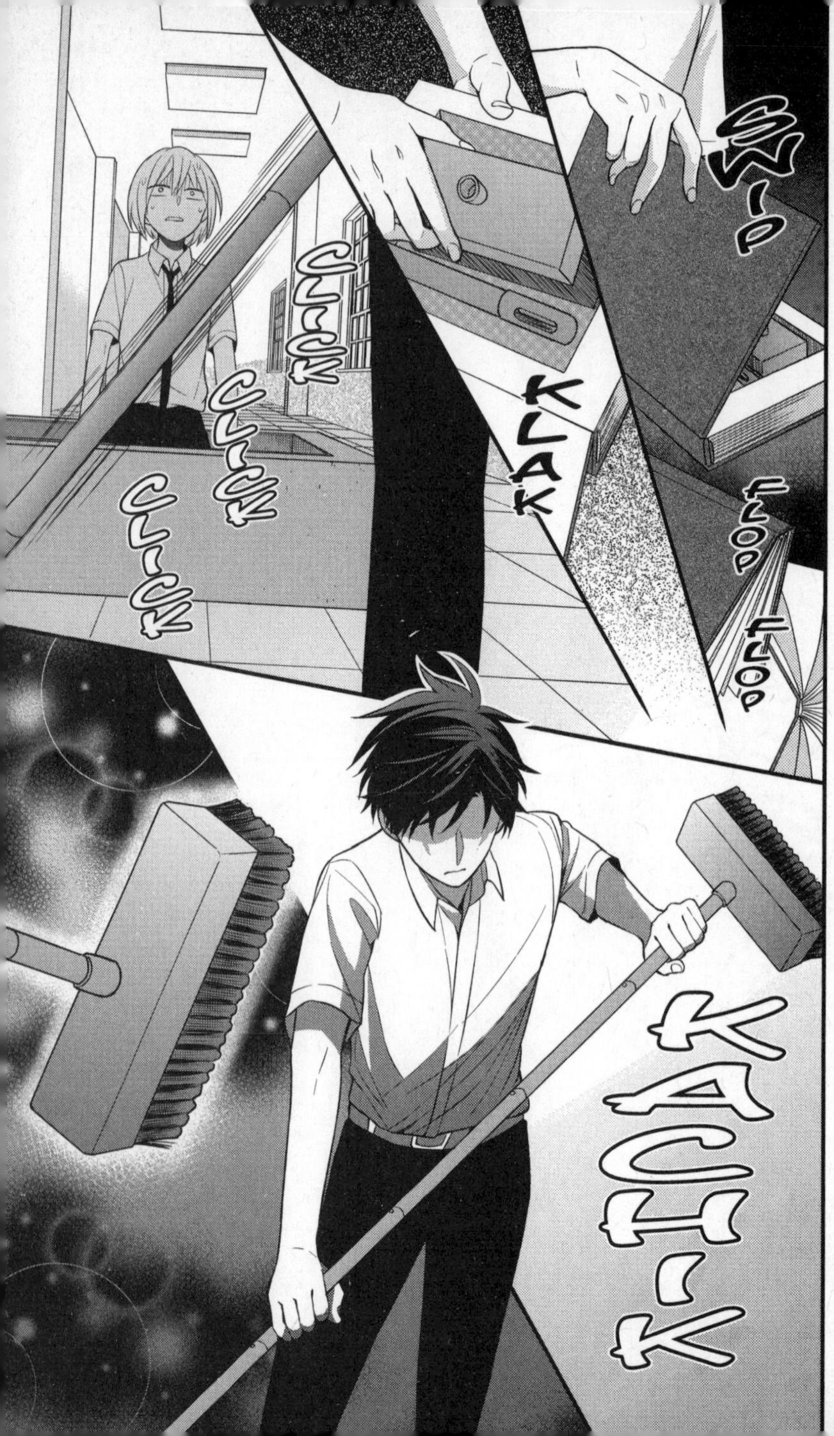
SWIP
KLAK
FLOP
FLOP
CLICK
CLICK
CLICK
KACHIK

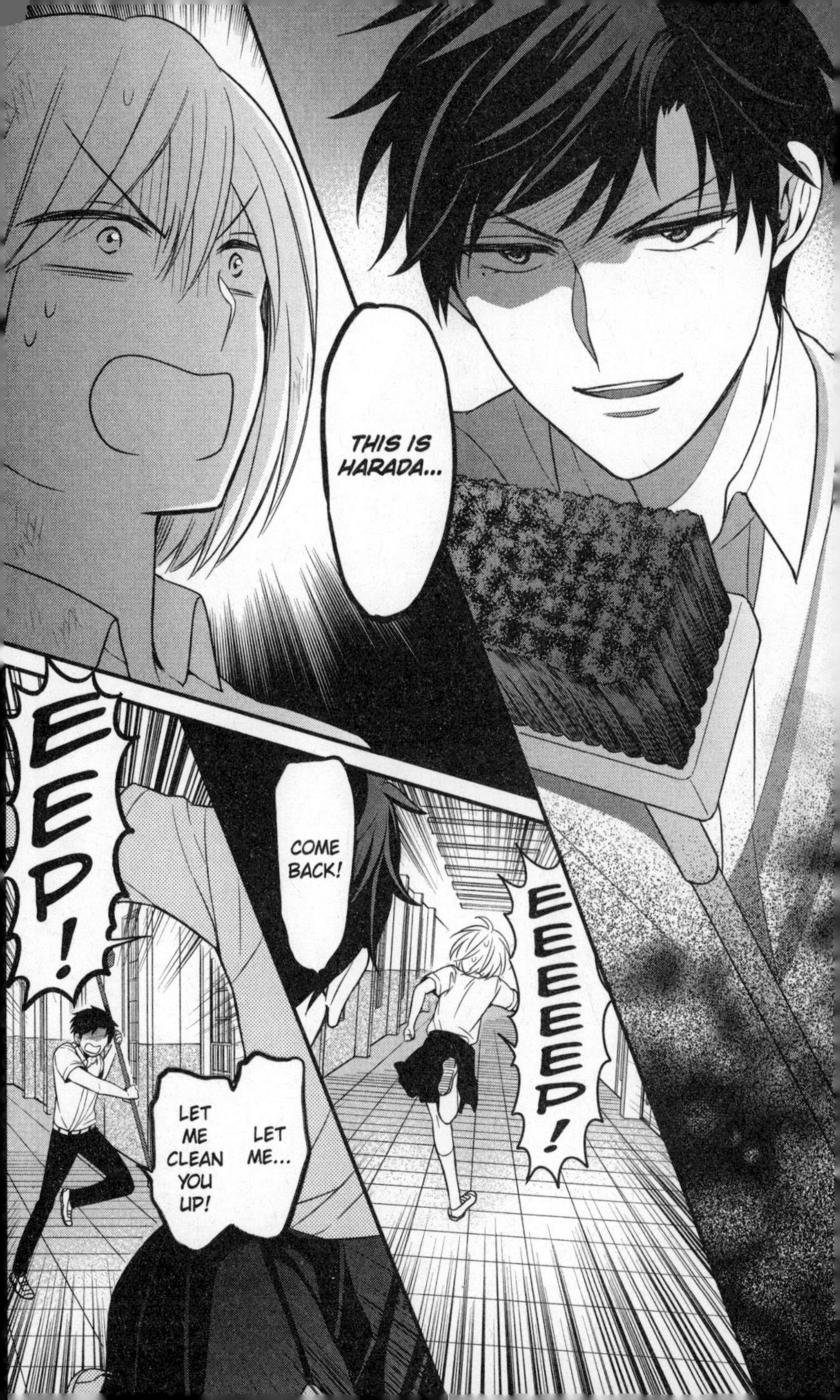
THIS IS HARADA...
EEEEEEP!
COME BACK!
EEP!
LET ME...
LET ME CLEAN YOU UP!

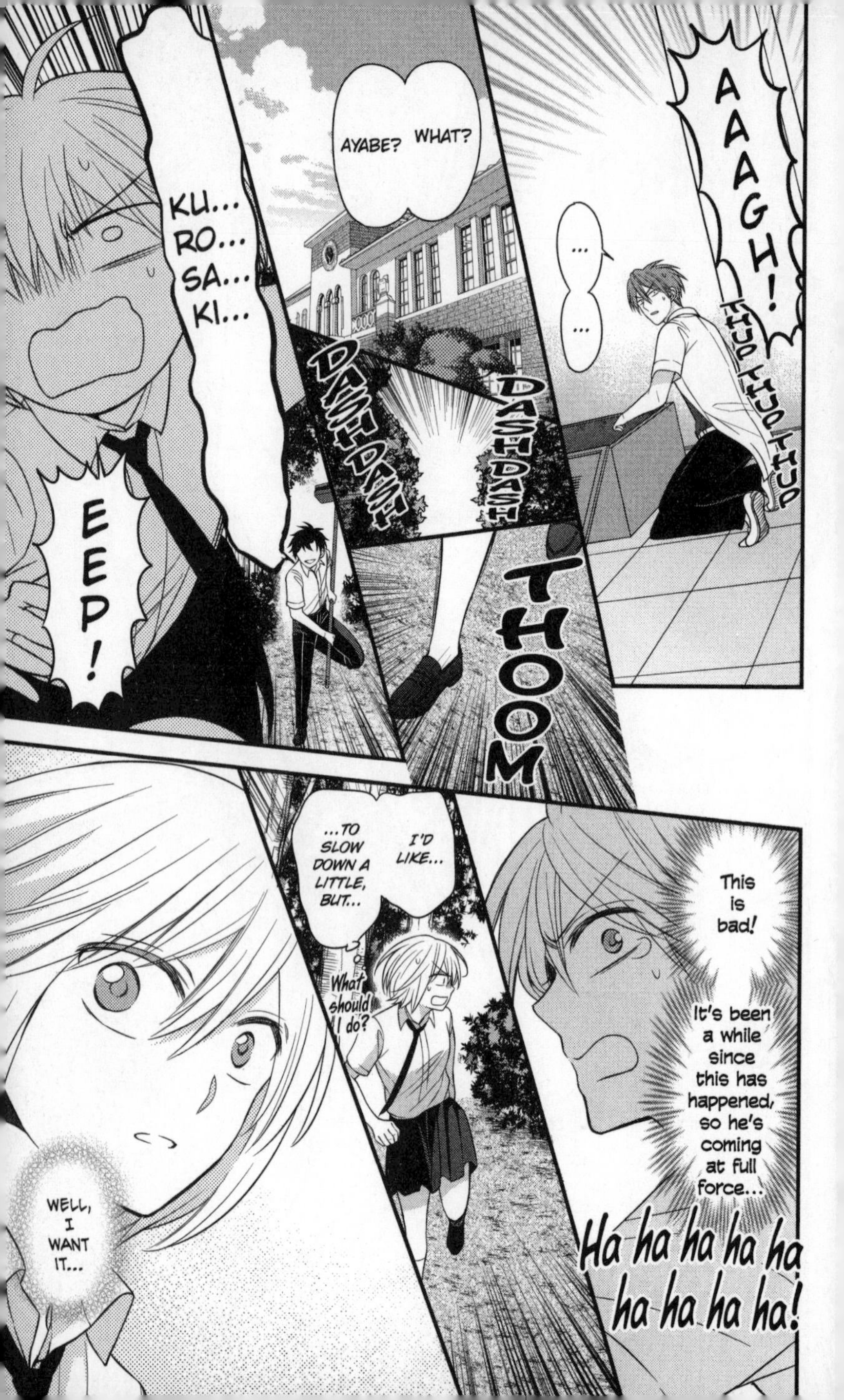

AAAAGH!
THUP THUP THUP THUP
...
...
AYABE? WHAT?
DASH DASH
DASH DASH
THOOM
KU... RO... SA... KI...
EEP!
This is bad!
It's been a while since this has happened, so he's coming at full force...
Ha ha ha ha ha ha ha ha ha ha!
I'D LIKE...
...TO SLOW DOWN A LITTLE, BUT...
What should I do?
WELL, I WANT IT...

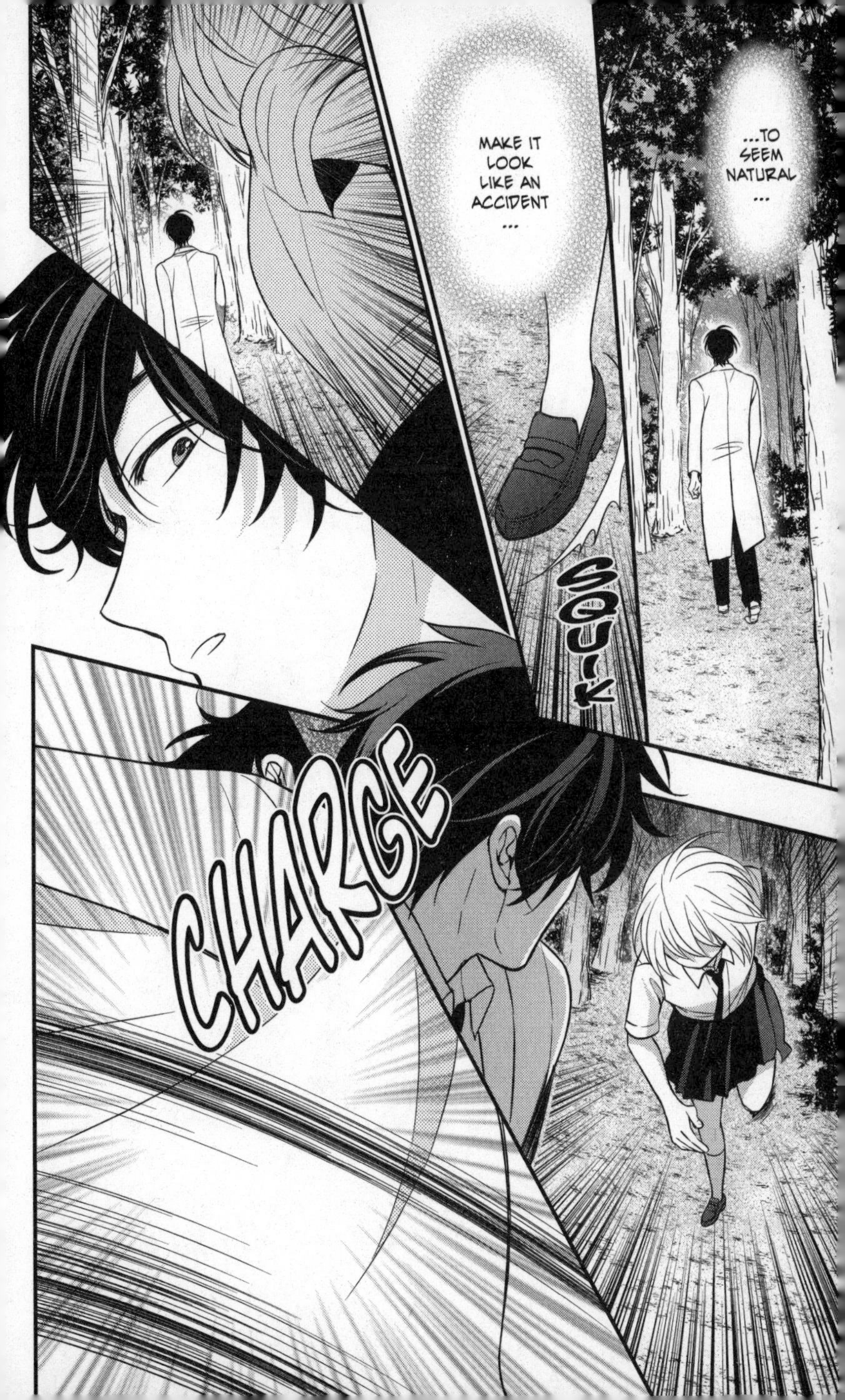
...TO SEEM NATURAL ...
MAKE IT LOOK LIKE AN ACCIDENT ...
SQUI-K
CHARGE

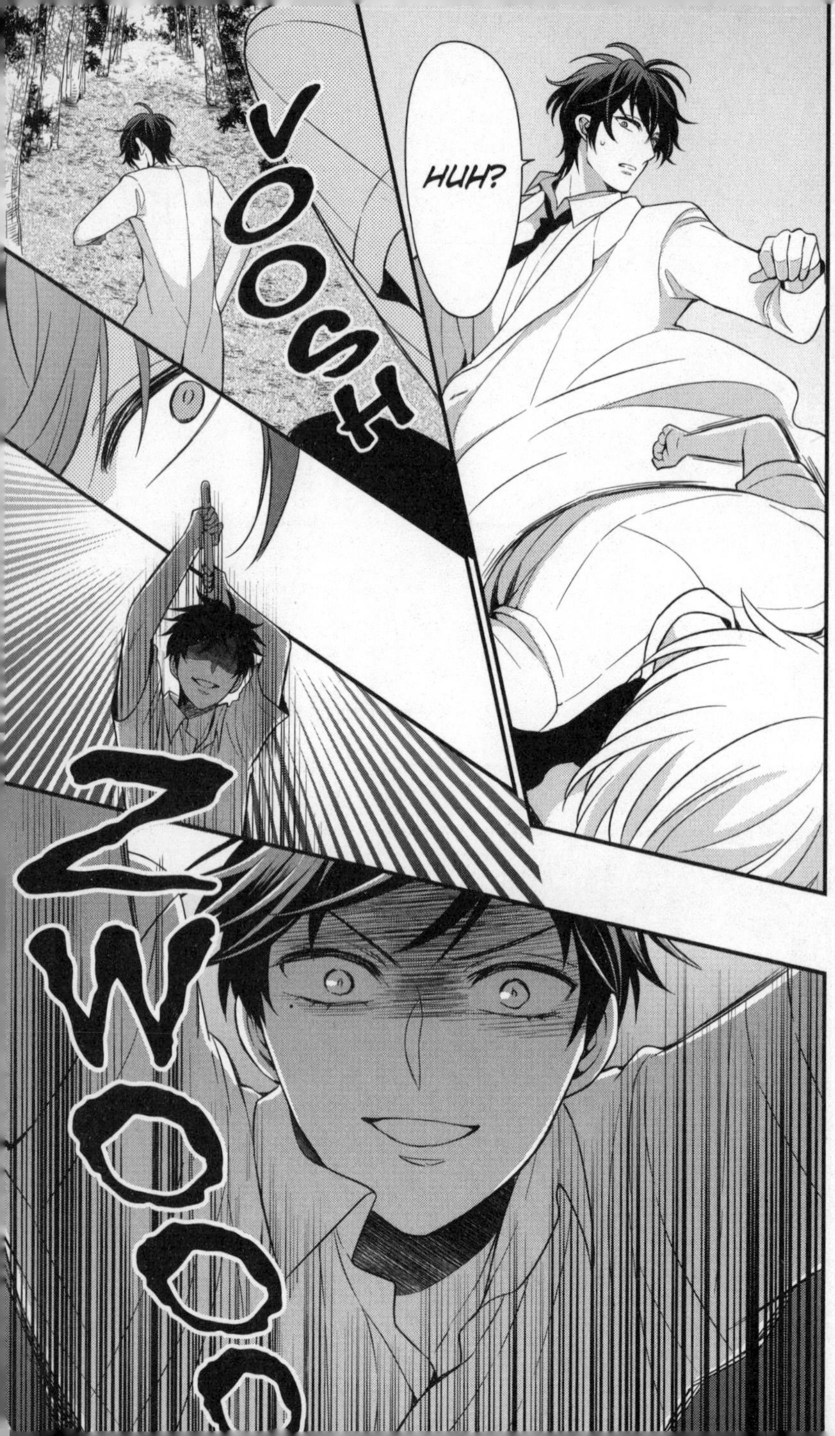
HUH?
VOOSH
ZWOOO

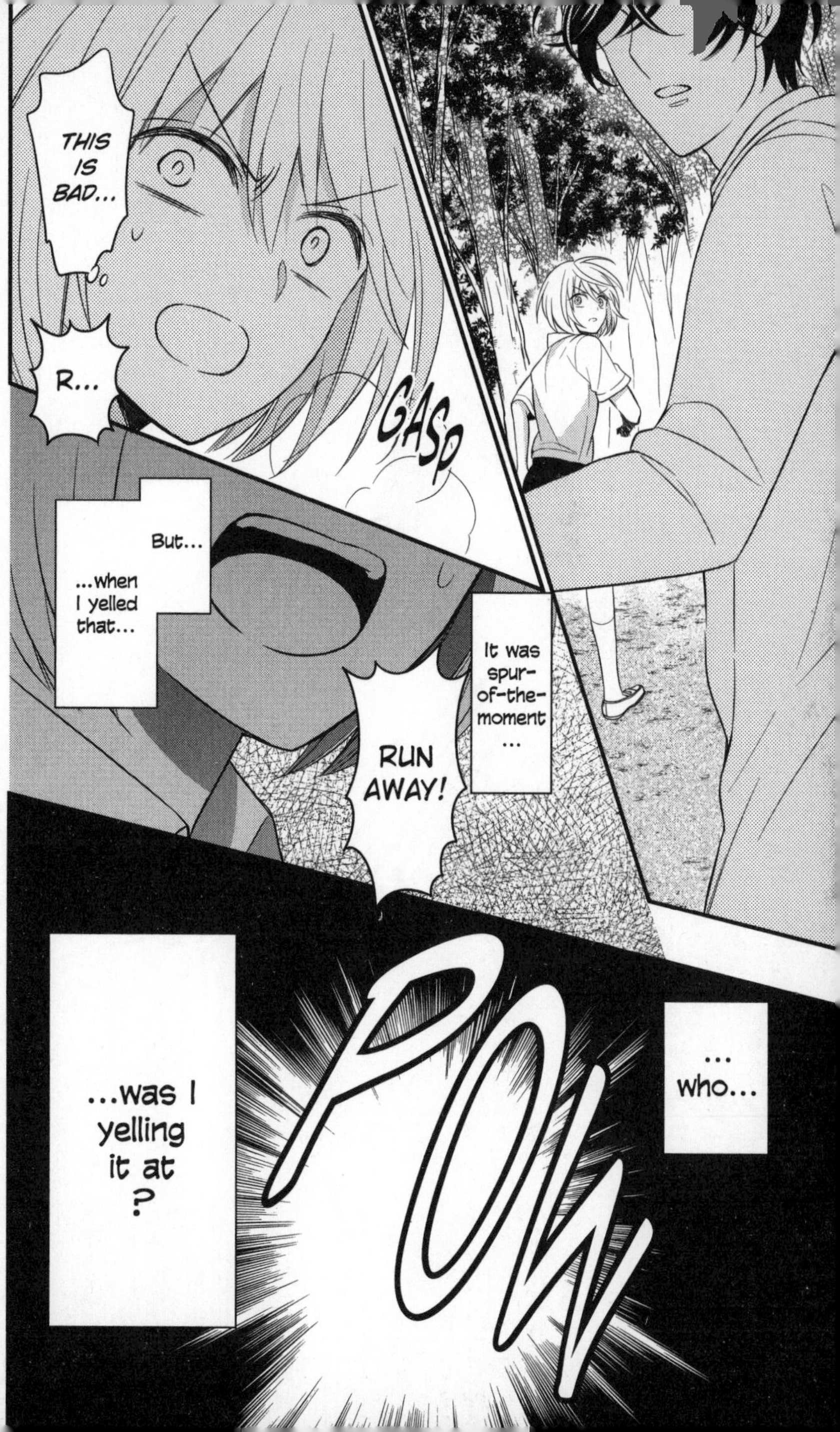
THIS IS BAD...
R...
GASP
It was spur-of-the-moment...
RUN AWAY!
But...
...when I yelled that...
...who...
POW
...was I yelling it at?

Chapter 146

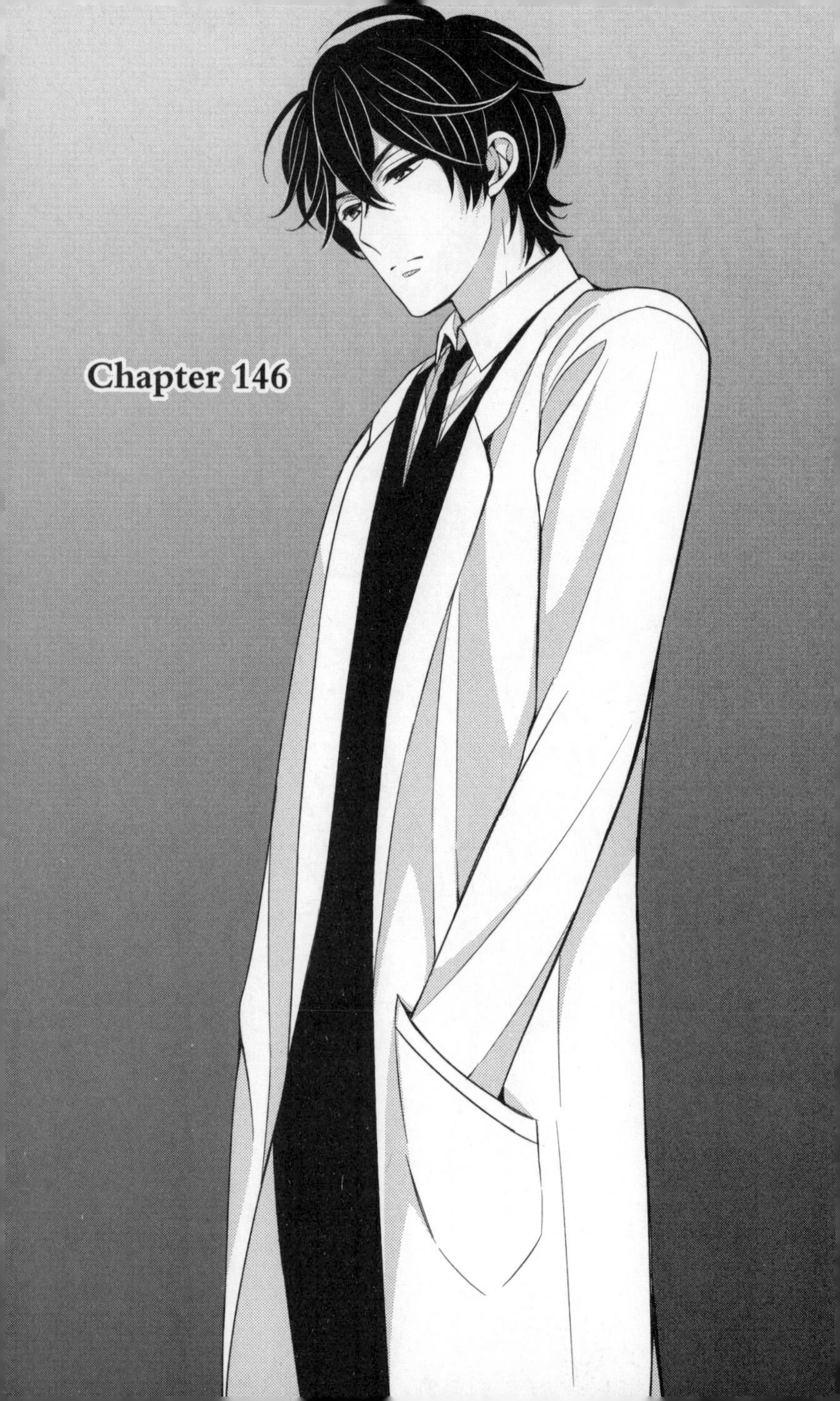

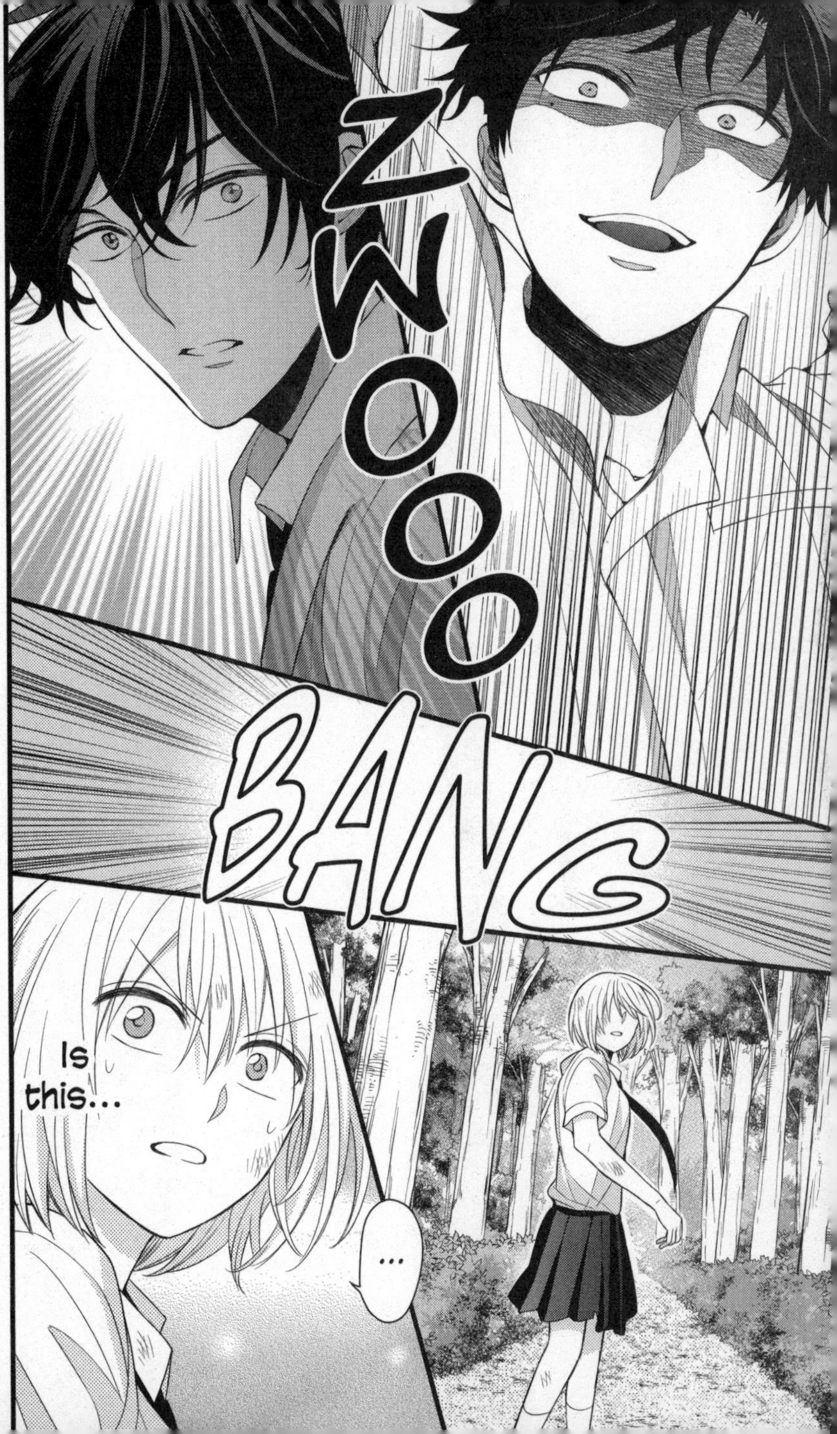
ZWOOO
BANG
...
Is this...

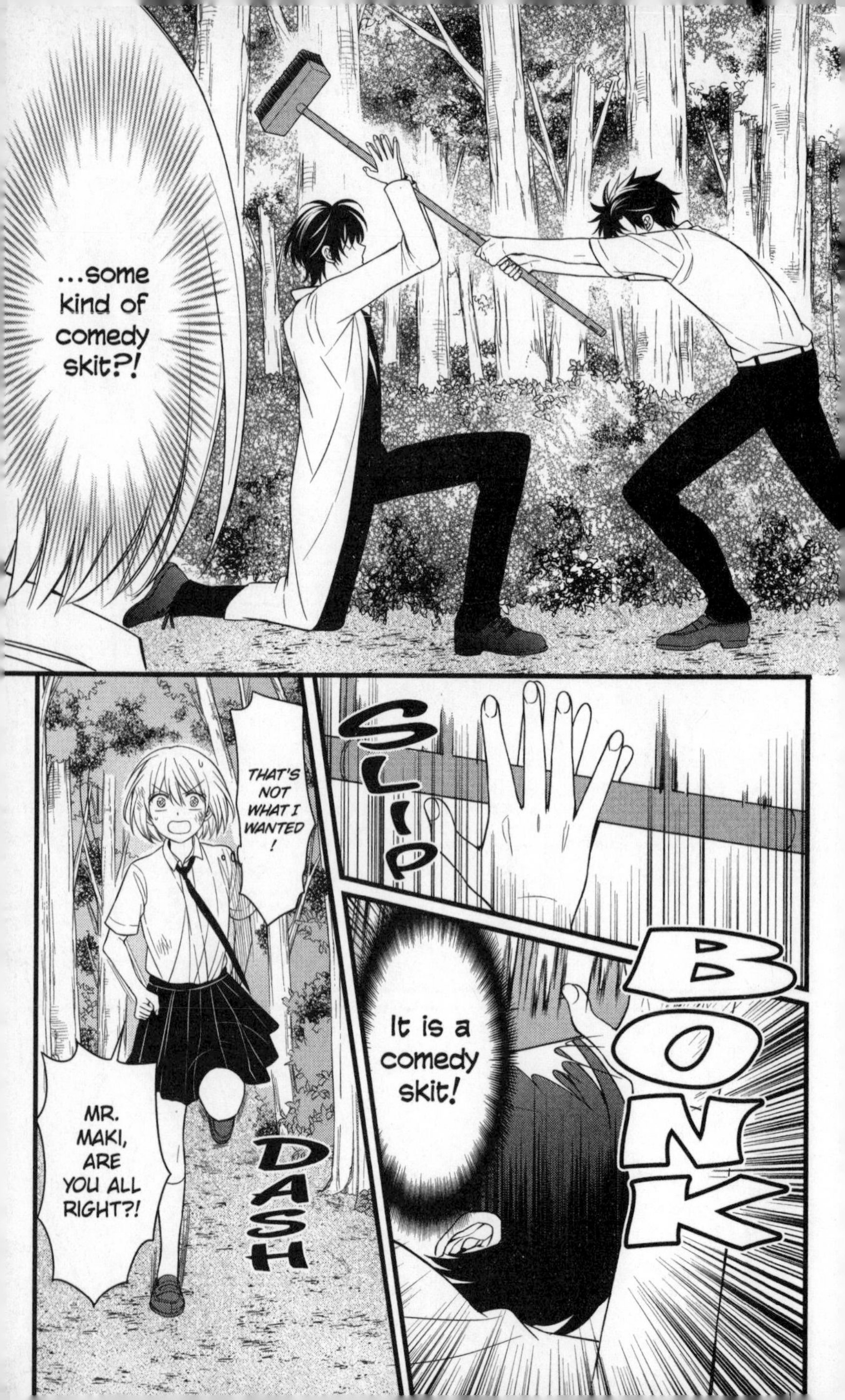
...some kind of comedy skit?!
SLIP
BONK
It is a comedy skit!
THAT'S NOT WHAT I WANTED!
MR. MAKI, ARE YOU ALL RIGHT?!
DASH

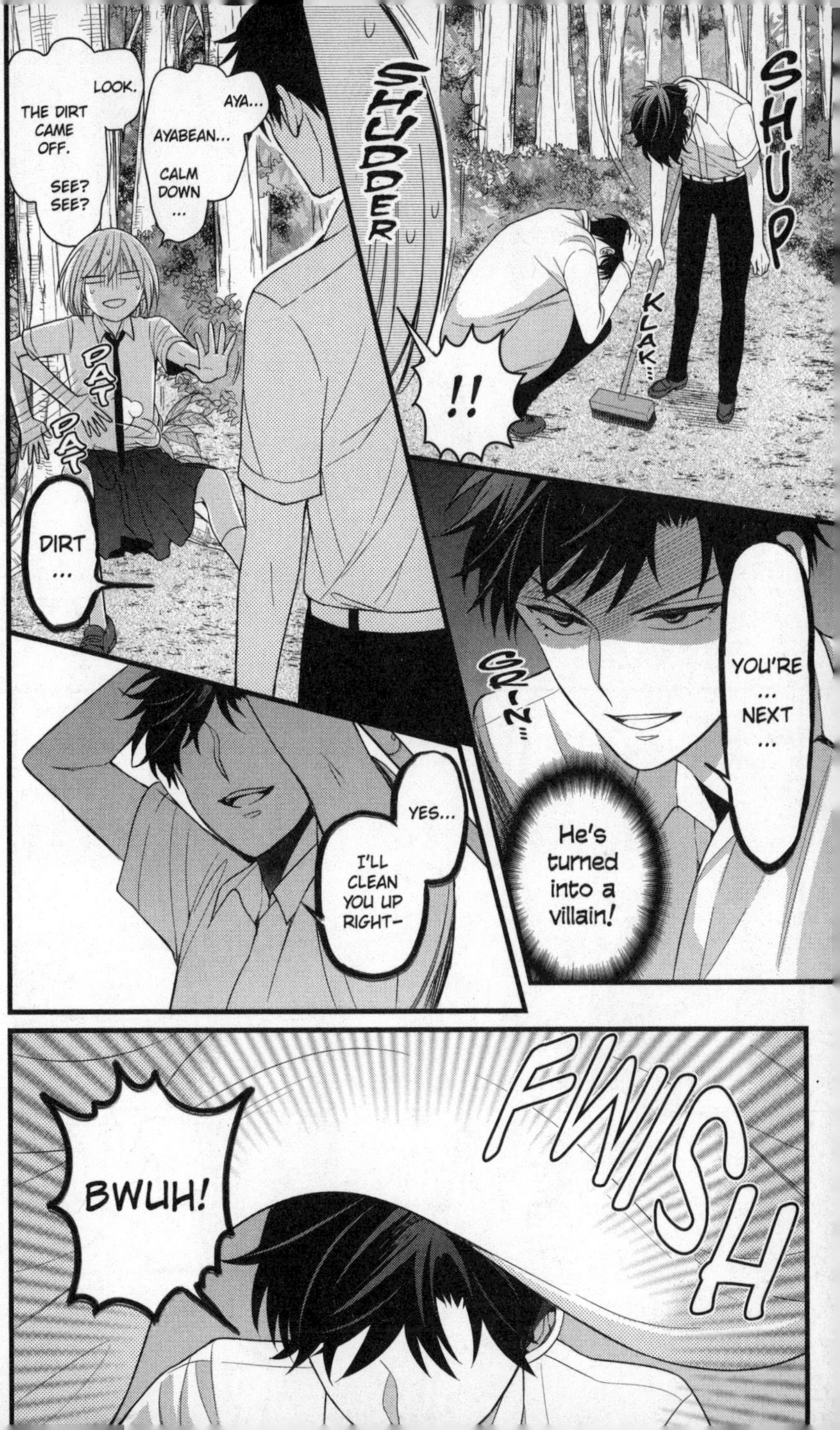
SHUP
KLAK...
!!
SHUDDER
AYA... AYABEAN... CALM DOWN...
LOOK. THE DIRT CAME OFF. SEE? SEE?
PAT PAT
DIRT...
GRIN...
YOU'RE... NEXT...
He's turned into a villain!
YES... I'LL CLEAN YOU UP RIGHT-
FWISH
BWUH!

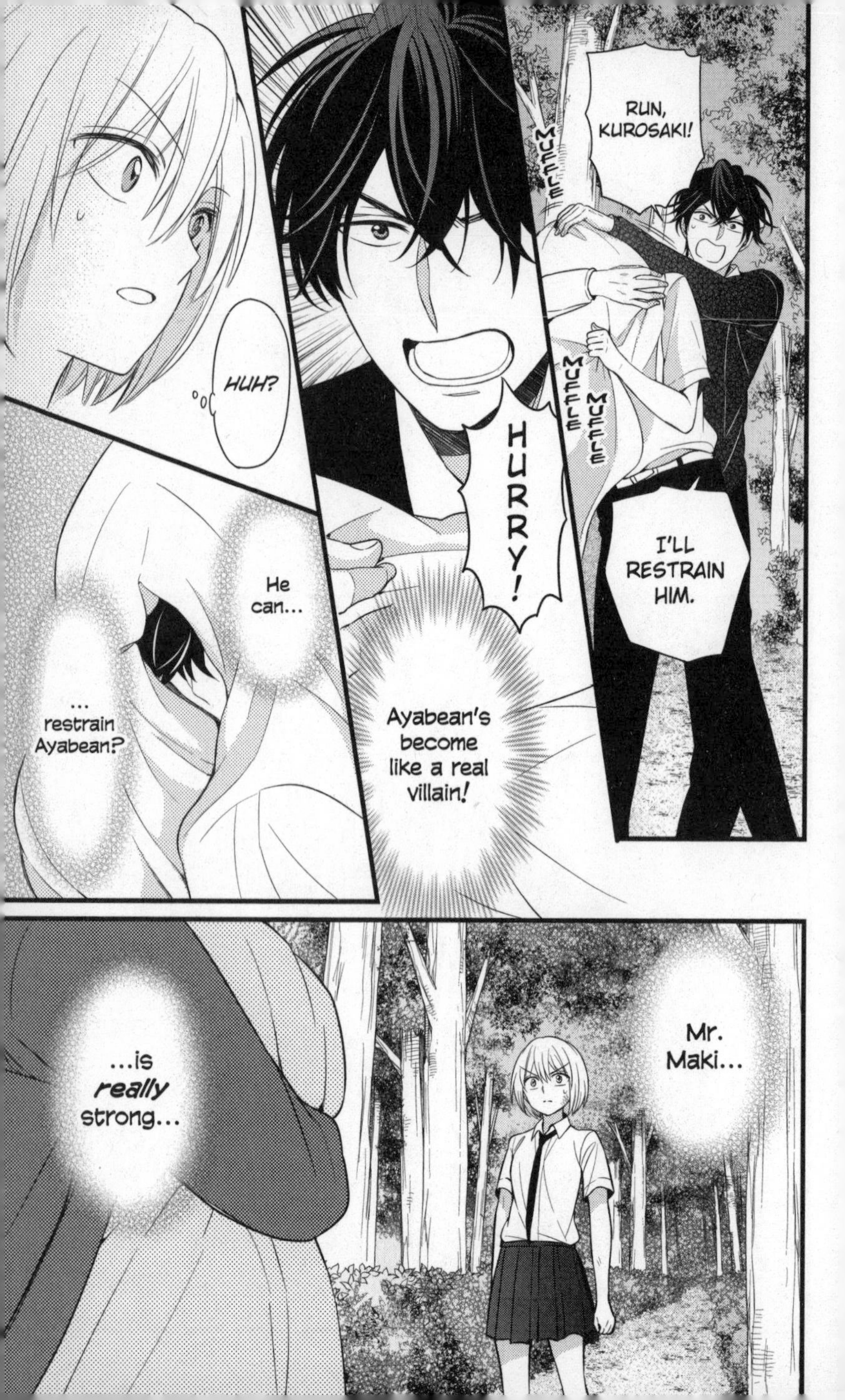
RUN, KUROSAKI!
MUFFLE
MUFFLE MUFFLE
I'LL RESTRAIN HIM.
HURRY!
Ayabean's become like a real villain!
HUH?
He can...
...restrain Ayabean?
Mr. Maki...
...is *really* strong...

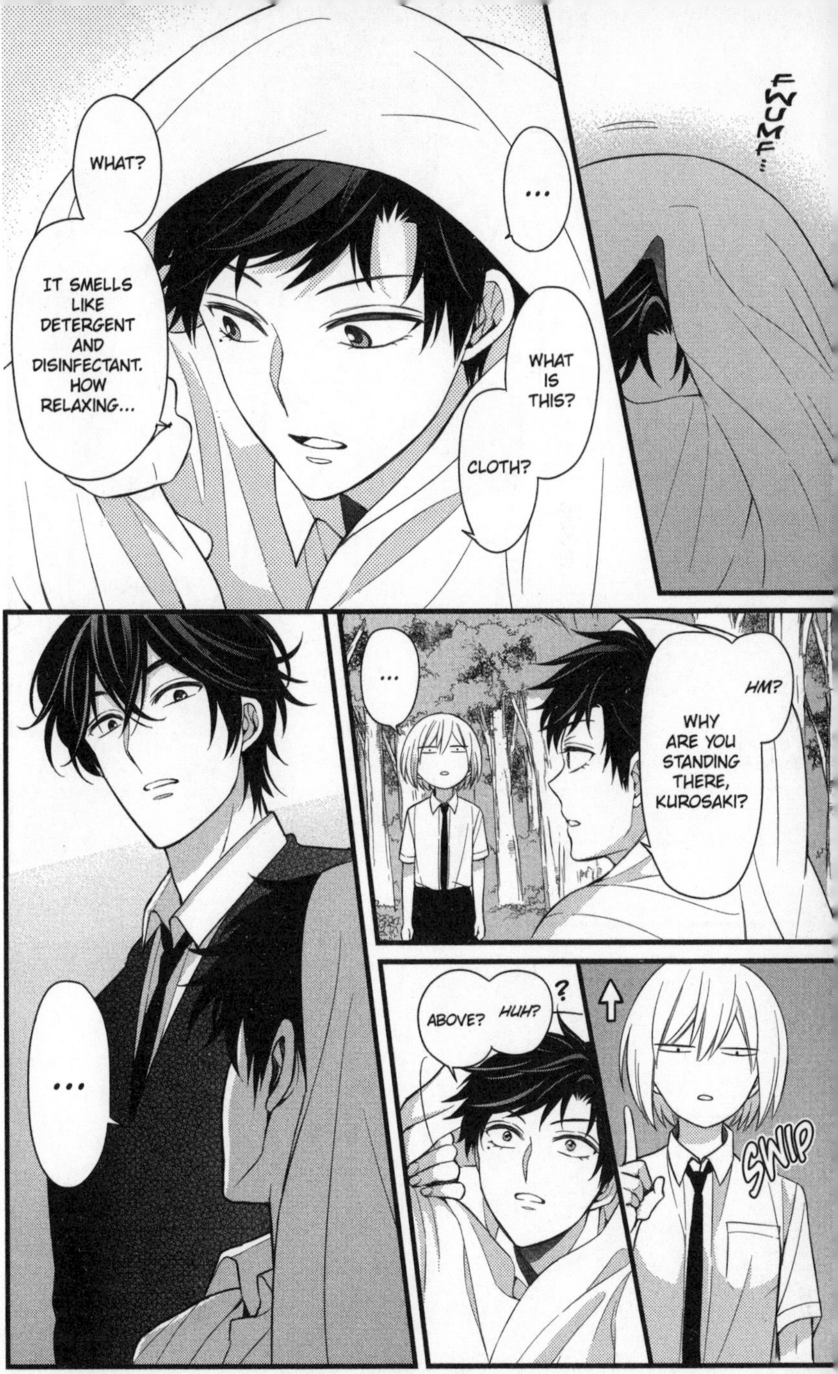
FWUMF...
...
WHAT IS THIS?
CLOTH?
WHAT?
IT SMELLS LIKE DETERGENT AND DISINFECTANT. HOW RELAXING...
HM?
WHY ARE YOU STANDING THERE, KUROSAKI?
...
?
HUH?
ABOVE?
SWIP
...

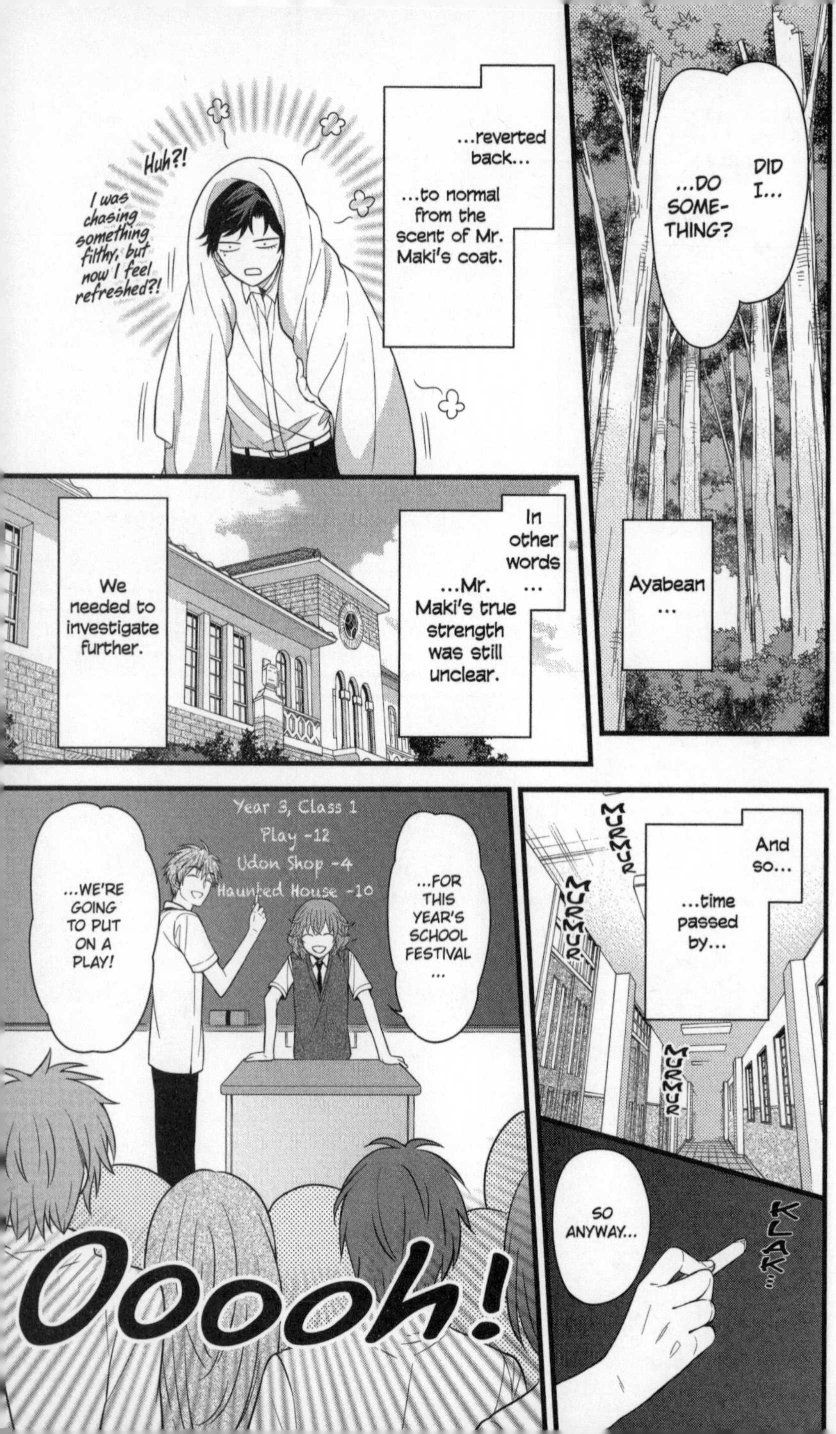
DID I...
...DO SOMETHING?
Ayabean...
...reverted back...
...to normal from the scent of Mr. Maki's coat.
Huh?!
I was chasing something filthy, but now I feel refreshed?!
In other words...
...Mr. Maki's true strength was still unclear.
We needed to investigate further.
And so...
...time passed by...
MURMUR
MURMUR
MURMUR
SO ANYWAY...
KLAK...
Year 3, Class 1
Play -12
Udon Shop -4
Haunted House -10
...FOR THIS YEAR'S SCHOOL FESTIVAL...
...WE'RE GOING TO PUT ON A PLAY!
Ooooh!

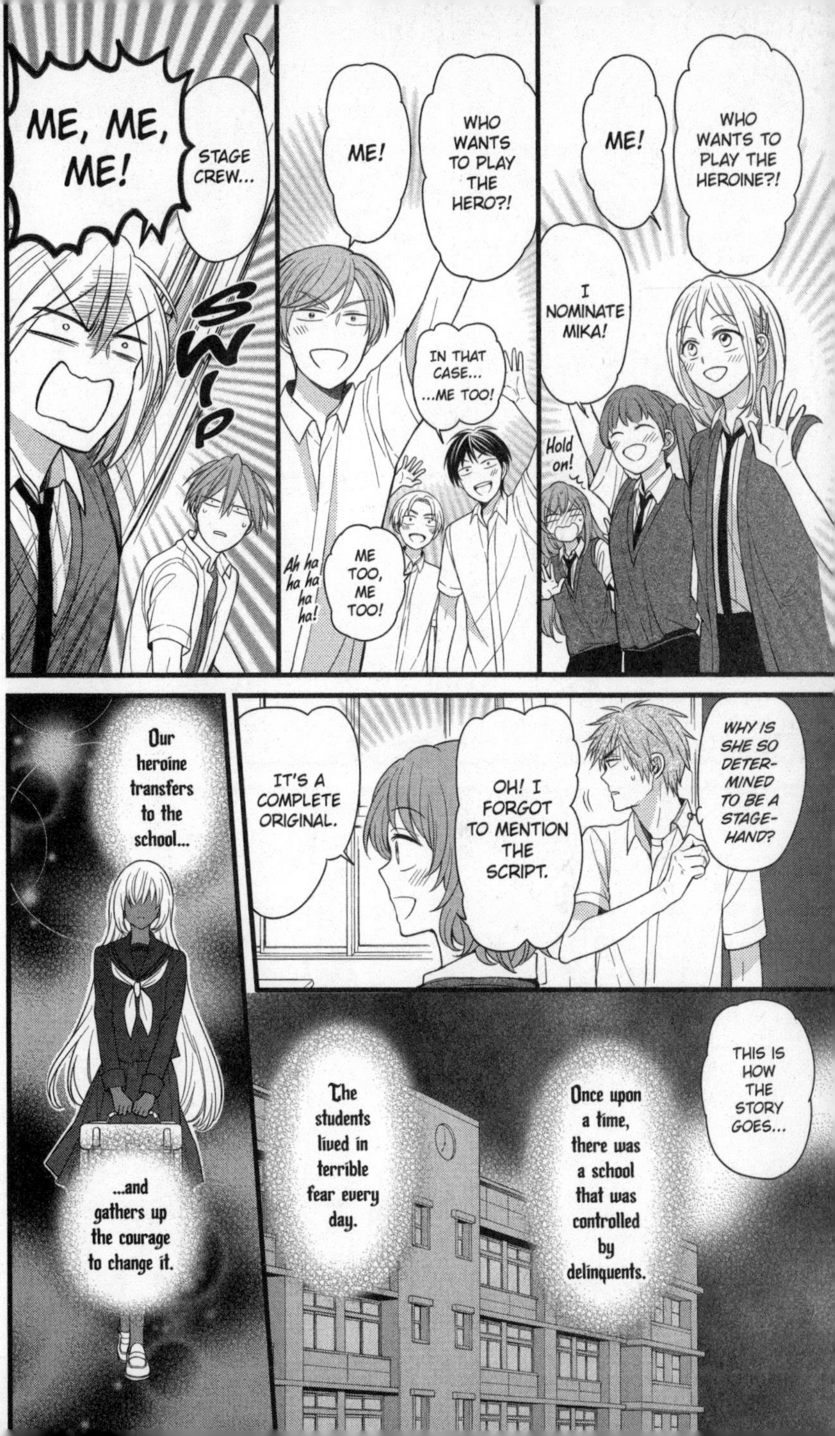
WHO WANTS TO PLAY THE HEROINE?!
ME!
I NOMINATE MIKA!
Hold on!
WHO WANTS TO PLAY THE HERO?!
ME!
IN THAT CASE... ...ME TOO!
ME TOO, ME TOO!
Ah ha ha ha ha ha!
STAGE CREW...
ME, ME, ME!
SWIP
WHY IS SHE SO DETERMINED TO BE A STAGEHAND?
OH! I FORGOT TO MENTION THE SCRIPT.
IT'S A COMPLETE ORIGINAL.
THIS IS HOW THE STORY GOES...
Once upon a time, there was a school that was controlled by delinquents.
The students lived in terrible fear every day.
Our heroine transfers to the school...
...and gathers up the courage to change it.

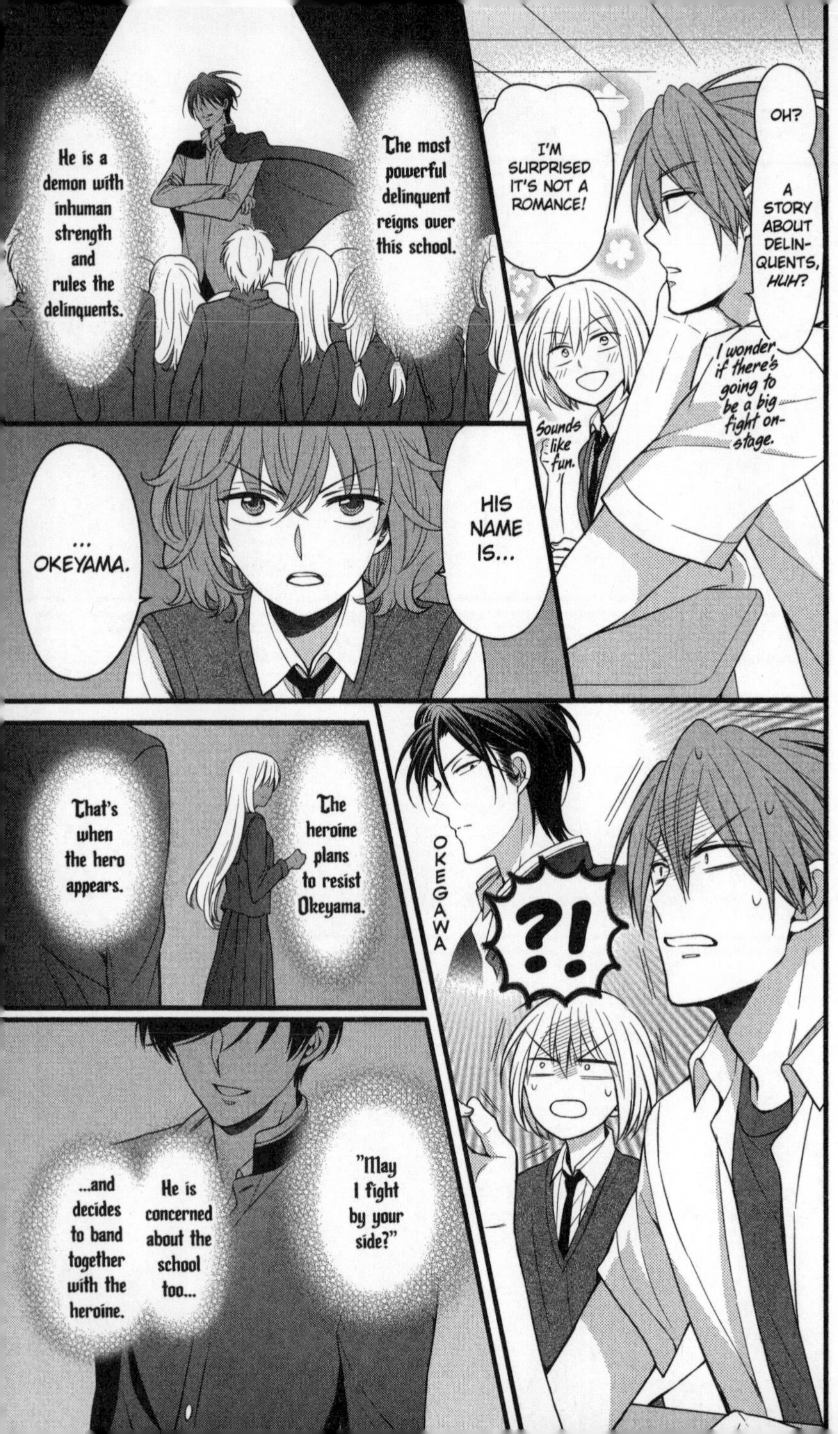
OH?
A STORY ABOUT DELINQUENTS, HUH?
I'M SURPRISED IT'S NOT A ROMANCE!
I wonder if there's going to be a big fight on-stage.
Sounds like fun.
The most powerful delinquent reigns over this school.
He is a demon with inhuman strength and rules the delinquents.
HIS NAME IS...
...OKEYAMA.
OKEGAWA
?!
The heroine plans to resist Okeyama.
That's when the hero appears.
"May I fight by your side?"
He is concerned about the school too...
...and decides to band together with the heroine.

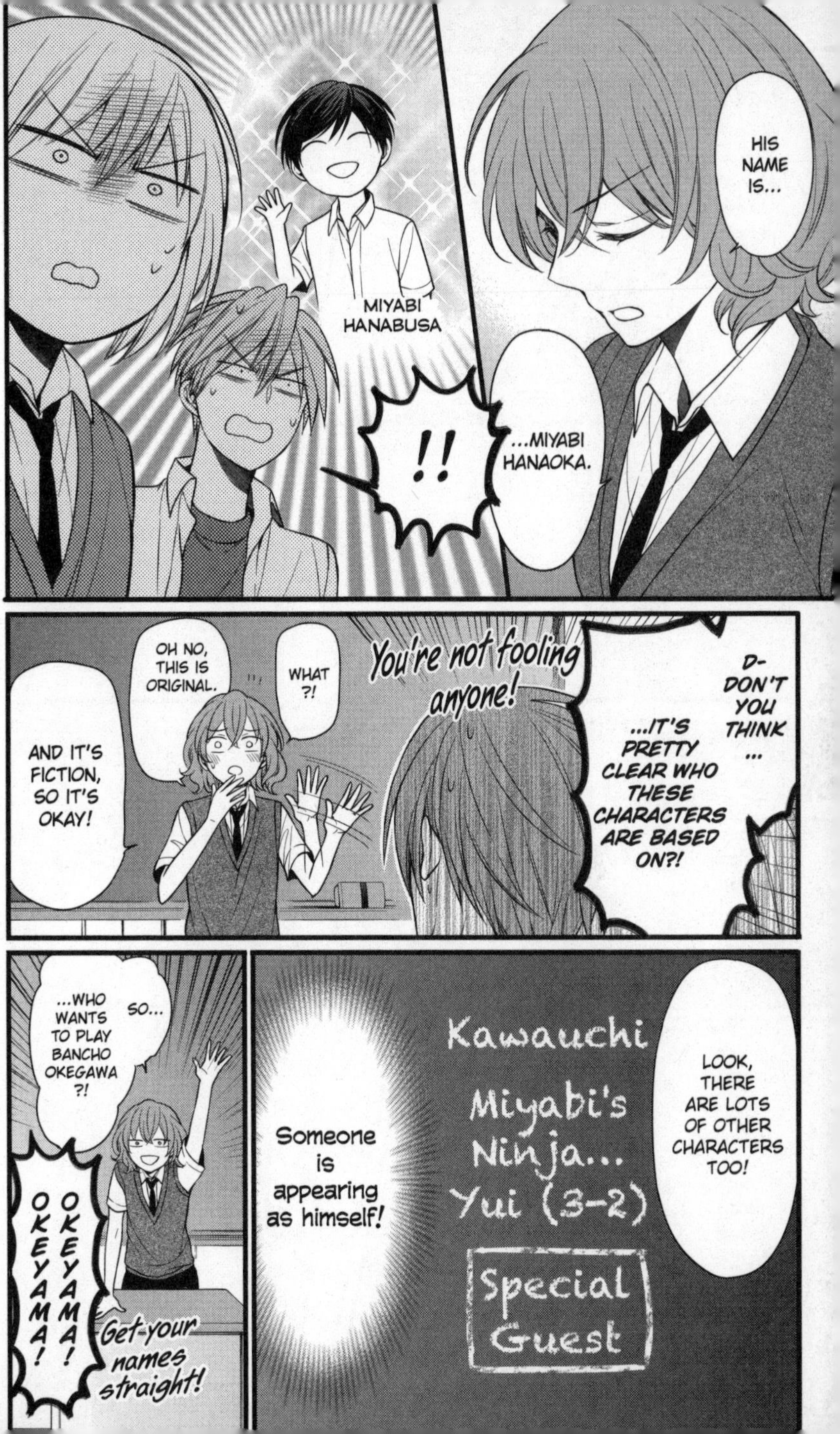
HIS NAME IS...
...MIYABI HANAOKA.
!!
MIYABI HANABUSA
D-DON'T YOU THINK...
...IT'S PRETTY CLEAR WHO THESE CHARACTERS ARE BASED ON?!
You're not fooling anyone!
WHAT?!
OH NO, THIS IS ORIGINAL.
AND IT'S FICTION, SO IT'S OKAY!
LOOK, THERE ARE LOTS OF OTHER CHARACTERS TOO!
Kawauchi
Miyabi's Ninja... Yui (3-2)
Special Guest
Someone is appearing as himself!
SO...
...WHO WANTS TO PLAY BANCHO OKEGAWA?!
OKEYAMA!
OKEYAMA!
Get your names straight!

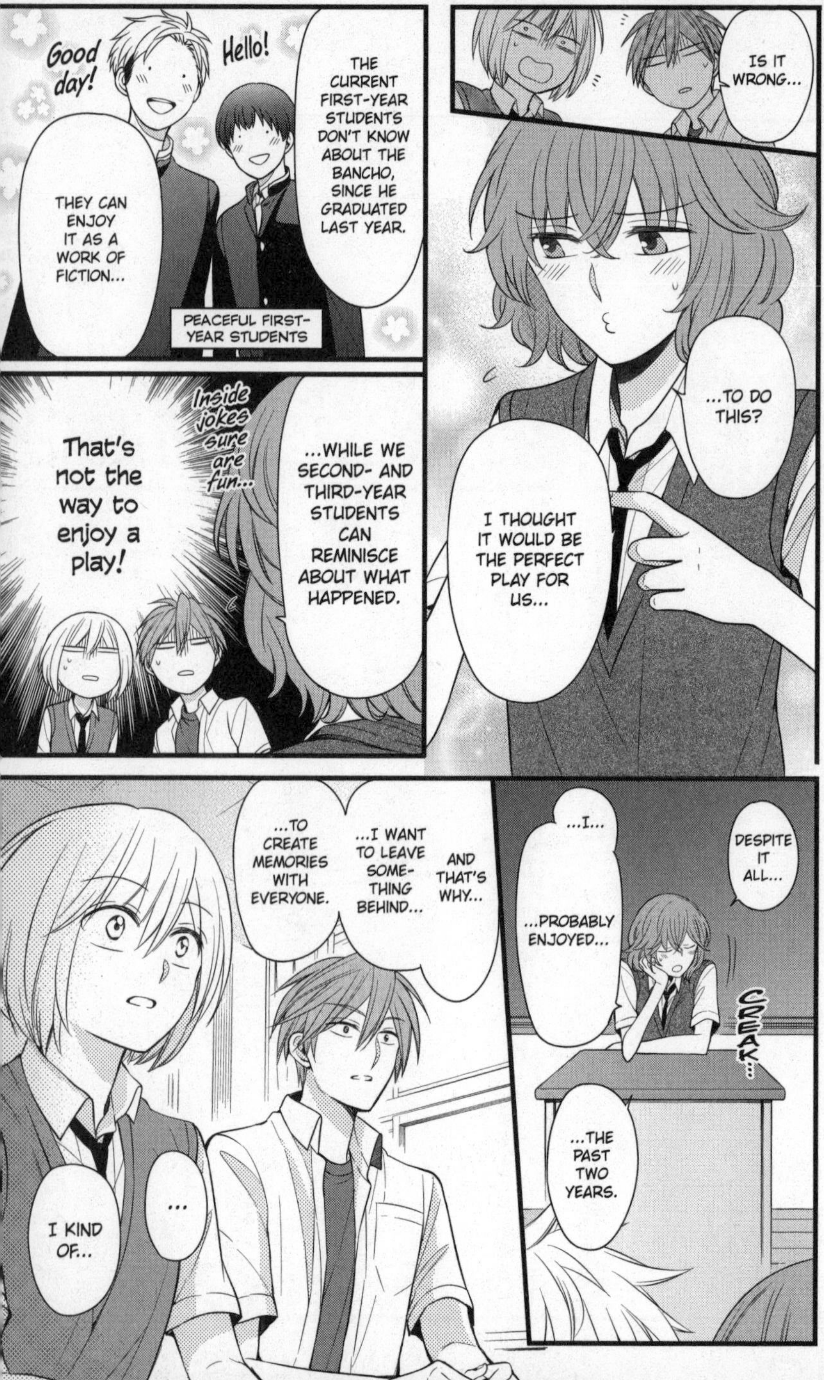
IS IT WRONG...
...TO DO THIS?
I THOUGHT IT WOULD BE THE PERFECT PLAY FOR US...
THE CURRENT FIRST-YEAR STUDENTS DON'T KNOW ABOUT THE BANCHO, SINCE HE GRADUATED LAST YEAR.
Hello!
Good day!
THEY CAN ENJOY IT AS A WORK OF FICTION...
PEACEFUL FIRST-YEAR STUDENTS
...WHILE WE SECOND- AND THIRD-YEAR STUDENTS CAN REMINISCE ABOUT WHAT HAPPENED.
Inside jokes sure are fun...
That's not the way to enjoy a play!
DESPITE IT ALL...
...I...
...PROBABLY ENJOYED...
CREAK...
...THE PAST TWO YEARS.
AND THAT'S WHY...
...I WANT TO LEAVE SOMETHING BEHIND...
...TO CREATE MEMORIES WITH EVERYONE.
...
I KIND OF...

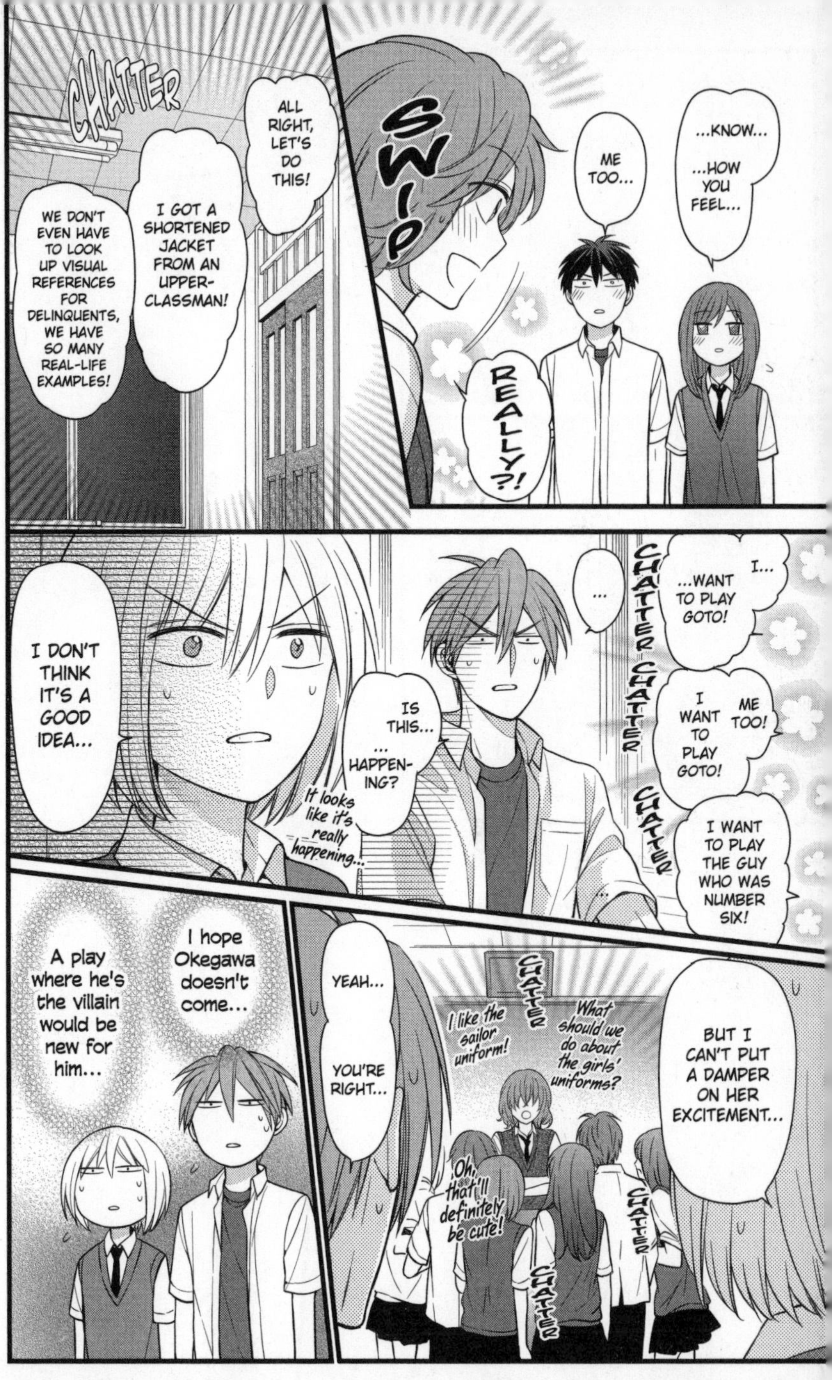
...KNOW... ...HOW YOU FEEL...
ME TOO...
SWIP
REALLY?!
ALL RIGHT, LET'S DO THIS!
CHATTER
I GOT A SHORTENED JACKET FROM AN UPPER-CLASSMAN!
WE DON'T EVEN HAVE TO LOOK UP VISUAL REFERENCES FOR DELINQUENTS, WE HAVE SO MANY REAL-LIFE EXAMPLES!
I... ...WANT TO PLAY GOTO!
ME TOO!
I WANT TO PLAY GOTO!
I WANT TO PLAY THE GUY WHO WAS NUMBER SIX!
CHATTER CHATTER CHATTER
CHATTER
...
IS THIS... ...HAPPENING?
It looks like it's really happening...
I DON'T THINK IT'S A GOOD IDEA...
BUT I CAN'T PUT A DAMPER ON HER EXCITEMENT...
CHATTER
What should we do about the girls' uniforms?
I like the sailor uniform!
CHATTER
Oh, that'll definitely be cute!
CHATTER
YEAH...
YOU'RE RIGHT...
I hope Okegawa doesn't come...
A play where he's the villain would be new for him...

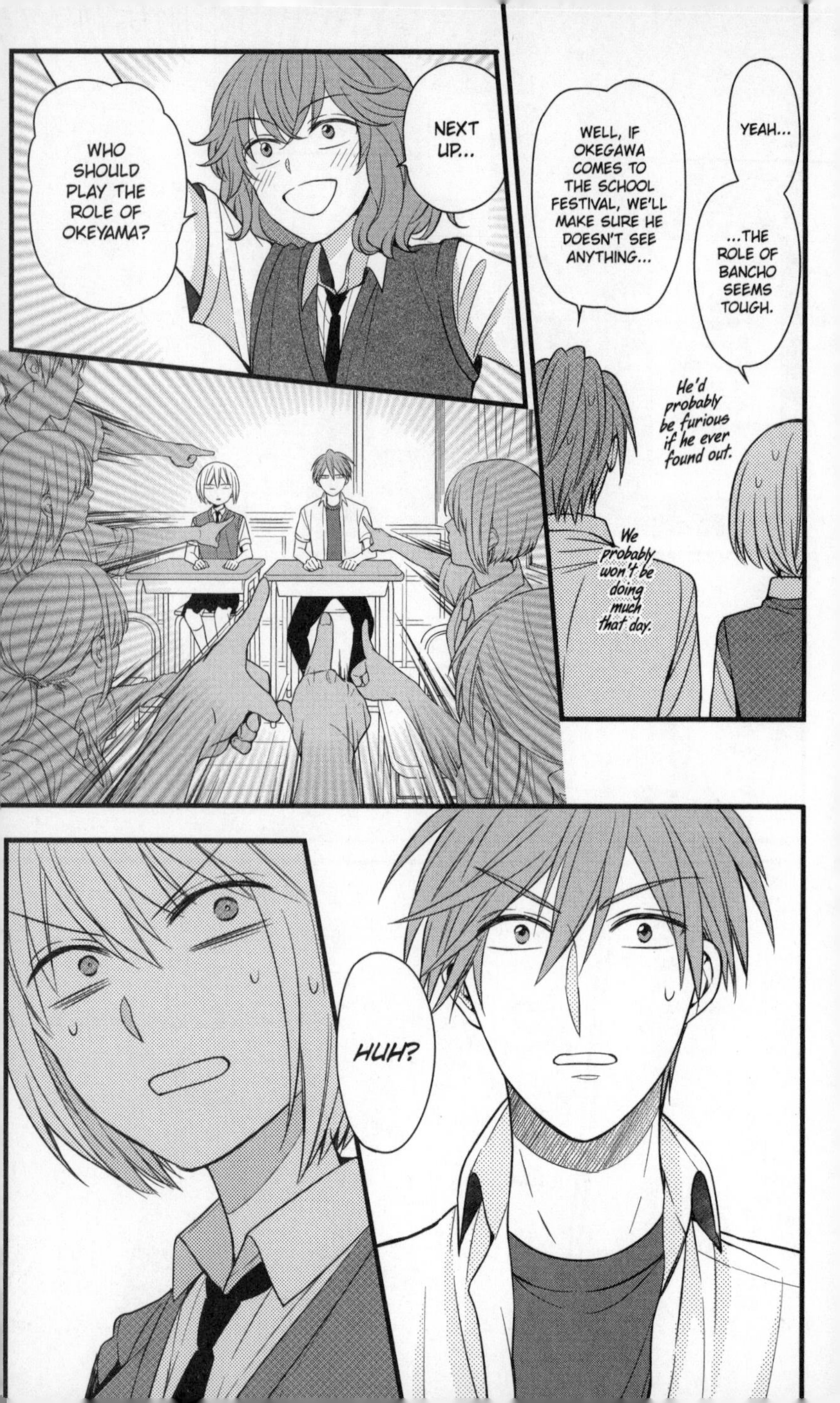
YEAH...
...THE ROLE OF BANCHO SEEMS TOUGH.
WELL, IF OKEGAWA COMES TO THE SCHOOL FESTIVAL, WE'LL MAKE SURE HE DOESN'T SEE ANYTHING...
He'd probably be furious if he ever found out.
We probably won't be doing much that day.
NEXT UP...
WHO SHOULD PLAY THE ROLE OF OKEYAMA?
HUH?

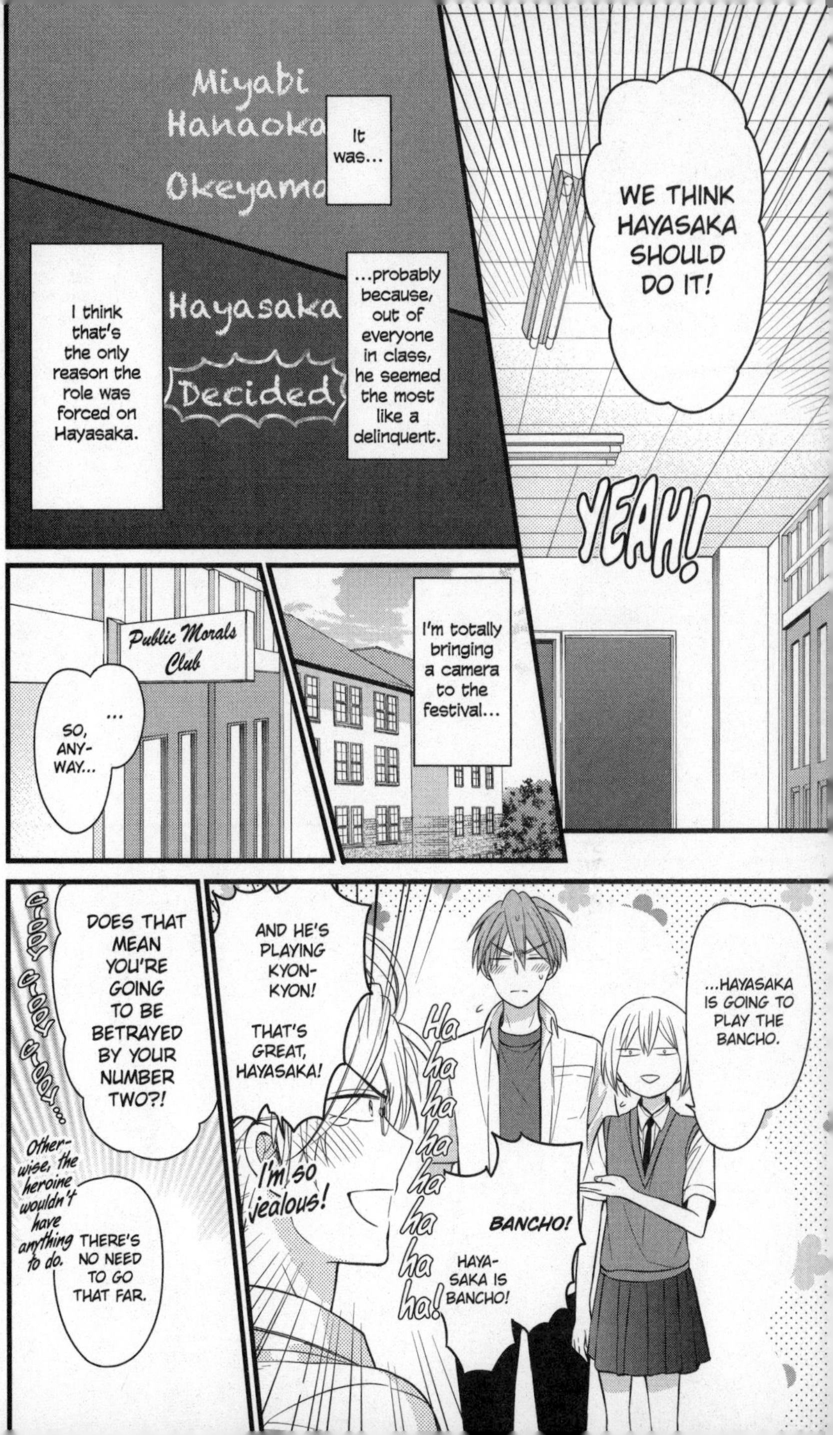
WE THINK HAYASAKA SHOULD DO IT!
YEAH!
Miyabi Hanaoka Okeyama
It was...
Hayasaka
Decided
...probably because, out of everyone in class, he seemed the most like a delinquent.
I think that's the only reason the role was forced on Hayasaka.
I'm totally bringing a camera to the festival...
Public Morals Club
... SO, ANYWAY...
...HAYASAKA IS GOING TO PLAY THE BANCHO.
BANCHO!
HAYA-SAKA IS BANCHO!
Ha ha ha ha ha ha ha ha ha ha!
AND HE'S PLAYING KYON-KYON! THAT'S GREAT, HAYASAKA!
I'm so jealous!
DOES THAT MEAN YOU'RE GOING TO BE BETRAYED BY YOUR NUMBER TWO?!
G-DOY G-DOY G-DOY...
THERE'S NO NEED TO GO THAT FAR.
Other-wise, the heroine wouldn't have anything to do.

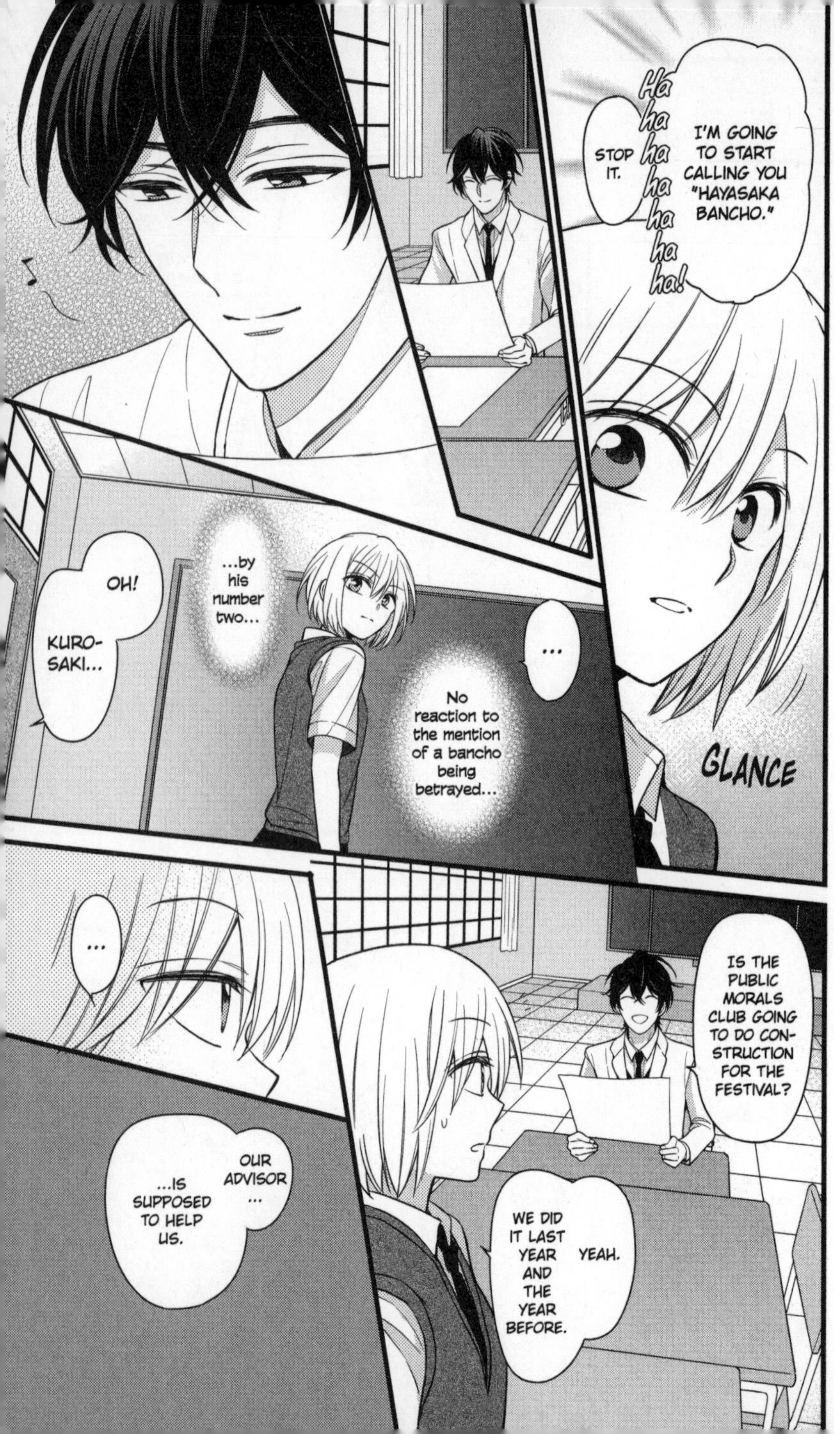
I'M GOING TO START CALLING YOU "HAYASAKA BANCHO."
Ha ha ha ha ha ha ha!
STOP IT.
GLANCE
...
No reaction to the mention of a bancho being betrayed...
...by his number two...
OH!
KURO-SAKI...
IS THE PUBLIC MORALS CLUB GOING TO DO CON-STRUCTION FOR THE FESTIVAL?
YEAH.
WE DID IT LAST YEAR AND THE YEAR BEFORE.
...
OUR ADVISOR...
...IS SUPPOSED TO HELP US.

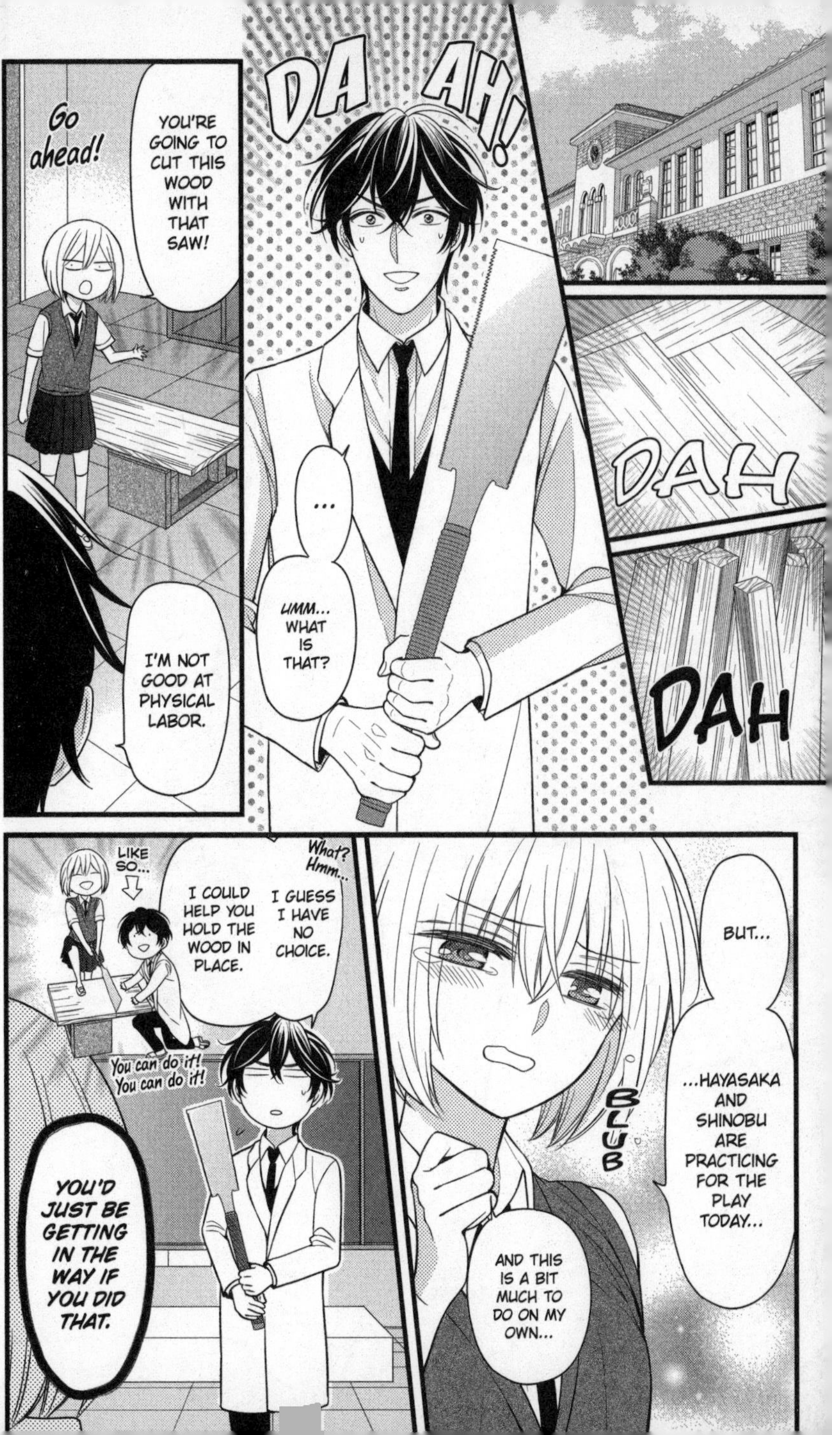
DAH
DAH
DA AH!
...
UMM... WHAT IS THAT?
YOU'RE GOING TO CUT THIS WOOD WITH THAT SAW!
Go ahead!
I'M NOT GOOD AT PHYSICAL LABOR.
BUT...
...HAYASAKA AND SHINOBU ARE PRACTICING FOR THE PLAY TODAY...
BLUB
AND THIS IS A BIT MUCH TO DO ON MY OWN...
What? Hmm...
I GUESS I HAVE NO CHOICE.
I COULD HELP YOU HOLD THE WOOD IN PLACE.
LIKE SO...
You can do it! You can do it!
YOU'D JUST BE GETTING IN THE WAY IF YOU DID THAT.

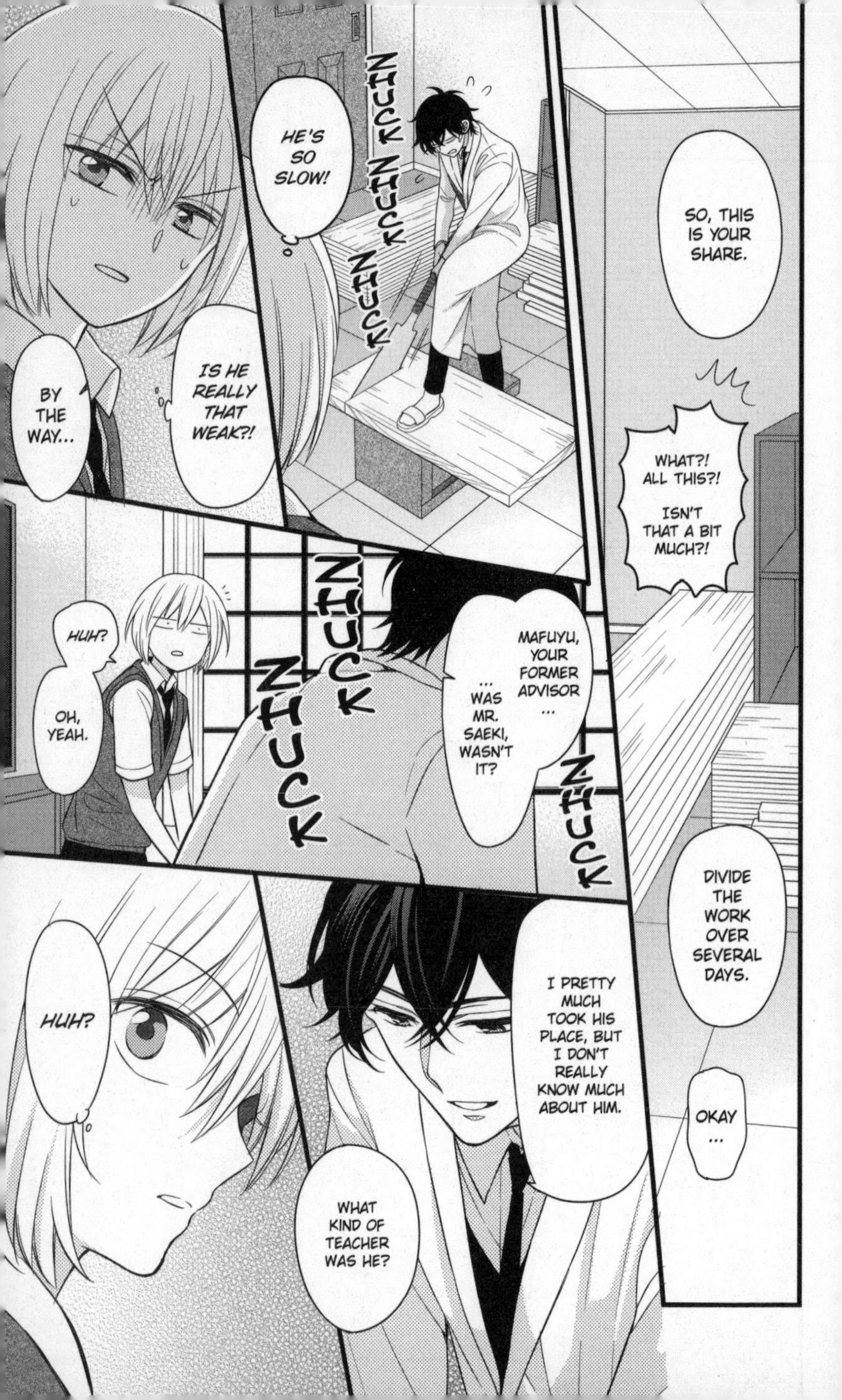
SO, THIS IS YOUR SHARE.
WHAT?! ALL THIS?! ISN'T THAT A BIT MUCH?!
DIVIDE THE WORK OVER SEVERAL DAYS.
OKAY ...
ZHUCK ZHUCK ZHUCK ZHUCK
HE'S SO SLOW!
IS HE REALLY THAT WEAK?!
BY THE WAY...
ZHUCK ZHUCK ZHUCK
MAFUYU, YOUR FORMER ADVISOR ...
... WAS MR. SAEKI, WASN'T IT?
HUH?
OH, YEAH.
I PRETTY MUCH TOOK HIS PLACE, BUT I DON'T REALLY KNOW MUCH ABOUT HIM.
WHAT KIND OF TEACHER WAS HE?
HUH?

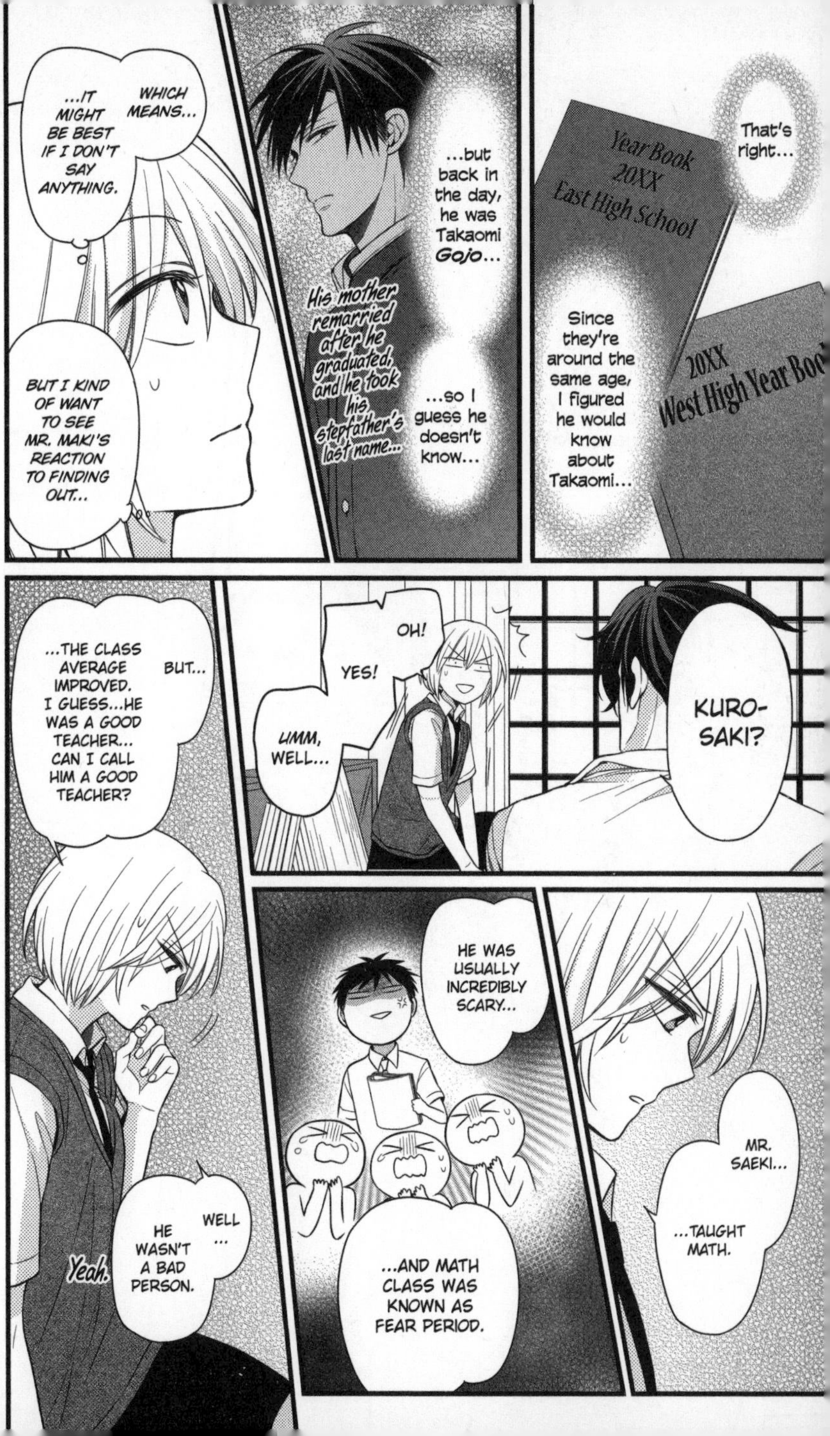
That's right...
Year Book
20XX
East High School
Since they're around the same age, I figured he would know about Takaomi...
20XX
West High Year Boo
...but back in the day, he was Takaomi Gojo...
His mother remarried after he graduated, and he took his stepfather's last name...
...so I guess he doesn't know...
WHICH MEANS...
...IT MIGHT BE BEST IF I DON'T SAY ANYTHING.
BUT I KIND OF WANT TO SEE MR. MAKI'S REACTION TO FINDING OUT...
KURO-SAKI?
OH!
YES!
UMM, WELL...
MR. SAEKI...
...TAUGHT MATH.
HE WAS USUALLY INCREDIBLY SCARY...
...AND MATH CLASS WAS KNOWN AS FEAR PERIOD.
BUT...
...THE CLASS AVERAGE IMPROVED. I GUESS...HE WAS A GOOD TEACHER... CAN I CALL HIM A GOOD TEACHER?
WELL...
HE WASN'T A BAD PERSON.
Yeah.

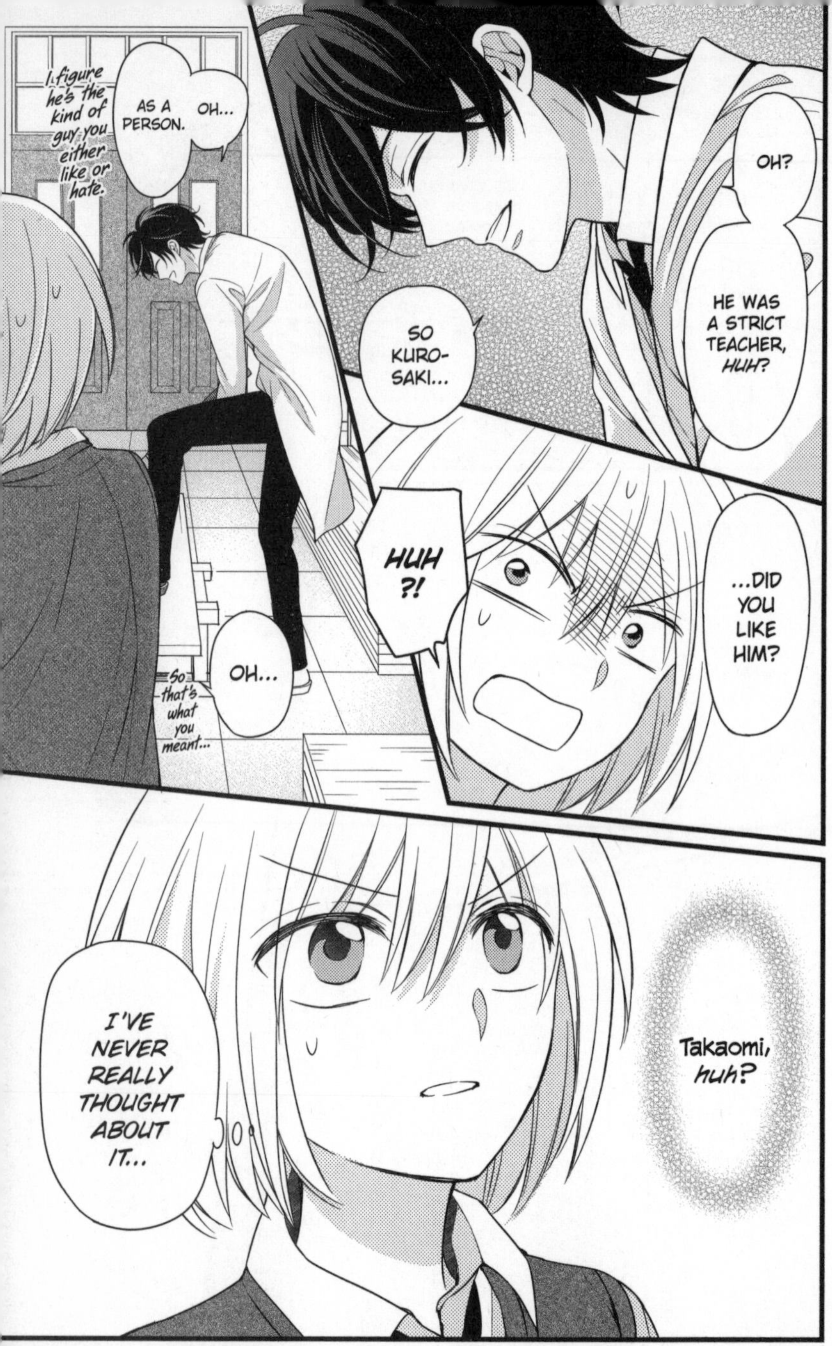
OH?
HE WAS A STRICT TEACHER, HUH?
SO KURO-SAKI...
...DID YOU LIKE HIM?
HUH ?!
OH...
AS A PERSON.
I figure he's the kind of guy you either like or hate.
OH...
So that's what you meant...
Takaomi, huh?
I'VE NEVER REALLY THOUGHT ABOUT IT...

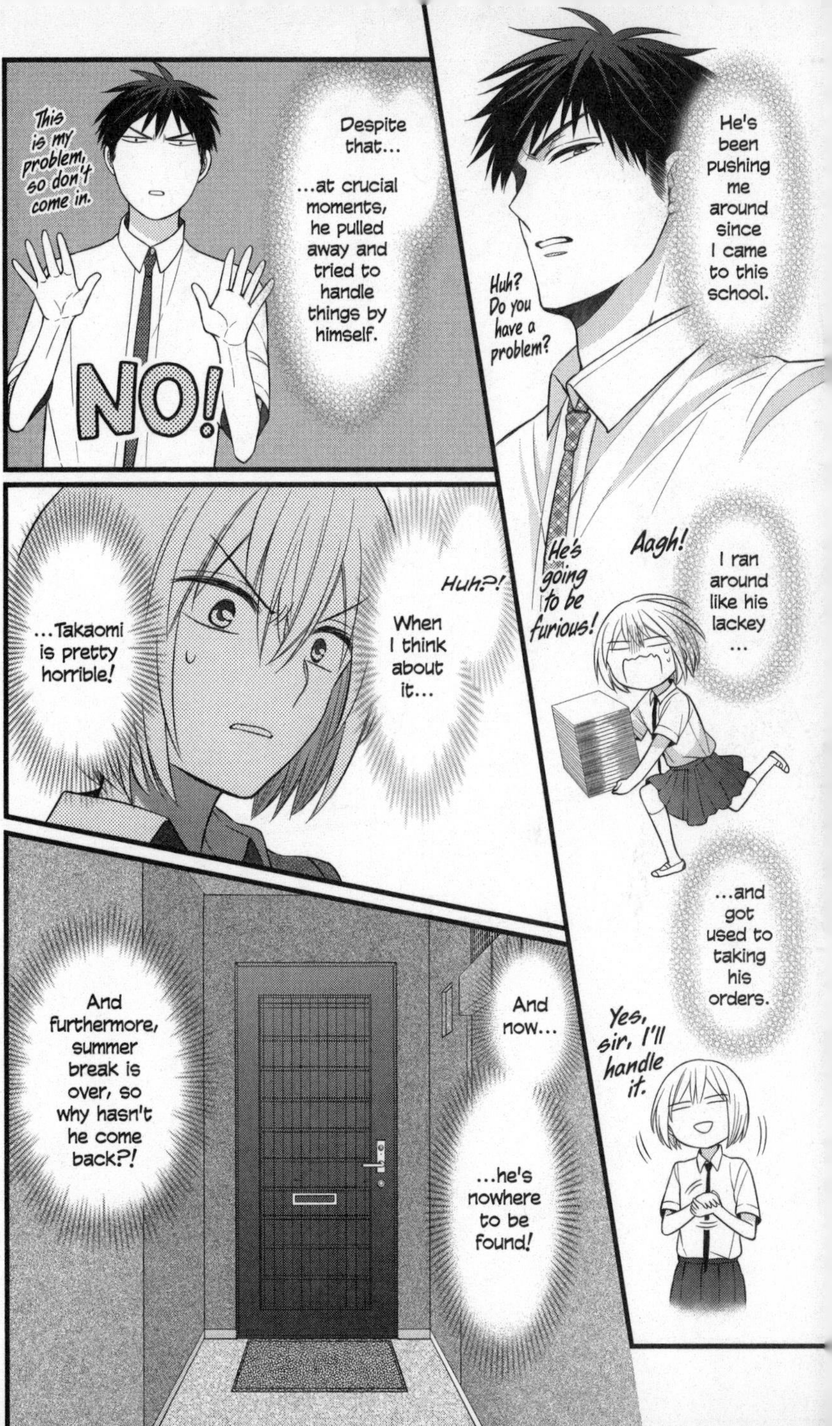
He's been pushing me around since I came to this school.
Huh? Do you have a problem?
I ran around like his lackey...
Aagh!
He's going to be furious!
...and got used to taking his orders.
Yes, sir, I'll handle it.
Despite that...
...at crucial moments, he pulled away and tried to handle things by himself.
This is my problem, so don't come in.
NO!
When I think about it...
Huh?!
...Takaomi is pretty horrible!
And now...
...he's nowhere to be found!
And furthermore, summer break is over, so why hasn't he come back?!

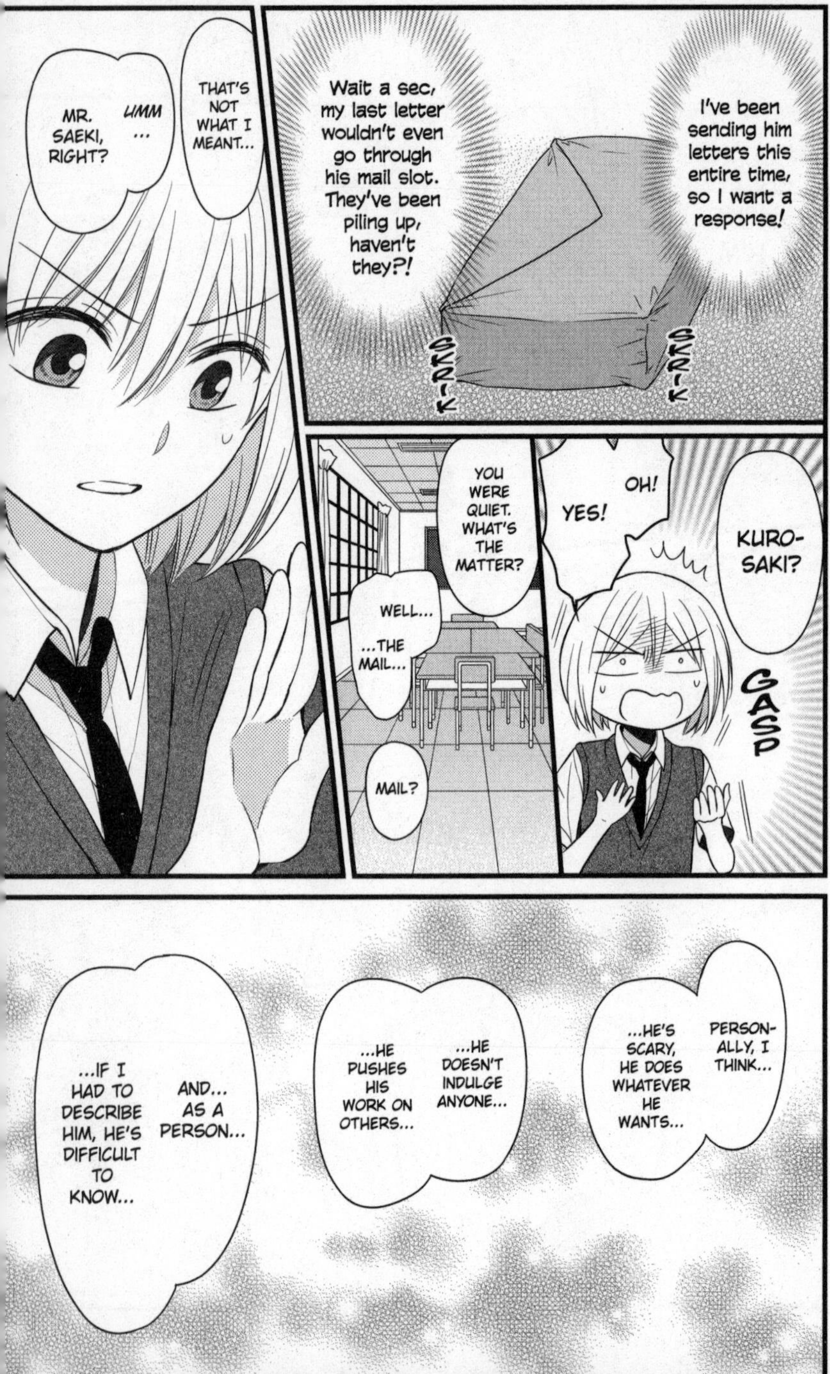
I've been sending him letters this entire time, so I want a response!
Wait a sec, my last letter wouldn't even go through his mail slot. They've been piling up, haven't they?!
SKRIK
SKRIK
KURO-SAKI?
OH!
YES!
GASP
YOU WERE QUIET. WHAT'S THE MATTER?
WELL...
...THE MAIL...
MAIL?
THAT'S NOT WHAT I MEANT...
UMM...
MR. SAEKI, RIGHT?
PERSON-ALLY, I THINK...
...HE'S SCARY, HE DOES WHATEVER HE WANTS...
...HE DOESN'T INDULGE ANYONE...
...HE PUSHES HIS WORK ON OTHERS...
AND... AS A PERSON...
...IF I HAD TO DESCRIBE HIM, HE'S DIFFICULT TO KNOW...

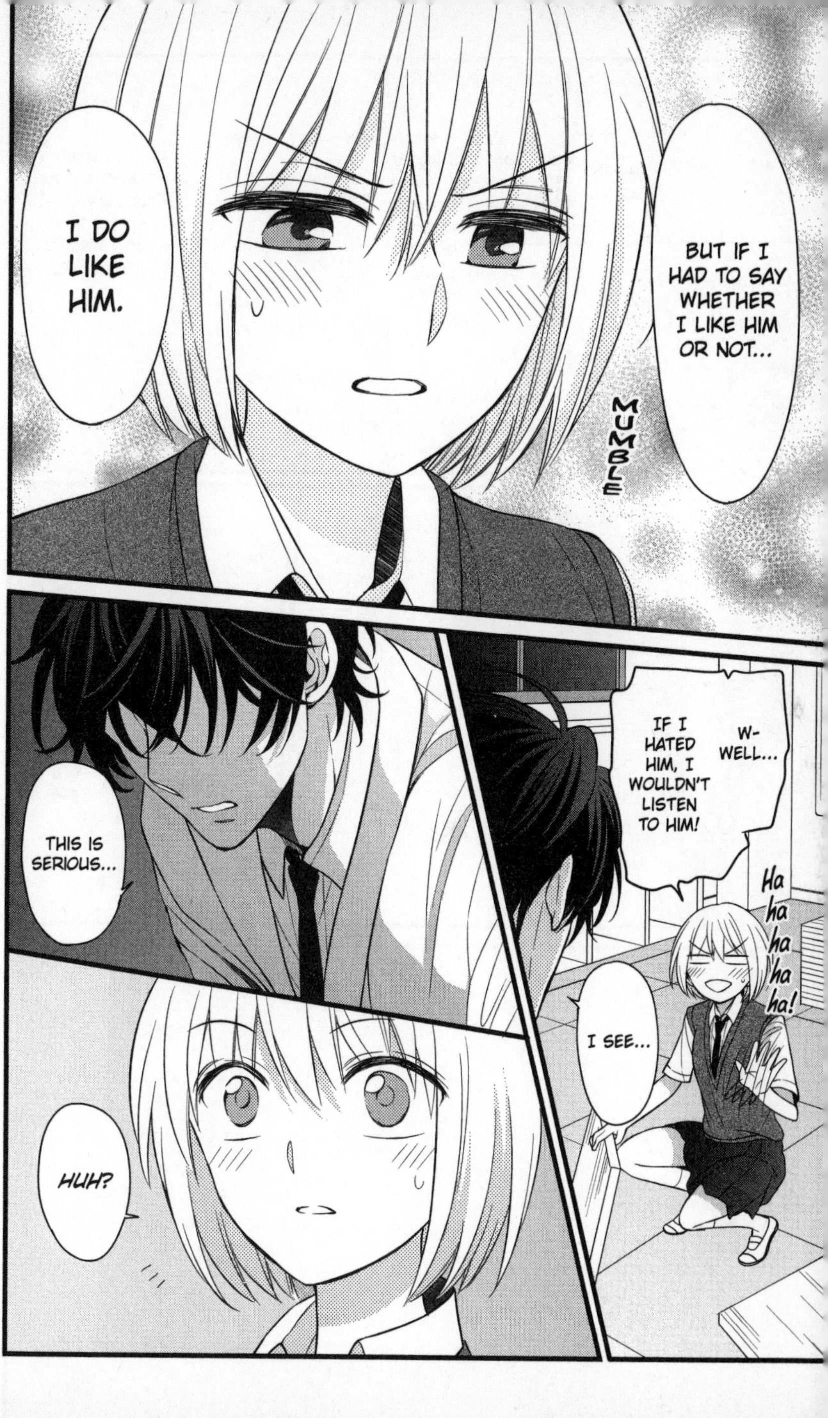
BUT IF I HAD TO SAY WHETHER I LIKE HIM OR NOT...
MUMBLE
I DO LIKE HIM.
W-WELL...
IF I HATED HIM, I WOULDN'T LISTEN TO HIM!
Ha ha ha ha ha!
I SEE...
THIS IS SERIOUS...
HUH?

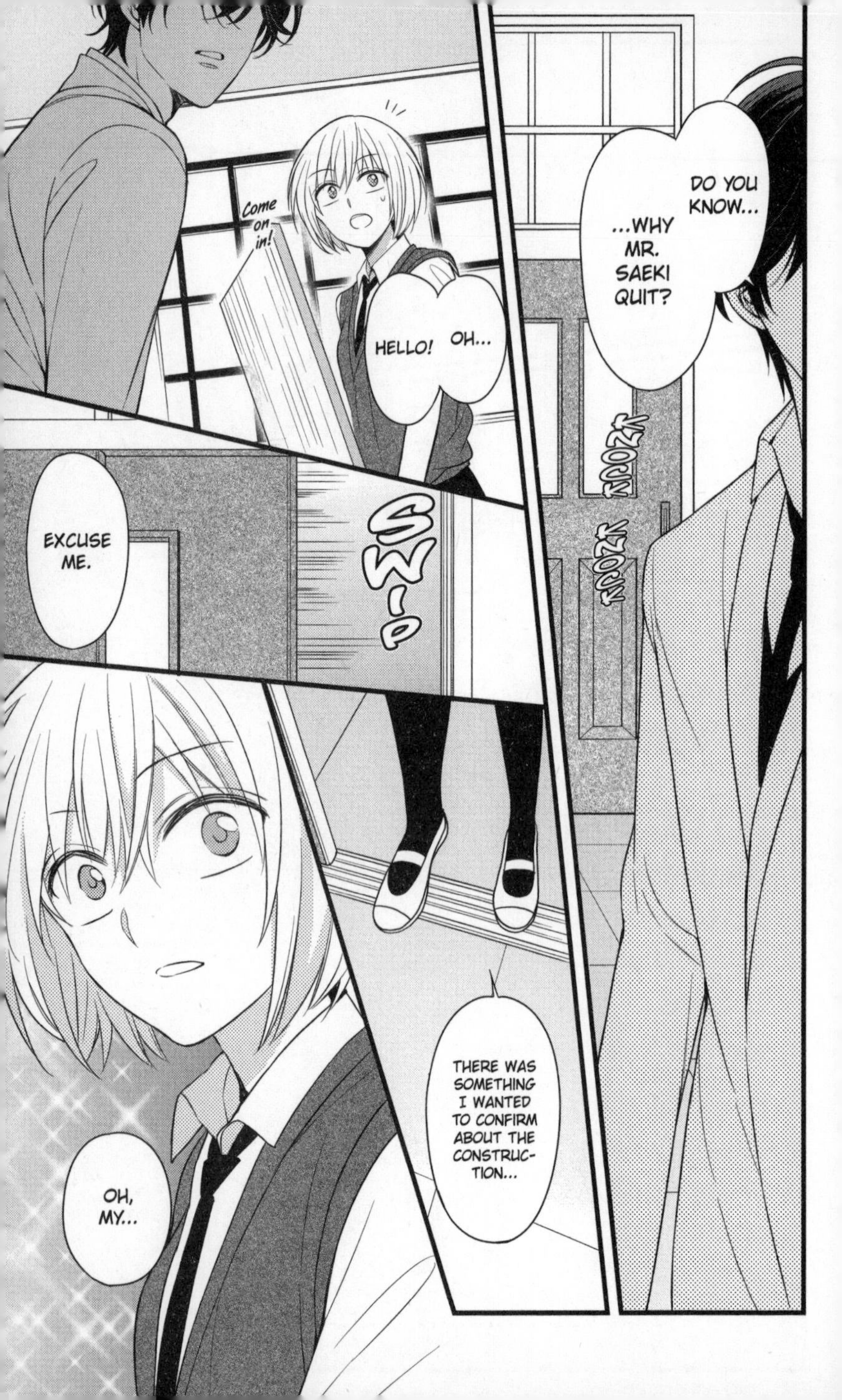
DO YOU KNOW...
...WHY MR. SAEKI QUIT?
VROOM
VROOM
Come on in!
OH... HELLO!
SWIP
EXCUSE ME.
THERE WAS SOMETHING I WANTED TO CONFIRM ABOUT THE CONSTRUC-TION...
OH, MY...

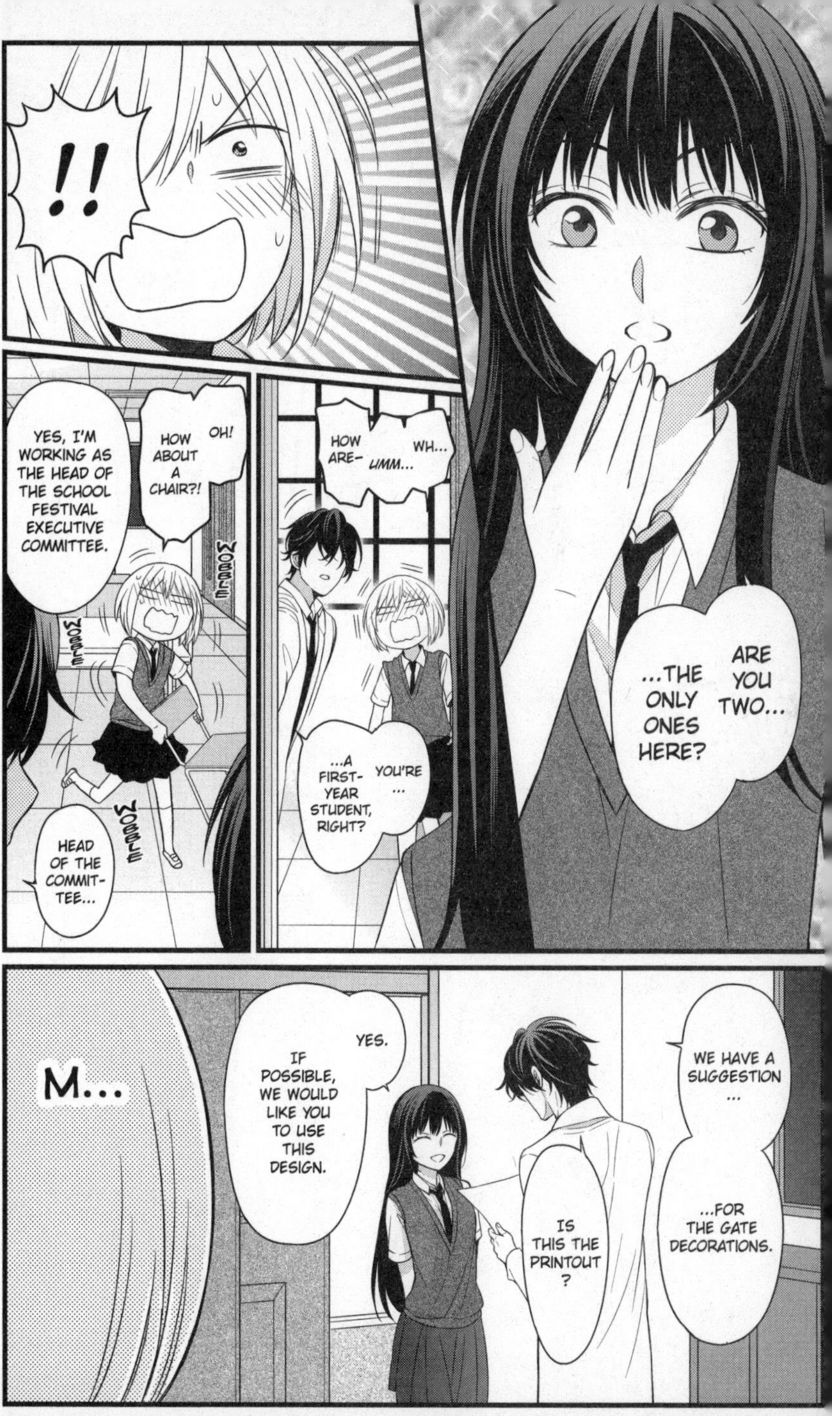
ARE YOU TWO...
...THE ONLY ONES HERE?
!!
WH... UMM... HOW ARE-
YOU'RE ...
...A FIRST-YEAR STUDENT, RIGHT?
OH! HOW ABOUT A CHAIR?!
YES, I'M WORKING AS THE HEAD OF THE SCHOOL FESTIVAL EXECUTIVE COMMITTEE.
WOBBLE
WOBBLE
WOBBLE
HEAD OF THE COMMIT-TEE...
WE HAVE A SUGGESTION ...
YES. IF POSSIBLE, WE WOULD LIKE YOU TO USE THIS DESIGN.
...FOR THE GATE DECORATIONS.
IS THIS THE PRINTOUT ?
M...

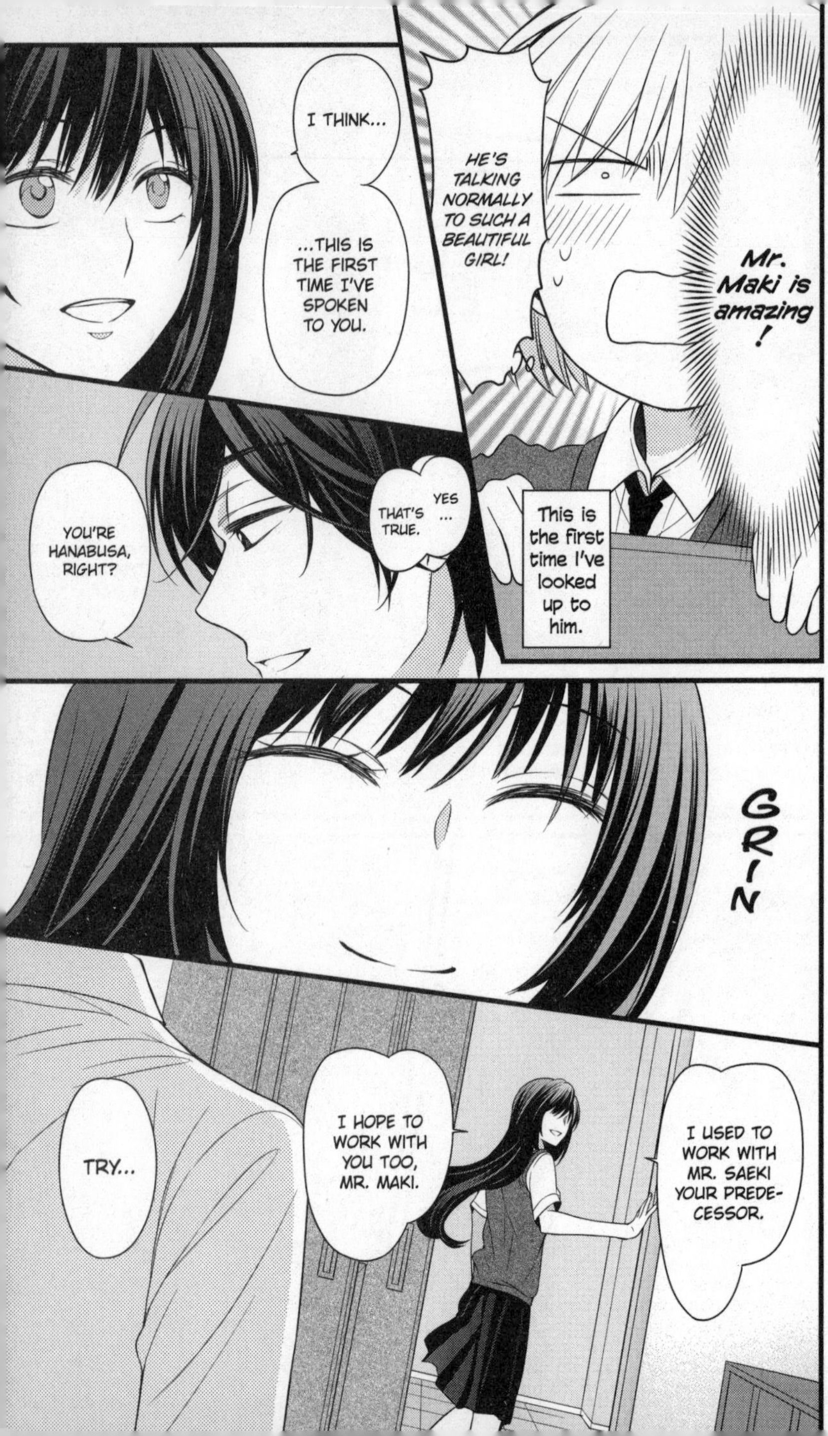
HE'S TALKING NORMALLY TO SUCH A BEAUTIFUL GIRL!
Mr. Maki is amazing!
This is the first time I've looked up to him.
I THINK...
...THIS IS THE FIRST TIME I'VE SPOKEN TO YOU.
YES... THAT'S TRUE.
YOU'RE HANABUSA, RIGHT?
GRIN
I USED TO WORK WITH MR. SAEKI YOUR PREDE-CESSOR.
I HOPE TO WORK WITH YOU TOO, MR. MAKI.
TRY...

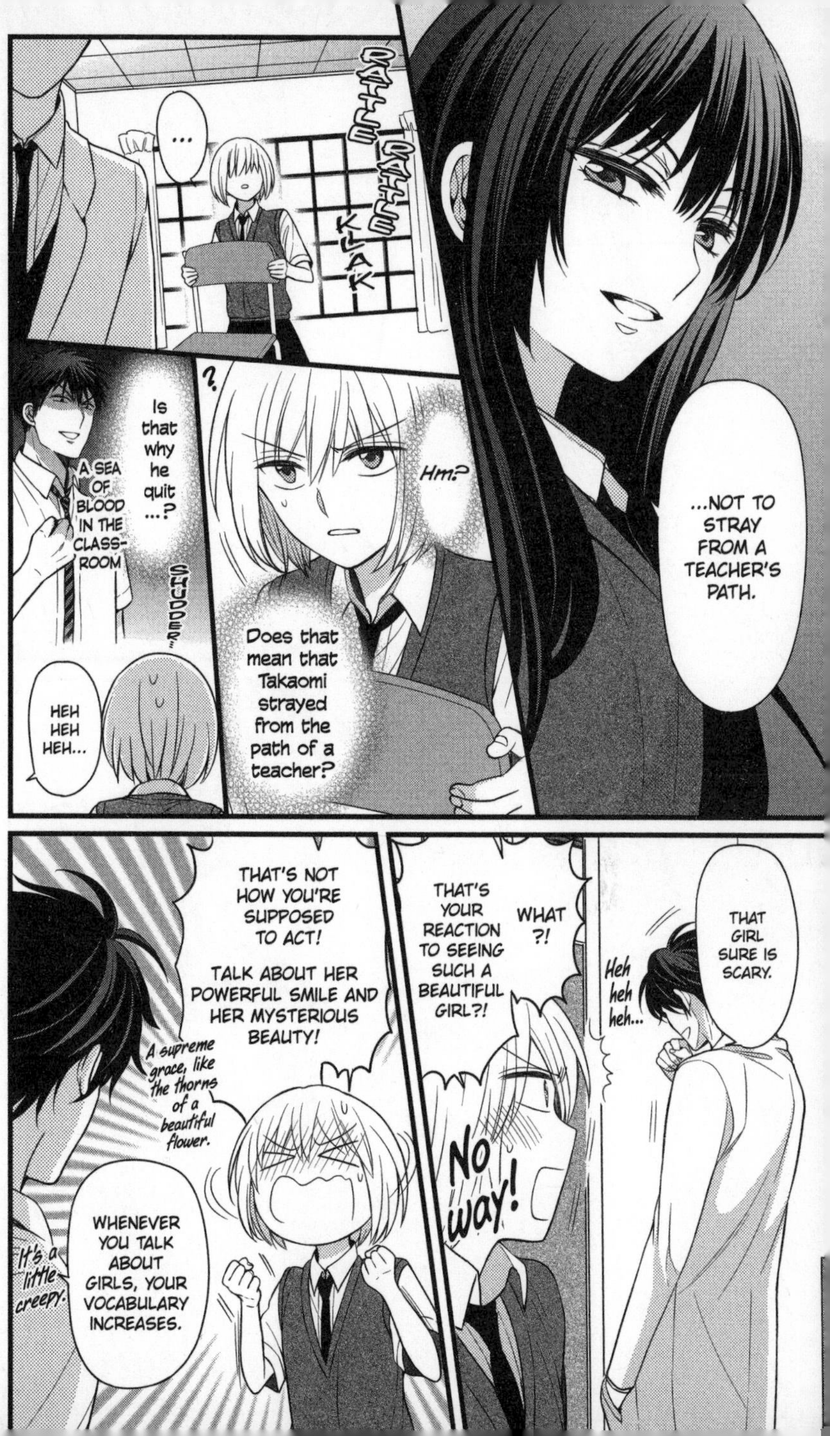
...NOT TO STRAY FROM A TEACHER'S PATH.
RATTLE RATTLE
KLAK
...
?
Hm?
Does that mean that Takaomi strayed from the path of a teacher?
Is that why he quit ...?
A SEA OF BLOOD IN THE CLASS-ROOM
SHUDDER...
HEH HEH HEH...
THAT GIRL SURE IS SCARY.
Heh heh heh...
WHAT ?!
THAT'S YOUR REACTION TO SEEING SUCH A BEAUTIFUL GIRL?!
No way!
THAT'S NOT HOW YOU'RE SUPPOSED TO ACT!
TALK ABOUT HER POWERFUL SMILE AND HER MYSTERIOUS BEAUTY!
A supreme grace, like the thorns of a beautiful flower.
WHENEVER YOU TALK ABOUT GIRLS, YOUR VOCABULARY INCREASES.
It's a little creepy.

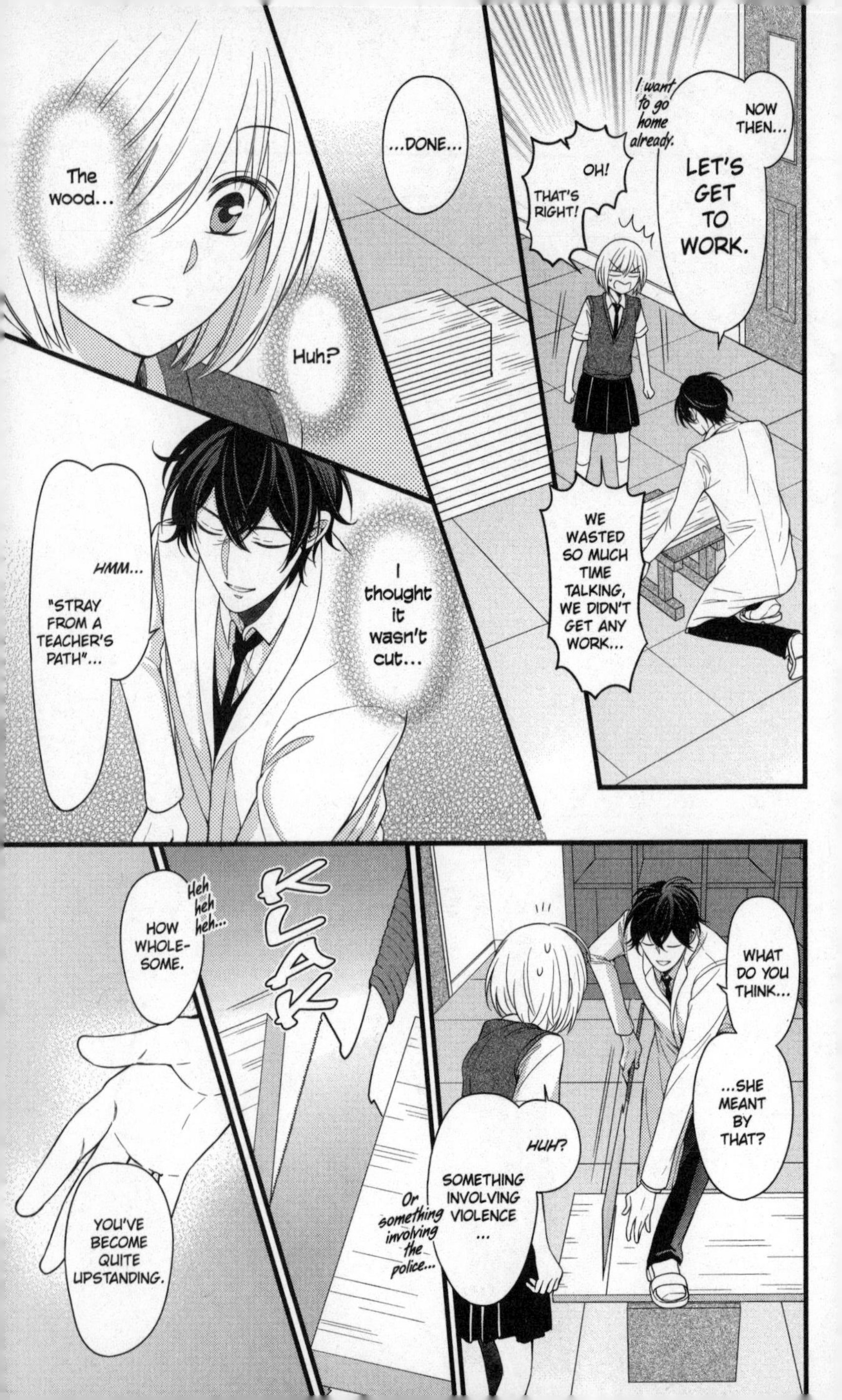

NOW THEN... LET'S GET TO WORK.
I want to go home already.
OH! THAT'S RIGHT!
WE WASTED SO MUCH TIME TALKING, WE DIDN'T GET ANY WORK...
...DONE...
The wood...
Huh?
I thought it wasn't cut...
HMM... "STRAY FROM A TEACHER'S PATH"...
WHAT DO YOU THINK...
...SHE MEANT BY THAT?
HUH?
SOMETHING INVOLVING VIOLENCE ...
Or something involving the police...
KLAK
Heh heh heh...
HOW WHOLE-SOME.
YOU'VE BECOME QUITE UPSTANDING.

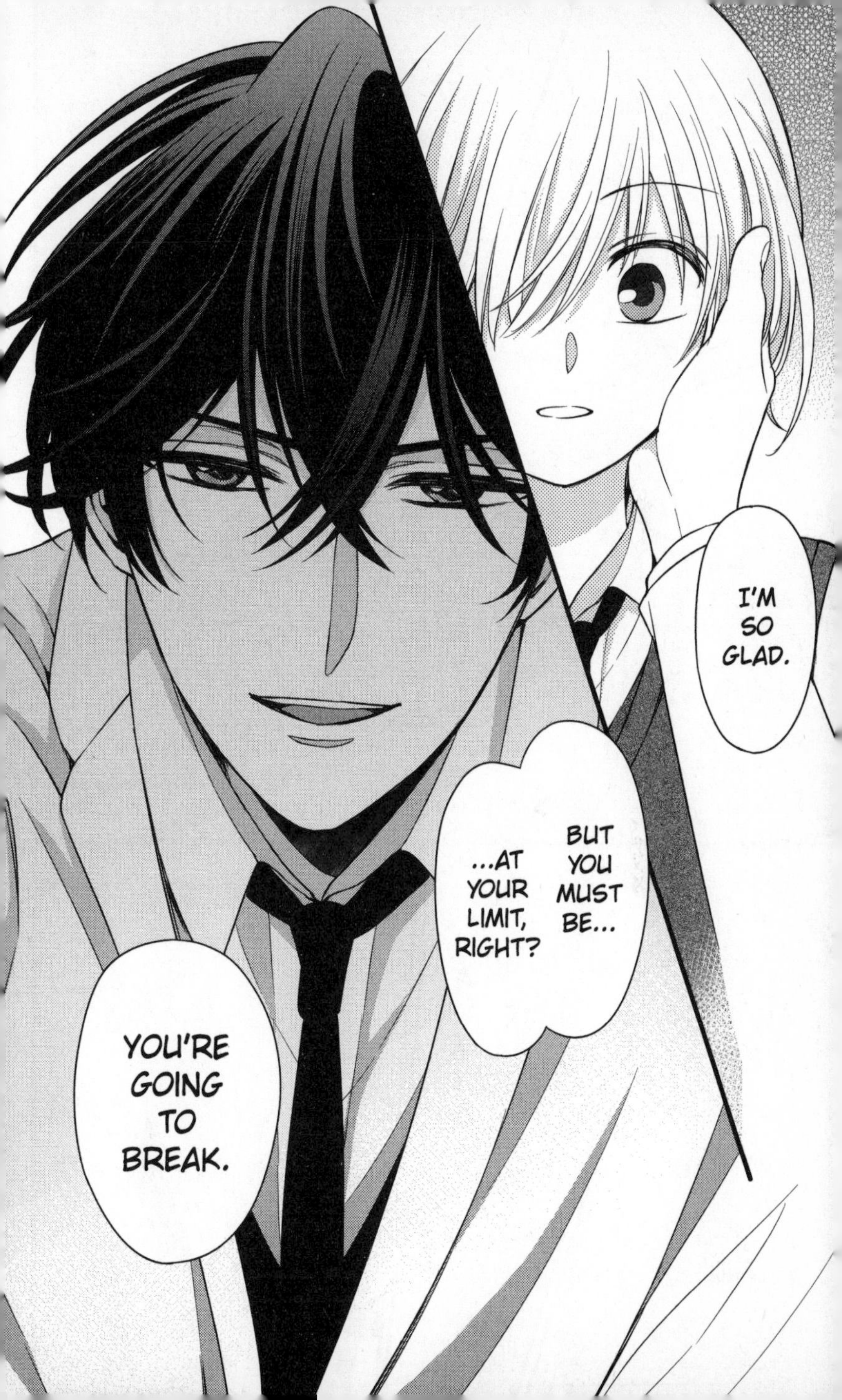
I'M SO GLAD.
BUT YOU MUST BE...
...AT YOUR LIMIT, RIGHT?
YOU'RE GOING TO BREAK.

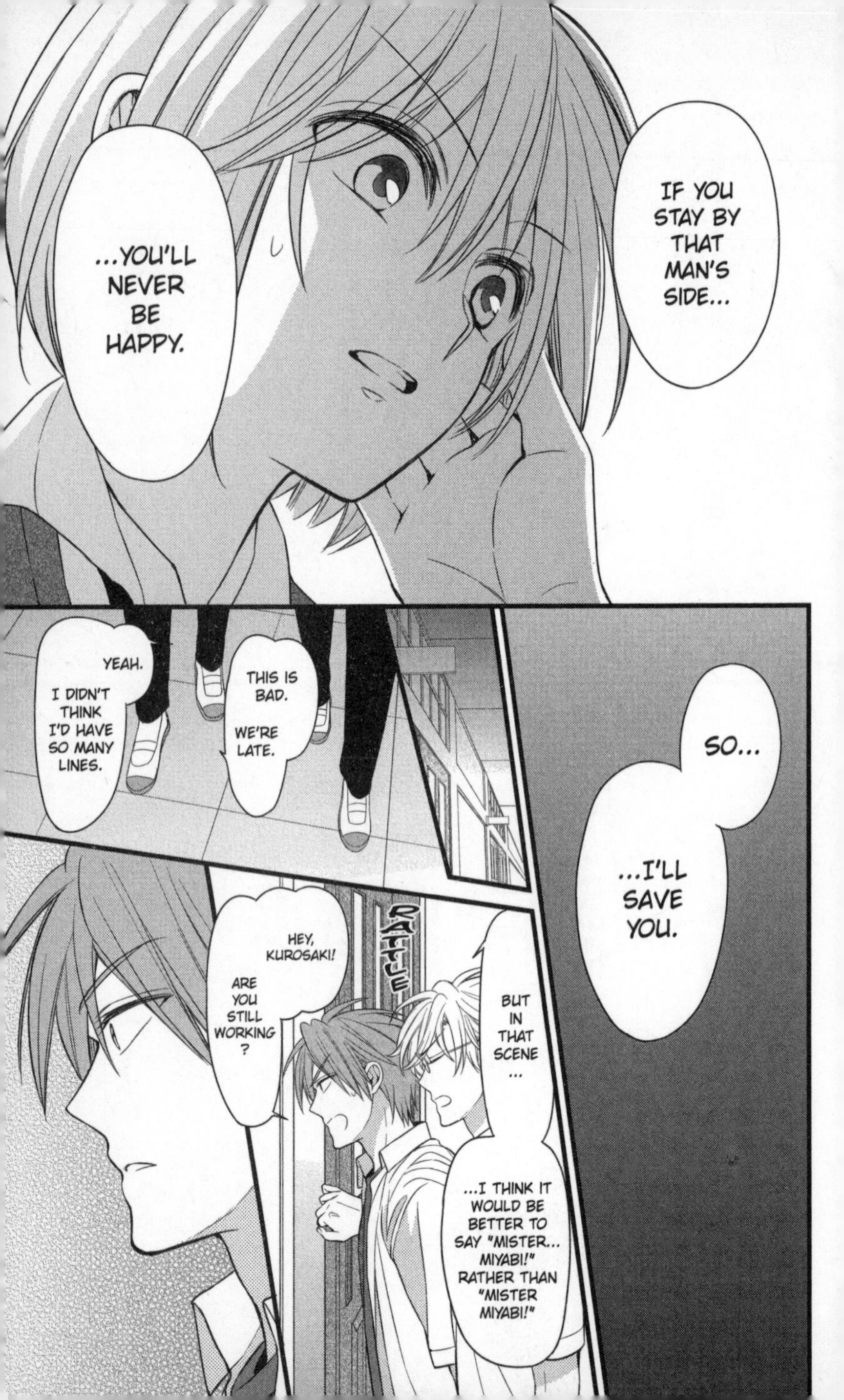
IF YOU STAY BY THAT MAN'S SIDE...
...YOU'LL NEVER BE HAPPY.
SO...
...I'LL SAVE YOU.
THIS IS BAD. WE'RE LATE.
YEAH. I DIDN'T THINK I'D HAVE SO MANY LINES.
RATTLE
BUT IN THAT SCENE...
...I THINK IT WOULD BE BETTER TO SAY "MISTER... MIYABI!" RATHER THAN "MISTER MIYABI!"
HEY, KUROSAKI! ARE YOU STILL WORKING?

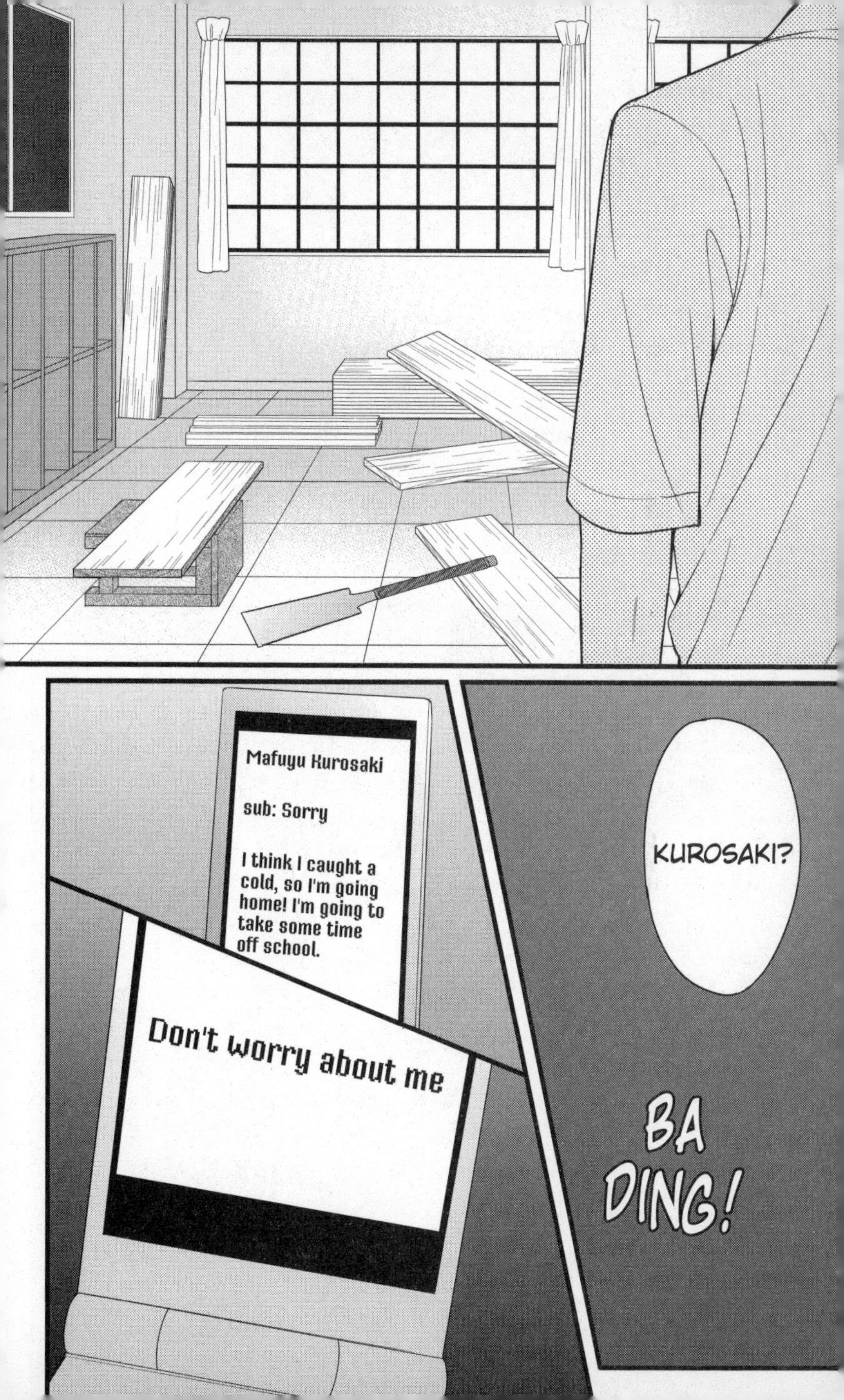
KUROSAKI?
BA DING!
Mafuyu Kurosaki
sub: Sorry
I think I caught a cold, so I'm going home! I'm going to take some time off school.
Don't worry about me

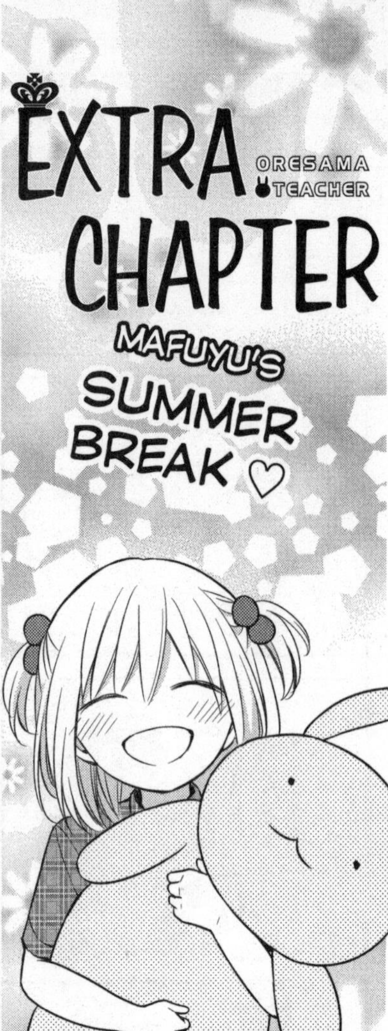
EXTRA CHAPTER
ORESAMA TEACHER
MAFUYU'S SUMMER BREAK ♡

MAFUYU'S INVITATION ♡

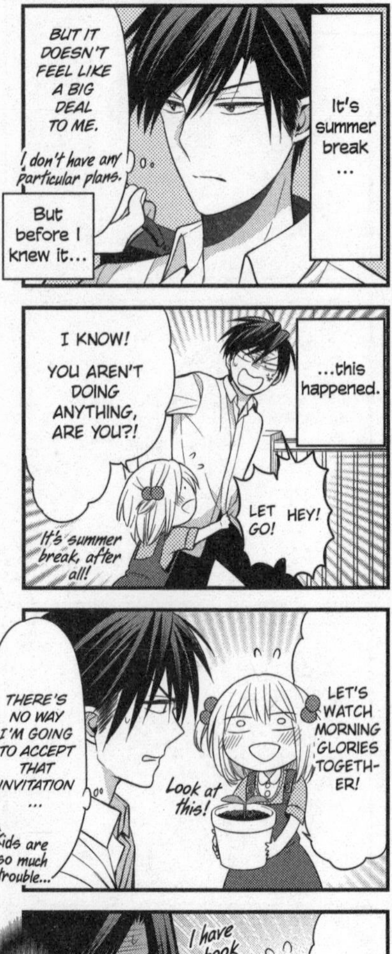
It's summer break ...
BUT IT DOESN'T FEEL LIKE A BIG DEAL TO ME.
I don't have any particular plans.
But before I knew it...
...this happened.
I KNOW! YOU AREN'T DOING ANYTHING, ARE YOU?!
HEY!
LET GO!
It's summer break, after all!
LET'S WATCH MORNING GLORIES TOGETH-ER!
Look at this!
THERE'S NO WAY I'M GOING TO ACCEPT THAT INVITATION ...
Kids are so much trouble...
WORK ON A RESEARCH PROJECT WITH ME!
I have a book report too!
This kid...
...is trying to make me do her home-work...

WHAT YOU CAN TELL FROM THE SUMMARY

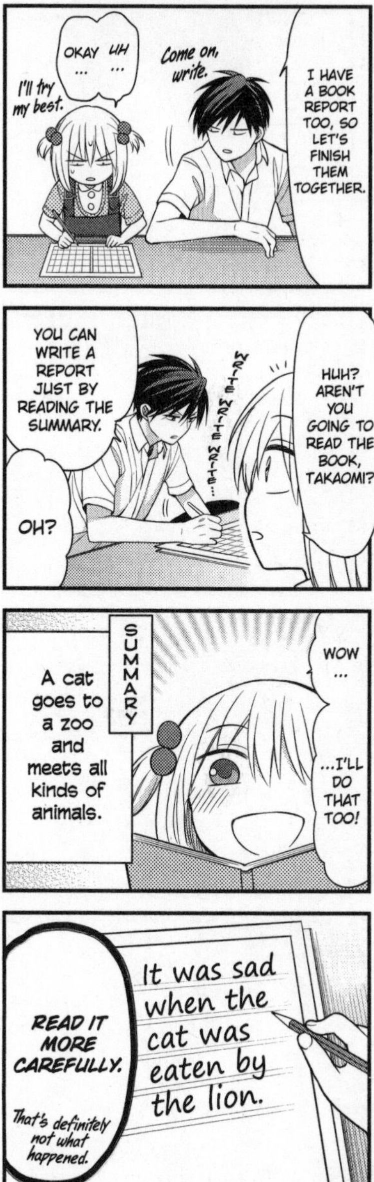
I HAVE A BOOK REPORT TOO, SO LET'S FINISH THEM TOGETHER.
Come on, write.
OKAY ... UH ...
I'll try my best.
HUH? AREN'T YOU GOING TO READ THE BOOK, TAKAOMI?
WRITE WRITE WRITE...
YOU CAN WRITE A REPORT JUST BY READING THE SUMMARY.
OH?
WOW ...
...I'LL DO THAT TOO!
SUMMARY
A cat goes to a zoo and meets all kinds of animals.
It was sad when the cat was eaten by the lion.
READ IT MORE CAREFULLY.
That's definitely not what happened.

FUN MATH

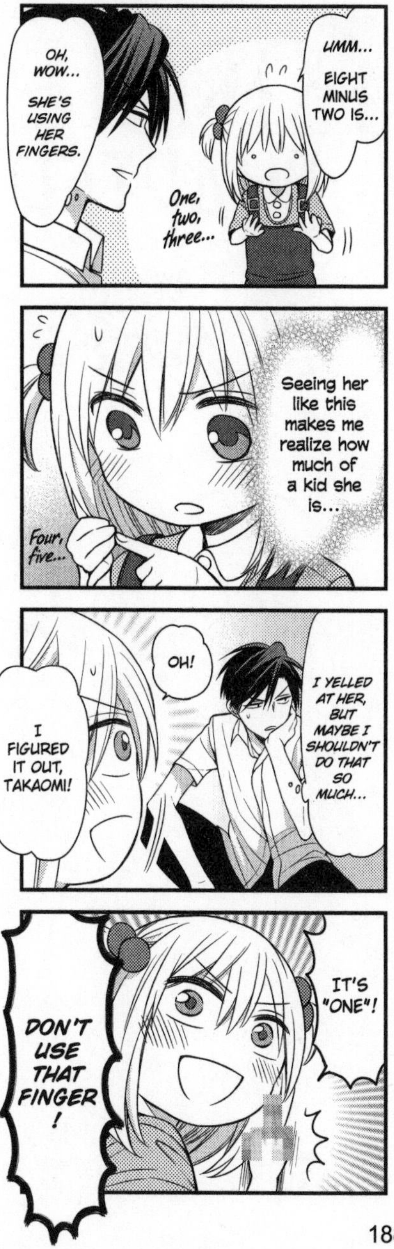
UMM... EIGHT MINUS TWO IS...
One, two, three...
OH, WOW... SHE'S USING HER FINGERS.
Seeing her like this makes me realize how much of a kid she is...
Four, five...
I YELLED AT HER, BUT MAYBE I SHOULDN'T DO THAT SO MUCH...
OH!
I FIGURED IT OUT, TAKAOMI!
IT'S "ONE"!
DON'T USE THAT FINGER!

GIVE ME A REWARD

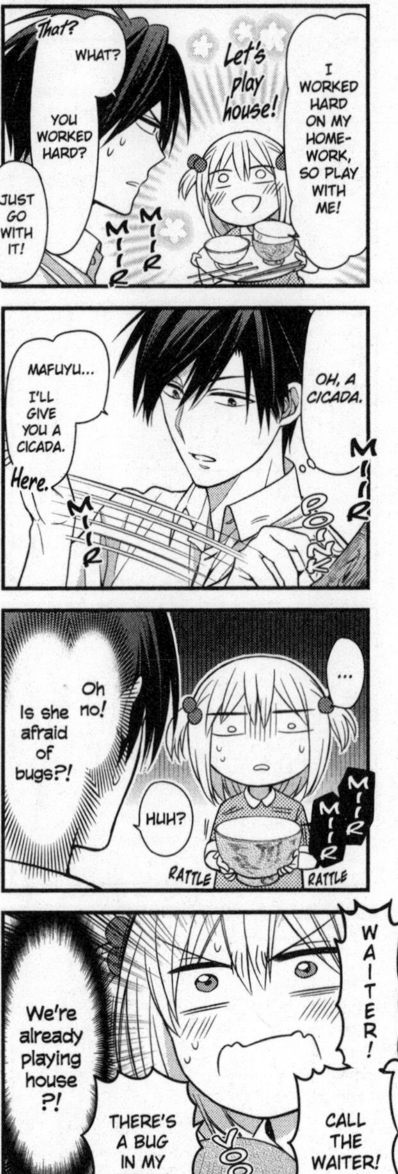
I WORKED HARD ON MY HOMEWORK, SO PLAY WITH ME!
Let's play house!
WHAT?
That?
YOU WORKED HARD?
JUST GO WITH IT!
MIIR
MIIR
OH, A CICADA.
MIIR
MAFUYU... I'LL GIVE YOU A CICADA.
Here.
MIIR
...
Oh no!
Is she afraid of bugs?!
HUH?
MIIR
MIIR
RATTLE
RATTLE
WAITER!
CALL THE WAITER!
We're already playing house?!
THERE'S A BUG IN MY BOWL!

A DELINQUENT AND A CHILD

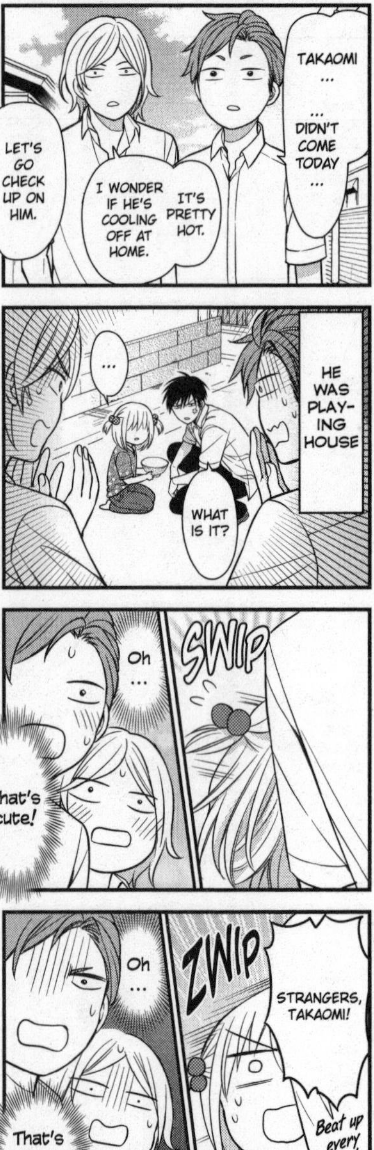
TAKAOMI... ...DIDN'T COME TODAY...
IT'S PRETTY HOT.
I WONDER IF HE'S COOLING OFF AT HOME.
LET'S GO CHECK UP ON HIM.
HE WAS PLAYING HOUSE
...
WHAT IS IT?
SWIP
Oh...
That's cute!
STRANGERS, TAKAOMI!
ZWIP
Beat up every last one of them!
Oh...
That's *not* cute!

MY STUPID DOG

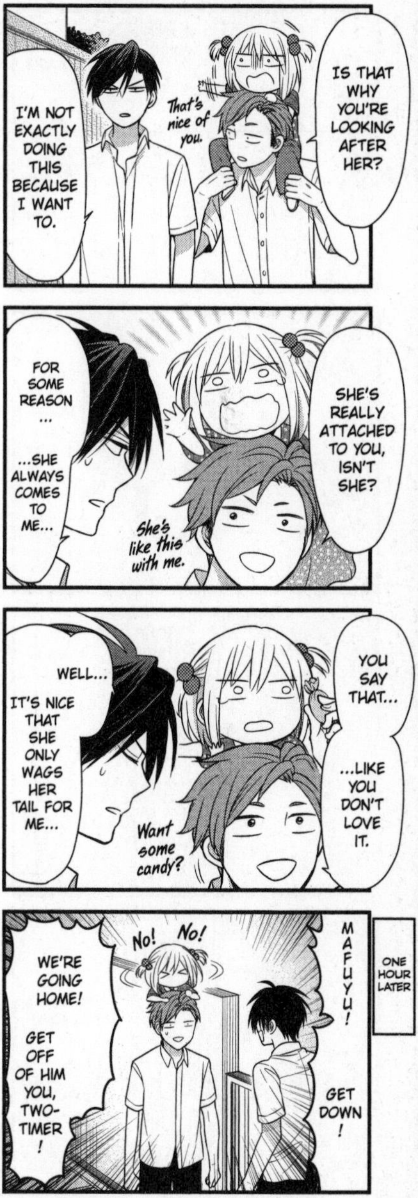
IS THAT WHY YOU'RE LOOKING AFTER HER?
That's nice of you.
I'M NOT EXACTLY DOING THIS BECAUSE I WANT TO.
SHE'S REALLY ATTACHED TO YOU, ISN'T SHE?
FOR SOME REASON...
...SHE ALWAYS COMES TO ME...
She's like this with me.
YOU SAY THAT...
...LIKE YOU DON'T LOVE IT.
WELL...
IT'S NICE THAT SHE ONLY WAGS HER TAIL FOR ME...
Want some candy?
ONE HOUR LATER
MAFUYU!
GET DOWN!
No! No!
WE'RE GOING HOME!
GET OFF OF HIM YOU, TWO-TIMER!

A RECORD OF CRIMES

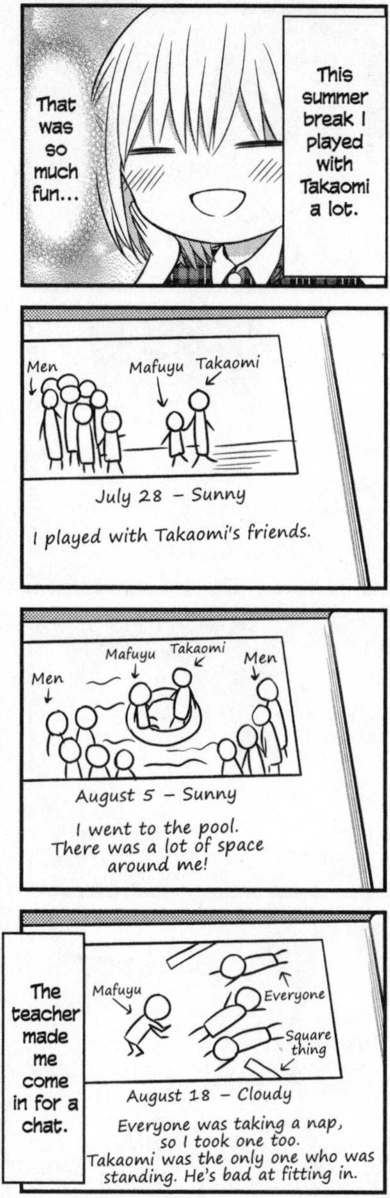
This summer break I played with Takaomi a lot.
That was so much fun...
Takaomi
Mafuyu
Men
July 28 – Sunny
I played with Takaomi's friends.
Men
Takaomi
Mafuyu
Men
August 5 – Sunny
I went to the pool. There was a lot of space around me!
Everyone
Square thing
Mafuyu
August 18 – Cloudy
Everyone was taking a nap, so I took one too. Takaomi was the only one who was standing. He's bad at fitting in.
The teacher made me come in for a chat.

2ND ORESAMA TEACHER CHARACTER CONTEST RESULTS!

THANK YOU FOR ALL THE VOTES!

ORESAMA TEACHER HAS BEEN RUNNING FOR OVER TEN YEARS! TO CELEBRATE THIS MAJOR MILESTONE, WE PRESENT TO YOU THE CONTEST RESULTS!

AFTER HITTING TEN CONTINUOUS YEARS OF PUBLICATION IN THE SUMMER OF 2017, WE RAN A POPULARITY POLL WHERE READERS CHOSE THEIR TOP THREE FAVORITE CHARACTERS. THE POLL WAS IN *HANA TO YUME* MAGAZINE AND ON A SPECIAL WEBSITE, AND THE RESULTS WERE ANNOUNCED IN *HANA TO YUME* ISSUE 21 (OCTOBER 2017).

11TH
581 VOTES
ASAHI SAKURADA
CROSSDRESSING AND UNDERWEAR! EVERYONE'S MASCOT!
12TH
360 VOTES
TOMOHIRO KAWAUCHI
A BELOVED, HOPELESS SUBORDINATE WITH A GREAT VOICE!
13TH
339 VOTES
KOTOBUKI OKUBO
IT'S PLEASING TO WATCH THIS UNLUCKY YOUNG MAN!
14TH
196 VOTES
AKI SHIBUYA
A CONSIDERATE UNDERCLASSMAN!
15TH
142 VOTES
KANON NONOGUCHI
HER ATTITUDE AND PIGTAILS MAKE HER REALLY POPULAR!
16TH
115 VOTES
MINATO KANGAWA
KANGAWA'S LITTLE SISTER ONLY APPEARS IN THE GRAPHIC NOVELS!
17TH
83 VOTES
WAKANA HOJO
18TH
66 VOTES
TAKUMI YAMASHITA
19TH
60 VOTES
TORIKICHI (JOSEPHINE)
NEKOMATA
20TH
42 VOTES
SHUNTARO KOSAKA

22nd place	23rd place	24th place
KENTO NOGAMI	SEIICHIRO MAKI	DAIKICHI GOTO
25th place	**26th place**	**27th place**
MASAYOSHI OMIYA	RUNA MOMOCHI	IZUMI TSUBAKI SENSEI
28th place	**29th place**	**30th place**
THE PERSON IN AYABE'S CLASS WHO REALLY LIKES YAKISOBA BREAD	RYUNOSUKE HIMEJI	ARISUGAWA & MARIKA

SO WHO SHINES AT THE TOP?!

THE TOP TEN ARE REVEALED ON THE NEXT PAGE!

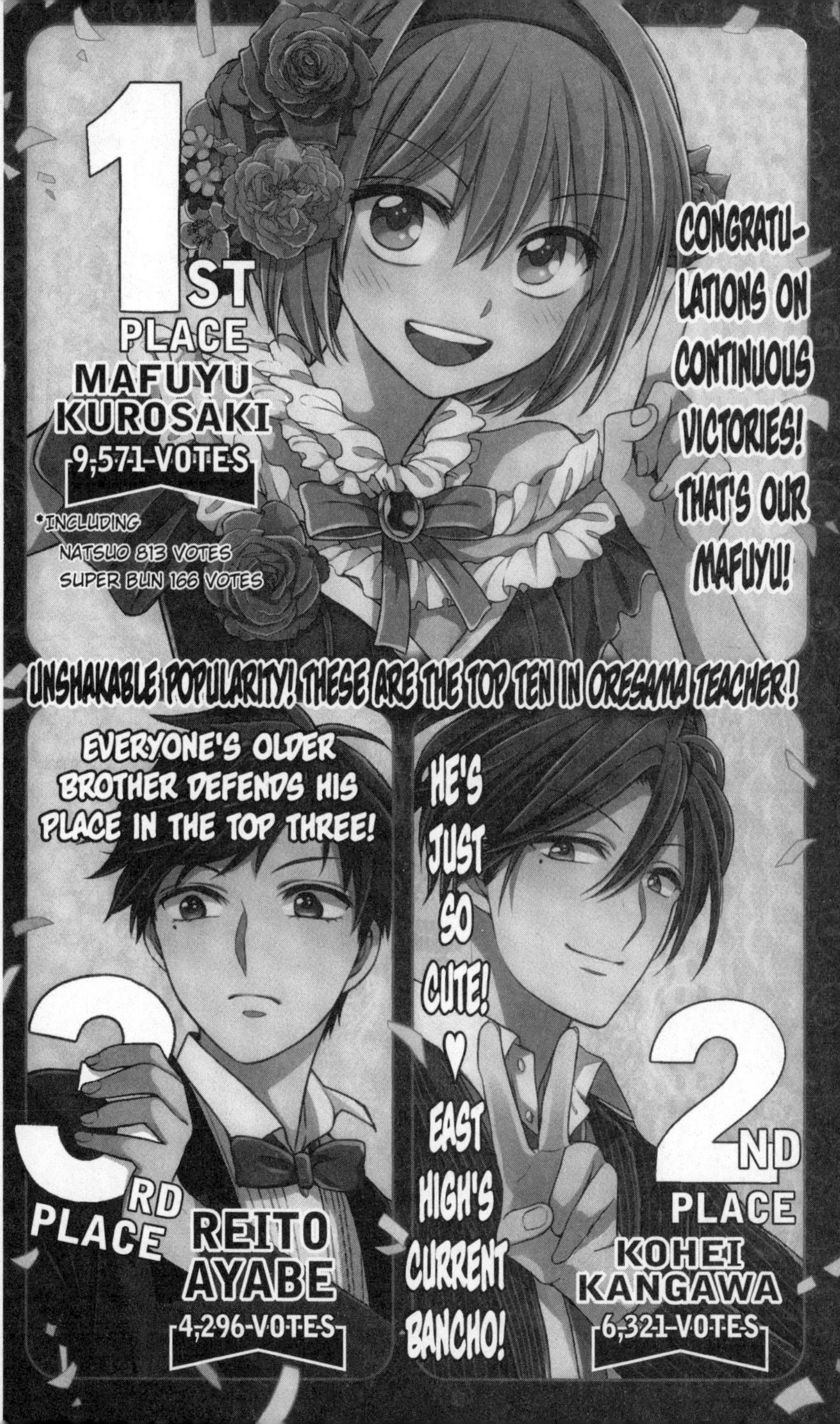
CONGRATU-LATIONS ON CONTINUOUS VICTORIES! THAT'S OUR MAFUYU!
1ST PLACE
MAFUYU KUROSAKI
9,571 VOTES
*INCLUDING NATSUO 813 VOTES SUPER BUN 166 VOTES
UNSHAKABLE POPULARITY! THESE ARE THE TOP TEN IN ORESAMA TEACHER!
HE'S JUST SO CUTE! ♥
EAST HIGH'S CURRENT BANCHO!
2ND PLACE
KOHEI KANGAWA
6,321 VOTES
EVERYONE'S OLDER BROTHER DEFENDS HIS PLACE IN THE TOP THREE!
3RD PLACE
REITO AYABE
4,296 VOTES

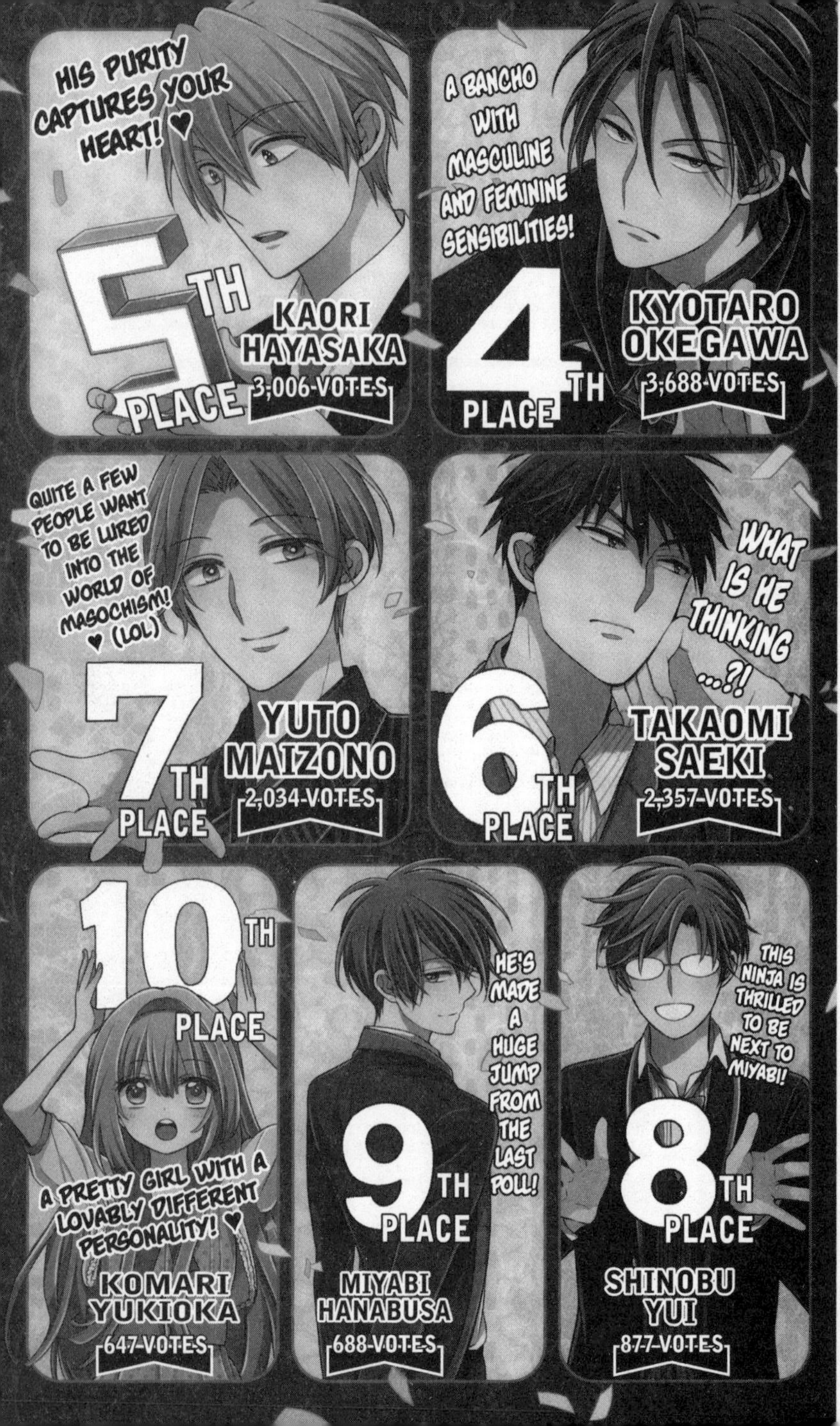
A BANCHO WITH MASCULINE AND FEMININE SENSIBILITIES!
4TH PLACE
KYOTARO OKEGAWA
3,688 VOTES
HIS PURITY CAPTURES YOUR HEART! ♥
5TH PLACE
KAORI HAYASAKA
3,006 VOTES
WHAT IS HE THINKING ...?!
6TH PLACE
TAKAOMI SAEKI
2,357 VOTES
QUITE A FEW PEOPLE WANT TO BE LURED INTO THE WORLD OF MASOCHISM! ♥ (LOL)
7TH PLACE
YUTO MAIZONO
2,034 VOTES
THIS NINJA IS THRILLED TO BE NEXT TO MIYABI!
8TH PLACE
SHINOBU YUI
877 VOTES
HE'S MADE A HUGE JUMP FROM THE LAST POLL!
9TH PLACE
MIYABI HANABUSA
688 VOTES
10TH PLACE
A PRETTY GIRL WITH A LOVABLY DIFFERENT PERSONALITY! ♥
KOMARI YUKIOKA
647 VOTES

2ND CHARACTER CONTEST

MESSAGES OF SUPPORT FROM PASSIONATE FANS ♥

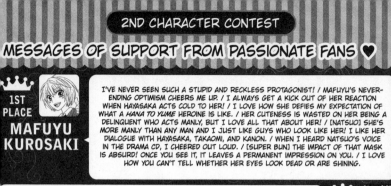

1ST PLACE
MAFUYU KUROSAKI

I'VE NEVER SEEN SUCH A STUPID AND RECKLESS PROTAGONIST! / MAFUYU'S NEVER-ENDING OPTIMISM CHEERS ME UP. / I ALWAYS GET A KICK OUT OF HER REACTION WHEN HAYASAKA ACTS COLD TO HER! / I LOVE HOW SHE DEFIES MY EXPECTATION OF WHAT A *HANA TO YUME* HEROINE IS LIKE. / HER CUTENESS IS WASTED ON HER BEING A DELINQUENT WHO ACTS MANLY, BUT I LOVE ALL THAT ABOUT HER! / [NATSUO] SHE'S MORE MANLY THAN ANY MAN AND I JUST LIKE GUYS WHO LOOK LIKE HER! I LIKE HER DIALOGUE WITH HAYASAKA, TAKAOMI, AND KANON. / WHEN I HEARD NATSUO'S VOICE IN THE DRAMA CD, I CHEERED OUT LOUD. / [SUPER BUN] THE IMPACT OF THAT MASK IS ABSURD! ONCE YOU SEE IT, IT LEAVES A PERMANENT IMPRESSION ON YOU. / I LOVE HOW YOU CAN'T TELL WHETHER HER EYES LOOK DEAD OR ARE SHINING.

2ND PLACE
KOHEI KANGAWA

HE'S JUST SO CUTE. / THE BEST UNDERCLASSMAN. SEEING HIM TURN HAPPY AND SAD OVER MAFUYU TRIGGERS MY MATERNAL INSTINCTS. I LIKED HIS EXPRESSION WHEN HE SAID "I WANTED YOU TO COME TO ME FIRST." / I COMPLETELY FELL IN LOVE WITH KANGAWA IN VOLUME 7, CHAPTER 38. SINCE THEN, I ALWAYS LOOK FORWARD TO THE TIMES WHEN MAFUYU RETURNS TO HER HOMETOWN! / THOSE PUPPY-DOG EYES... THAT SEXY MOLE UNDER HIS EYE... / IT'S SO CUTE HOW HE TURNS RED ALL THE TIME. / I CAN'T GET ENOUGH OF SEEING KANGAWA TURN RED.

3RD PLACE
REITO AYABE

LOWER EYELASHES, A MOLE UNDER HIS RIGHT EYE, AND THAT KANSAI ACCENT... I REALLY LIKE THE WAY HE LOOKS. / HE'S A GOOD PERSON WHO CARES FOR HIS FAMILY! I WANT TO PLAY WITH HIS SIBLINGS. / THE FACT THAT HE CAN COOK AND CLEAN EARNS HIM A LOT OF POINTS. IN THE DRAMA CD, I LOVED THE FACT THAT HE DIDN'T MEASURE THE INGREDIENTS WHEN MAKING SWEETS. / HIS CLEANING MODE IS THE BEST! / IT'S SO CUTE THAT HE NAMES HIS CLEANING EQUIPMENT. / I WAS SO TOUCHED BY HOW MUCH HE LOVES THE GUITAR CASE THAT STUDENT COUNCIL PRESIDENT HANABUSA GAVE HIM.

4TH PLACE
KYOTARO OKEGAWA

I USED TO THINK HE WAS A SCARY, FORMIDABLE PERSON, BUT BETWEEN THE MASCOT CHARACTER, THE PIGEON PEN-PALS AND FLUNKING A YEAR...HE'S THE PRINCE OF DEFYING EXPECTATIONS! A TON OF AMUSING THINGS KEEP HAPPENING TO HIM. / HE'S REALLY CUTE WITH HIS HAIR DOWN! HIS FAIRY-TALE LETTERS ARE TOO CUTE! IT'S THE BEST WHEN HE BEATS PEOPLE UP FOR NO REASON! / I LAUGHED THE MOST AT THE MORSE CODE STORY. THAT WAS MY FAVORITE. / OKEGAWA HAS RATHER FEMININE SENSIBILITIES AND HE GETS NERVOUS ABOUT MAFUYU. IT MAKES ME REALIZE I'M READING A GIRLS' COMIC.

5TH PLACE
KAORI HAYASAKA

I THINK IT'S THE FACT THAT HE'S TSUNDERE! / BECAUSE OF HAYASAKA, I BECAME OBSESSED WITH TSUNDERE. / I LIKE THAT HE'S SERIOUS AND SHOWS UP AT CLASS AND MORNING MEETINGS. / I LIKE HIM EVEN MORE NOW THAT WE KNOW ABOUT HIS FAMILY AND HIS PAST! / HE WAS REALLY CUTE WHEN HE BLUSHED AFTER HE WAS COMPLIMENTED ON HIS HAIR.

6TH PLACE
TAKAOMI SAEKI

A TEACHER WHO'S HANDSOME AND GOOD AT FIGHTING IS JUST TOO POWERFUL. (LOL) I ALSO LOVE TAKAOMI WHEN HE WAS A HIGH SCHOOL STUDENT! / I LOVE THE JOKES ABOUT THE STRUGGLES OF BEING A TEACHER AND BEING AN ADULT. / HE CARES FOR HIS GRANDFATHER AND IS SURPRISINGLY KIND. AND HE LOOKS GREAT IN A SUIT! I WANT HIM TO PAT MY HEAD. (LOL)

7TH PLACE
YUTO MAIZONO

I LOST IT WHEN I SAW THAT HIS CHARACTER INTRODUCTIONS DESCRIBED HIM AS "THE ONE WHO LURES YOU INTO THE WORLD OF MASOCHISM." / I LIKED HIM EVEN MORE AFTER THE TEST OF COURAGE STORY. / HIS UNWAVERING WEIRDNESS AND HIS SOMEWHAT ELEGANT MYSTERIOUSNESS IS QUITE WONDERFUL.

8TH PLACE
SHINOBU YUI

HE'S A REAL PAIN IN THE ASS! (PRAISE) / IT'S REALLY CUTE THAT HE LOVES MIYABI AND WATCHING HIM MAKES ME FEEL BETTER! / IT'S NOT FAIR THAT HE SOMETIMES LOOKS REALLY HANDSOME!

9TH PLACE
MIYABI HANABUSA

I LOVE THE COOL THINGS HE DOES AS COUNCIL PRESIDENT AND THE WAY HE INNOCENTLY PLAYS AROUND. / AT FIRST, HE WAS MYSTERIOUS AND SCARY, BUT HIS LOVE FOR THE STUDENT COUNCIL IS DEEP AND WONDERFUL. I CRIED AT VOLUME 22.

10TH PLACE
KOMARI YUKIOKA

I LOVE THE WAY SHE TALKS AND THE THINGS SHE TALKS ABOUT DESPITE HER LOOKS! / THE WAY SHE CHARGES AT SHIBUYA IS HONEST AND CUTE! / THE LAME WAY SHE RUNS LIKE AN OLD MAN IS CUTE!

THANK YOU VERY MUCH FOR ALL THE VOTES AND MESSAGES!
I HOPE YOU CONTINUE TO SUPPORT *ORESAMA TEACHER*! ♥

STOP IT

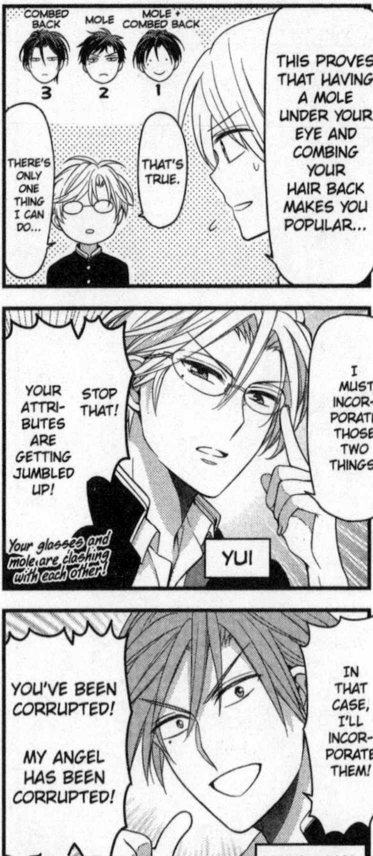
THIS PROVES THAT HAVING A MOLE UNDER YOUR EYE AND COMBING YOUR HAIR BACK MAKES YOU POPULAR...
MOLE + COMBED BACK
MOLE
COMBED BACK
1
2
3
THAT'S TRUE.
THERE'S ONLY ONE THING I CAN DO...
I MUST INCORPORATE THOSE TWO THINGS.
YUI
STOP THAT!
YOUR ATTRIBUTES ARE GETTING JUMBLED UP!
Your glasses and mole are clashing with each other!
IN THAT CASE, I'LL INCORPORATE THEM!
HAYASAKA
YOU'VE BEEN CORRUPTED!
MY ANGEL HAS BEEN CORRUPTED!
This is unforgivable!
I'VE INCORPORATED THEM TOO.
MIYABI
I'M HAVING PROBLEMS TELLING WHO YOU ARE!

PLEASE STOP

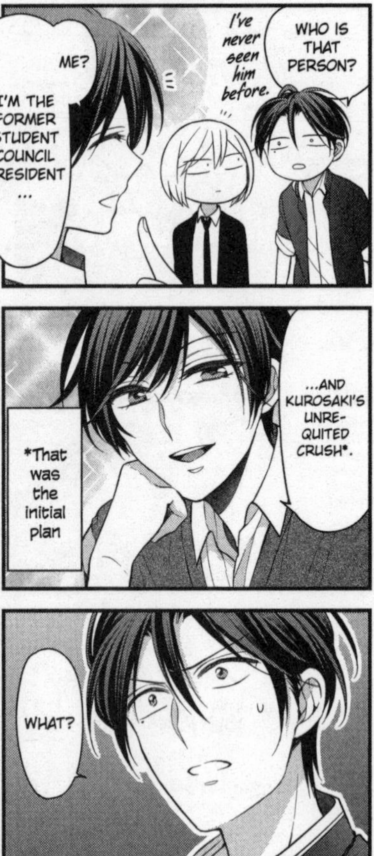
WHO IS THAT PERSON?
I've never seen him before.
ME?
I'M THE FORMER STUDENT COUNCIL PRESIDENT ...
...AND KUROSAKI'S UNREQUITED CRUSH*.
*That was the initial plan
WHAT?
MAFUYU, I'VE CHANGED MY LOOK!
What do you think?!
I'M HAVING PROBLEMS TELLING WHO YOU ARE!
Stop it!

COMPARED TO THE LAST TIME

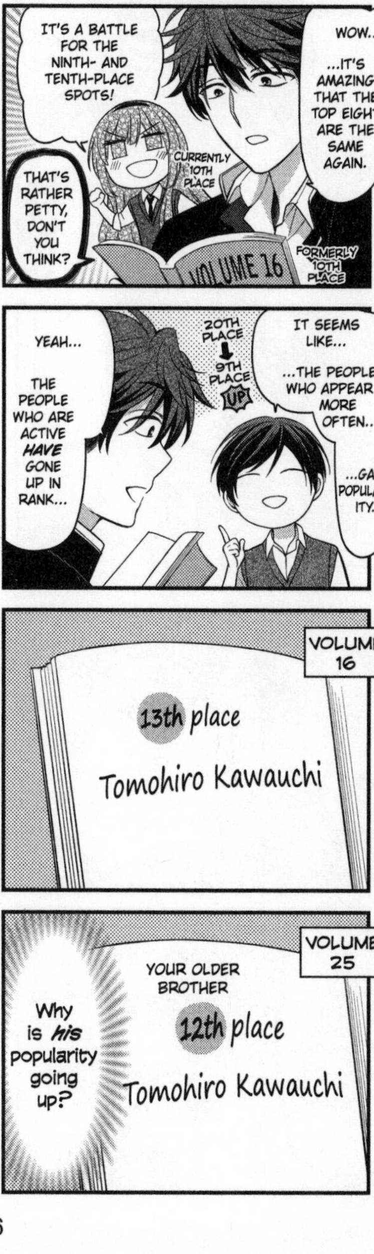
WOW... ...IT'S AMAZING THAT THE TOP EIGHT ARE THE SAME AGAIN.
FORMERLY 10TH PLACE
IT'S A BATTLE FOR THE NINTH- AND TENTH-PLACE SPOTS!
CURRENTLY 10TH PLACE
THAT'S RATHER PETTY, DON'T YOU THINK?
VOLUME 16
IT SEEMS LIKE... ...THE PEOPLE WHO APPEAR MORE OFTEN...
...GAIN POPULAR-ITY.
20TH PLACE
9TH PLACE
UP
YEAH...
THE PEOPLE WHO ARE ACTIVE *HAVE* GONE UP IN RANK...
VOLUME 16
13th place
Tomohiro Kawauchi
VOLUME 25
YOUR OLDER BROTHER
12th place
Tomohiro Kawauchi
Why is *his* popularity going up?

YOUR OLDER BROTHER

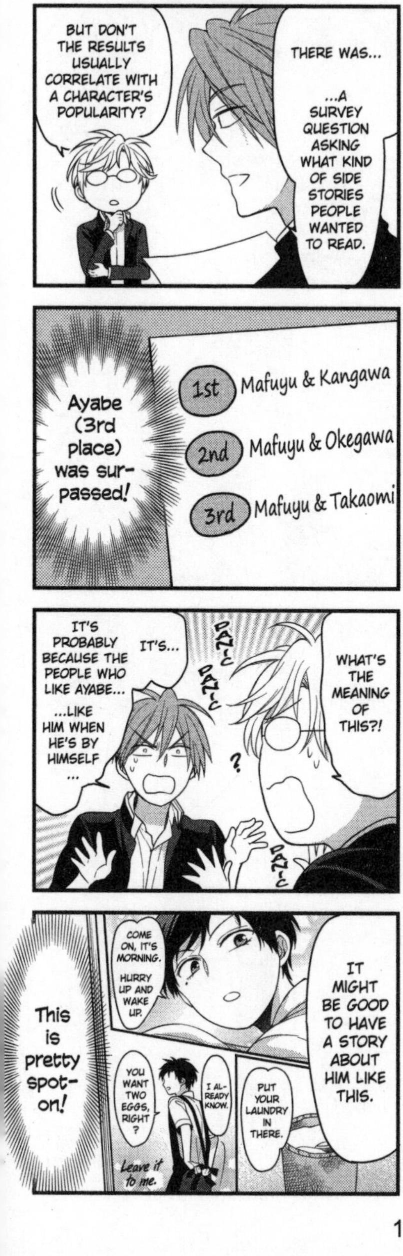
THERE WAS...
...A SURVEY QUESTION ASKING WHAT KIND OF SIDE STORIES PEOPLE WANTED TO READ.
BUT DON'T THE RESULTS USUALLY CORRELATE WITH A CHARACTER'S POPULARITY?
1st Mafuyu & Kangawa
2nd Mafuyu & Okegawa
3rd Mafuyu & Takaomi
Ayabe (3rd place) was sur-passed!
WHAT'S THE MEANING OF THIS?!
PANIC PANIC
?
IT'S...
IT'S PROBABLY BECAUSE THE PEOPLE WHO LIKE AYABE...
...LIKE HIM WHEN HE'S BY HIMSELF...
PANIC
IT MIGHT BE GOOD TO HAVE A STORY ABOUT HIM LIKE THIS.
COME ON, IT'S MORNING. HURRY UP AND WAKE UP.
PUT YOUR LAUNDRY IN THERE.
I AL-READY KNOW.
YOU WANT TWO EGGS, RIGHT?
Leave it to me.
This is pretty spot-on!

UNEXPECTED

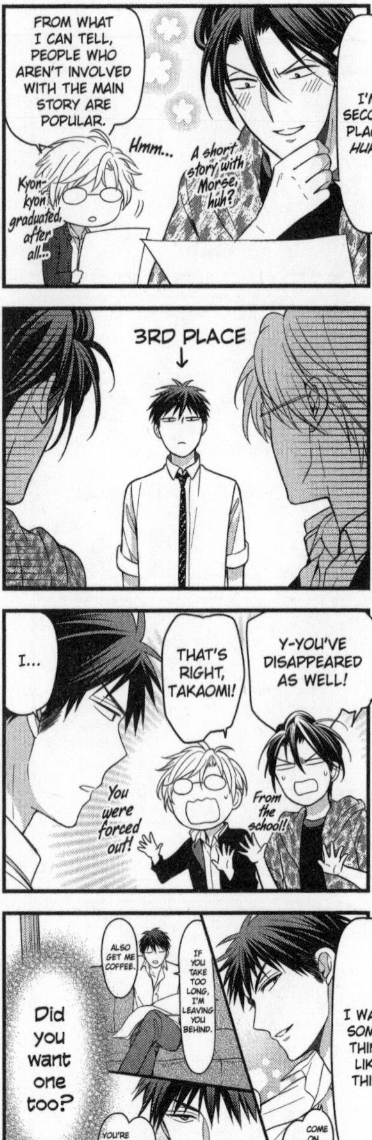

I'M SECOND PLACE, HUH?
A short story with Morse, huh?
Hmm...
FROM WHAT I CAN TELL, PEOPLE WHO AREN'T INVOLVED WITH THE MAIN STORY ARE POPULAR.
Kyon-kyon graduated, after all...
3RD PLACE ↓
Y-YOU'VE DISAPPEARED AS WELL!
From the school!!
THAT'S RIGHT, TAKAOMI!
You were forced out!
I...
I WANT SOMETHING LIKE THIS.
IF YOU TAKE TOO LONG, I'M LEAVING YOU BEHIND.
ALSO GET ME COFFEE.
COME ON... IT'S MORNING.
POUR ME A CUP.
YOU'RE GOOD AT THAT, RIGHT?
Did you want one too?

A SMART-ALECK CONCERN

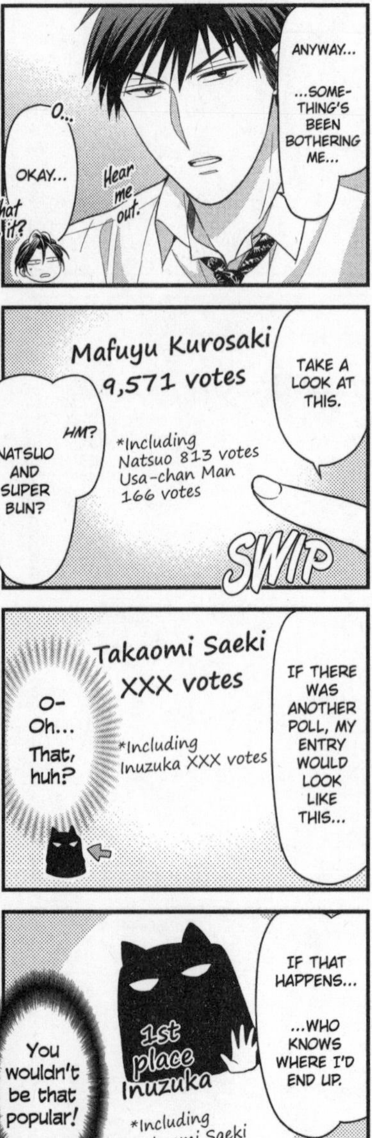

ANYWAY...
...SOMETHING'S BEEN BOTHERING ME...
Hear me out.
O... OKAY...
What is it?
TAKE A LOOK AT THIS.
Mafuyu Kurosaki 9,571 votes
*Including Natsuo 813 votes Usa-chan Man 166 votes
SWIP
HM? NATSUO AND SUPER BUN?
IF THERE WAS ANOTHER POLL, MY ENTRY WOULD LOOK LIKE THIS...
Takaomi Saeki XXX votes
*Including Inuzuka XXX votes
O-Oh... That, huh?
IF THAT HAPPENS...
...WHO KNOWS WHERE I'D END UP.
1st place Inuzuka
*Including Takaomi Saeki XXX votes
You can't see my face...
You wouldn't be that popular!

THE MAN WHO QUIETLY GETS VOTES

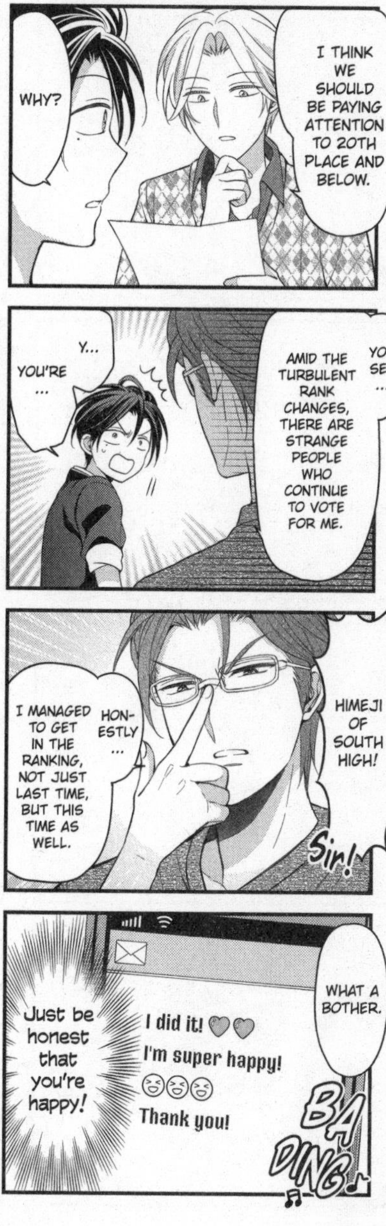
I THINK WE SHOULD BE PAYING ATTENTION TO 20TH PLACE AND BELOW.
WHY?
YOU SEE ...
AMID THE TURBULENT RANK CHANGES, THERE ARE STRANGE PEOPLE WHO CONTINUE TO VOTE FOR ME.
Y... YOU'RE ...
HIMEJI OF SOUTH HIGH!
Sir!
HON-ESTLY ...
I MANAGED TO GET IN THE RANKING, NOT JUST LAST TIME, BUT THIS TIME AS WELL.
WHAT A BOTHER.
BA DING
I did it!
I'm super happy!
Thank you!
Just be honest that you're happy!

A MAN WHO LEARNS

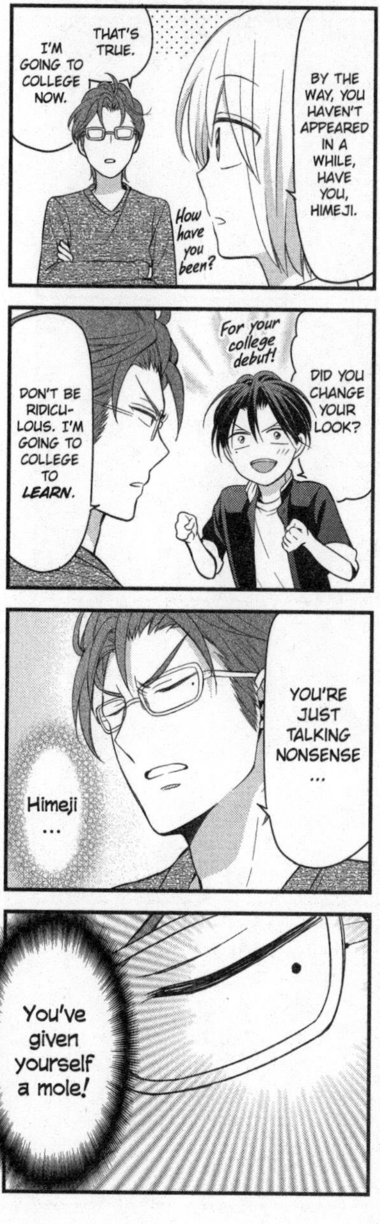
BY THE WAY, YOU HAVEN'T APPEARED IN A WHILE, HAVE YOU, HIMEJI.
How have you been?
THAT'S TRUE.
I'M GOING TO COLLEGE NOW.
DID YOU CHANGE YOUR LOOK?
For your college debut!
DON'T BE RIDICU-LOUS. I'M GOING TO COLLEGE TO LEARN.
YOU'RE JUST TALKING NONSENSE ...
Himeji ...
You've given yourself a mole!

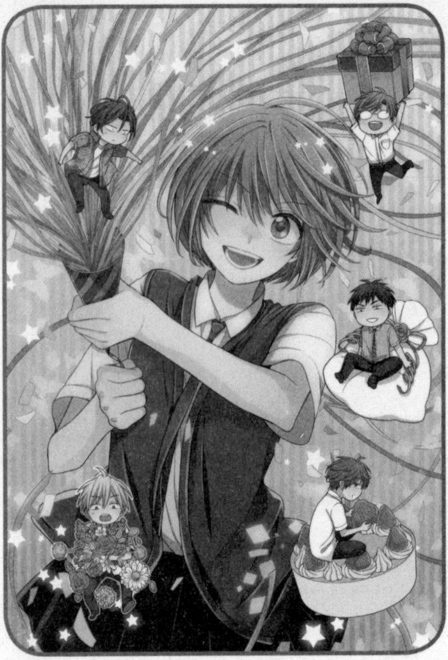

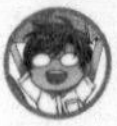

We have the results of our tenth anniversary character popularity poll!
I'm really eager to find out where I ranked! Hurry up and take a look!
The first character poll results are in volume 16, so it might be fun to compare them!
Hmm… First place is… Well, that makes sense… Second place is… *Hmm*… So that's how it is…
Hey, you there! Don't say things haven't changed!

Izumi Tsubaki began drawing manga in her first year of high school. She was soon selected to be in the top ten of *Hana to Yume's* HMC (*Hana to Yume* Mangaka Course), and subsequently won *Hana to Yume's* Big Challenge contest. Her debut title, *Chijimete Distance* (Shrink the Distance), ran in 2002 in *Hana to Yume* magazine, issue 17. Her other works include *The Magic Touch* (*Oyayubi kara Romance*) and*Oresama Teacher*, which she is currently working on.

ORESAMA TEACHER
Vol. 25
Shojo Beat Edition

STORY AND ART BY
Izumi Tsubaki

English Translation & Adaptation/JN Productions
Touch-up Art & Lettering/Eric Erbes
Design/Yukiko Whitley
Editor/Pancha Diaz

ORESAMA TEACHER by Izumi Tsubaki © Izumi Tsubaki 2018
All rights reserved. First published in Japan in 2018 by HAKUSENSHA, Inc., Tokyo.
English language translation rights arranged with HAKUSENSHA, Inc., Tokyo.

Printed in the U.S.A.

Published by VIZ Media, LLC
P.O. Box 77010
San Francisco, CA 94107

10 9 8 7 6 5 4 3 2 1
First printing, February 2019

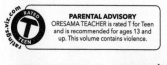

viz.com   shojobeat.com